BLACK AMERICAN
CINEMA

AFI Film Readers
a series edited by
Edward Branigan and Charles Wolfe

Psychoanalysis and Cinema
E. Ann Kaplan, editor

Fabrications: Costume and the Female Body
Jane Gaines and Charlotte Herzog, editors

Sound Theory/Sound Practice
Rick Altman, editor

Film Theory Goes to the Movies
Jim Collins, Hilary Radner, and Ava Preacher Collins, editors

Theorizing Documentary
Michael Renov, editor

The American Film Institute
P.O. Box 27999
2021 North Western Avenue
Los Angeles, California 90027

BLACK AMERICAN
CINEMA

EDITED BY

MANTHIA DIAWARA

ROUTLEDGE

New York • London

Published in 1993 by

Routledge
29 West 35 Street
New York, NY 10001

Published in Great Britain by

Routledge
11 New Fetter Lane
London EC4P 4EE

The editor wishes to acknowledge *Screen* magazine for permission to reprint "Black Spectatorship: Problems of Identification and Resistance" in this volume. A version of bell hooks's "The Oppositional Gaze: Black Female Spectatorship" appears in her book, *Black Looks,* South End Press: Boston, 1982.

Printed in the United States of America on acid free paper.

Library of Congress Cataloging in Publication Data

Black American cinema : aesthetics and spectatorship / edited by
 Manthia Diawara.
     p.   cm. — (AFI film readers)
  Includes bibliographical references and index.
  ISBN 0-415-90396-3. — ISBN 0-415-90397-1
  1. Afro-Americans in motion pictures. 2. Afro-American motion
picture producers and directors. 3. Experimental films—United
States—History and criticism. I. Diawara, Manthia, 1953–   .
II. Series.
PN1995.9.N4B45   1993
791.43'6520396073—dc20   92-32907
                                                              CIP

British Library Cataloguing in Publication Data also available

Contents

Acknowledgments   vii

Preface   ix

Black Aesthetics

1. Black American Cinema: The New Realism
    Manthia Diawara   3

2. "Twoness" in the Style of Oscar Micheaux
    J. Ronald Green   26

3. Fire and Desire: Race, Melodrama, and Oscar Micheaux
    Jane Gaines   49

4. Oscar Micheaux: The Story Continues
    Thomas Cripps   71

5. The Black Writer in Hollywood, Circa 1930: The Case of
    Wallace Thurman
    Phyllis Klotman   80

6. Is *Car Wash* a Black Musical?
    Richard Dyer   93

7. The Los Angeles School of Black Filmmakers
    Ntongela Masilela   107

8. Reading the Signs, Empowering the Eye: *Daughters of the Dust*
    and the Black Independent Cinema Movement
    Toni Cade Bambara   118

9. Spike Lee at the Movies
   Amiri Baraka   145

10. Spike Lee and the Commerce of Culture
    Houston A. Baker, Jr.   154

11. The Ironies of Palace-Subaltern Discourse
    Clyde Taylor   177

12. Looking for Modernism
    Henry Louis Gates, Jr.   200

Black Spectatorship

13. Black Spectatorship: Problems of Identification and Resistance
    Manthia Diawara   211

14. The Harlem Theatre: Black Film Exhibition in Austin, Texas:
    1920–1973
    Dan Streible   221

15. The Black Image in Protective Custody: Hollywood's Biracial
    Buddy Films of the Eighties
    Ed Guerrero   237

16. The Construction of Black Sexuality: Towards Normalizing
    the Black Cinematic Experience
    Jacquie Jones   247

17. Race, Gender, and Psychoanalysis in Forties Film: *Lost
    Boundaries, Home of the Brave,* and *The Quiet One*
    Michele Wallace   257

18. Reading Through the Text: The Black Woman as Audience
    Jacqueline Bobo   272

19. The Oppositional Gaze: Black Female Spectators
    bell hooks   288

    Bibliography
    Stephen M. Best   303

    List of Contributors   311

    Index   313

Acknowledgments

Several people helped me to lift this project from the ground. I thank Toni Cade Bambara and Clyde Taylor for encouraging me with the initial idea. The two of them taught me most of what I know in Black cultural studies. I am grateful to all the contributors to the book. They took time away from their busy schedules to write for my project. I owe them. I thank Edward Branigan and Chuck Wolfe for encouraging me with the project; for reading every chapter in the book; for editorial advice, and for their gallant patience. My thanks also go to Louis Massiah, Mbye Cham, Mansita, Daman, and Regina Austin.

Preface

Manthia Diawara

This book examines Black American cinema from two perspectives. Contributors to the first part derive a Black film aesthetic by focusing on the Black artist, his or her representation of the Black imaginary, and his or her place within broader communities. In these essays the modes of existence of a Black film culture are linked to Black institutions, nationalist versus integrationist politics, Black American literature and literary criticism, and issues of realism in representation. Contributors to the second part address the thorny issue of film spectatorship. In doing so, they bring into view another dimension of the Black film experience, one encompassing a history of film reception, generic expectations, patterns of spectatorial identification, and the possibility of political resistance.

Black American Cinema is unique for revealing continuities among independent Black filmmakers, from Oscar Micheaux (see essays by Ron Green and Jane Gaines) to Charles Burnett (Ntongela Masilela), Spike Lee (Amiri Baraka and Houston Baker, Jr.), John Singleton, and Julie Dash (Toni Cade Bambara and myself). Analyses of Black writers and directors who are often simplistically dismissed for selling out to Hollywood demonstrate both the influence of Hollywood's "master narrative" on the work of Black artists and their surreptitious infiltration of the film industry, changing the complexion of Hollywood cinema in the process. Phyllis Klotman takes as a test case the career of Wallace Thurman, a Black playwright who worked as a screenwriter in Hollywood in the 1930s. Richard Dyer explores the development of a Black musical aesthetic in movies from the early years of sound through the 1976 comedy, *Car Wash*. Beyond the constraints of Hollywood, moreover, a global view of Black filmmaking is provided by Masilela, Bambara, and Henry Louis

Gates, Jr., all of whom pursue ties between new Black *auteurs* and film-makers from the diaspora (Africa, Europe, and Latin and Central America). Focusing on discourses of irony and appropriation in Black cinema, Gates and Clyde Taylor also suggest that the topic of Black film aesthetics cannot be divorced from the productive efforts of the spectator who works with and upon the film image. Essays in the second part of the volume confront the question of Black spectatorship head on. If, as Ed Guerrero proposes, the image of Blacks on screen appears in the "protective custody" of Hollywood, perhaps other dimensions to the representation of Black life can be reclaimed at the site of reception. Dan Streible alerts us to this possibility in his social history of Black film exhibition in Austin, Texas, as do several other contributors who probe the theoretical implications of their own encounters with specific films. I offer some tentative ideas concerning problems of identification and resistance for the Black spectator in my analysis of the notorious "Gus" sequence from *The Birth of a Nation.* Subsequent articles explore a wider range of issues, with particular stress placed on gender constructions for and by the Black female spectator, a topic examined by Jacquie Jones, Michele Wallace, Jacqueline Bobo, and bell hooks.

In this book, issues of race, gender, and class are explored on both sides of the production-reception divide. Through stratagems of appropriation and resistance, spectators—and filmmakers who assume and anticipate the role of the spectator—reinterpret traditions of filmmaking, thus making possible the Black American cinema of the future.

Black Aesthetics

1

Black American Cinema: The New Realism

Manthia Diawara

The release of D. W. Griffith's *The Birth of a Nation* in 1915 defined for the first time the side that Hollywood was to take in the war to represent Black people in America. In *The Birth of a Nation*, D. W. Griffith, later a founding member of United Artists, created and fixed an image of Blackness that was necessary for racist America's fight against Black people. *The Birth of a Nation* constitutes the grammar book for Hollywood's representation of Black manhood and womanhood, its obsession with miscegenation, and its fixing of Black people within certain spaces, such as kitchens, and into certain supporting roles, such as criminals, on the screen. White people must occupy the center, leaving Black people with only one choice—to exist in relation to Whiteness. *The Birth of a Nation* is the master text that suppressed the real contours of Black history and culture on movie screens, screens monopolized by the major motion picture companies of America.

Griffith's film also put Black people and White liberals on the defensive, inaugurating a plethora of historical and critical writings against *The Birth of a Nation*, and overdetermining a new genre, produced exclusively for Black audiences, called race films. More insidiously, however, the racial conflict depicted in *The Birth of Nation* became Hollywood's only way of talking about Black people. In other words, whenever Black people appeared on Hollywood screens, from *The Birth of a Nation* to *Guess Who's Coming to Dinner?* to *The Color Purple*, they are represented as a problem, a thorn in America's heel. Hollywood's Blacks exist primarily for White spectators whose comfort and understanding the films must seek, whether they thematize exotic images dancing and singing on the screen, or images constructed to narrate a racial drama, or images of pimps and muggers. With *The Birth of a Nation* came the ban on Blacks

3

participating in bourgeois humanism on Hollywood screens. In other words, there are no simple stories about Black people loving each other, hating each other, or enjoying their private possessions without reference to the White world, because the spaces of those stories are occupied by newer forms of race relation stories which have been overdetermined by Griffith's master text.

The relations between Black independent cinema and the Hollywood cinema just described above parallel those between Blackness and Americanness; the dichotomy between the so-called marked cultures and unmarked cultures; but also the relations between "high art" and "low art." The complexity of these relations is such that every independent filmmaker's dream is to make films for Hollywood where she/he will have access to the resources of the studios and the movie theaters. On the other hand, the independents often use an aesthetic and moral high ground to repudiate mainstream cinema, which is dismissed as populist, racist, sexist, and reactionary. Furthermore, a look at the relations between Oscar Micheaux and the Hollywood "race films," Melvin Van Peebles and the Blaxploitation films, Charles Burnett (*Killer of Sheep*), Haile Gerima (*Bush Mama*), and Spike Lee and the rethematization of urban life in such films as *City of Hope, Grand Canyon, Boyz N the Hood,* and *Straight Out of Brooklyn* reveals that mainstream cinema constantly feeds on independent cinema and appropriates its themes and narrative forms.

Some of the most prominent Black film historians and critics, such as Albert Johnson, Donald Bogle, and Thomas Cripps, emphasize mainly mainstream cinema when discussing Black films. With the exception of a few breakthrough films, such as those by Micheaux, Van Peebles, and Lee, these historians are primarily concerned with the issues of integration and race relations in mainstream films, Black actors and actresses on the big screen, and the construction of stereotypes in Hollywood films. They rarely pay attention to independent cinema, which includes far more Black directors than Hollywood, and in which aesthetics, political concerns such as authorship and spectatorship, and the politics of representation with respect to Black cinema are more prevalent. Critics and historians such as Clyde Taylor, Toni Cade Bambara, Phyllis Klotman, and Gladstone Yearwood are the first to focus on Black independent cinema as a subject of study. More recently, the *Black Film Review* has assumed the preeminent role in Black film history and criticism.

Hollywood's block-booking system prevents independently produced films from reaching movie theaters and large audiences. This may be one reason why film historians and critics neglect independent cinema: some film magazines, such as *Cineaste,* adopt a policy of accepting only reviews of films that have been distributed and seen by their readers. It is also possible to argue that Black independent cinema has remained marginal until now because its language, not unlike the language of most independent films, is metafilmic, often nationalistic, and not "pleasurable" to consumers accustomed to mainstream Hollywood products. Black independent cinema, like most independent film practices, approaches film as a research tool. The filmmakers investigate the possibilities of representing alternative Black images on the screen; bringing to the foreground issues central to Black communities in America; criticizing sexism and homophobia in the Black community; and deploying Afrafemcentric discourses that empower Black women. The narratives of such films are not always linear; the characters represent a tapestry of voices from W. E. B. DuBois, Frantz Fanon, Toni Morrison, Malcolm X, Martin Luther King, Jr., Karl Marx, Angela Davis, Alice Walker, and Zora Neale Hurston. Even what passes as documentary in Black independent films, like *The Bombing of Osage Avenue* (Louis Massiah), is an artistic reconstruction of archival footage and "real" events.

What is, therefore, the Black independent cinema, and what constitutes its influence on mainstream cinema? The French appropriately refer to independent cinema as *cinema d'art et essai*. In France, the government sponsors such a cinema by imposing a distribution tax on commercial films. The *cinema d'art et essai* is less concerned about recouping its cost of production and making a profit; its main emphasis is toward artistic development, documenting an area of research, and delineating a certain philosophy of the world. In the late 1950s, a group of French youth, who were dissatisfied with commercial films and wanted to make their own films, mobilized private and personal funds along with government funds to produce low-budget films. The result is well known today as the French New Wave, considered by some as one of the pivotal moments in film history.

As an alternative to commercial cinema, which emphasized the well-made story, acting, and the personality of the actor, the New Wave put in the foreground the director, whom it raised to the same artistic level as the author of a painting, a novel, or a poem; the New Wave also demystified the notion of the well-made story by experimenting with different ways of telling the same story, and by deconstructing the notion of actor and acting. Jean-Luc Godard's *Breathless* (1959), for example, is famous for its reinsertion of the "jump-cut" as a valid narrative device. The jump-cut, which was avoided in Hollywood films in order not to disrupt the spectator with "unnecessary" repetitions, has today become a powerful narrative device used by directors such as Spike Lee, who redefines it and uses it to describe the repetition and the sameness in racial and sexual stereotyping. In *Do the Right Thing* (1988) Lee uses the same angle to repeat several shots of Blacks, Italians, Jews, and Koreans repeating racial stereotypes, unlike Godard, who uses the same image twice from the same angle. Lee practices the same device in *She's Gotta Have It* (1985) to construct sexual stereotypes among young Black males.

This example of the New Wave reveals that independent filmmakers come to their vocation for at least two reasons: one political, and the other artistic. Politically, they are dissatisfied with commercial cinema's lack of courage to address certain issues. They feel that they have to make their own films if they want to see those issues on the screen. Artistically, they want to explore new ways of telling stories; they want to experiment with the camera, the most powerful invention of modern times, and engage the infinite possibilities of storytelling. There are other examples of alternative or independent cinemas that occupy important places in the history of film. The Italian Neorealism, the Brazilian Cinema Novo, and the Argentinian Third Cinema have all created alternative narrative techniques that were at first unknown to commercial cinemas, but are claimed today as part of traditional narrative practices.

Similarly, the cloning of Hollywood's mind to Black history and culture, which do not revolve around White people, is the reason why most Black filmmakers since Oscar Micheaux have turned first to the independent sector. Since Oscar Micheaux, Black independents have pioneered creating alternative images of Blacks on the screen, constructing new narrative forms derived from Black literature and folklore, and denouncing racism, sexism and homophobia in American culture.

This is not, however, to romanticize the independent practice. Micheaux made his films by selling personal property and borrowing money from friends. Still today, independent filmmaking causes many people to become poor. It takes more than six years for some filmmakers to gather the money for one film. Charles Burnett's *To Sleep With Anger,* and Julie Dash's *Daughters of the Dust* came only after arduous years of fundraising. Haile Gerima has been trying to raise funds for *Nunu* for several years now. We have not yet seen second features by talented directors such as Billy Woodberry (*Bless Their Little Hearts*), Larry Clark (*Passing Through*), Alile Sharon Larkin (*A Different Image*), and Warrington Hudlin (*Street Corner Stories*). Spike Lee sums up the harsh reality of independent production as follows:

When I went to film school, I knew I did not want to have my films shown only during Black History Month in February or at libraries. I wanted them to have a wide distribution. And I did not want to spend four or five years trying to piecemeal together the money for my films. I did my first film, *She's Gotta Have It,* independently for $175,000. We had a grant from the New York State Council on the Arts and were raising money the whole time we were shooting. We shot the film in twelve days. The next stage was to get it out of the lab. Then, the most critical part was when I had to hole up in my little apartment to get it cut. I took about two months to do that. I had no money coming in, so I had to hold off the debtors because I knew if I had enough time to at least get it in good enough shape to show, we could have some investor screenings, and that's what happened. We got it blown up to 35mm for a film festival. What you have to do is to try to get a distributor. You enter as many film festivals as you can.[1]

Black independent cinema is any Black-produced film outside the constraints of the major studios. The filmmakers' independence from Hollywood enables them to put on the screen Black lives and concerns that derive from the complexity of Black communities. Independent films provide alternative ways of knowing Black people that differ from the fixed stereotypes of Blacks in Hollywood. The ideal spectators of the films are those interested in Black people's perspectives on American culture. White people and Whiteness are marginalized in the films, while central positions are relegated to Black people, Black communities, and diasporic experiences. For example, the aesthetics of uplifting the race in a film like *The Scar of Shame* (1928, The Colored Players) concern particularly Black spectators, whom the filmmakers' stated mission is to entertain and educate. The film posits Black upper-class culture as that which should be emulated by lower-class Blacks in order to humanize themselves. Unlike Hollywood films of that time, which identified with the ideal White male, the camera in *The Scar of Shame* identifies with the position of the Black bourgeoisie. The film is precious today as a document of Black bourgeois ways of being in the 1920s and 1930s. Crucially, it constitutes, with Oscar Micheaux's films, a genre of Black independent cinema which puts Black people and their culture at the center as subjects of narrative development; in these films, Black people are neither marginalized as a problem, nor singled out as villainous stereotypes such as Hollywood constructs in its films.

Contemporary independent films continue the same effort of inquiring into Black subjectivities, the heterogeneity of Black lives, the Black family, class and gender relations, and diasporic aesthetics. Recently, independent Black women filmmakers such as Kathleen Collins (*Losing Ground*), Alile Sharon Larkin (*A Different Image*), Ayoka Chenzira (*Zajota: the Boogie Spirit*), Julie Dash (*Daughters of the Dust*), and Zeinabu Davis (*A Powerful Thang*) have explored such themes as Black womanhood and spirituality, diaspora art and music, and Afrocentric aesthetics. Black manhood, the urban landscape, unemployment and the Black family are thematized in films like *Sweet Sweetback's Baaaaadassss Song* (Van Peebles), *Killer of Sheep* (Burnett), *Bless Their Little Hearts* (Woodberry), *Serving Two Masters* (Tim Lewis), *Street Corner Stories* (Warrington Hudlin), *Chame-*

leon Street (Wendell Harris), and *Ashes and Embers* (Haile Gerima). The themes of sexuality and homophobia are depicted in *Tongues Untied* (Marlon Riggs), *Storme: Lady of the Jewel Box* (Michelle Parkerson), *She's Gotta Have It* (Spike Lee), *Ganja and Hess* (Bill Gunn), *Splash* (Thomas Harris), and *She Don't Fade* (Cheryl Dunye). The major Black documentary artists, such as William Greaves, Louis Massiah, Camille Billops, and Sinclair Bourne, have also enriched the documentary genre by focusing their cameras on Black people in order to reconstruct history, celebrating Black writers and activists, and giving voice to people who are overlooked by television news and mainstream documentaries.

Two Paradigms of Black Cinema Aesthetics

In her contribution to this volume, Jane Gaines defines Oscar Micheaux's editing style as follows: "Perhaps to elude any attempt to essentialize it, we could treat this style as more of an ingenious solution to the impossible demands of the conventions of classical Hollywood style, shortcuts produced by the exigencies of economics, certainly, but also modifications produced by an independent who had nothing at stake in strict adherence to Hollywood grammar." Gaines goes on to posit that Micheaux's "freewheeling cinematic grammar" constitutes both a misreading and an improvement upon Hollywood logic. Clearly, Micheaux's "imperfect" cinema (to borrow a term from Julio Garcia Espinoza), which misreads and improves upon Hollywood logic, is a powerful metaphor for the way in which African-Americans survived and continue to survive within a hostile economic and racist system, and used the elements of that survival as raw material to humanize and improve upon American modernism. Micheaux's "loose editing," like the improvisation of jazz, surprises and delights the spectator with forbidden images of America that Hollywood's America conceals from its space. In so far as the classical Hollywood narrative proceeds by concealment of space, Micheaux's "imperfect" narrative constitutes an excess which reveals the cheat cuts, the other America artificially disguised by the Hollywood logic. It is in this sense that Gaines writes of improvement of film language by Micheaux. Another contributor to the volume, Ron Green, compares Micheaux's film style to Black English, and to jazz. His cinema is one of the first to endow African-Americans with cinematic voice and subjectivity through his uncovering of new spaces at the threshold of dominant cinema.

The first step in interpreting a Black film aesthetic must therefore be directed towards an analysis of the composition of the new shots discovered by Micheaux, and their potential effects on spectators. In this volume, Micheaux's films are discussed in an in-depth manner for the first time by Jane Gaines and Ron Green. Micheaux's legacy as an independent filmmaker not only includes his entrepreneurial style in raising money and making films outside the studios. He also turned his cameras towards Black people and the Black experience in a manner that did not interest Hollywood directors of race films. Crucially, Micheaux's camera positioned Black spectators on the same side as the Black middle-class ideology, acquiring for his films an aesthetic that was primarily specific to the ways of life of that class.

Similarly, in the 1970s, Melvin Van Peebles and Bill Gunn positioned spectators with respect to different imaginaries derived from the Black experience in America. In *Sweet Sweetback's Baadasssss Song,* Van Peebles thematizes Black nationalism by casting the Black community as an internal colony, and Sweetback, a pimp, as the hero of decolonization. In her contribution to this book, Toni Cade Bambara refers to *Sweet Sweetback* as "a case of Stagolee meets Fanon or Watermelon Man plays Bigger Thomas?" *Sweet Sweetback* is about policing and surveillance of Black communities, and the existentialist struggle of the film's main character, a Black man. As Bambara notices, Bigger Thomas is not the only literary reference in the film; it also draws on the theme of the running Black man in *Invisible Man,* which is collapsed into a transformed Hollywood stereotype of the Black stud. As such, *Sweet Sweetback* is famous as the paradigmatic text for the 1970s Blaxploitation films. The theme of the Black man running from the law or from Black-on-Black crime, which links Van Peebles to such Black American writers as Richard Wright, Ralph Ellison, and Chester Himes, is also echoed in 1990s films like *Juice, Straight Out of Brooklyn,* and *Boyz N The Hood,* not to mention *New Jack City,* a film directed by Van Peebles's son, Mario Van Peebles.

Sweet Sweetback's aesthetic draws on the logic of Black nationalism as the basis of value judgment, and defines itself by positioning the spectator to identify with the Black male hero of the film. Bambara rightly criticizes the centrality of Black manhood at the expense of women in *Sweet Sweetback,* but recognizes nationalist narratives as enabling strategies for survival, empowerment, and self-determination. As Sweetback is helped to escape from the police by one Black person after another, the nationalist discourse of the film transforms the ghetto, where Black people are objects, into the community, where they affirm their subjecthood. To put it in Bambara's words, "Occupying the same geographical terrain are the *ghetto,* where we are penned up in concentration-camp horror, and the *community,* where we enact daily rituals of group validation in a liberated zone."

In *Ganja and Hess,* Bill Gunn aestheticizes the Black imaginary by placing the spectator on the same side as the Black church. The spectator draws pleasure from the film through the confrontation between the ideology of the Black church and vampirism, addiction to drugs and sex, and materialism. *Ganja and Hess* is perhaps the most beautifully shot Black film, and the most daring with respect to pushing different passions to their limits. The Black artist, Meda (played by Bill Gunn himself), is a nihilist who advocates total silence because, as a Black person, his art is always already overdetermined by race in America. The love scenes in the film are commingled with vampiristic gestures that are attractive and repulsive at the same time. At the Cannes Film Festival in 1973, Gunn's daring camera angles during one of the loves scenes brought spectators to joy, applauding and screaming "Bravo! Bravo!" in the middle of the film. *Ganja and Hess* also pushes the classical narrative to the threshold by framing a frontal nude image of a Black man coming out of a swimming pool and running toward a window where a woman, Ganja (Marlene Clarke), smilingly awaits him.

What is radical about both *Ganja and Hess* and *Sweet Sweetback* is their formal positioning of Black characters and Black cultures at the center of the screen, creating a sense of defamiliarization of the classical film language. The two films also inaugurate for Black cinema two narrative tracks with regard to time and space. While *Ganja and Hess* is cyclical, going back and forth between pre-Christian time and the time after Christ, *Sweet Sweetback* is a linear recording of the progress of Black liberation struggle.

With regard to Black aesthetics, it is possible to put in the same category as *Ganja and Hess* such films as *A Powerful Thang* (Davis), *Daughters of the Dust* (Dash), *Losing Ground* (Collins), *Killer of Sheep* and *To Sleep with Anger* (Burnett), *Tongues Untied* (Riggs), and *She's Gotta Have It* (Lee). These films are concerned with the specificity of identity, the empowerment of Black people through mise-en-scène, and the rewriting of American history. Their narratives contain rhythmic and repetitious shots, going back and forth between the past and the present. Their themes involve Black folklore, religion, and the oral traditions which link Black Americans to the African diaspora. The narrative style is symbolic.

Sweet Sweetback, on the other hand, defines its aesthetics through recourse to the realistic style in film. The story line develops within the logic of continuity editing, and the characters look ordinary. The film presents itself as a mirror on a Black community under siege. The real effect is reinforced throughout the film by events which are motivated by racial and gendered causes. The sound track and the costumes link the film to a specific epoch in the Civil Rights Movement. Unlike the first category of films, which uses the symbolic style and concerns itself with the past, *Sweet Sweetback* makes the movement toward the future-present by confronting its characters with obstacles ahead of them. Other films in this category include *Cooley High* (Michael Schultz), *House Party* (Reginald Hudlin), *Chameleon Street* (Harris), *Passing Through* (Clark), *Do*

The Right Thing (Lee), *Straight Out of Brooklyn* (Rich), *Juice* (Ernest Dickerson), and *Boyz N The Hood* (Singleton). These lists are neither exhaustive nor fixed. The realist category has more in common with the classical Hollywood narrative, with its quest for the formation of the family and individual freedom, and its teleological trajectory (beginning, middle, and end). The symbolic narratives have more in common with Black expressive forms like jazz, and with novels by such writers as Toni Cade Bambara, Alice Walker, and Toni Morrison, which stop time to render audible and visible Black voices and characters that have been suppressed by centuries of Eurocentrism.

The comparison of the narrative styles deployed by *Sweet Sweetback* and *Ganja and Hess*[2] is useful in order to link the action-oriented *Sweet Sweetback* to modernism, and the reflexive style of *Ganja and Hess* to postmodernism. *Sweet Sweetback* defines its Afro-modernism through a performative critique of the exclusion of Blacks from reaping the fruits of American modernity and liberal democracy. *Ganja and Hess* is a postmodern text which weaves together a time of pre-Christian Africa, a time of Christ's Second Coming in the Black church, and a time of liberated Black women. Crucially, therefore, the repetition of history as played out on the grid of the Black diaspora is important to the definition of Gunn's film language. Through the repetition of these Black times in the film, Bill Gunn defines a Black aesthetic that puts in the same space African spirituality, European vampire stories, the Black church, addiction to drugs, and liberated feminist desires.

The New Black Films

It is easy to see the symbolic, reflexive, and expressive styles in films such as *Killer of Sheep* and *Daughters of the Dust,* and the active, materially grounded, and linear styles in *Boyz N the Hood.* But before looking more closely at these films, it is important to put into some perspective the ways in which Black films posit their specificity by challenging the construction of time and space in Hollywood films. It is only in this sense that arguments can begin about whether they displace, debunk, or reinforce the formulaic verisimilitude of Hollywood.

The way in which a filmmaker selects a location and organizes that location in front of the camera is generally referred to in film studies as mise-en-scène. Spatial narration in classical cinema makes sense through a hierarchical disposition of objects on the screen. Thus space is related to power and powerlessness, in so far as those who occupy the center of the screen are usually more powerful than those situated in the background or completely absent from the screen. I have described here Black people's relation to spatially situated images in Hollywood cinema. When Black people are absent from the screen, they read it as a symbol of their absence from the America constructed by Hollywood. When they are present on the screen, they are less powerful and less virtuous than the White man who usually occupies the center. Hollywood films have regularly tried to resolve this American dilemma, either through token or symbolic representation of Blacks where they are absent—for instance, the mad Black scientist in *Terminator 2;* or through a substitution of less virtuous Blacks by positive images of Blacks—for instance, *Grand Canyon* or *The Cosby Show.* But it seems to me that neither symbolic representation nor positive images sufficiently address the specificity of Black ways of life, and how they might enter in relation to other Americans on the Hollywood screen. Symbolic representation and positive images serve the function of plotting Black people in White space and White power, keeping the real contours of the Black community outside Hollywood.

The construction of time is similarly problematic in the classical narrative. White men drive time from the East to the West, conquering wilderness and removing obstacles out of time's way. Thus the "once upon a time" which begins every story in Hollywood also posits an initial obstacle in front of a White person who has to remove it in order for the story to continue, and for the conquest ideology of Whiteness to prevail. The concept of beginning, middle, and end, in itself, is universal to storytelling. The difference here is that Hollywood is only interested in White people's stories (White times), and Black people enter these times mostly as obstacles to their progress, or as supporting casts for the main White characters. "Once upon a time" is a traditional storytelling device which the storyteller uses to evoke the origin of a people, their ways of life, and the role of the individual in the society. The notion of *rite de passage* is a useful concept for describing the individual's separation from or incorporation into a social time. The classical narrative in cinema adheres to this basic ideological formula in order to tell White people's stories in Hollywood. It seems that White times in Hollywood have no effect on Black people and their communities: whether they play the role of a negative or positive stereotype, Black people neither grow nor change in the Hollywood stories. Because there is a dearth of Black people's stories in Hollywood that do not revolve around White times, television series such as *Roots,* and films such as *Do the Right Thing,* which situate spectators from the perspective of a Black "once upon a time," are taken out of proportion, celebrated by Blacks as authentic histories, and debunked by Whites as controversial.

To return again to the comparison between *Sweet Sweetback* and *Ganja and Hess,* it is easy to see how important time and space are to defining the cinematic styles they each extol. The preponderance of space in films such as *Ganja and Hess* reveals the hierarchies of power among the characters, but it also reveals the preoccupation of this style of Black cinema with the creation of space on the screen for Black voices, Black history and Black culture. As I will show later with a discussion of space in *Daughters of the Dust,* Black films use spatial narration as a way of revealing and linking Black spaces that have been separated and suppressed by White times, and as a means of validating Black culture. In other words, spatial narration is a filmmaking of cultural restoration, a way for Black filmmakers to reconstruct Black history, and to posit specific ways of being Black Americans in the United States.

The emphasis on time, on the other hand, reveals the Black American as he/she engenders him/herself amid the material conditions of everyday life in the American society. In films like *Sweet Sweetback* and *Boyz N the Hood,* where a linear narrative time dominates, the characters are depicted in continuous activities, unlike the space-based narratives, where the past constantly interrupts the present, and repetitions and cyclicality define narration. Crucially, whereas the space-oriented narratives can be said to center Black characters on the screen, and therefore empower them, the Black-times narratives link the progress of time to Black characters, and make times exist for the purpose of defining their needs and their desires. Whereas the space-based narratives are expressive and celebratory of Black culture, the time-based narratives are existentialist performances of Black people against policing, racism, and genocide. I would like now to turn to *Daughters of the Dust* and *Boyz N the Hood* to illustrate the point.

Space and Identity: Black Expressive Style in *Daughters of the Dust*

> I am the first and the last
> I am the honored one and the scorned one
> I am the whore and the holy one
> I am the wife and the virgin
> I am the barren one and many are my daughters. . . .
> I am the silence that you cannot understand. . . .
> I am the utterance of my name.
>
> *(Daughters of the Dust)*

I have argued that the Hollywood classical narrative often articulates time and space through recourse to a discriminating gaze toward American Blacks. When the story is driven by time and action, it is usually White times. I'll say more about this in my discussion below of *Boyz N the Hood.* Similarly, when spatial considerations dominate the production of the story, the purpose is usually to empower White men. Common sense reveals that characters that are more often on the screen, or occupy the center of the frame, command more narrative authority than those that are in the background, on the sides, or completely absent from the frame. By presence, here, I have in mind first of all the literal presence of White characters in most of the shots that constitute the typical Hollywood film, which helps to define these characters as heroes of the story. There is also the symbolic presence through which narrative authority for the organization of space is attributed to certain characters in the story. These devices of spatial narration are effective in linking characters with spaces, and in revealing space occupancy as a form of empowerment. For example, through the character played by Robert Duval in *Apocalypse Now,* Francis Ford Coppola parodies the power associated with White male actors such as John Wayne as they are framed at the center of the screen.

There is preponderance of spatial narration in Julie Dash's *Daughters of the Dust.* Black women and men occupy every frame of the film, linking Black identity to a place called Ibo Landing in the Sea Islands of South Carolina, and, more importantly, empowering Black women and their ways of life. On a surface and literal level, the wide appeal of the film for Black women depends on the positioning of the women characters as bigger than life in the middle of the screen, which mirrors the beautiful landscape of Ibo Landing. Black women see themselves on the screen, richly adorned, with different hues of Blackness and Black hair styles, and flaunting their culture. In *Daughters of the Dust,* the screen belongs to Black women. At a deeper level, where space and time are combined into a narrative, Julie Dash emphasizes spatial narration as a conduit to Black self-expressivity, a storytelling device which interrogates identity, memory, and Black ways of life. *Daughters of the Dust* stops time at 1902, when the story was set, and uses the canvas of Ibo Landing in the Sea Islands to glance backward to slavery, the Middle Passage, African religions, Christianity, Islam, the print media, photography, moving pictures, and African-American folkways, as elements with which Black people must come to terms in order to glance forward as citizens of the United States. In other words, the film asks us to know ourselves first, know where we came from, before knowing where we are going. To put it in yet another way, Ibo Landing is a symbolic space in which African-Americans can articulate their relation to Africa, the Middle Passage, and the survival of Black people and their ways of life in America. Crucially, the themes of survival, the memories of African religions and ways of life which enter into conflict with Christianity and European ways of life, and the film's proposal of syncretism as a way out, are narrativized from Black women's points of view. I want to take more time here to show how Julie Dash uses women's voices to make these themes compatible with the space of Ibo Landing.

The conflict in the film concerns the migration of the Peazant family from Ibo Landing of the Sea Islands to the North. At first the conflict is set in binary terms. For those who support the migration North, the space of Ibo Landing is primitive, full of people who worship the sun, the moon, and the river. The North therefore promises literacy, Christianity and progress. For Grandma Nana and the Unborn Child who link their identity to the space of Ibo Landing, the North represents the destruction of the family, disconnection from the ancestors, and the loss of identity for the children. For Grandma Nana, Ibo Landing is where the ancestors watch over the living, protect them, and guide them. It is in this sense that Nana does not want the family reunion to be a farewell party between those who are leaving and those staying. She prepares herself to give them something that they "can take North with [them] along with [their] big dreams."

As filmic space, Ibo Landing is the link between Africa and America. Or, to put it another way, Ibo Landing is Africa in America. According to the film, it is where the last slaves landed. *Daughters of the Dust* also argues that it is where African-Americans remained isolated from the mainland of Georgia and South Carolina, and "created and maintained a distinct imaginative and original African-American culture." The Peazant family must therefore learn the terms of their belonging to Ibo Landing, which will be an example of African-American belonging to America, and must use the space of Ibo Landing to validate their identities as Americans of a distinctive culture. It is interesting to notice here that, unlike the Hollywood narratives which claim space only as a process of self-empowerment, *Daughters of the Dust* acknowledges through the letter that Iona receives from her Indian lover that the space belonged to the Indians first.

Weaving the voices of Grandma Nana, the Unborn Child, and Eula (the mother of the Unborn Child) through the spaces of Ibo Landing, Julie Dash creates a narrative that connects Africa to America, the past to the present. Using African ancestor figures as her narrative grid, she places Grandma Nana at the center of her story, and constructs oppositional characters around her. On the one hand we have Haagar, Viola, the bible lady, and Eli, who is Eula's husband; on the other hand we have Yellow Mary, Eula, and Iona, who is Haagar's daughter. We have characters who are alike and who constitute reincarnations of ancestor figures with similar dispositions; and characters who are contraries of one another, and therefore require the intervention of the ancestors to bring peace and harmony.

Grandma Nana is the oldest person on the island. She spends most of her time visiting the graveyard where the ancestors are buried, and by the water which is a dwelling place of the spirits of the ancestors. I do not have enough space here to discuss the significance of water in *Daughters of the Dust.* But it is crucial to point out the recurring Middle Passage theme of Africans walking on water to go back to Africa. As an intertextual religious space, the use of water by Grandma Nana to communicate with the gods echoes *Yeelen* by Souleymane Cissé, where the mother baths with milk in the middle of the river and asks the Goddess to protect her son. *Daughters* also reminds us of *Testament* by Black Audio Film/Video Collective, in which the characters walk into the middle of the river or visit graveyards in order to unlock the secret of the past. It would also be interesting to investigate the use of water in vases and on altars as a representation of Voodoo in *Daughters* and in *Dreaming Rivers* by Sankofa Film/Video Collective.

Daughters depicts the survival of African religious practices in Ibo Landing through Grandma Nana in other ways as well. She can hear the calls of the spirits, and, therefore, works with the Unborn Child to keep the family together. She teaches Eli about the core of African ancestor worship: "It's up to the living to keep in touch with the dead, Eli. Man's power don't end with death. We just move on to another place; a place where we go and watch over our living family. Respect your elders, respect your family, respect your ancestors."

A recourse to religion is central to the understanding of *Daughters of the Dust*. For Grandma Nana, ancestor worship provides the strongest stability for the Black family in America and Africa. Unlike Christianity and Islam, which are teleological and reserve the final reward for the end in Heaven, the ancestors in Grandma Nana's belief system just move to another world and watch over their living descendants. The children are the reincarnation of the ancestors, and this makes them precious to the adults whose fathers and grandfathers have joined the land of the ancestors. The Unborn Child in the film is one such reincarnation. She is doubled not only in the figure of Grandma Nana herself, but also in the young girl with tribal scars who appears with her mother in one of the flashbacks. She travels through time, and she is present at different settings in the film: we see her among the first generation of Africans working with indigo dye, and we see her in a 1902 setting among children playing in the sand. Like the ancestors, her role is one of a mediator in the family. It is in this sense that Grandma Nana states that for Africans, the ancestors and the children are the most sacred elements of society.

Julie Dash also uses the religious theme of reincarnation, and links the Unborn Child to African-American survival during slavery, genocide, and the rape of Black women. In the film, the theme of the Peazant family's disintegration entailed by the migration to the North is replayed in the subtheme of Eli's self-exile from his wife, Eula, because she's carrying a child that Eli does not consider his. Eli's first reaction to Eula's pregnancy is to become an iconoclast toward the ancestor belief system that Grandma Nana wants to maintain. He puts into question the religion and culture he has received from childhood to adulthood. In other words: How can this happen to him, who has played by the rules? How come the gods are not avenging his misfortune? Subsequently, he picks up his ax and proceeds to smash all the fetishes that he had previously revered.

Grandma Nana finds an answer to Eli's blasphemous questions in her belief system. She links Eula's pregnancy to the condition of Black women in slavery who were raped, denied motherhood rights, and treated like animals. At the same time, the power and complexity of Black people come from their ability to maintain the sacredness of the womb by restoring to the group the children of interracial rape. Grandma Nana uses ancestor worship, and the place of children in it, to appropriate the baby Eula is carrying. By doing so, she bends the filiative and patriarchal rules Eli maintains in order to disavow the Unborn Child. For Grandma Nana, Eli, too, must learn the process of cleansing rape from the child's name, and making it his own child. Grandma Nana argues that the womb is as sacred as the ancestors, and that the Unborn Child is sent by the ancestors, precisely at this critical juncture in Ibo Landing's history, to ensure survival: "You need this one, Eli, to make the family stronger like it used to be." It is interesting to note the spatial organization as Grandma Nana talks to Eli. As the oldest person in the Peazant family, her role is that of a teacher. As she speaks to Eli, the space revealed on the screen is that of children playing games on the beach. The narrative implication here is that the children are the audience of her teaching. At one point during the children's game, the film changes to a slow motion. As the children fall on top of one another, we hear screaming and groaning, which remind us of the Middle Passage during which hundreds of Africans were piled on top of each other in the cabins of slave ships. The implication of Grandma Nana's teaching is that, just as captured Africans were thrown together during that painful time of the Middle Passage, Blacks today must see themselves in the same boat, and fight together to "make the family stronger."

Eli's questions about the paternity and, therefore, the race of the Unborn Child also touch on the issues of light skin and dark skin, pure blood and mixed blood, superior and inferior; in short, we are dealing with racism among Blacks. It is in this sense that Yellow Mary is ostracized by Haagar and Viola, who use her light complexion as a sign of betrayal and try to banish her from Ibo Landing. For Grandma Nana, Yellow Mary and the Unborn Child contribute to the survival and maintenance of Black people in America, because their presence makes Blackness diverse and complex. Black survival in America confounds and embarrasses both Whiteness and essentialist notions of pure Africans. Julie Dash puts onto stage one of the most beautiful and powerful scenes in the film to illustrate this point. Haagar and others have been chastising Yellow Mary for not being Black enough, when Eula stands up and delivers a speech worthy of an ancestor figure. The mise-en-scène of this sequence reveals Black women in all their powers, as Eula reminds Haagar that no one is Blacker or purer than anyone else, and warns her and Viola about the wrath of the gods, if they were to continue their gesture of expelling Yellow Mary out of the race. Spatial representation again becomes paramount, because Eula's speech is directed to the on-screen audience of the Peazant family, as well as the off-screen spectators.

I have discussed so far the ways in which *Daughters of the Dust* uses African belief systems as the center which enables Black women and men to articulate their identities on the space of Ibo Landing. Grandma Nana, particularly, posits the ancestor worship system as a text which holds together the world of Ibo Landing and provides answers to practical daily problems. A crucial question remains: whether the belief in ancestors can coexist with other belief systems, such as Christianity and Islam, on and off the island? At first, religious systems seem to be opposed in *Daughters of the Dust*. Bilal, who is Muslim, is opposed to the Baptists, who think that their God is better. Viola and Haagar use Christianity to elevate themselves above Grandma Nana. They see ancestor worship as an idolatry which is confined to Ibo Landing. They look to the North as a sign of enlightenment and Christian salvation.

Clearly, Julie Dash represents all these belief systems on the space of Ibo Landing not to show the fixity of different religions, and their essentialist nature, but to propose all of them as part of what makes Black people in America complex. Toward the end of the film Grandma Nana brings together the different belief systems, when she ties together the Bible and a sacred object from her own religion, and asks every one to kiss the hybridized Bible before departing from the island. This syncretic move is her way of mixing up the religions in Ibo Landing, and activating their combined power to protect those who are moving North. Earlier in the film she commands Eli to "celebrate our ways" when he goes North. The syncretic move is therefore also a survival tactic for the African ways of life up North.

Arguably, another reason for deploying ancestor worship (and casting Grandma Nana at the center in the film) is to reveal its usable power in holding the Black family together. Placing women at the center of the frame is also Julie Dash's way of creating space for Black people in modernity, and is her redefinition of Black images in their relation to such modern tools as still photography, newspapers, and moving pictures. Julie Dash's spatial narrative style inextricably combines the identities of her characters with the landscape of Ibo Landing. Her mise-en-scène of Grandma Nana, Haagar, Yellow Mary, and Eula in the center of the frame makes the space theirs, and their possession of the space makes them bigger than life. They become so associated with the space of Ibo Landing, through close-ups of various sorts, that it becomes difficult to imagine Ibo Landing now without the faces of these Black women. Analogically speaking, it is like imagining America in Western films without the faces of John Wayne, Kirk Douglas, and Gary Cooper.

The spatial narrative style of *Daughters of the Dust* enables Julie Dash to claim America as the land of Black people, to plot Africanism in American ways of life, and to make intelligible African voices that were rendered inarticulate. To return to the thematization of religion in the film, Julie Dash has made manifest an Africanism that was repressed for centuries, but that refused to die. As Grandma Nana states, "those African ancestors sneak up on you when you least suspect them." With her revival of ancestor worship as a narrative grid, as a point of reference for different themes in the film, Julie Dash has ignited the fire of love and caring among Black people. The path between the ancestors and the womb constitutes a Black structure of feeling, a caring handed down from generation to generation, which commands us to care for our children. In an article entitled "Nihilism and Black America," Cornel West proposes "a politics of conversion" as a way out of the carelessness of Black-on-Black crime, and as a protection against "market-driven corporate enterprises, and white supremacism." For West,

> The genius of our black foremothers and forefathers was to create powerful buffers to ward off the nihilistic threat, to equip black folk with cultural armor to beat back the demons of hopelessness, meaning-lessness, and lovelessness. . . . These traditions consist primarily of black religious and civic institutions that sustained familial and communal networks of support.[3]

Perhaps Julie Dash's theory of ancestor worship should be among those institutions that constitute Black structures of feeling; as Grandma Nana puts it, let the ancestors guide us and protect us.

Black Times, Black Stories: *Boyz N the Hood*

> Either they don't know, or don't show, or don't care about what's going on in the 'Hood. (*Boyz N the Hood*)

To return now to *Boyz N the Hood,* I would like to illustrate its emphasis on time and movement as a way of defining an alternative Black film language different from the spatial and expressive language of *Daughters of the Dust.* Like *Daughters of the Dust, Boyz N the Hood* begins with a well-defined date. But unlike *Daughters of the Dust,* which is set in 1902 and looks into the past as a way of unfolding its story, *Boyz N the Hood* starts in 1984, and continues for more than seven years into the future. *Daughters of the Dust* is about Black peoples' reconstitution of the memories of the past; it is a film about identity, and the celebration of Black ways of life. *Boyz N the Hood,* on the other hand, is a rite of passage film, a film about the Black man's journey in America. The story line is linear in *Boyz N the Hood,* whereas *Daughters of the Dust* unfolds in a circular manner.

In films like *Boyz N the Hood, Juice, Straight Out of Brooklyn,* and *Deep Cover,* the narrative time coincides with the development of the lives of the characters in the films. Many of these films begin with the childhood of the main characters, who then enter into adulthood, and face many obstacles in their lives. These films produce an effect of realism by creating an overlap between the rite of passage into manhood and the narrative time of the story. The notion of rite of passage, which defines the individual's relation to time in terms of separation from or incorporation into society, helps us to understand the use of narrative time in a film like *Boyz N the hood.* The beginning, middle, and end of *Boyz N the Hood* constitute episodes that mark the young protagonist's incorporation into the many levels of society. In fact, the structure of the film is common to African-American folktales, as well as to the classical cinema. It is as follows: A boy has to go on a journey in order to avert an imminent danger. He travels to the home of a relative or friend (uncle, aunt, father, mother, wise man, and so on) who teaches him, or helps him to overcome the obstacle. At the end, he removes the danger, and his nation (or community, or family) gets stronger with him. This skeletal structure is common to texts as diverse as *The Epic of Sunjata* (D. T. Niane), the *Aeneid* (Virgil), and *The Narrative of the Life of Frederick Douglass* (Douglass), as well as to the Hollywood Western genre, the martial art films, and the Rocky films with Silvester Stallone. The literal journey in time and space overlaps with the symbolic journey of the rite of passage. Typically, this type of storytelling addresses moments of crisis, and the need to build a better society.

The moment of crisis is symbolized in *Boyz N the Hood* by the opening statistical information, which states that "One out of every twenty-one Black American males will be murdered in their lifetime. Most will die at the hands of another Black male." Thus, *Boyz N the Hood* is a cautionary tale about the passage into manhood, and about the development of a politics of caring for the lives of Black males. More specifically, it is about Tre Styles (Cuba Gouldings), the main character, and his relation to the obstacles that he encounters on his way to manhood. Crucially, the major distractive forces in the film are the police, gang life, and the lack of supervision for the youth. To shield Tre from these obstacles, his mother sends him to live with his father, whose teaching will guide him through the many rites of passage toward manhood.[4]

The film is divided into three episodes, and each episode ends with rituals of separation and transition. In the first episode the ritual ends with Tre leaving his mother (first symbol of weaning) and friends behind. The story of this episode implies that most of the friends he leaves behind will not make it. On the way to his father's house, Tre's mother says, "I don't want you to end up dead, or in jail, or drunk standing in front of one of these liquor stores." The second episode ends with Doughboy's (Ice Cube) arrest by the police, who take him to the juvenile detention camp. The third episode ends with the death of Ricky Baker, Doughboy, and many other Black males. At the end of each episode, Tre moves to a higher understanding of life.

Let us now focus on one of the episodes in order to show its internal conflicts, and the specific elements that enter into play to prevent the passage of young Black males into manhood and caring for the community. I will choose the first episode because it introduces the spectator to most of the obstacles which are complicated and repeated in the other episodes. The film opens with a shot in which the camera zooms in on a stop sign until it fills the screen. We see a plane fly over the roofs, and the next shot reveals Tre and three other young kids walking to school. The subtitles say: "South Central LA, 1984." The children walk by a one-way street sign. This sign, too, is depicted in close-up as the camera travels above to establish the crossroad. Then the four kids take a direction facing a wrong-way sign. They travel on that road and see a crime scene that is circled by a plastic ribbon with the words: "Police Line Do Not Cross." Inside the police line there are three posters of President Ronald Reagan with a sign saying: "Reagan/Bush, Four More Years." The kids cross the police line, as one of them moves closer to the Reagan posters. At that moment a rhythmic and violent editing reveals each of the posters in close-up with the sound of a gunshot. There are bullet holes in the poster. In the next scene, the kids are in a classroom where the students' artworks on the wall reflect the imagery of policing: drawings of a Los Angeles Police Department helicopter looking down on people, a police car, a coffin, and a poster of wanted men. Tre disrupts a lesson on the Pilgrims, and when the teacher asks him to teach the class, he points to the map of Africa and states that: "Africa is the place where the body of the first man was found." This is a reference to the multiculturalism debate not only across the curriculum, but also in rap music, and in the press. Tre's lesson ends with a fight between himself and another boy. The following shot begins with Tre walking home. He passes a group of young Black males shooting dice. They break into a fight. As Tre crosses the street to go home, he is almost run over by a blue car which presumably is driven by gang members. His mother is on the telephone talking to the teacher about the fight and Tre's suspension. The editing of the soundtrack is interesting in this scene. As

Tre walks past the men shooting dice, their noise is placed in the background, and we hear in the foreground the conversation between Tre's mother and the teacher. This editing device unites different spaces through their sharing of the same sound. For example, later in the film, the community is shown as one when people in different places listen to the same rap song. (Similarly, in *Do the Right Thing,* Spike Lee uses the DJ and his music to unite the community.) The last scene in this episode involves Tre and his mother driving to his father's house. They pass by liquor stores and junkies standing by the doors. The mother reassures Tre that she loves him, and will do anything to keep him from ending up in jail, or standing in the streets in front of liquor stores.

Signs (Stop, One Way, Wrong Way, LAPD, Liquor Store, POLICE LINE DO NOT CROSS, and so on) play an important role in limiting the movement of people in South Central Los Angeles. Showing the airplane flying over the roofs not only indicates where we are in LA, but also suggests the freedom associated with flying away from such an enclosed space. Black American literature often draws on the theme of flying to construct desire for liberated spaces: Bigger Thomas of *Native Son* (Richard Wright) sees flying as a way out of the ghetto of South Side Chicago; Milkman of *Song of Solomon* (Morrison) reenacts the myth of flying Americans in order to free himself from an unwanted situation.

The signs become control tools for the police, in the way that they limit individual freedom of movement in the "hood." They also define the hood as a ghetto by using surveillance from above and outside to take agency away from people in the community. In fact, *Boyz N the Hood* is about the dispute over agency and control of the community that pits the protagonist and his allies against gang members and the police. The drawings of helicopters, police cars, and wanted men show how the police surveillance has penetrated the imaginary even of schoolchildren in the hood. Later on in the film, helicopter noise, police sirens, and police brutality are revealed to be as menacing and distracting to people in the hood as drugs and gang violence.

The dispute over the control of the hood is also a dispute over images. The police need to convince themselves and the media that every Black person is a potential gang member, armed and dangerous, in order to continue the policing of the hood in a terroristic and militaristic manner. For the Black policeman in the film, the life of a Black person is not worth much: "one less nigger out in the street and we won't have to worry about him." It is by making the gang members and other people in the hood accept this stereotype of themselves that the community is transformed into a ghetto, a place where Black life is not worth much. It seems to me that *Boyz N the Hood* blames the rise of crime and the people's feeling of being trapped in the hood on a conspiracy among the gang members, the police, the liquor stores, and Reagan. Indeed, the film raises questions of human rights violation when gang warfare and police brutality collude to prevent people from moving around freely, sleeping, or studying.

On the other hand, Tre's struggle to gain agency also coincides with his passage to manhood, and the development of a politics of caring for the community. *Boyz N the Hood,* in this respect, is one of the most didactic Black films. The other contenders are *Deep Cover,* and perhaps some rap videos which espouse a politics of identification with lawbreakers against the police.[5] The didacticism of *Boyz N the Hood* emanates from the film's attempt to teach Tre not to accept the police's and the media's stereotype of him and other young Black males as worthless; and to teach him to care for his community and reclaim it from both the gangs and the police. Didactic film language abounds in the film. We see it when the camera lingers on the liquor stores and homeless people, as Tre and his mother drive to his father's house. The mother, in one of the first instances of teaching Tre in the film, states that she loves him and that is why she is taking him out of this environment. Earlier in the same episode, we also saw the Reagan posters interpreted in a didactic manner, so as to blame him for the decay of the urban community. The posters are situated in the same environment as the murder scene.

However, Tre's father, more than the didactic camera and editing styles, is the central figure of judgment in the film. He calls the Black policeman "brother" in order to teach him, in the presence of Tre, how to care about other Black people; he delivers lessons on sex education, Black-on-Black crimes, the dumping of drugs in the Black community, gentrification, and the importance of Black-owned businesses in the Black community. He earns the nickname of preacher, and Tre's friends describe him as a sort of "Malcolm/Farrakhan" figure. Crucially, his teachings help Tre to develop a politics of caring, to stay in school, and more importantly, to stay alive. It is revealing in this sense that a didactic and slow-paced film like *Boyz N the Hood* can be entertaining and pleasurable at the same time.

The New Black Realism

Realism as a cinematic style is often claimed to describe films like *Boyz N the Hood, Juice,* and *Straight Out of Brooklyn.* When I taught *Boyz N the Hood,* my students talked about it in terms of realism: "What happened in the film happens everyday in America." "It is like it really is in South Central LA." "It describes policing in a realistic manner." "The characters on the screen look like the young people in the movie theater." "It captures gang life like it is." "It shows Black males as an endangered species." "I liked its depiction of liquor stores in the Black community." "I identified with Ice Cube's character because I know guys like that back home."

Clearly, there is something in the narrative of films like *Boyz N the Hood* and *Straight Out of Brooklyn* that links them, to put it in Aristotelian terms, to existent reality in Black communities. In my class, some students argued that these films use hip hop culture, which is the new Black youth culture and the most important youth culture in America today. Thus, the characters look *real* because they dress in the style of hip hop, talk the lingo of hip hop, practice its world view toward the police and women, and are played by rap stars such as Ice Cube. Furthermore, the films thematize an advocacy for Black males, whom they describe as endangered species, in the same way that rap groups such as Public Enemy sing in defense of Black males.

It seems to me, therefore, that the films are about Black males' initiation into manhood, the obstacles encountered that often result in death and separation, and the successful transition of some into manhood and responsibility toward the community. In *Juice,* for example, of the four young boys who perform the ritual of growing up, two die, one is seriously injured by a gun shot, and only one seems to have been successfully incorporated into society. Removing obstacles out of Black males' way is also the central theme of *Chameleon Street, Straight Out of Brooklyn, Deep Cover* and *Boyz N the Hood.*

In *Deep Cover,* the ritual of manhood involves the main character's exposure of a genocide plotted by drug dealers in Latin America and the highest officials in the US government against the Black community. The real "deep cover" in *Deep Cover* is the recipe for caring for the community against genocidal forces like White supremacists, drugs, and Black-on-Black crime. The removal of obstacles out of the main character's way leads to the discovery of the politics of caring to the Black community. In this film, as in many new Black realism films, to be a man is to be responsible for the Black community, and to protect it against the aforementioned dangers. John (Larry Fishburne), a cop working undercover as a drug dealer, enters in an intriguing relationship with a Black detective (Clarence Williams), who plays the born-again policeman. The religious policeman keeps reminding John of his responsibility to the community, and John laughs at him. Toward the end of the film, when the character played by Clarence Williams gets shot, John is united with him by the force of caring, and realizes that he must fight both the drug dealers and the police to protect his own.

A key difference between the new Black realism films and the Blaxploitation series of the 1970s lies in character development through rites of passage in the new films. Unlike the static characters of the Blaxploitation series, the characters of the new realism films change with the enfolding of the story line. As characters move obstacles out of their way, they grow into men, and develop a politics of caring for the community. The new realism films imitate the existent reality of urban life in America. Just as in real life the youth are pulled between hip hop life style, gang life, and education, we see in the films neighborhoods that are pulled between gang members, rappers, and education-prone kids. For the black youth, the passage into manhood is also a dangerous enterprise which leads to death both in reality and in film.

Notes

1. Janice Mosier Richolson, "He's Gotta Have It: An Interview with Spike Lee," in *Cineaste*, Vol. 28, No. 4, (1992), p. 14.

2. For more on the aesthetics of *Sweet Sweetback* and *Ganja and Hess*, see the important book, *Black Cinema Aesthetics: Issues in Independent Black Filmmaking*, edited by Gladstone L. Yearwood, Athens: Ohio University Center for Afro-American Studies, 1982; Tommy L. Lott "A No-Theory Theory of Contemporary Black Cinema," in *Black American Literature Forum* 25/2 (1991); and Manthia Diawara and Phyllis Klotman, "*Ganja and Hess:* Vampires, Sex, and Addictions," in *Black American Literature Forum* 25/2 (1991).

3. Cornel West, "Nihilism in Black America," in *Dissent* (Spring 1991), 223.

4. Clearly, there is a put-down of Black women in the rhetoric used to send Tre to his father's house. For an excellent critique of female-bashing in the film see Jacquie Jones, "The Ghetto Aesthetic," in *Wide Angle*, Volume 13, Nos. 3 & 4 (1991), 32–43.

5. See Regina Austin, " 'The Black Community,' Its Lawbreakers and a Politics of Identification," in *Southern California Law Review* (May 1992), for a thorough discussion of Black peoples' identification with the community and its lawbreakers.

2

"Twoness" in the Style of Oscar Micheaux

J. Ronald Green

Many critics and historians have been impressed by Oscar Micheaux's long, productive career. Micheaux produced over thirty independent feature films, as well as seven long novels, released over three decades. Few critics, however, have respected his work, and most would probably agree with James Nesteby, who has said in his work, *Black Images in American Films,* that the films are "racked by uneven talents and close budgets."[1] Nevertheless, I have been attracted to Micheaux's work since I first saw *Ten Minutes to Live* about ten years ago, and I am aware of other filmmakers and critics, such as Ken Jacobs and Thom Andersen, who appreciate his films.

Much of the character of Micheaux's work arises from his poor production values, which in turn arose from local economic conditions during production. Detailed discussions of his production values and the aesthetics of "poor cinema" are beyond the space limitations of this essay; here I will discuss Micheaux's style as reflecting a struggle with an equally fundamental problem of cultural identity that W. E. B. DuBois called "twoness."

Twoness

Thomas Cripps's ground-breaking book on the history of race movies, *Slow Fade to Black,*[2] has stood largely unchallenged as the major statement about the value of early films made by and for Black audiences, which were called race movies. Cripps's monumental effort in locating and interpreting primary and secondary source materials relating to Black cinema—along with pioneering efforts by Donald Bogle and Daniel J. Leab[3]—has opened to view a whole ethnic cinema that was previously

invisible. Cripps's thesis, founded on the historical phenomenon of assimilation, on the myth of the American melting pot, and on Black cinema as
a "problem" of nonassimilation, defined the territory and some major
issues of race movies. The "slow fade to black" thesis is an enormously
important contribution to the history of cinema. The critical work in this
history, however, is ill-founded and damaging to its own thesis.

Cripps ends his study at 1942, and on a positive note, by celebrating
the written agreement reached by "delegates of the National Association
for the Advancement of Colored People and the heads of several Hollywood studios" who "met and codified some social changes and procedures":

> The studios agreed to abandon pejorative racial roles, to place Negroes
> in positions as extras they could reasonably be expected to occupy in
> society, and to begin the slow task of integrating blacks into the ranks
> of studio technicians.[4]

In closing his introductory chapter, thus capping his whole thesis, Cripps
wrote:

> The 1942 agreement accomplished far more than allowing a few blacks
> to appear in roles that were not overtly racist. It changed the whole
> tone and nature of Hollywood's response to the Afro-American's role
> in film and, by extension, in American life as well.[5]

The problem with the optimism of this denouement is that it purports
to be an answer to a problem that Cripps himself has initially and repeatedly
presented as a non-Hollywood, as well as a Hollywood, problem. Early in
Slow Fade to Black, Cripps identified a debilitating dilemma for Black
film in America, a dilemma he said was associated closely with what
W. E. B. DuBois termed a "twoness" of American racial codes: African-
Americans, that is, face the possibility of two social identities at the same
time, whose relations to each other are strained, but which each Black
American must somehow resolve individually for herself or himself. The
models for the two conflicting identities are to be found firstly in the
dominant White culture that cannot be ignored, and secondly, in the ethnic
Black culture of their Afrocentric group. Twoness recognizes a need to
retain Black ethnic identity in the face of assimilation. Assimilation seemed
necessary for survival in America, but it presented a problem for the
retention of African identity. The 1942 Agreement addresses only assimilation, half the stated problem. One might hope that the assimilation of
Blacks would "Africanize" Hollywood, but there is little historical evidence relating to the assimilation of Black or other ethnic groups to support

such a hope. Any success derived from the 1942 agreement in integrating Blacks into the Hollywood culture industry would appear to be a gain for one side of the twoness dilemma but a loss for the other side. We see more positive black characters on television today, for example, but their African ethnicity is virtually erased.

Cripps presents the twoness problem in the following way:

> Perhaps the most illuminating element in the black struggle for an indigenous cinema was the attempt of the Negro press to create a black aesthetic. Such writers as Lester Walton, Harry Levette, and half a dozen more wrestled with the duality—the "twoness," as W. E. B. DuBois put it—of American racial codes as they impinged on the cinema. Was the Negro to be a unique American with an "eternal tom-tom beating in his breast [sic]," [Langston Hughes, "The Negro Artist and the Racial Mountain," Nation, June 23, 1926, p. 694] or was he to be a "lamp-blacked Anglo-Saxon" [George S. Schuyler, "The Negro Art Hokum," Nation, June 16, 1926, p. 662]?[6] By 1942 the critics had turned away from race movies and now supported Hollywood and the NAACP as the most effective means to bring about proper depiction of blacks on the screen. The keenest of these writers recognized that, for all their symbolic value as black enterprise, race movies tended to acquiesce in segregation, place white cupidity off-limits as a theme, rehash many stereotypes for which Hollywood had been blamed, set black against black, and imitate white movies.[7]

The solution to the twoness dilemma that is implied by this important paragraph is a poor one. After hearing that "the most illuminating element in the black struggle for an indigenous cinema was the attempt of the Negro press to create a black aesthetic," we learn that the illuminating aspect is that the attempt failed. The fact that by "1942 the critics had turned away from race movies and now supported Hollywood and the NAACP as the most effective means to bring about proper depiction of blacks on the screen" was scant cause for celebration. Hollywood has done a notoriously poor job of representing "outsiders." Any success by Blacks in Hollywood could be expected to come at the expense of important concessions. Hollywood's treatment of other ethnic groups, including White ones, should be taken into account before founding a whole thesis of Black representation on the 1942 agreements.

Still, Hollywood certainly should be held responsible for its extreme and peculiar misrepresentation of Blacks. The efforts of DuBois and the NAACP resulting in the 1942 agreements were necessary and laudable; but they should not be characterized as sufficient. As critics, we should do well to avoid the mistake that DuBois himself made, which Cripps has replicated in his thesis. DuBois presented the paradigmatic notion of twoness in the first few pages of *The Souls of Black Folk:*

> After the Egyptian and Indian, the Greek and Roman, the Teuton and Mongolian, the Negro is a sort of seventh son, born with a veil, and gifted with second-sight in this American world,—a world which yields him no true self-consciousness, but only lets him see himself through the revelation of the other world. It is a peculiar sensation, this double-consciousness, this sense of always looking at one's soul by the tape of a world that looks on in amused contempt and pity. One ever feels his twoness,—an American, a Negro; two souls, two thoughts, two unreconciled strivings; two warring ideals in one dark body, whose dogged strength alone keeps it from being torn asunder.[8]

Having identified double-consciousness, DuBois cast it solely in the role of problem when it can also be seen as a competence. Robert A. Bone, in *The Negro Novel in America,* thoroughly castigated DuBois for his critique of the Harlem School, placing DuBois among the "Negro middle class who believed that 'unassimilable' elements in the race should be hidden, and not exposed to public view in sordid novels."[9] Bone treated DuBois as a principal figure in his chapter titled, "The Rear Guard," he grouped DuBois with "spokesmen of Negro Philistia," and he placed DuBois first among the leadership of a "conservative faction."[10] Given the general high regard for DuBois (which includes my own), this judgment is perhaps too strong. One immediately wants to balance Bone's remarks with the equally true image of DuBois as: a Black nationalist (though not a separatist or Garveyite); a defined and accomplished antagonist against the color line as both an intellectual and a Weberian-cum-Marxist activist; and a frank critic with a complex understanding of American society, if not of American art. Bone recognized that it

> may seem strange to speak of DuBois, with his militant Negro nationalism and his fellow-traveling politics, as a conservative. Nevertheless, his emotional tirades against the Harlem School, when he was editor of *Crisis,* plainly reveal the strength of his attachment to the Victorian tradition. It is well to remember that DuBois was already in his mid-fifties at the beginning of the Negro Renaissance.[11]

The issue of twoness is important for an understanding of Micheaux, of race movies, and of Cripps's thesis about them. DuBois's idea of twoness implies wretched imposition and a threatened identity: "two warring ideals in one dark body, whose dogged strength alone keeps it from being torn asunder." DuBois's examples, however, of six first-born sons (Egyptians and Indians, Greek and Roman, Teuton and Mongolian) who do have an identity with no veil, can be seen as more complex exampla than DuBois intended. On the one hand, all of them are vigorous masters of their own destinies, and also conquerors, builders of nations and empires, and masters of the destinies of others. On the other hand, all of them are also conquered and colonized peoples. Twoness characterizes all their ethoses: Egyptian identity must account for Egypt's own subjection by Turkey, France and Britain; India was subjected by Macedonia and Britain; Greece by Macedonia and Rome; Rome by the Goths, the Byzantines, and the French; the Teutons by the Reformation and the Americans; and Mongolia by Japan. There is a twoness in all these identities that includes both mastery and subjection. The point here is not to suggest that DuBois's twoness is not a uniquely difficult situation to bear, but rather that some aspects of it resemble master/subject relationships that occur in the identities of most cultures and groups. The fact of the color line in America in one sense gives African-Americans important knowledge— the local knowledge of both master and subject at the same time. The United States is the dominant country in the world, directly and indirectly responsible for numerous colonial, neocolonial, and authoritarian regimes. African-Americans are American citizens, but, because of the color line, are in a position to understand two sides of American hegemony.

Though, as DuBois said, twoness may not be an enviable state (the value of the knowledge of twoness in no way *justifies* the color line), twoness is a knowledge worth having. The value of such knowledge justifies not only the study of Micheaux, but the place of race movies in any canon that claims to represent the dialectical aspects of American hegemony.[12] The twoness explored by Black filmmakers such as Oscar Micheaux has its own integrity and is, conceptually and effectually, an integral part of the history of American cinema.

Cripps has proposed that the future of Black cinema, and Black criticism and spectatorship, lies properly with Hollywood. He has tried hard to find works of artistic value created by what he calls the Black underground outside Hollywood, which included Micheaux and the Colored Players. But Cripps concluded that no Black producer was sufficiently capitalized to produce good films, and that Hollywood was sufficiently capitalized to co-opt any successful idea produced by Black producers of race movies— hence the negative aspect of the meaning of "slow fade to black"—the slow fade-*out* of the *independent* Black producer. Cripps also concluded that Black interests must, consequently, turn to Hollywood and try to integrate it—hence the positive aspect of his meaning of "slow fade"— the slow fade-*in* of the *Hollywood* Black producer.

Cripps answers the twoness dilemma by opting for assimilation, which represents one side of that dilemma. There is no evidence, however, that Hollywood can handle—in the interest of any group seeking assimilation—differences of identity as significant as the color line, economic status exploitation, patriarchal sexism, or sexual taboo. Cripps's answer is therefore inadequate. Hollywood does not take the lead in celebrating significant difference. For such leadership in cinema, one must look to the undercapitalized and always unassimilated independents.

If Cripps could write off Black independent race movies by saying, as he did in the conclusion of his introduction quoted above, that Black-produced cinema acquiesced in segregation, placed White cupidity off-limits as a theme, rehashed many stereotypes for which Hollywood had been blamed, set Black against Black, and imitated White movies, it is because he accepted without question the aesthetics of assimilation. He hoped that the assimilation of Blacks in Hollywood (the slow fade-in) would change those aesthetics, would Africanize the Americans as much as Americanize the Africans. But Hollywood is still the aesthetic legacy of Griffith, of racism and patriarchy, reflecting and representing domination while erasing or mollifying subjection. Hollywood aesthetics were designed and are operated by and for those who have already settled any struggle with twoness.

Micheaux's Reception

No extant Micheaux film looks much like a well-made Hollywood film. The closest to the model may be *Body and Soul* (1924), the film picked by the Directors Guild of America to be shown at the recent ceremony honoring their selection of Micheaux for their Lifetime Achievement Award. Cripps has been intolerant of the deviation of Micheaux's style from that of Hollywood; his conclusions in *Slow Fade to Black* still represent a consensus on Micheaux's accomplishment.

Cripps has described the pervasive, typical "mistakes" in Micheaux's style, and has shown that the Micheaux company was aware of them but unable to correct them because of the prohibitive expense of higher shooting ratios, retakes, master shots, and professional editing. The apparatus of Cripps's own critical assessment, however, is founded on the unresolved contradiction of twoness. At the beginning of his discussion of Micheaux, Cripps described the central dilemma for Micheaux (and Black-produced race movies) as the "temptation to make mirror images of white movies [in which case] . . . success itself might be a false god for Negroes."[13] Throughout the discussions on Micheaux, Cripps uses the term "mirror images" to signify this problem.

This perspicacious identification of what is at stake in race movies, and in Micheaux's work, is unresolved by Cripps's treatment, however. Instead of holding up this lantern of contradiction to illuminate the struggle of Black filmmakers and critics, Cripps alternated in his loyalties from one side of that contradiction to the other. At times, Cripps recognized that Black filmmakers are in a "fight against Hollywood,"[14] and disagreed with Black critics who expressed their Eastern cultural snobbery at the expense of racial solidarity. Cripps calls attention to the problem of regional snobbery with this example from the *Amsterdam News:* "[Our] people in New York, used to the best pictures, do not accept Micheaux."[15] (One might call this "dicty"[16] criticism.) Cripps noted that it was unfortunate that the New York critics took this critical stance, since it helped to kill a nascent tendency in the Black press and Black middle class to accept the work of Black moviemakers. The lack of support in New York may or may not have been unfortunate. We are left wondering whether or not to agree with Cripps, because he has not provided us with the criteria to resolve the historical judgment. Why would it have been better for "the proposed union of moviemen with the black bourgeoisie" to succeed,[17] if the danger of producing mirror images of White filmmaking was an unavoidable result? How did Cripps avoid contradictory values here? How do we proceed to discuss Micheaux or the phenomenon of race movies at all until we can say something about the possible outcomes of the dilemma of "twoness"?

Cripps's case against Black critics continued; he has written that

> Roi Ottley, a major figure among black newspapermen, called forth even less precise objections and settled for a rhetorical broad racial boosterism:
>
> "The Green Pastures" will no doubt, receive magnificent and glowing accounts in the Negro press . . . and unhappily so for the Negro public. . . . Negro newspapers on the whole have a false sense of values. . . . They seem to work from the promise that anytime a Negro appears in a play or picture which the whites have produced it should be applauded regardless of its merits. . . . This department goes on record as feeling that Oscar Micheaux, with his inferior equipment, would have produced a better picture.[18]

It is pointless to blame criticism such as Ottley's for contributing to the demise of Black independent race movies, for several reasons. First, because Ottley's position exemplified the attitude toward race movies that Micheaux himself wanted to encourage—frank but helpful critique. Second, Ottley rejected out of hand the propriety of an apartheid system, in which White people make movies for Black people. If all Black critics had taken that position, and if readers of the Black press had supported that position, then Hollywood and White independents would not have been able to kill the Black film movement. Hollywood would have been recognized as a rich monstrosity, whose view of Blacks was not worthy of critique but only of rejection.

Third, Ottley suggested by the phrasing of his idea—"Micheaux, with his inferior equipment, would have produced a better picture"—that low production values can make "better" movies. (I treat low production values as an aspect of style in a forthcoming essay, "Oscar Micheaux and Production Values.")

Importantly, Cripps explained why turning the production of Black culture (in the form of Black musicals) over to White production companies drove the Black producers out of business. Cripps says:

> The compromise solutions offered by Hollywood in its slick, bright packages seemed enough for hungry Negro audiences. *Variety,* whose editors rarely asked bookers to take risks, challenged exhibitors to overcome the hot-weather opening of *The Green Pastures.* . . . But few black or white critics, producers, and writers shared those early hopes. . . . Because *Hearts in Dixie, Hallelujah!,* and *The Green Pastures* failed to do top-dollar business, the possibilities of black life on film were lost on moviemakers.[19]

Cripps's analysis here was leading toward a condemnation of the phenomenon of White production of Black musicals. However, some of Cripps's language (for example, "those early hopes that had stirred," and "the possibilities . . . were lost") suggested that some substantial basis for hope had existed in the apartheid arrangement. His descriptive analysis of *The Green Pastures* was aimed at identifying such a basis for hope.[20]

Cripps's critical stance here—White studio disinterest and timidity plus "Black accommodation" to slick compromises as the cause of a failed opportunity to produce Black movies in a White industry—seemed again to accept only one side of the dilemma of Black production. He seemed to be regretting an opportunity for successful moviemaking without positing what success might mean and how it might avoid DuBois's dilemma of twoness. And in his argument Cripps blamed two examples of criticism from the Black press of that time (Matthews and Ottley) that seem to suggest the most responsible approach toward the dilemma. The two critics that Cripps criticized were insisting that no matter what the technical and stylistic problems, the only future for the production of Black culture was through Black people, and the only future for Black films was through Black filmmakers. Technical "problems" then would become technical characteristics, elements of style and texture, as in an Elijah Pierce sculpture. "Mistakes" must then be proven as mistakes according to explicit criteria derived from the Black folk culture or the African-American culture of the maker (whether rural or urban, working- or middle-class)—the culture of twoness—not criteria derived from the apartheid Hollywood industry. Once such an antiapartheid approach constitutes a norm, the occasional cross-cultural productions, such as *The Cool World* (1964) by Shirley Clarke, and *The Quiet One* (1948) by Sidney Meyers and written by James Agee (all White artists), can be seen as gifts, not as models for the production or representation of Black culture. Similarly, anything in the features of *The Green Pastures, Hallelujah!*, or *Carmen Jones* that might seem good or pleasing to Black audiences might be accepted or rejected without any implication that those films are examples of how Black culture is produced or represented.

Cripps critically analyzed several Micheaux films. The critical stance of these analyses can be found in his general introduction to Micheaux's work:

> For twenty years [Micheaux] carried the movement in the face of apathy and mockery; in spite of an amateurish, almost naive artlessness. Like the comedians Jerry Lewis and Harry Langdon and the tragedian John Barrymore, he suffered for want of a firm hand to lend discipline to his craft. Eccentrically, he could ascend to peaks of bizarre excess and then insert unmatching cutaway shots. He would create a mood with a fine back-lighted shot; then his limited budget would force him to cut to a lame, ill-lighted mistake that would have ended on the cutting room floor of a major studio.[21]

There are several problems with this paragraph. It seems to reject without discussion the value of the "amateurish" and the "naive" in art, or at least seems to relegate the amateur and the naive to the realm of the "artless." But, in relation to Hollywood slickness, the amateur and the naive are saving graces; they produce qualities conducive to an art Hollywood does not value. Just as Black African art and African-American music were important in breaking the arrogant hegemony of decadent classicisms after the turn of the century, Black filmmaking might have helped bring life and reality to Hollywood classicism a few years later. It could still do so today. On the other side of the dilemma of the color line, it is of little importance that black music helped reanimate White music, or that Black cinema could have done the same for Hollywood; Black American music stands on its own, and so does Black cinema.[22]

Cripps's reference to Jerry Lewis's need of a "firm hand to lend discipline to his craft" is debatable and depends on which independently produced Jerry Lewis films are meant. There is considerable room for argument about where Lewis's personal taste and choices served him well and where they did not; but there is little room for argument that Lewis's genius was well served by his decision to go independent. If he made some terrible films, they are balanced by films of astounding insight, such as *The Nutty Professor* (1963), that no one else could have imagined.

One needs more specificity for a critique of Cripps's description of Lewis's and of Micheaux's style. When Cripps noted that Micheaux "could ascend to peaks of bizarre excess and then insert unmatched cutaway shots," Cripps seemed to be valorizing the bizarre excess, since he refers to its occurrences as "peaks," and then seemed to be disdaining the cutaway shots through the use of the term "unmatching." To judge whether we agree with this scheme of values, we need to know more about both the bizarre excess and the cutaway shots to which he referred. However, we can infer that Cripps believed narrative films should use the conventions of matching. We might even infer that, since match cutting is a convention of the well-made Hollywood film, brought to perfection by Griffith, Cripps accepted the conventions of that cinema.

But it is not necessary to assume the conventions of Hollywood as the basis of narrative cinema. Cripps had already stated that Micheaux and other Black independents were in a fight against Hollywood, that the temptation for Black producers was to make mirror images of White movies. Cripps complained that the viewers and critics in New York who were "used to the best pictures" were exercising "regional snobbery" in rejecting Micheaux. He reported that "the keenest critics turned away from race movies" partly because they were imitating White movies.[23] What would a "good" Black cinema look like, then, assuming it did not imitate classical White cinema? Cripps did not pose that question; rather he tended to assume the criteria for classical cinema to be universal. Yet any student of world cinema knows that there are many examples of narrative cinema that assume formal and operational principles other than those of the classic Hollywood film. Many of those films have been successful at reaching an appreciative and supportive audience, a non-mass audience which understands varieties of individualistic, cultural, or ethnic forms and semiotic codes. There are all sorts of ways, for example, that Black independent filmmakers can and do make movies, just as Black musicians, preachers, and writers showed there were different ways to make improvisational music, oral jeremiad, and narratives that could both be understood by their own cultures and later be celebrated by Eurocentric cultures. The contribution of these forms to art and to pleasure has been the greater for their ethnic authenticity and can only be diminished by any forced concessions toward classicism. The symphonic music of Ellington, for example, in its slickness and classicism, poorly represents his contribution, not only to African-American culture, but to Eurocentric and world culture—this in spite of his obvious need of and pleasure in producing classical Western music and Eurocentric jazz. Ellington's best music remains his earlier, European-influenced but nevertheless Afrocentric jazz, such as "Mood Indigo" (1930) and "Ko-Ko" (1940), rather than his later,

African-influenced but nevertheless Euro-centric symphonic suites, such as "Afro-Eurasian Eclipse" (1971) or the sacred concerts.

The fact that Black independent race movies failed commercially is very important, and much of Cripps's study is crucial to an understanding of that failure. Though commercial failure is not equivalent to artistic failure, Cripps's extensive negative appraisals of several of Micheaux's films not unreasonably suggest that commercial failure was at least partly the result of artistic failure. In his discussion of Micheaux's *The Notorius Elinor Lee* (1940), for example, Cripps wrote that this film "had proven that for race movies to be viable they must be good." The use of the term "good" should warn us, as J. L. Austin warned us, to "remember what the philosophers have said about the word 'good.' "[24] Austin called it, like the term "real," a "substantive-hungry" term:

> . . . what about 'good'? We have here a variety of gaps crying out for substantives—'A good *what?*', 'Good *at* what?'—a good book perhaps, but not a good novel; good at pruning roses, but not good at mending cars.[25]

Since Cripps failed to define criteria for the *kind* of cinema that would constitute a solution to the problem of twoness, there is no foundation for a good Black cinema. Cripps backed up his use of the term "good" with analytic details that are subjective and inadequately explained—for example, " . . . a flat succession of long shots and poorly choreographed closeups." We are asked to trust that we would agree that the succession of long shots is "flat" and the close-ups "poorly" choreographed. But in fact, Cripps's qualifiers are not trustworthy, nor are his descriptions of Micheaux's films, as we shall see below. So again we note that Cripps's historical work on Black cinema is crucial, but his critical work on the films was ill-founded and damaging to his own thesis.

The first Micheaux film Cripps evaluated as narrative art was *The Symbol of the Unconquered* (1921), which he calls

> a mindless scattergun that was [according to an article in the *Competitor* in 1921] to be part of "one of the greatest vitalizing forces in race adjustment," a promoter of racial understanding, an indictment of the KKK, a "thrilling and realistic" melodrama, a lesson in "the folly of color, both within and without the race," a love story, a quest for oil-bearing land, and a pointed assault on "passing" Negroes.[26]

We are supposed to accept this list of themes as evidence that the film is mindless and scattergun. Cripps's critique, however, does not appear to be based on a viewing of the film. His footnote references to the quotation above and his references to the same film elsewhere in the book (page 180) are based on an article written about the film in 1921, not on the film itself; that article is the apparent source of his knowledge. In fact, I have not been able to locate evidence of an extant print of the film.

Also, once again we are given no criteria for assessing Cripps's judgment about the film. We are asked to accept that the film's apparent attempt to deal with many issues (large and small, public and private) is inherently scattergun and mindless. Does he mean that single movies cannot deal with many themes and issues? Would he include the films of D. W. Griffith, Akira Kurosawa, or Jean-Luc Godard under that proscription? Could we not apply Cripps's abstract of the themes in Micheaux's *The Symbol of the Unconquered* to Griffith's *The Birth of a Nation* (1915), and turn it (mutatis mutandis) into White supremacist praise? The following, for example, is my own parody of Cripps's abstract transformed into "praise" for Griffith's film:

> *Birth of a Nation* was a brilliant integration of one of the greatest vitalizing forces in racial relations, a promoter of racial loyalty and faith, an indictment of carpetbagging reconstruction, a thrilling melodrama, a realistic history lesson, a parable on the folly of color-blindness both in the North and the South, a love story, a quest for a lost agrarian aristocracy, and a pointed assault on the shameful sexual consequences of Northern liberalism.

Griffith and Thomas Dixon (the Yale University roommate of Woodrow Wilson and a Southern racist who wrote the book on which Griffith's film was based) would surely approve of such a valuative description of their work. Most film scholars would agree that all the themes mentioned are major concerns of the film. What is it about *The Birth of a Nation* that would prevent Cripps from assessing it as a "mindless scattergun" of intentions, rather than the masterpiece of White supremacist propaganda and the apotheosis of Hollywoodian teleology that it is generally accepted to be? What distinguishes "mindless scattergun" from "epic thematic richness"? Perhaps Cripps would want to defend the coherency of Griffith's film, and spell out the incoherence that he has perceived in the written description of Micheaux's film, but he has not done so.

The lack of criteria to be used for evaluation and the lack of salient descriptive detail in Cripps's critique of *The Symbol of the Unconquered* is typical of every critique of Micheaux's films in Cripps's book. On the very next page Cripps noted:

> And when [Micheaux] was short of cash he was not above an occasional exploitation of gullible Negro audiences. *Within Our Gates,* his treatment of the Leo Frank lynching case, reappeared a year later as

The Gunsaulus Mystery, a "whodunnit" probably patched together from old "outtakes" or merely retitled and rereleased.[27]

Once again, neither of these two films was extant when Cripps wrote his critique.[28] Cripps was speculating, somewhat wildly, since his charge that Micheaux used extensive outtakes or rereleased the older film under a new title can be disproved easily by examining the credits of the two films, in which we find only one actor common to both, Evelyn Preer. Perhaps the credits were not available before Cripps published his book, nevertheless, the speculation appears to have been groundless and seems careless and ill founded. Once again, there are no criteria to help us understand why the use of outtakes would be inherently conducive to "bad" filmmaking, even if Micheaux had done what Cripps suggests. As it happens, one of the most interesting aspects of Micheaux's work is his constant recycling of his material throughout his films and his novels— his obsessions and his dreams keep recurring, mutating and modulating, accruing density and performing variations.

Cripps next discussed at some length a film that is extant and viewable in at least one version, *Body and Soul* (1924), which he said "represented the highest level of achievement for Micheaux."[29] Cripps had several positive comments about this film, for example, "Robeson's preacher . . . enlarged the role into complex parts . . . [bringing] power to the gambler's cynical smile and to the preacher's practical piety." Our ability to make sense of this characterization of Robeson's presence, however, depends on our understanding which version of the film is being discussed. Cripps introduced it as the "second version," but there is no definitive documentation in Cripps's book of the history of the existence of particular, identifiable versions of this film. The only extant version cited is a print at the George Eastman House archive, dated 1925. The 1925 dating would seem to indicate that this was a later version (possibly the "second version" to which Cripps refers), which was subjected to reediting at the insistence of the New York board of censors before release was granted, thus "bearing white fingermarks."[30] If we are to infer that Cripps's reference is to the print at George Eastman House, his description of Robeson's roles bears very little resemblance to those in that version, for in that version the Robeson character is split between a "bad" preacher who is also a gambler and ex-convict, and a "good" look-alike brother who is an inventor and entrepreneur and who triumphs in the end. There is no sense to be made of "the preacher's practical piety" since there is no piety in that role. While it may be true that Robeson's role was "enlarged . . . into complex parts," it is impossible to assume what those parts are and who enlarged them until the historical dust is blown off the mystery of the various versions of this film.

It is difficult to trust Cripps's descriptive work. In *Body and Soul,* Cripps describes the daughter waking from the dream, whereas the Eastman House print (and, I suspect, every other possible version) shows the mother as the dreamer. Cripps seems to have paid insufficient attention to the film texts themselves, thus compounding the more basic problem of the general absence of valuative criteria. The critical discussions in *Slow Fade to Black* of other Micheaux films are similarly hampered.

This critique of Cripps's assessment of Micheaux would be unnecessary if his book were not generally accepted as a standard reference on Black cinema, and if Cripps had presented his artistic judgments more tentatively. Cripps only appears to have laid the groundwork of evidence for his almost completely negative evaluation of Micheaux's artistic accomplishment, for his groundwork is faulty. That fact does not imply, in and of itself, that Cripps is wrong, simply that the case he seems to have nailed shut is still wide open. Since many books and articles that discuss Micheaux have tended to agree with Cripps, it is clear that there is something about Micheaux's work that invites disdain and dismissal. Anyone who has seen the work will understand that response. The fact that Micheaux's films seem so rough and amateurish, compared to the standard of Hollywood and Europe, probably explains why the negative case against Micheaux as artist has been so poorly constructed. Micheaux's "inadequacies" seem just obvious to anyone who assumes most of the criteria of classical Hollywood film.

Micheaux, however, was a deeply thoughtful and important filmmaker in several ways, which the next part of this essay will begin to explore. He did not assume Hollywood standards, nor must we. We must, in fact, look at the films themselves more closely to articulate their values according to paradigms, some of which may be other than those of White cinema. White cinema is important to Micheaux's work, and to the understanding of it, certainly, but White cinema is not a determinant model. Micheaux's production values and style were appropriate to his circumstances. They can be considered artistically limiting only in the way that the super-refined style and the high production values of *Gone With the Wind* (1939) are artistically limiting.

Micheaux's Style

The struggle itself, with twoness, remains of primary interest. To the extent that the struggle can be significantly located in Hollywood, Hollywood film is of interest. But, instead of turning too quickly to Hollywood, either to place hopes or prove fears, I want to begin an examination of Micheaux's style.

Micheaux's treatment of racial issues was much more sophisticated than has been generally noticed.[31] As stated previously, Cripps concluded that "race movies tended to acquiesce in segregation, place white cupidity off-limits as a theme, rehash many stereotypes . . . , set black against black, and imitate white movies."[32] I believe these attributes are incorrectly characterized as failures, as regards Micheaux; he explored just those issues, among others. Full discussion on Cripps's list of failures must wait for another occasion, but it is nevertheless safe to say that Hollywood could not be expected to be able to deal with these issues, or most other issues Micheaux explored, at the level he wanted to explore them. It is equally improbable that Hollywood's style would ever reflect such sensitivity to twoness and contradiction as Micheaux's style does.

According to Neal Gabler's thesis in *An Empire of Their Own,*[33] Hollywood was constructed almost entirely by immigrants who wanted desperately to assimilate to the characteristics of the founding groups of Europe and New England. Hollywood was created and its style was designed to create an empire of illusion that would do just that—turn immigrants into the image of the power elite, the "New England-Wall Street-Middle West money,"[34] American through the ideals and aesthetics of Hollywood movies.

One difficulty of the American industrial revolution was that both the labor and consumer markets (pretty much the same groups by the time mass production reached its maturity) were radically fragmented. The factories and urban centers were attracting new ethnic groups all the time, including the Southern Blacks who were in the midst of their greatest migration northward. This is about the time when Griffith and Micheaux were getting underway. Hollywood, itself seeking a dependable mass market, began trying to assimilate the new urban diversity. In order to cover over the substantive near-impossibility of such a job, Hollywood developed a style of gloss, illusionism, and closure.

Micheaux's style might be understood better as a retention of early film traits, from before the advent of glossy illusionism, then as a failed imitation of White movies. His style is more closely related to the glossing of a text than the glossing over of a rough surface. If we are to accept a nonassimilative style that glosses a living struggle with twoness, and if twoness, as DuBois said, threatens the dark body with "being torn asunder," then we must expect a style that reflects double-consciousness and struggle.

One example of such a style is found in Micheaux's treatment of a minor character in *The Girl from Chicago* (1932): the sister of Mary Austin.[35] Mary Austin is a middle-aged Southern Black woman who runs a boarding house in the small town of Batesburg, Mississippi (reminiscent of the Patesville of *The Conjure Woman,* 1899, by Black writer Charles Chesnutt). She wishes to send her sister North to seek her fortune as a singer; Austin's boarding-house savings are all set aside for that purpose. When Norma Shephard, the female lead in the film, arrives in town to take up her position as a new teacher, she stays at Austin's boarding house. The boarding house is the setting for most of the action in the first half of the film, since it also temporarily houses the male lead, Alonzo White, who eventually captures the villain there, saving Norma.

The first five minutes of the film are composed of some thirty short- and medium-length shots—averaging about ten seconds each, with one take of about sixty seconds—full of disturbing content (peonage and potential seduction or rape) as well as disturbing style (flagrantly discontinuous matching, expressionistic shooting, some awkward blocking and acting and some practically comic, but also illusion-rending, audio glitches). Then there occurs a shot sequence of over three minutes in which Mary Austin, in medium shot, stands beside her sister, who, seated in the foreground at the piano, performs an entire song. The transition to this shot is accented on the leading side of the cut by a shot of the villain, Jeff Ballinger's car exiting screen right, and on the trailing side of the cut by a strong piano tone that is struck a fraction of a beat after the cut to the scene in question. Thus we spring, via syncopation, into this shot sequence out of a particularly fragmented experience. Mary Austin's sister sings "Blue Lagoon" in an impressive, but imperfect, light-operatic voice. Partly because the recording quality is low, the voice seems to break up occasionally, and the humble upright piano sounds tinny. The single-point lighting that falls off to darkness, and the hard, live acoustics seem consistent with the low production values and discontinuities in editing, and the declamatory acting style of the previous scene. The effect produced is bound to be excruciating or inappropriately comic to anyone demanding Hollywood production qualities.

Yet for anyone sympathetic to the economic status of the characters, for whom we are meant to care, and for whom there is no narrative reason for us not to care at this point, this shot sequence is realistic and appealing. There is both hope and pathos in the desires of the two sisters, which are well expressed in the "grain" of this untrained, but beautiful voice, and in the style of its representation.[36] There is integrity in the unity of time, place, and action that sets this song apart as a vignette for our appreciation and a haven from surrounding confusion; the title and theme of the song reinforce the effect of haven. The hopes and fears in this scene are stylistically represented in the contrasts: confusion versus unity of shooting and editing; roughness of audio recording and of untrained voice versus smoothness of the vocal talent and the self-confidence of the singer.

Even though there is pathos as well as hope, the scene is not pathetic. Pathos does not dominate, since some Black singers, writers, dancers, musicians, and composers were making it in Chicago and Harlem at the time. Jazz, blues, jazz dance, and the Harlem Renaissance were in full flower in 1932. In the second half of *The Girl from Chicago,* most of the primary and secondary characters move to Harlem. The line "Home to Harlem!" uttered by Alonzo in celebration of the move from Batesburg to Harlem is an inside reference to a famous novel of that title by one of the leading lights of the Harlem renaissance, Claude McKay. Many of those who succeeded during the renaissance period were not "New Negroes," or eastern-educated dickty-styled ("high-toned") artists, and many of those who were at least partly dickty were loyal to their humble origins in the South, as was Zora Neale Hurston, for example. Mary Austin's sister's song of the blue lagoon is more dickty, certainly, than Bessie Smith's or Billie Holiday's songs, but the success of Smith and Holiday lend credibility to the Austin family's hopes. Micheaux's scene represents the hopes and fears of the migration realistically, which Hollywood has never done.

There are several possible objections to this scene. It is possible to object that the sister's voice is not a "good" one, that it breaks in places— so did Louis Armstrong's and Bob Dylan's, although their style was more ironic. Armstrong and Dylan were not always ironic, but to the extent that they were, it was part of what made them great. Mary Austin's sister, however, is not meant to represent greatness—she represents hope and pathos, and she may yet learn irony too. There is "hope" for her.

It is possible to object that the shot is too dark. But so is the work of many photographers, such as Edward Steichen, W. Eugene Smith, Bill Brandt, and many of the philosophical photographers of the 1960s. Wynn Bullock has described darkroom techniques intended to produce a darker overall tone to some photographic printing than would likely be produced by an amateur photographer. In the photo-secessionist movement of Micheaux's own period, dark printing tones were sought in order to replicate the saturation of lithographs and other traditional academic art.[37] More importantly, the darkness of Micheaux's shot serves its representation of an interior scene in a depression-era, lower-middle-class house of American Victorian or Southern Gothic origins, a house that would typically be dark, compartmentalized into small rooms, and run-down. To light this scene strongly and from the classical three points would give an inappropriately glossy effect. Had Micheaux had the capital to shoot "correctly," the scene might have changed stylistically from subtly tragic to merely mediocre. It may be difficult to see the tragedy of such a scene, but, from the point of view of the filmmaker, the talent and potential success represented is grand. That grandness, combined with an element of fear, and the possibilities of failure that are inherent in the style of the film and explored in the themes and narrative events of the second half, produce a tragic overtone.

It is possible to object that Micheaux's shot is grainy. Yet shots in cinema verité and direct cinema, semi-documentary, Neorealism, New Wave, and underground styles are often grainy. All those styles are accepted (though they were not originally) as mature, purposeful, and effective. They became accepted stylistically as appropriate to the circumstances of their production and to representational systems, once those were understood. The grain in Micheaux's shot reflects lower-middle-class tawdriness and material thinness, approximating the economic status of the boarding house and of the film's producer. Micheaux's interiors are reminiscent of the Farm Security Administration photographs of the Southern poor (those of tenant farmers, for example, by photographers Walker Evans and Russell Lee). The content represented in Micheaux is lower-middle-class instead of poor—the boarding house is plain and run-down, but not dirty and falling apart like the FSA tenant farmhouses. The style of Micheaux's shots is closer to the production style and aesthetics of the subjects than Evans's and Lee's style is to the style and aesthetics of their subjects. Micheaux's dark, grainy shots look like the faded, halftone newspaper and magazine art that decorate the sharecroppers' houses in Evans's and Lee's photographs. Evans and Lee reproduced those sharecroppers' interiors, but they represented them through their own styles of photography, which were often elegant and well produced. Micheaux as a producer was closer to the economic status and the style of his subjects.

It is possible to object that the piano in this shot sequence is tinny and out of tune and is presented as such without irony, thus becoming ludicrous—yet the piano in one of Benny Carter's jazz groups, "Benny Carter and His Swing Quintet," is tinny and out of tune and is not used ironically. The instruments in Carter's "Waltzing the Blues" and "Jingle Bells" sound, in relation to earlier jazz, like the "original instruments" movement of Gustav Leonhardt and Nikolaus Harnoncourt in classical music today.[38] Benny Carter has spent much of his career writing music and arrangements for very smooth orchestras and for slick Hollywood films and mainstream television programs and commercials. His choice of "tinny" original instruments for some of his recording sessions was aesthetically legitimate, and resulted in some of his most engaging work. Micheaux's performers and instruments were also legitimate, in spite of the fact that Micheaux's choices were more bound by economic constraints.[39]

After Mary Austin's sister's song ends, the shot sequence continues with Austin congratulating her sister on the perfection of her performance and lamenting the lack of financial resources that prevent her from sending her sister to Chicago to pursue a career. Austin strikes her open hand with her fist and says "If I only had a few more boarders, I could soon send you." Mary Austin's references to her own lack of financial resources can be understood to express the anguish of any "producer" or manager of talent—such as Micheaux himself. Micheaux's production values and style in this shot can be read as part of a representation of desire for financial means; that is, Micheaux has presented Mary Austin as having a problem similar to his own, and thus the production values and style themselves become a contributing theme in the narrative. The question of Micheaux's style, that is, becomes itself a theme treated by the film, as does the struggle for twoness inherent in the style of all race movies but absent from the style of the Hollywood films produced for Black audiences.

How the themes of production financing and representations of twoness may be developed and resolved I leave for the moment to the interested reader to explore. I can suggest the following avenues: (1) There are several more set-piece singing sequences in the film, two of them in the boarding house in the first half of the film, the others in nightclubs in Harlem in the second half. Each of those set in the boarding house is presented in a style different from that of the original, and each from that of the other. Those three sequences might be understood as a progression, in which the stylistic changes and the narrative meanings constitute a development of underlying theme of the struggle with twoness. In these three sequences, the style becomes progressively fragmented in ways related to the introduction or intrusion of significant new characters. The intercutting becomes very confusing, the matching of the eyeline vectors of glances becomes complex and unorthodox, at one point placing the audience in the position of a spying "snitch" by use of a direct glance— a shot of the singer, Wade Washington, looking straight at the camera.

(2) The direct glance is used at several other points of the narrative, with poignancy. When Alonzo and Norma declare their feelings for each other and conspire to keep their relationship dark, they look at the camera. When they discuss Liza Hatfield's lover of the second half of the film, the numbers racket magnate, Gomez, during the "rupture" in Liza's song (this scene is discussed below), they refer to him as "furtive." While emphasizing the term "furtive," they speak directly to the camera. These direct glances may be seen as a representation of direct speech, of integrity and good faith, through a simple, pseudo-theatrical address to the audience. They can also be seen as part of a style that is less illusionistic and glossy than that of Hollywood, that does not attempt suture.

(3) The whole production, so to speak, moves to Harlem in the middle of the movie. This might be considered a serious flaw in the film, because the move seems to hack the narrative in two, and the Harlem story becomes a seemingly gratuitous second beginning for all the characters. Some story lines are tied off completely, while others are taken up again later. The extreme and messy break is not gratuitous, however, but is integral in ways related to the theme of production financing. The break represents the great migration itself, which occurred before the depression when

thousands of ambitious Blacks moved from the agrarian, rural, poorly capitalized South to the industrial, urban, well-capitalized North. People went North to get jobs (personal and household financing), but also to seek their fortune as artists and entrepreneurs (production opportunities and production financing). Mary Austin and her sister, as well as Alonzo and Norma, are among the characters in *The Girl from Chicago* who go North.

(4) There are several production numbers in the second half of the film, the most important of which features the eponymous girl from Chicago, Liza Hatfield, as the lead chanteuse of a jazz band. This sequence echoes the earlier "production number" in the boarding house. Liza Hatfield represents the "wrong" approach to the twoness problem and to production values and style. Narrative anticipation builds around her production number as the film's male lead, Alonzo White, in conversation with Norma, calls Liza exotic and strange, partly because Liza is reputed to be returning from a successful career in Paris and is of unknown African-American origin. Liza's production number is deeply ruptured by a cut-away from the lead-in music to another long discussion of her by Alonzo and Norma at their nightclub table. The cutaway is one of those time-extending, non-continuity edits discussed by Eisenstein—when Alonzo's and Norma's discussion ends and we return to the production number, the music continues from the same point we left it, as a long take without further interruption. The song, "Love is a Rhapsody," is intended to be seductive and polished. Although the production number recalls Mary's sister's performance in some ways—the long take of a female vocal performance—Liza's number is distinguished in many ways from Mary's sister's, most relevantly by its representation of higher production values. Since Liza turns out to be the central problem in the film, her relation to explicitly higher production values—those of Paris and of the Radium Club where she sings in Harlem—than those of the "good" characters, we have some evidence for an evaluation and narrative conclusion about the theme of production financing for African-Americans struggling with twoness. The glossier production number, though it is enjoyed by Alonzo and is meant for the enjoyment of Micheaux's audience, is located in a realm of villainy, furtiveness, and seduction.

My case is not that Micheaux intended every aspect of his style, but that the style is appropriate to and worthy of his situation and his issues, and that, therefore, his accomplishment was greater than has been recognized. Micheaux's style has served important themes and has provided a complex but worthy answer to the twoness dilemma. Micheaux has represented both the hope for and dangers of assimilation. He has compared the hopes of one amateur singer and the accomplishments of one professional singer, and has incorporated ideas about the production financing and stylistic values of each. The relatively high financing and stylistic values are associated with Liza Hatfield, a virtual prostitute; the lower production values are associated with the hopes of a character with undeveloped talent and personal integrity. Micheaux associates his own undeveloped style and personal integrity with both these modes, as a hope and a fear. He would like to be able to assimilate into both aspects of the American culture, but he represents that assimilation as dangerous, as well as attractive, for his group. The idea of a dangerous attraction is one reflection of the struggle with twoness in African-American assimilation, a struggle embodied in a style "whose dogged strength alone keeps it from being torn asunder."[40]

Notes

1. Nesteby, *Black Images in American Films, 1896–1954: The Interplay Between Civil Rights and Film Culture* (New York: Lanham, 1982).

2. Thomas Cripps, *Slow Fade to Black* (London: Oxford University Press, 1977).

3. Donald Bogle, *Toms, Coons, Mulattoes, Mammies & Bucks* (New York: Viking, 1973); Daniel J. Leab, *From Sambo to Superspade: The Black Experience in Motion Pictures* (Boston: Houghton Mifflin, 1975).

4. Cripps, *Slow Fade*, 3.

5. Cripps, *Slow Fade*, 7.

6. I include the full references for Schuyler and Hughes because Cripps, in his footnote, has attributed the Schuyler quotation to Hughes and vice versa, and Cripps has reversed the dates of the articles, placing the Hughes instead of the Schuyler article on June 16. Moreover, the quotation from Hughes is inaccurate—in the original article the line reads "the eternal tom-tom beating in the *Negro soul* (emphasis added)" rather than "Negro breast." It was not clear to me until I read the original Hughes article that Hughes intended the reference to the tom-tom to be *unambiguously positive* and in no way ironic, as the remainder of the quotation makes clear: "—the tom-tom of revolt against weariness in a white world, a world of subway trains, and work, work, work; the tom-tom of joy and laughter, and pain swallowed in a smile." I have no doubt Cripps understood this correctly, but I offer the point to readers who might misread its meaning, as I did at first.

7. Cripps, *Slow Fade*, 6.

8. W. E. B. Dubois, *The Souls of Black Folk*, in *Three Negro Classics* (New York: Avon, 1965), 214–15.

9. Robert A. Bone, *The Negro Novel in America*, rev. ed. (New Haven: Yale University Press, 1965), 95.

10. Bone, *Negro Novel*, 95.

11. Bone, *Negro Novel*, 100.

12. Regarding hegemony and Micheaux, Jane Gaines, in her essay, "Fire and Desire: Race, Melodrama, and Oscar Micheaux," (published elsewhere in this volume) says: "Discussing the value of Gramsci for ethnic studies, Stuart Hill emphasizes that the utility of the concept is in the way hegemony explains the " 'subjection" of the

victims of racism to the mystification of the very racist ideologies which imprison and define them. [Hall, "Gramsci's Relevance for the Study of Race and Ethnicity," *Journal of Communication Inquiry* 10: 2 (Summer 1986) 27].' Thus it seems to me that there is sufficient theoretical justification for going beyond the early dismissal of Micheaux on the basis of race hatred. The jury is still out on Oscar Micheaux."

13. Cripps, *Slow Fade,* 172.

14. Cripps, *Slow Fade,* 180.

15. Unnamed critic, in Cripps, *Slow Fade,* 180.

16. See "dicky" (defined as "high-toned Negro") in the index of Bone, *The Negro Novel,* 275. In discussing the dicky theme in Jean Toomer's novel, *Cane,* Bone says "whiteness presses on [the blacks] from all sides. The 'dicky' Negro, and especially the near-white, who are most nearly assimilated to white civilization, bear the brunt of repression and denial, vacillating constantly between two identities [p. 84]."

17. Cripps, *Slow Fade,* 180.

18. Cripps, *Slow Fade,* 260–61.

19. Cripps, *Slow Fade,* 261.

20. Cripps, *Slow Fade,* 258–260.

21. Cripps, *Slow Fade,* 183.

22. Any analogy between Black music and Black cinema must take into consideration the exponentially greater economic requirements of even low-production-value cinema, as Jane Gaines points out in her essay on Micheaux elsewhere in this volume. Cinema is almost necessarily bourgeois in the economic scale or status required for its production. To the extent that Black independent cinemas do emerge and survive, I believe the analogy with music is instructive, and I will extend it in another essay. Any bourgeois American aspects of style are likely to be mixed with African aspects, as the dilemma of twoness suggests, and thus cinemas of significant difference remain possible and interesting.

23. Cripps, *Slow Fade,* 6.

24. J. L. Austin, *Sense and Sensibilia* (New York: Oxford University Press, 1962), 64.

25. Austin, *Sense,* 71.

26. Cripps, *Slow Fade,* 190.

27. Cripps, *Slow Fade,* 191.

28. *Within Our Gates* has recently been discovered in Spain, with a new title, *La Negra,* and with Spanish subtitles; it has been delivered to the Library of Congress and is the subject of Jane Gaines's article elsewhere in this book.

29. Cripps, *Slow Fade,* 191.

30. Cripps, *Slow Fade,* 191–92.

31. See, for example, J. Ronald Green and Horace Neal, Jr., "Oscar Micheaux and Racial Slur: A Response to 'The Rediscovery of Oscar Micheaux'," *Journal of Film and Video,* 40: 4 (Fall 1988), 66–71.

32. Cripps, *Slow Fade,* 6.

33. Neal Gabler, *An Empire of Their Own: How the Jews Invented Hollywood* (New York: Crown Publishers, 1988).

34. Gabler, *Empire*, 5.

35. I chose *The Girl from Chicago* partly because it is not one of his "better" films, from the point of view of Hollywood style.

36. The "grain" of Micheaux's style is analogous in some ways to the grain of Panzera's voice, and the polished and perfect style of Hollywood is analogous to Fischer-Dieskau's voice, as characterized in Roland Barthes' famous essay, "The Grain of the Voice," in *Image-Music-Text*, ed. and trans., Stephen Heath (New York: Hill and Wang, 1977).

37. Thanks to John Fergus-Jean and Ardine Nelson for the photography examples.

38. A review of one of the major recording projects of the original-instruments movement points to some criticism of the movement that is reminiscent of the criticism of race movies: " . . . even sympathetic scholars could find the Leonhardt-Harnoncourt approach disconcerting, what with its clipped non-legato articulations, its rhythmic alterations and dislocations, its easily satirized dynamic bulges, its brusquely punctuated recitatives, its flippant tempos, not to mention the tiny forces, the green and sickly-sounding boy soprano soloists, above all the recalcitrant, sometimes ill-tuned 'original instruments.'

    "Some were downright indignant at the loss of traditional scale and weight. The venerable musicologist Paul Henry Lang blasted the 'frail performances with inadequate ensembles. . . .' " Richard Taruskin, "Facing Up, Finally, To Bach's Dark Vision," *New York Times* (January 27, 1991), H25.

    In defense of the original-instruments movement, the same review says: "Mr. Harnoncourt's style has taken on attributes that 'performance practice' alone could never have vouchsafed. They can only have come from those 'contemptible' Lutheran texts and their unaccommodating polemic. His increasingly hortatory and unbeautiful way of performing Bach reached a peak about halfway through the series, and the intervening decade has done nothing to lessen its power to shock—or disgust. If you seek contact with the essential Bach at full hideous strength, Mr. Harnoncourt's performances remain the only place to go." Taruskin, H28.

    For our purposes, race movies are the only place to go.

39. The question of whether Micheaux had the talent of a Benny Carter or a Louis Armstrong remains open, but is not relevant to this point of style. The evaluation of Micheaux's accomplishment is just beginning; we are just beginning to discuss valuative criteria.

40. DuBois, *Souls*, 215.

3

Fire and Desire: Race, Melodrama, and Oscar Micheaux

Jane Gaines

If D. W. Griffith's *Birth of a Nation* (1913) was history "written with lightning," Oscar Micheaux's *Within Our Gates* (1919) was history written in smoke.[1] When the African-American independent film producer's second feature was first exhibited in major American cities, Black as well as White communities treated it like a time bomb. The same Black communities which had welcomed Micheaux's first film, *The Homesteader* (1918), and applauded the success of the Micheaux Book and Film Company, protested against *Within Our Gates*. In Chicago, the Methodist Episcopal Ministers' Alliance committee, comprised of representatives of both races, took their case against exhibiting the film to the mayor and the chief of police.[2]

The request for a permit to show the film had been denied after the first screening, but a more liberal group, arguing for the social value of the film's subject matter, prevailed after a second screening. The film opened at the Vendome Theatre in Chicago on January 12, 1920. But the protest against it continued up until the hour before the film opened.[3] Why? What kinds of scenes could represent such a danger to public safety in 1920? And what issue could unify White and Black churches in this way?

In January 1920, *Within Our Gates* was caught up in a riot-lynching linkage which characterized American race relations in the 1920s. Because of this linkage (both real and imagined), the film's release offers another case study of the way symbolic events (inflected as socially dangerous) can become inextricably mixed up with the events themselves, especially during racially sensitized moments in history. Micheaux's film included a sequence depicting the hanging and burning of two innocent African-Americans—a man and his wife. The sequence may have been no more than a short scene in a flashback, filling in the history of mulatta heroine

Sylvia Landry, and may have only had minor relevance to the central narrative, but the relation of such a controversial segment to the narrative whole often becomes irrelevant when such a moving image is singled out by public discourse in this way. Released in the US the year after the "red summer" of 1919, the film encountered especially active resistance in Chicago, where in July, 1919, police indifference to a White gang's drowning of a Black teenager had set off a chain of South Side riots.[4] In Shreveport, Louisiana, the Star Theatre refused to book the film because of its "nasty story."[5] Even in Omaha, Nebraska, Lincoln Motion Pictures head George P. Johnson explained the poor attendance at an August return engagement of the film as due to the fact that the film reminded people of the events of the year before.[6] And in New Orleans, police reported that nine Negroes were lynched in the film.[7]

In several cities, Micheaux was required by officials to edit out parts of the film, but even this continual recutting doesn't explain the wild discrepancies in viewers' reports.[8] The groups that wanted an outright ban on exhibiting Micheaux's film saw little results from their direct appeals to city officials, whose peace-making solution was to require these cuts. But the case of *Within Our Gates* brings home one of the lessons of the NAACP campaign against *The Birth of a Nation*. Whereas *protest* against a film in this period did not mean that it would be banned (and it might even insure that it drew crowds), the threat of a race *riot* meant that exhibitors and city officials would cooperate to keep a film off the screen.[9]

What suggests comparison between *Within Our Gates* and *The Birth of a Nation* is, of course, primarily the caldron of protest around racial imagery into which both films were flung. However, in almost every other way, Micheaux's film is the antithesis of *Birth,* especially in its middle-class, Black-centered view of American society. Also, in contrast to the NAACP protest around *The Birth of a Nation* (centered upon a notion of falsehood in representation), the *Within Our Gates* controversy implicitly focussed on the fear of "too much truth." This status quo discourse on "truth," however, made no reference to the political realities of Southern lynch-mob justice. Such mob justice, it should be remembered, had actually contributed to the instability of Northern cities, crowded in 1919 with Blacks who had left Southern towns in the aftermath of lynchings. The attempt to ban screenings of Micheaux's film, then, was an attempt to silence the protest against lynching, but also a law-and-order move to suppress active protest against worsening housing and employment conditions in the North. *Within Our Gates* was thus historically linked to fear of cataclysmic social change, a linkage obfuscated by the smoke screen of "race riot." And here is where the difference between the fate of this film and that of *The Birth of a Nation* is so revealing. While Griffith's "masterpiece" was enshrined, Micheaux's answer to it was "run out of town," so to speak. While the White supremacist version of the Civil War survived, Micheaux's African-American history lesson disappeared and was classified by film scholars as "lost." Seventy years later, a 35mm print version of *Within Our Gates,* now called *La Negra,* was finally returned to the Library of Congress from Europe.

So what follows is an analysis of *La Negra,* the only extant version of *Within Our Gates.* This is a work which has had two cultural lives: the first, in the US in the troubled year of its early exhibition, and the second, on the continent, where Spanish audiences would have seen it as a "strange tale of the American South." Somewhat like the trade in abolitionist literature, which fled an inhospitable climate of race-terror to seek publication in Britain, this film is part of that traffic of banned discourse which has historically crossed the Atlantic along with African-American intellectuals, themselves fleeing discrimination. In 1990, the film returned to the US with Spanish intertitles, producing our estranged culture as a very strange text.

Our cultural heritage, then, is returned to us in another language, producing a text that is literally unreadable for monolingual US speakers of English—African-American and Euro-American English speakers alike. And ironically, only the Spanish-speaking, second largest US minority can properly "read" this film text, a strange turn given the history of the first "illiterate" immigrant audiences who learned the English language as well as US cultural codes in the early moving picture theatres. The English speaker is "illiterate" in the face of this silent film within which the intertitles are crucial narrative markers, within a silent film that alternates between linguistic and iconic signification. The non-diegetic (other-worldly) narrator of the realm of the intertitles, signs to the English-speaking reader to no avail. But the Euro-American English speaker is doubly illiterate here. He is handicapped by his linguistic deficiency as well as his ignorance of African-American history and culture, the knowledge of which is basic to understanding the moving picture story told to the viewer through the articulation of Black bodies in dramatic space.

And finally I should mention the difficulty of analyzing even this version of Micheaux's 1919 film, most likely a skeleton of the original, but an original that had never been integrally whole, shredded as it was by censors' cuts in the year of its US exhibition. My analysis, however, is not a lament for an original text or an original moment of reception; rather it treats *La Negra* as Micheaux's final text, and assumes that it is structurally similar to the motion picture that disturbed so many in 1920. Just as one could argue that *La Negra* is significantly changed, one could also argue that it is as much a *Within Our Gates* text as any other since the "original" prints exhibited in Chicago, New Orleans, and Omaha may not have been the same. Given this textual fluctuation, it also stands to reason that if *La Negra* is unlike the print of *Within Our Gates* shown to Chicago censors in 1919, this "original" film could just as well have been more tame as it could have been more graphic than *La Negra.* We may never know. But for me the controversy is sufficient justification for focusing on the lynching story. My exaggeration of its relative importance in the narrative should be understood as a reprise of that earlier exaggeration.

This is not to say that the lynching story (which is not integral to the narrative) isn't connected to the whole in any way. As told by Sylvia's cousin Alma to her suitor Dr. Vivian, the lynching story is offered as an explanation for Sylvia's reluctance to marry this successful Black doctor. Rather than serving any direct narrative purpose, then, the story functions as a kind of exorcism of the past. Tagged on as it is to the end of the film, it seems structurally tangential rather than central. Once Sylvia's history is told, the film cuts to final shots of the heroine with Dr. Vivian who reconciles her to a more optimistic point of view, arguing that Black participation in World War I has changed the meaning of American patriotism for Blacks. The optimistic nationalism that ends the film, then, depends upon seeing the scenes of racial injustice as relegated to the past, not conceivable in the present of the film's contemporary story, ostensibly the present of the film's year of release.

We are supposing, as I have said, that *La Negra* is structurally similar to the film that was shown in the US in 1920. However, this assumption still presents us with some mysteries. Why, despite the controversy, was the film promoted in terms of the minor lynching story in city after city? Why do none of the existing publicity materials mention the "uplift" narrative dealing with Sylvia Landry's efforts to raise money for a school in the South? Instead of featuring this respectable narrative, the advertising for the film hawks "Who Killed Phillip Girdlstone?" and promises, in addition to the solution of the mystery, a "Spectacular Screen Version of the Most Sensational Story on the Race Question Since Uncle Tom's Cabin."[10] This, then, must be the key—lynching as spectacular attraction. For, more than anything, Micheaux was an accomplished showman.

But in the tradition of *Uncle Tom's Cabin,* spectacle and emotion go hand in hand.[11] The film-within-the-film of *La Negra* is also a small sentimental melodrama—so complete, it is as though one were viewing an entire D. W. Griffith short dropped down within a silent feature. Not surprisingly, the lynching narrative owes its basic formal structure to Griffith, even while its rhetorical structure produces the antithesis of *The Birth of a Nation*—that is, the history of Reconstruction from the Black point of view. Wealthy planter Felipe Gridlstone (Philip Girdlestone) is unwilling to settle accounts with Black sharecropper Gaspar (Jasper)

Landry who has earned the $685 needed to repay his debt to the planter. A fight ensues when Landry urges the villain Gridlstone to treat him fairly. But we see that Landry isn't alone in his feeling of animosity toward the cruel landowner. A poor White cracker, seeing his opportunity to get rid of the hated Gridlstone, shoots the aristocrat through the window. The blame falls on Landry. Gridlstone's meddlesome Black butler Efrain ("Eph"/Ephrain) has been watching the interview with the sharecropper, but hasn't seen the shooting and thus sounds the alarm that it is Landry who has murdered old Gridlstone. Landry, his wife, his young son Emilio (Emil), and his grown daughter Sylvia flee to the woods with the lynch mob on their trail.

Lynching as Peculiarly American

Seldom have African-American and Euro-American versions of social reality been more at odds than in the historical case of lynching. In White American popular mythology, a lynching is a hanging, punishment meted out to Negro men who had sexual relations with White women. Technically, however, lynching refers to an enforcement of justice outside the law that could involve any number of brutal punishments from burning to tarring and feathering. Even despite the attempts to educate Whites about the full implications of lynching, first by Black journalist Ida B. Wells in the 1880s and later by White reformers like Southerner Jessie Daniel Ames, the post-Civil War rape and lynching mythology has persisted for Whites even into the present. For Black Americans, however, the situation is significantly different, since from the 1880s there has been a strong literary and journalistic effort to write lynching sagas as a form of protest against the practice. A comparison of Micheaux's banned version of Southern injustice with the White mythology, then, needs to locate the terms of this dialogue, this ideological battle in the realm of representation.

Broader accounts of lynching tell us that it is a uniquely American phenomenon, evolving out a tradition of vigilantism going back to the Revolutionary War. Because of the long association with racial issues, it is not well known that the first victims of "lynch law," that is, mob justice, were White. The practice that reached its height in 1877, then, was adapted from a preexisting tradition, but with a significant difference: The sadistic punishments inflicted on Blacks during the period of Reconstruction raised the ante for brutal acts as never before. And, as Jacqueline Dowd Hall tells us, there seemed to be a direct relationship between the increase in economic tensions and the sadism of the acts against Negroes that included burning alive and torture as well as emasculation.[12]

The act of lynching, then, is a classic displacement—a radical adjustment in which something of peripheral importance comes to occupy a central position. Here, the central economic concern is shifted onto the sexual, or, the threat to real property gets transposed as the threat to symbolic property—White womanhood. But, to follow the Freudian dream metaphor further, it is not the taboo *sexual* thought that is repressed, it is the *economic* motive that is unspeakable. Sex (even when there was none) was historically asserted and "money" was denied. But to figure the economic basis of lynching too abstractly risks overlooking the unusual mix of multiple causes of the phenomenon. For lynching can be productively seen as overdetermined in both the Freudian and the Marxian senses.[13]

Ritualized lynching, like Freud's dream element, is the product of a whole cluster of historical causes, so tangled, inverted, and disguised, that one can never hope to trace the phenomenon back to a single source. Functioning like Althusser's overdetermined superstructural phenomenon, the links between lynching and the economic base are so varied and multilayered as to seem hopelessly indeterminate.[14] However, in the 1920s, the scattershot determinations of a lynching climate clustered around four main social developments: the extension of voting rights to Black men and the question of votes for women; returning World War I veterans seeking jobs; Black competition for jobs and Black economic successes; and consensual interracial sexual relations.

I also say scattershot "causes" to emphasize the way mob justice came down—the utter arbitrariness of the trumped-up justifications for lynching—the nonsense of the charges against Southern Negroes. It seemed, says Hall in her study of the anti-lynching crusade, that the "transgression of a whole range of nebulous taboos" could result in brutal beating or even hanging for the incredulous Black. And this "justice" was also indiscriminate since, given the "brushfire" effect, it often didn't matter if the Black person accused of the crime could not be found. If the crowd had worked up an appetite for Black flesh, any convenient Negro might be executed.[15] Micheaux gives us this informed view of the lynch mob in his portrait of the victimization of Gridlstone's servant Eph, who, having encouraged the mob to look for Landry, is himself grabbed as a substitute when they fail to find the accused.

Perhaps Micheaux's portrait of the lynch mob is his signal achievement in this film, for he chooses to show what Blacks knew and Northern Whites refused to believe. He shows the total barbarism of the White mob. The more astounding reports collected by Ida B. Wells confirm that lynch mobs decapitated bodies and took the parts as trophies, invented obscene tortures, and burned victims after hanging them. Women and children were not sheltered from these horrors, but participated in the horrid revelry.[16] And here is where Micheaux is at his boldest—the mob he gives us is not the usual cadre of town bullies. White women and children also wield sticks and torches in some of the most unsettlingly beautiful scenes in silent cinema of the late teens. Micheaux's day-for-night shooting renders a grotesque black silhouette against a light sky—a kind of multi-limbed spiked monster spiral from background to foreground—attacking and receding in a dynamic use of screen depth. It is all the better that these scenes are also shot in such crisp focus, for what they portray is nothing more nor less than White people as savages. The accusation of "primitivism" is turned back onto White Southern culture.

Yes, this is lynching as sensational spectacle. But we should consider how it is significantly different from lynching as public spectacle, the gruesome ritual that functioned as social control and warning to Blacks. Contrast this with the White-staged ritual Micheaux's screen representation of Southern lynching, that was intended to work in the opposite way on the same Black public. For Micheaux, to reveal these horrors was *not* to contain and control through terror. As his publicity asserted, this "Preachment of Race Prejudice and the Glaring Injustices Practiced Upon Our People" was to "Hold you Spellbound" and offer you details that would make you "Grit Your Teeth in Silent Indignation."[17] In the same spirit as *Uncle Tom's Cabin,* Micheaux's film was meant less to inspire action or race solidarity than to work as a kind of moral self-affirmation. As I have argued before, much of the appeal of "race movies" had to do with their melodramatic structure, that is, the fictional scheme of things in which the power structure is inverted.[18] Melodrama elevates the weak above the powerful by putting them on a higher moral ground. Micheaux's spectacle of lynching, then, was rhetorically organized to encourage the feeling of righteous indignation in the Black spectator.

The Politics of Cross-Cutting

To these ends, Micheaux makes exceedingly haunting uses of cross-cutting, alternating the lynching scene with the attempted rape of Sylvia, and it is this pattern that I want to discuss in detail since it tells us so much about the way African-American artists have historically used melodramatic devices. As I have noted, Micheaux characterizes the White mob as crazed and barbarically cruel—so cruel that even innocents—women and children—are its victims. Landry's wife is dragged forward and beaten by the mob, and the noose is placed around her neck and the neck of her young son, although the boy wriggles out of it and narrowly escapes on a horse. That the man and wife are to be hanged together is signalled by one of the most unsettling images in the history of African-American cinema: a low-angle close-up of a wooden bar frames two dangling ropes against a cloudy sky. This abstraction, as it stands in for the horrible tragedy, is then used by Micheaux as a kind of gruesome punctuation in the cross-cut sequence that culminates the lynching scenario.

The fate of the family is thus established as one line of action, a line which splits into two when the film cuts from the lynchers starting a fire to Sylvia Landry, returning to the family's house for provisions, unaware of the plight of her family. In the same shot of Sylvia gathering supplies, she is discovered by Felipe Girdlstone's elderly brother Armando (Armand) who has joined the search for his brother's killer. From the shot establishing Sylvia's danger, the film cuts back to the shot of the ghostly post, this time seen with one noose cut and the other still dangling. Even more strange, a second shot of the noose being cut is upside down, producing an eerie defiance of gravity—the rope stretching toward the sky. Between the shot of the one rope cut and the next shot of both ropes cut is an intertitle: "Still not satisfied with the poor victims burned in the bonfire, Girdlstone goes looking for Sylvia." That is, before the victims have been represented as hanged and burned, Girdlstone has examined their bodies. I will want to return to the "error" of this title momentarily since it is interesting for the way in which it contradicts the temporal conventionally associated with cross-cutting—the assumption that this form of shot alternation indicates simultaneity. Following this assumption, the sequence represents a time frame in which Sylvia is being molested *at the same moment* in which her parents are being executed for crimes they did not commit.

Although Armando Girdlstone's taunting of Sylvia is alternated with shots of the hanging, the systematic cross-cutting pattern begins with the conflict between the characters. Here, the struggle is interrupted five times with shots of the mob burning the bodies in a raging bonfire. I say "interrupted," but there are any number of other ways in which the relationship between the two or more lines of action in a parallel editing pattern can be described. We might say, for instance, that they are "interwoven," which could indicate that the lines of action are measured out more or less equally. But here I want to emphasize how the parallel narration really works to produce a contrast between the two events. Although a strict reading of the time relations set up by the intertitle tells us that the mob has already completed its terrible work by the time Armando reaches Sylvia, the hanging segment renders moot any rigid linearity of this kind. What matters is that Micheaux has used the connotations of simultaneity to give the attack on Sylvia an additional charge. Yes, the narration tells us that the rape and the lynching are coincident, but it also says that there is an even closer connection between the fire and the desire. In the struggle, Sylvia and her attacker circle the table, her clothes are ripped from her shoulder, she throws a vase at him, and finally she faints. The scene is thus symbolically charged as a reenactment of the White patriarch's

ravishment of Black womanhood, reminding viewers of all of the clandes-
tine forced sexual acts that produced the mulatto population of the American South.[19]

The issue of the temporal order of the lynching sequence gives us
an opportunity to ask some additional questions about cross-cutting as
melodramatic form. What does it contribute to the affect? How does this
device manage melodramatic material? It is arguable that cross-cutting as
a form may have special meaning for the disenfranchised because of the
way the device inscribes power relationships. Although it is often noted,
as I have said, that melodrama empowers the socially inferior by awarding
them moral superiority, there are ways in which, contrary to this, cross-
cutting puts the viewer in a helpless position. Which is it in this case? As
Tom Gunning discusses the technique of cross-cutting, it is clearly marked
by the intervention of a storyteller who is in the position to manipulate the
narrative, and especially to play on audience sensibilities by "withholding"
parts of the story.[20] But if, in this case, "withholding" pieces of narrative
information doesn't put Black spectators in a controlling position, perhaps
it puts them in a familiar position, which would mean that Sylvia's fate
(in which they cannot intervene) allows a replay of the futility of the
African-American historical condition. Once more, Blacks look on while
the White patriarch exerts his sexual prerogative. But the scene may still
afford pleasure for Blacks because although the White master appears to
be prevailing, Sylvia effectively resists and eludes him again and again.
The pleasure this resistance affords may be like the satisfaction offered
by Harriet A. Jacobs's *Incidents in the Life of a Slave Girl* where Linda
Brent (the author's fictionalized self), manages to thwart the sexual
advances of her master over the course of the entire book.[21] In this
important slave narrative, the odds of escaping from her master's vindictive
grip and finding safety in the North for herself and her children are piled
up against Linda Brent, exponentially increased. Characteristic of much
African-American and abolitionist literature of the late nineteenth and
early twentieth centuries is this narrative "piling on" of the overwhelming
odds against freedom and safety (which is not to suggest that this isn't an
accurate portrayal of the condition of enslaved peoples whose lives were
daily defined by attempts to survive humanly impossible tests).

One of the features abolitionist fiction borrows most effectively from
the melodrama form that predates it is this almost mathematical measure-
ment of outcomes. Life's agonies are played back as the embattled forces
of virtue meet the vile antagonists of virtue, a confrontation *timed* to
the second and rhythmically orchestrated. No device exemplifies this
mathematical feature of melodrama more than narrative coincidence, and
cross-cutting at its most effective is really an exercise in coincidence. To
return to coincidence, however, and by so doing to take it seriously, is to

return to the very device that has been cited so often as proof of the "lowness" of melodrama form. Was the form maligned because audiences (readers as well as viewers) were insulted by what they thought was the affront to realism that narrative coincidence represents? Does the use of coincidence for some imply a naive reader? In spite of the critical dismissal of such narrative maneuvers, theatre critic Eric Bentley, in a relatively early defense of theatre melodrama, has claimed that "outrageous coincidence" is the "essence of melodrama."[22] It is, he says, like farce because of the way in which it "revels in absurdity." While I approve of Bentley's championing of "outrageous coincidence," I am not sure that "absurdity" best describes the amazing coincidences in Griffith's last-minute rescues or the many astounding lucky moments in both the novels and films of Oscar Micheaux. For I suspect that the swift turn of events that equalizes the unequal, and the symmetrical plot development which evens scores, may only be absurd and nonsensical to those in power. In his list of melodramatic devices which might be seen by some film theorists as exceeding the constraints of classical narrative economy, Rick Altman mentions a reliance on coincidence along with spectacle and episodic presentation.[23] If he is right that "coincidence" is problematic excess, that it is not characteristic of classical text construction (and I think he is), does he mean that it is seen as illogical, overblown, or just indulgent? Because in terms of narrative theory, coincidence is not an overindulgence, but rather a highly economical solution for the storyteller. Thematic designs and narrative lines can be neatly unified through a coincidental unforeseen intersection of events—for that is what coincidence is—incidents coinciding to bring about swift change. And here, "swift" needs as much emphasis as "change," for coincidence brings about that astonishing narrative quickening that Todorov says is produced most effectively by supernatural forces.[24]

Coincidence may be "excess," then, but not because it exceeds narrative economy. It must be "excess" for some other reason. Consider that coincidence is perceived as "low" and "outrageous" (sometimes illogical) when it is surprising and miraculous, when it is sudden and unmotivated (that is without justification or preparation). And to continue my argument about the appeal to the powerless, consider also how coincidence is really a secular version of divine intervention, the only intervention that can rescue the powerless in the unjust world of social realist fiction. To illustrate this from *La Negra,* I might point to the series of coincidences by which Sylvia comes to receive the much-needed money to keep open Piney Woods School for Negroes in the South. On a fund-raising trip to Boston, a tramp steals her purse and is quickly seen and apprehended by Dr. Vivian, the man to whom she becomes romantically attached. Next, Sylvia is hit by a car as she dashes to save a child who has run into the street. Coincidentally, the woman to whom the car belongs is an extremely wealthy suffragette who is sympathetic to Sylvia's cause. Although a visiting Southern matron tries to dissuade her friend, the Boston suffragette decides to give the school not just the needed $5,000 but $50,000.

The miracle of coincidence is indifferent to marketplace measures of merit and worth. Instead, melodramatic coincidence dispenses rewards and punishments according to the motives of the heart, a standard directly at odds with work-world values. And so it may be the redistribution of rewards according to this alternative scheme that drags melodrama down in the cultural regard. Could it be that this is one of those places where what we have come to call the "contradictions of capitalism" may be manifest? That the deep asymmetry of a culture that espouses two systems of reward (corresponding with the old public sphere/private sphere division) shows up when the reward systems are seen to be at odds with one another? African-Americans have historically stood a better chance of triumphing in fictional worlds (certainly since the publication of William Wells Brown's *Clotel: Or, the President's Daughter* in 1853). In the fictional world of *La Negra*, Sylvia, the tragic mulatta, survives unscathed and is rewarded with a $50,000 gift from heaven.

But this alternative moral scheme of the home and hearth that depends so thoroughly on the pattern of "little" miracles also depends upon comparisons. The concurrent events balanced through cross-cutting are not only interwoven and matched, but contrasted, as best seen in D. W. Griffith's contrast dramas, where the emphasis is not on developing action but on social inequality. I'm thinking here of the scenes in *The Usurer* (1910) and *A Corner in Wheat* (1909) where the helpless are shown suffering (waiting in breadlines and being evicted) in shots alternated with corpulent capitalists toasting their own successes. At least one film historian has argued that such contrast implies a cause-and-effect relation.[25] Seen in this way, in one move (the "rescue" of the homeless or the "last gasp" of the Wheat King drowning in his own grain bin), syntagmatic causality may be complimented by paradigmatic causality. The linear chain of events as well as contrast implied in alternating shots bear out the assertion that the Usurer and the Wheat King *caused* the suffering and the death of innocent people.

Melodrama Form and African-American Fiction

There is still some question as to whether Griffith's parallelism is equal to the job the form will need to do for a social conscious African-American cinema. With these issues in mind, let us return to Sylvia cornered by the White patriarch. Micheaux's scene uses the classic double play of silent film melodrama, that is, a parallel concurrence of events (the "rape" and the lynching) as well as a coincidence that unifies the two lines of action. And this is a coincidence that asks viewers to accept an improbability which is so farfetched that it could *only* be seen to happen if it were, indeed, "the truth," which the adage tells us is "always stranger than fiction." So it is that in the act of ripping Sylvia's dress, Gridlstone discovers a telling birthmark on her breast: the mark is proof that he may be sexually assaulting his own daughter. I say "may be" because the wording of the Spanish title following is somewhat oblique: "Una cicatriz que tenia en el pecho la salvo de la legitimo matrimonio con una mujer de su raza y luego adoptada por los Landry." The ambiguity of the pronoun is still not resolved in English translation: "A scar that she had on her chest saved her dishonor because on discovering it Gridlstone knew that Sylvia was his daughter which he had in legitimate marriage with a woman of her race and later adopted by the Landrys." Is Sylvia then saved from incestual rape?

Conventions of interpretation dictate that we not take intertitles at their word, especially since in this period titles are so often at odds with the dramatic thrust of the silent scenes within which they are inserted. But interpreting Micheaux's scene as "rape" also has a certain political signifi-cance since it can be understood as a reaction to that other controversial interracial sex scene—the "Gus chase scene" from *The Birth of a Nation*. Since Flora Cameron's flight from the free Black man Gus and her leap to death from the edge of a cliff have been historically called the "rape scene," (although she would jump rather than submit), it seems only fair that we should not hesitate to call Micheaux's point of view a representa-tion of "rape."[26] This allows us to see it as the long-muffled African-American retort to what Ida B. Wells condemned in 1892 as the "old threadbare lie that negro men rape white women."[27] Even more pertinently, the parallelism of the rape and the lynching scenes assert the historical connection between the rape of the Black woman and the lynching of the Black man, the double reaction of the Reconstruction period to Whites' nightmare vision of Blacks voting and owning property.

But in representing Sylvia's deflowering as incest, *La Negra* goes deeper than the specific historical moment of lynching, attacking as it does, the connecting roots of race, gender, and sexuality. For Gridlstone's attack on Sylvia stands in as protest against *all* of the master's sexual encounters with his own slave women, representing each and every encounter as an act of symbolic incest, since the paternalism of the plantation master encircled slaves in a concept of "my family, white and black."[28] Note, also, that Micheaux gives us a rescue sequence with no heroic rescue, no race to protect family honor and female purity.[29] In place of the Griffith-esque rescue, the race to protect family honor and female purity, Micheaux's film gives us a title telling us that Girdlstone had paid for

Sylvia's education but that even after his attack on her, he did not reveal that he was her father. Neither is it clear from the one shot of Armando in the contemporary portion of the film (an argument in Sylvia's bedroom) that he has revealed his identity to her. The abrupt cut from this title to the end of Alma's conversation with Dr. Vivian in the present, suggests that the doctor is offered as savior, that is, the new professional class (with education provided by philanthropic Whites) would "rescue" the Black race. This means that although the White patriarch cannot ride to the rescue when he himself is the real threat to the sanctity of the family, paradoxically (in the strategy of the Black middle class), he can still "save the day."

Am I making an argument for the radical nature of *La Negra* that I am gradually taking back? I have argued that Micheaux's film counters the White supremacist ideology of *The Birth of a Nation* in its images of the White lynch mob and the White patriarch's sexual assault on a Black woman. We have as well the historical evidence of the attempts to ban the film, which suggests that the hanging of innocent Negroes was incendiary imagery for Blacks as well as Whites, although in different ways. Clearly the film troubled ideological waters. And yet I want to ask whether there is a kind of formal tempering of this material which is the work of the devices of melodrama in the hands of the Black bourgeois. The most obvious criticism of the use of the tradition of *Uncle Tom's Cabin* (in which the nineteenth-century African-American novelists all worked) has been that its sentimentality is dishonest and that its catalogue of brutal acts is without justification, a criticism identified with James Baldwin, whose fury at Harriet Beecher Stowe had to do with the way, he said, she left "unanswered and unnoticed the only important question: what was it, after all, that moved her people to such deeds."[30]

However, without subtracting anything from the significance of Baldwin's question, we still need to ask if sentimental fiction is structurally equipped to answer this kind of question at all. Eisenstein, of course, wondered in 1944 if Griffith's parallel editing technique, with its contrasts of rich and poor (to which I have referred above), was capable of anything more than "liberal, slightly sentimental humanism." For Eisenstein, scenes paralleled through cross-cutting stood for a dualistic understanding of social class inequality that imagined poor and rich as moving toward "reconciliation." This visualized reconciliation, he argued, was as inaccessible and distant as the point of "infinity" where the parallel lines crossed.[31] What Eisenstein had in mind, of course, was a formal equivalent of Marxist dialectics—graphic clashes (mismatches) within and between his shot units—which could convey a "unity of opposites," the perfect symmetry of contradiction. To give an example closer to African-American history, the cinema that goes beyond Griffith's humanism would represent something more like Fanon's three "incongruent knowledges": body, race, ancestors.[32] Such incongruence (which defines race and class relations in US history), cannot be represented by means of Griffith's "mechanical parallelism" with its false reconciliation of the irreconcilable.[33]

Eisenstein's early attempt to define bourgeois cinema has been eclipsed by a more contemporary Marxist aesthetics that defines bourgeois form in terms of the illusionism of Hollywood-style continuity editing. Where what Eisenstein called bourgeois form was parallel montage (seen as a microcosm of the US class structure), what later Marxist theorists saw as bourgeois was the denial of cinematic formal devices. Following the logic of Jean-Luc Godard and others, if illusionistic cinema was bourgeois, radical cinema had to be anti-illusionistic—that is, it had to foreground its devices and, ideally, it also had to evidence the material conditions of its production. But for Eisenstein, Griffith's early cinema was bourgeois because (although it represented class) it could not represent class struggle. It was also patriarchal, but not in any of the ways patriarchal form has been identified by early feminist film theory, for Griffith's patriarchal provincialism was inherited from nineteenth-century melodrama and from Dickens in particular. For Eisenstein, the patriarchal as well as the bourgeois, then, was epitomized in the parallel montage sequence where traditional sentiment was harnessed to the mechanics of shot alternation.[34]

The most I would hope for here is that Micheaux might force a reconsideration of Eisenstein as well as D. W. Griffith. Eisenstein's position has been taken to mean that borrowing such a corrupted form means automatically reproducing the politics it embodies, and I would not want to abandon this argument entirely, especially since so much productive work in the last ten years of film theory has been premised on the form = politics equation. But the orthodoxy of counter-cinema's antidote to Hollywood has been challenged recently, and no more emphatically than by new Black British filmmakers.[35] And add to this the increasing theoretical importance of a developing Third Cinema whose early manifesto writers embraced a range of forms including the unfinished and "imperfect," the transitional and the "incomplete."[36] This move within the field represents such a total shuffling that it is almost as though we are left with no parameters. Hopefully, this state of things will invite attempts to develop new classification schemes as we start over again to ask the same questions about politics and aesthetics.[37] That the overdue consideration of Micheaux's filmmaking practice comes at this moment is fortunate, since these challenges to the counter-cinema model may stave off attempts to pigeonhole him in preexisting categories that could preempt exploration into the ways in which his own aesthetic might shape new paradigms. Fortunately, recent considerations of Micheaux do suggest that his maverick style confounds complacent assumptions about the connection between race, class, and aesthetic form. I want to turn next to the task of situating that existing work on Micheaux's film oeuvre.

African-American Culture and Bourgeois Cinema

The new Micheaux criticism suggests inventive ways to move beyond his reputation for creating unflattering characterizations of Blacks, as well as his reputation for technical amateurism and aesthetic poverty.[38] In a bold move, Jay Hoberman has located Micheaux in an avant-garde tradition, claiming that the results of his low-budget shooting produced "surreal" effects, and comparing his indifference to actors to Warhol's famous nondirection. Hoberman would like to place Micheaux outside the Hollywood tradition since he is seemingly "oblivious to the laws of cinematic continuity."[39] But here I would differ with Hoberman, arguing as I have that Micheaux should be situated in the classical Hollywood tradition which, after all, he so carefully studied and emulated. It is not so much that he broke with Hollywood conventions (as Hoberman argues) or even that he fell short of mastering them, but that he played "fast and loose" with classical style. As master of the unmotivated cut, it is almost as though he is saying that if, by 1918, audiences had learned to see discontinuous shots as fictional continuous space (always an approximation), then why couldn't they make sense of shots in a *really* rough approximation of that space?

Clearly, Micheaux's editing style was an ambitious improvisation with the few takes he had left after shooting at a low ratio, and this meant taking temporal license with the material, even pushing the limits of conventional temporalities. Here *Body and Soul* (1924), one of the few surviving examples of Micheaux's silent work, is exemplary for the way in which the director gives us not only the entire film as a dream-flashback, but two consecutive flashbacks within that dream. Thus, we are doubly deceived by the beautiful mulatta Isabelle's flashback "confessions" to her mother that the Reverend Isaiah Jenkins (Paul Robeson) raped her and stole her mother's money. The "confessions" within the dream are two steps removed from the overproductive mother's real fears for her daughter.[40] In addition, within this structure the temporal transitions are relatively unmarked, making it difficult for the viewer to be certain where scenes are located in time.

There is something about Micheaux's unmarked transitions and his temporal ambiguities as well as his unmotivated cuts that suggests that he is working in another mode. But does this mean that he is responding to the "call" of an indigenous African-American culture? I think not, and here I am as leery of linking Micheaux's unconventional style with any hint of an essential Black culture as I am with calling it prescient modernism. Perhaps to elude any attempt to essentialize it, we could treat this style as more of an ingenious solution to the impossible demands of the conventions of classical Hollywood style, shortcuts produced by the exigencies of economics, certainly, but also modifications produced by an independent who had nothing at stake in strict adherence to Hollywood grammar. And I do mean grammar, for if any comparison with African-American culture is useful, it may be with Black usage of standard English, which linguists have argued is a shortcut that often produces refinements of an awkward and illogical standard usage. Think, in this instance, of the Black usage modification of the state-of-being verb, "is," to "bes" or "it be" to give us "is" as a continuous state, an improvement of the standard tense that still follows its old logic.[41]

What I want to argue with this comparison is not the miracle of one marginalized group's cultural production so much as an off-centered attitude toward using conventional forms, whether standard Hollywood or standard English. To elaborate on my comparison, in both cases, it would seem, the dominant culture has seen nonstandard, aberrant usage as failure to achieve mastery, as "mistakes" needing correction, producing a "low production value" aesthetic that offends the dominant eye, or an aberrant grammar that offends the intolerant ear. But also in both cases, marginalized persons with less invested in rigid rules simplify these rules to their own ends.

An example of Micheaux's freewheeling cinematic grammar that is both spatial error and improvement upon Hollywood logic might be his use of the same close-up of one character in two different spaces. In *The Exile* (1931), for instance, Micheaux cuts to a close-up of the exquisite mulatta Agnes, who is unaware of her Ethiopian heritage and strangely attracted to the Black hero John Baptiste. Seen in an unidentified space, the close-up shows her reacting with pleasure to the presence of Baptiste, who is speaking with her father in the dining room. *After* the spatially ambiguous close-up, she enters the dining room and within that scene, Micheaux cuts to the same close-up seen before to show her continued interest in Baptiste. The result is somewhat disorienting for the viewer, who may be confused when Micheaux breaks continuity rules by using shots from one space in two distinctly different scenes. However, although the director may have broken a continuous-space rule, he has at the same time followed the logic of inserts (which *can* be shot in the context of one recreated space and cut into another, still successfully creating the illusion of continuous space within a scene).

In his discussion of Micheaux's style, Ron Green has argued that it could be seen as having the same relation to Hollywood classicism as African-American music has historically had to the classical musical style which it revitalized.[42] This seems a productive approach to the problem of form that offers the chance to theorize film in terms of music, but in such a comparison we should also be wary of the tendency to idealize an African-American cinema that might have seen a Golden Age analogous to the Golden Age of jazz in the 1920s. For analogies between film and other forms (especially linguistic signs) have a built-in tendency to gloss over economic realities, despite attempts by Marxist theory to see aesthetic forms as indelibly marked by the material conditions of their production. In contrast with the bare bones economics of African-American musical production that allowed a community of rhythmic interchange, capital-intensive motion picture production has historically precluded the use of these forms for all but a handful of Black entrepreneurs. This historical reality produces a predicament for Marxist theories of the relation between form and revolution, as exemplified by discussions of Third Cinema, for, as these discussions admit, motion picture economics has historically thrust filmmakers (no matter what their class origins) into the bourgeois class.[43]

It has already been well established that Micheaux epitomized the Black bourgeois class, and that his novels as well as his films are thematic tributes to individualism as well as testimonies to the possibility of transcending race and class handicaps.[44] The comparison with Micheaux as novelist and filmmaker points up the oddity of film critics' wishful tendency to consider early African-American cinema in relation to avant-garde practice, for, to my knowledge, no equivalent demand has ever been made on early African-American fiction writers, who as a whole worked within the conventions of narrative realism. Instead, recent approaches to this literature stress the way existing formulas were left intact at the same time that they were transformed, as in Hazel Carby's discussion of the way Francis E. W. Harper and other writers reconstructed the heroine of White sentimental fiction in their portrayals of the mulatta character.[45] Thus it is my sense that the key to Micheaux's cinematic formal style as well as his thematics is to be found in the way he transformed the existing without changing it. And to some degree this is one and the same as the fate of the Black bourgeois class, which has historically strived for a new order, but an order that is not substantially different from the one already in place.

However, there is much to be gained by an approach to Micheaux that insists upon qualifying his African-American heritage with his class position. First, understanding Micheaux's class position gives us a way around the prevalent charges of his own race hatred, the kind of charges that led to the Communist Party's boycott of *God's Stepchildren* (1937) on the basis of its damning portrait of a light-skinned mulatta whose deceitful attempts to reject her family and pass as White end in her tragic suicide.[46] But in the work of contemporary African-American theorists, such contempt is the product of internal conflict set in motion by the dual motors of dominant and subordinated cultures. And the African-American intellectual, says Cornel West, has been historically prone to this "double-consciousness," a theorization that seems close to the same "peculiar sensation" which W. E. B. Dubois called by the same name, that "sense of always looking at one's self through the eyes of others, of measuring one's soul by the tape of a world that looks on in amused contempt and pity."[47] It is not, then, that this consciousness is one's own or that the voice heard speaks for one's own culture—rather it speaks for the other culture which, in the case of the Black bourgeois, is also his own to the degree that he has been assimilated. It is really no wonder that the cultural products of an aspiring Black intellectual in this period gave us Black men as scoundrels, religious hypocrites, gamblers and sluggards, and Black women as madames, seductresses, and cheats. For he was seeing this Black culture through the eyes of the White culture, for which this vision of an irredeemable Black underclass was flattering and entirely functional.

While the operation of "double-consciousness" seems a fairly obvious way to explain Micheaux's offenses, it may be less obvious that the critique needs to be applied two ways. That is, we need to consider that the early Black culture critics were part of this same divided consciousness which produced the arguments that Blacks were really just like Whites and that Micheaux was at fault for showing negative images. This criticism, which had its most publicly visible moment in the protest around *The Birth of a Nation,* has been voided by recent work on the problem of the positive/negative formulation.[48] One would think that the popularization of Gramsci's concept of hegemony would have swept away this earlier formulation, would have rendered it out of date. For as a theory of hegemony explains how the oppressor's point of view is embraced by the oppressed (while this point of view does not serve them), the theory could also be said to lift all blame for negative self-imaging from colonized subjects themselves. Discussing the value of Gramsci for ethnic studies, Stuart Hall emphasizes that the utility of the concept is in the way hegemony explains the " 'subjection' of the victims of racism to the mystification of the very racist ideologies which imprison and define them."[49] Thus it seems to me that there is sufficient theoretical justification for going beyond the early dismissal of Micheaux on the basis of race hatred.[50] The jury is still out on Oscar Micheaux.

What I have suggested here is an approach to this important early African-American filmmaker and novelist which allows us to redeem him as well as critique him. But in some ways, to try to explain Micheaux in terms of melodramatic form is entirely too tidy. As I have shown, the doubleness of Black bourgeois consciousness finds its perfect expression in melodrama, the conflicted mode, the only mode within which (according to recent feminist theories) we can have classical realism and "progressive" subversion simultaneously.[51] Still, Micheaux introduces a new set of problems for melodrama as the mode of the disenfranchised, not the least of which is the question of what it meant historically for middle-class White women and middle-class Blacks to profit from fictions marketed to the less fortunate.

Notes

Thanks to Todd Boyd for the title, Ron Green for the George P. Johnson leads, and Celeste Fraser and Kathleen Newman for help with the intertitle translation.

1. The reference is to the famous quote from Woodrow Wilson. For more on the full story of the president's unusual relationship to this film see Michael Rogin, " 'The Sword Became a Flashing Vision': D. W. Griffith's *The Birth of a Nation*," *Representations* 9 (Winter 1985).

2. "Race Problem Play Raises Fuss in Chicago," *The Chicago Defender* (24 January 1920), George P. Johnson Collection, UCLA Special Collections, hereafter George P. Johnson Coll.

3. Ibid.

4. See David Burner, Elizabeth Fox-Genovese, Eugene D. Genovese, and Forrest McDonald, *An American Portrait: A History of the United States,* Vol. 2, 2nd ed. (New York: Charles Scribner's, 1985), 595–597; for placement of the 1919 Chicago race riot in the context of the year of the "Red Scare." Carl Sandburg, *The Chicago Race Riots: July, 1919* (New York: Harcourt, Brace and Howe, 1919).

5. Letter to D. Ireland Thomas, Jacksonville, Fla. from the manager of the Star Theatre, Shreveport, Louisiana (19 March 1920), George P. Johnson Coll.; Harry T. Sampson, *Blacks in Black and White: A Source Book on Black Films* (Metuchen, N.J.: Scarecrow, 1977), 47, says that the Star Theatre manager was White, and that his refusal to exhibit the film had to do with the fact that the New Orlans Superintendent of Police had sent him a copy of the letter referring to the "executing by hanging of about nine negroes" in the film. (See Note #7.)

6. Letter to Oscar Micheaux, Chicago Illinois, from George P. Johnson, Omaha, Nebraska (10 August 1920), George P. Johnson Coll.

7. Letter to Frank T. Monney, Superintendent of Police, from Capt. Theodore A. Ray, Special to Superintendent, New Orleans, Louisiana (10 March 1920), George P. Johnson Coll.

8. The primary sources in the George P. Johnson Collection make numerous references to sections of *Within Our Gates* as either cut out or replaced for one showing or another. But it is not just that the primary sources don't attest to a solid text. The secondary sources also differ even more basically about what the film portrayed. Thomas Cripps, *Slow Fade to Black: The Negro in American Film, 1900–1942* (London: Oxford University Press, 1977), 185, says that *Within Our Gates* is about the Leo Frank tragedy, the 1913 case in which a Jewish man was executed by a Southern lynch mob. In contrast, Sampson, 46–47, says that *The Gunsaulus Mystery* (1921) was about the Leo Frank murder case. Sampson quotes from a review of *Within Our Gates* which refers to a boy who dreams he is being lynched, a dream portrayed in such a way that on the screen "You see him hung up in the vanishing illusion."

9. Cripps, 64, refers to the exhibition of *The Birth of a Nation* in Oakland, where exhibitors paid groups to stage a boycott against the film because the protests were such effective publicity.

10. George P. Johnson Coll.

11. On Harriet Beecher Stowe's novel as sentimental fiction see Jane Tompkins, "Sentimental Power: *Uncle Tom's Cabin* and the Politics of Literary History," in *Feminist Criticism: Essays on Women, Literature, Theory,* ed. Elaine Showalter (New York: Pantheon Books, 1985).

12. Jacqueline Dowd Hall, *Revolt Against Chivalry: Jessie Daniel Ames and the Women's Campaign Against Lynching* (New York: Colorado University Press, 1979), 130–33.

13. See Sigmund Freud, "Jokes and Their Relation to the Unconscious," in *The Standard Edition of the Complete Psychological Works.* Trans. James Strachey (London: The Hogarth Press, 1959), 163.

14. See Louis Althusser, *For Marx,* trans. Ben Brewster (London: New Left Books, 1977), Part III.

15. Hall, 141; For the most complete account of this historical phenomenon see Arthur F. Raper, *The Tragedy of Lynching* (1933; rpt. New York: Negro Universities Press, 1969).

16. Ida B. Wells-Barnett, "Southern Horrors: Lynch Law in all its Phases" (1892) in *On Lynchings* (New York: Arno Press, 1969).

17. George P. Johnson Coll.

18. See my "*Scar of Shame:* Skin Color and Caste in Black Silent Melodrama." *Cinema Journal* 26: 4 (Summer 1987), 3–21, rpt. in *Imitations of Life: A Reader on Film and Television Melodrama,* ed. Marcia Landy (Detroit: Wayne State University Press, 1991).

19. Students in my classes have also pointed out that Armando's assault on Sylvia has a parallel in the scene in *The Birth of a Nation* in which Sylas Lynch stalks Elsie Stoneman.

20. Tom Gunning, "Weaving a Narrative: Style and Economic Background in Griffith's Biograph Films," in Elsaesser and Barker, 341.

21. Harriet A. Jacobs, *Incidents in the Life of a Slave Girl* (1861; rpt. Cambridge and London: Harvard University Press, 1987).

22. Eric Bentley, *The Life of the Drama* (New York: Atheneum, 1964), 201.

23. Rick Altman, "Dickens, Griffith, and Film Theory Today," *South Atlantic Quarterly* 88: 2 (Spring 1989), 342.

24. Tzvetan Todorov, *The Fantastic: A Structural Approach to a Literary Genre,* trans. Richard Howard (Ithaca: Cornell University Press, 1975), 166.

25. Gunning, 342.

26. Russell Merritt, "D. W. Griffith's *The Birth of a Nation:* Going After Little Sister," in *Close Viewings: An Anthology of New Film Criticism,* ed. Peter Lehman (Tallahassee: Florida State University Press, 1990); For an important analysis of why the Black spectator, although set up to view this scene as a "rape," might resist this reading, see Manthia Diawara, "Black Spectatorship: Problems of Identification and Resistance," *Screen* 29: 4 (Autumn 1988), 67–70.

27. Wells-Barnett, 11.

28. Elizabeth Fox-Genovese, *Within the Plantation Household: Black and White Women of the Old South* (Chapel Hill and London: The University of North Carolina Press, 1988), 101.

29. Nick Browne, "Griffith's Family Discourse: Griffith and Freud," in *Home is Where the Heart Is: Studies in Melodrama and the Woman's Film,* ed. Christine Gledhill (London: British Film Institute, 1987).

30. James Baldwin, *Notes on a Native Son* (New York: Dial Press, 1955), 14.

31. Sergi Eisenstein, *Film Form* (1949; rpt. New York: Harcourt Brace, 1977), 235.

32. Homi Bhabha, "The Other Question," *Screen* 24: 6 (November–December 1983), 32. Bhabha quotes Frantz Fanon, *Black Skin, White Masks,* trans. Charles Lam Markmann (New York: Grove Weidenfeld, 1967), 79:

> the corporeal schema crumbled, its place taken
> by a racial epidermal scheme. . . . It was no longer
> a question of being aware of my body in the third
> person but a triple person. . . . I was not given one,
> but two, three places.

33. Eisenstein, 233–35.

34. Eisenstein, 198, says:

> In order to understand Griffith, one must visualize
> an America made up of more than visions of speeding
> automobiles, streamlined trains, racing ticker tape,
> inexorable conveyor-belts. One is obliged to
> comprehend this second side of America as well—America
> the traditional, the patriarchal, the provincial. And
> then you will be considerably less astonished by this
> link between Griffith and Dickens. . . . The threads of
> both these Americas are interwoven in the style and
> personality of Griffith—as in the most fantastic of
> his own parallel montage sequences.

More recently, both Rick Altman and Miriam Hansen have suggested that cross-cutting in Griffith may not be as politically complicit as Eisenstein first thought. Based on Altman's earlier consideration of *The Lonely Villa* (1909), Hansen argues about *Intolerance* (1916) that Griffith's oppositions are not as stable as we might think. Cross-cutting is quite capable of setting up binarisms that it then proceeds to undermine. More needs to be done with this provocative suggestion. Certainly this explains the breakdown whereby patriarchial oppressor becomes savior. But does the form also support the American ideology that the poor can become rich (and vice versa)? See Rick Altman, *"The Lonely Villa* and Griffith's Paradigmatic Style," *Quarterly Review of Film Studies* 6: 2 (Spring 1981), 123–34; Miriam Hansen, *Babel and Babylon: Spectatorship in American Silent Film* (Cambridge: Harvard University Press, 1991), 223.

35. See Isaac Julien, as quoted in Coco Fusco, *Young, British, and Black: The Work of Sankofa and Black Audio Film Collective* (Buffalo, N.Y.: Hallwalls/Contemporary Arts Center, 1988), 32.

36. Paul Willemen, "The Third Cinema Question: Notes and Reflections," in *Questions of Third Cinema,* eds. Jim Pines and Paul Willemen (London: British Film Institute, 1989), 9; See also Kobena Mercer, "Diaspora Culture and the Dialogic Imagination:

The Aesthetics of Black Independent Film in Britain," in *Blackframes: Critical Perspectives on Black Independent Cinema* (London and Cambridge, Mass.: MIT Press, 1988), 59; Julio Garcia Espinosa, "For an Imperfect Cinema," in *Twenty-Five Years of the New Latin American Cinema,* ed. Michael Chanan (London: BFI/Channel 4 Television, 1983).

37. Willemen, 15.

38. A good example of this is Cripps, 183.

39. Jay Hoberman, "A Forgotten Black Cinema Resurfaces," *Village Voice* (17 November, 1975), 86–7.

40. Richard Dyer, *Heavenly Bodies: Film Stars and Society* (London: Macmillan, 1987), 115, interprets the film this way.

41. Geneva Smitherman, *Talkin' and Testifin': The Language of Black America* (Detroit: Wayne State, 1977).

42. See Ron Green, " 'Twoness' in the Style of Oscar Micheaux," in this collection.

43. Willemen, 9.

44. Joseph A. Young, *Black Novelist as White Racist: The Myth of Black Inferiority in the Novels of Oscar Micheaux* (Westwood, Ct: Greenwood Press, 1989).

45. Hazel Carby, *Reconstructing Womanhood: The Emergence of the Afro-American Woman Novelist* (New York: Oxford University Press, 1987).

46. Hoberman, 88.

47. Cornel West, "The New Cultural Politics of Difference," in *Out There: Marginalization and Contemporary Cultures,* eds. Russell Ferguson, Martha Gever, Trinh T. Minh-ha, and Cornel West (Cambridge, Mass. and London: The MIT Press, 1990), 28; W. E. Burghardt DuBois (1903, rpt. New York: Signet, 1969), 45.

48. See, for instance, Steve Neale, "The Same Old Story: Stereotypes and Difference," *Screen Education* 32/33 (Autumn/Winter 1979–80).

49. Stuart Hall, "Gramsci's Relevance for the Study of Race and Ethnicity," *Journal of Communication Inquiry* 10: 2 (Summer 1986), 27; Albert Memmi articulated the concept of hegemony in his own way before Gramsci became fashionable. See *Dominated Man: Notes Towards a Portrait* (New York: Orion Press, 1968), 20:

We have already met the well-behaved colonized, the Good
Spirit. He becomes in reality, like them, an accessory.
after the fact of his own oppression.

50. Young, 146, is to my knowledge the first to go beyond the early condemnation of Micheaux through the use of Fanon's understanding of the colonized subject's alienated psyche.

51. Christine Gledhill, "The Melodramatic Field: An Investigation," *Home is Where the Heart Is: Studies in Melodrama and the Woman's Film,* ed. Christine Gledhill (London: British Film Institute, 1987), 13.

4

Oscar Micheaux: The Story Continues

Thomas Cripps

Professor Ronald Green is, of course, correct in calling for an ongoing probe of the work of the African-American novelist and moviemaker, Oscar Micheaux. He, Professor Jane Gaines of Duke University, and others have begun a newsletter meant for the growing number of Micheaux scholars, a long-overdue research organ. Micheaux's "lost" movies continue to turn up: back in the 1970s I identified one in the Cineteca España in Madrid; Professor Richard Grupenhoff of Glassboro State College in New Jersey came upon another one, *Veiled Aristocrats,* only last year; and yet another, *The Symbol of the Unconquered,* was shown at the Museum of Modern Art only days after this was written. And as Green writes, even if we found no more such films, our analysis of the canon that survives is far from "nailed shut." Moreover, we now have a new baggage of theoretical tools drawn from feminist studies, Freud, Marx, a generation of French and German linguists and social critics, and their advocates in the pages of *Screen* and *Cahiers du Cinema.*

Micheaux as we know him came to light only twenty years ago in books that, in the main, were conceived fully a quarter of a century ago. I am thinking, of course, of Donald Bogle's archly titled *Toms, Coons, Mulattoes, Mammies & Bucks* (1973), Daniel J. Leab's *From Sambo to Superspade* (1975), and my own *Slow Fade to Black* (1977); books, it should be said, Green has reckoned as having "pioneered" in opening a heretofore "invisible" field, indeed "a whole new ethnic cinema."

Unfortunately, this first rush to judgment brought no outpouring of "race movie" (those made for Black audiences) scholarship. In the same decade that saw the books into print, I wrote a piece for *Black American Literature Forum* in which I urged a goal that Green seems to share: that "black genre film cannot be judged on its aesthetic merits alone, for its message may reach its audience in spite of its artistic naivete, or even because of it. . . . [A] plausibly rendered anatomy of black life often meant more to black audiences than aesthetic considerations."[1] A few years later, in Gladstone L. Yearwood's book, *Black Cinema Aesthetics,* I tried to put a fine point on it, one only just being heeded by academic writers, including Professor Green. "The need for a critical canon of past black filmmaking grows more urgent," I wrote in 1980. "So far, the most prolific black filmmaker, Micheaux, who generated paroxysms of angry debate during his own lifetime, has inspired only legend-making and the naming of festivals and theatres."[2]

So far, Micheaux scholars might find this a ground for agreement. At issue, however, has been a standard against which to reckon with Micheaux's work (and that of Spencer Williams and his other age-cohorts) that both takes into account his playing to a discrete, minority audience and his reliance upon resources and techniques apart from classical Hollywood style. Perhaps with unseemly wambling, I have tried to face these facts of Micheaux's life by having it both ways: he was important to Black filmmaking, while at the same time much of his work is a historical and cultural treasure rather than an aesthetic one. As I wrote in a review of the *American Film institute Catalogue* (1971): "Uneven, and often terrible in quality, they are the dreamlike authentic voices of a self-taught black man who tried to speak to Afro-America." At issue, then, is the still inchoate process of formulating an aesthetic through which to encounter both the social significance of Micheaux, as well as his cinematic achievement: a long way to go, from what I have read so far. About which, more later. For the moment, we might all take heart from how far scholarship has come. On the occasion of my signing the contract for the book that became *Slow Fade to Black,* the late and distinguished historian of African America and a friend of many years, Elliott Rudwick, wisecracked: "After Stepin Fetchit and Hattie McDaniel what is there."

Rudwick was correct if not prescient in that before us—Bogle, Leab, and me—Micheaux had been forgotten and unjustly tossed upon Trotsky's ashbin of history. And yet, even though we celebrated him for his fortitude in standing up to Hollywood while staying obtusely apart from it, we were also agreed that his work (that we knew of at the time) was at best cavalier in its attention to the conventions of moviemaking, by which we meant Hollywood moviemaking, the same standard by which Micheaux's own Black critics and audiences judged him. To Bogle he was a looming presence, an impresario of the old school, sweeping into bookers' offices in his fur coat and wide-brimmed hats, but also no more than a maker of movies "similar to the Hollywood product" that were doomed by circumstance to be "technically inferior." His *Birthright,* for example, though focused on " 'uplift,' " seemed only "silly and sly." Leab gave him only a half-dozen pages and a reluctant sense that the "sad fact" of his distance from both technique and distribution systems left a canon that "cannot be considered outstanding."[3] We also knew in restoring Micheaux to a fresh audience that the fate of the historian is to be revised and to be reckoned "old hat," much as Ferdinand Braudel, a founder of the "Annales" school of writing history from the bottom up, and author of the famous *The Mediterranean and the Mediterranean World in the Age of Philip II* (1949), felt as each new generation read his work, at first finding his claims for his "new" history "imprudent," then as the movement took hold, finding him merely "timid." Yet, as he wrote: "This is the way of the research world and I should be the last to complain."[4] Not that every historian faces an identical fate. The historical inventory of the ages constitutes a sort of intellectual supermarket from which writers may choose what suits their purposes. For example, dozens of historians, including Green, have picked off the rack W. E. B. DuBois's famous characterization of African-American sensibility as a "twoness," one part Black, one part White. But that was DuBois in 1903, in the midst of a long life that included a role in the National Association for the Advancement of Colored People (NAACP), editing its organ *The Crisis,* and advocacy of groups ranging from various socialist sects to Woodrow Wilson's Democratic Party. Thus in 1917, at the height of World War I, he urged that the African-American "put himself into the turmoil and work effectively for a new democracy that shall know no color," a sentiment that colored his famous "Close Ranks" editorial and appeared to abandon both the notion of twoness as well as his commitment to fighting racism.[5] The point here, of course, is that there were many DuBoises in his long life, and that if an idea lifted from one part seems to make too-good-to-be-true sense of our own time, perhaps we, remote from its time, are expecting the document too easily to give us access to its meaning. As Robert Darnton warns in *The Great Cat Massacre,* if we too readily "get" the joke drawn from an older time, perhaps we have missed entirely its originally intended meaning: like Green's finding of DuBois's "twoness" to be an ideological "mistake," in that its author saw it "solely in the role of a problem when it can also be seen as a competence." But the reader should also know that when DuBois wrote in 1903, the Black press was vibrant with almost weekly news of Republican Party appointments of Blacks to federal offices and many other gestures designed to, as Theodore Roosevelt said, "hold open the door of hope for" Black America. Never mind that these hopes were dashed even before Woodrow Wilson restored the Southern Democratic Party to the White House. Events allowed DuBois to embrace such hopes for improving the lot of African-Americans that he was precluded from clinging to "twoness" as a form of "competence."[6]

At the risk of seeming to drag Bogle and Leab to the guillotine with me, one might point out that a densely rich era of similar great promise at least half formed our books. The previous decade had borne witness to the rise of Martin Luther King, and his ringing hope for Black and White children to walk hand in hand, as well as Malcolm X's hajji to Mecca, which resulted in his deeply felt, broadened interracial vision. Moreover, our ploughing of similar fields of research led us into fleeting moments when Hollywood too had seemed to "hold open the door of hope." Not that we agreed on the enduring impact of these eras—the coming of sound which brought with it *Hallelujah!*, *Hearts of Dixie,* and Bessie Smith's brief (and only) movie; the trove of wartime movies with their Black roles that had arisen as a direct result of NAACP pressure; the ensuing "message movie" era in which racial liberalism had become momentarily marketable. But we all knew that these movies were accompanied by uncommonly bold social changes in the form of Franklin Roosevelt's "black cabinet," the opening of the Lincoln Memorial to Marian Anderson after she had been snubbed in a bid to sing in Constitution Hall, the executively created Fair Employment Practices Commission in the wake of A. Philip Randolph's threatened March on Washington of 1940, and after the war, the startlingly bold report on American racism and its antidotes embodied in Harry Truman's Civil Rights Commission Report of 1947, along with the Democratic platform and a film that were derived from it. Of course, Bogle and Leab carried their work even further toward the present and examined the era that had followed in the train of Melvin Van Peebles's *Sweet Sweetback's Baadasssss Song.*

To miss this generational setting and its intellectual stimulation is to ignore every precept of the "new" history and to settle for journalism. I belabor this point because at stake is the dismissing of older work, mine in particular in this instance, without reference to context. Green asserts, for example, that I "Write off black independent race movies . . . because [I] accepted the aesthetics of assimilation" and of Hollywood with its "aesthetic legacy of Griffith, of racism and patriarchy, reflecting and representing domination while erasing or mollifying subjection." This phrasing is not entirely clear to me, but does it mean to say that Hollywood as an institution remains as it was in 1915 when *The Birth of a Nation* was released? I hope not. At that time, self-evidently, the Directors Guild of America (DGA) had not been founded but if it had been, surely no Black members would have been enrolled. A glance at only one index of change, the current directory of the DGA, reveals roughly nine columns of "minority" members (not all of them Black), at roughly sixty-seven names per column, for a total of some six hundred dues-paying members other than "White." The women's list runs to twenty-five columns or about 1,675 names, some of whom are crosslisted also as Black.[7] These figures appeared in tandem with national movie magazines that have featured a

Black and female managerial establishment. These figures and corresponding rosters of other guilds are kept in part at least for purposes of taking Federally mandated "affirmative action" by those in search of minority personnel. Such numbers and the work arising from their presence in Hollywood belie the simplistic portrayal of it as a warren of "Griffith, racism, and patriarchy." Such rhetoric seems particularly overdrawn in the light of the DGA's showing of Micheaux's *Body and Soul* (1924) at the time it gave him posthumously its Lifetime Achievement Award. The DGA's award raises yet another paradox in the light of Green's disapproval of the treatment of Micheaux in *Slow Fade to Black:* what other book could the DGA have turned to for the details of Micheaux's long and honorably fought career other than, perhaps, the briefer treatments in Bogle and Leab?

In arguing that works of history speak from the mood—"the ideology," in newspeak—of their times as well as the times that form their subject, a few matters of actual book-making must be raised. First, a boom in "Black Studies" publishing had reached its peak, but movies were rarely included as fit subjects. Jervis Anderson's *New Yorker* essay that appeared in book form as *This was Harlem* (1981), a "cultural portrait," mentioned a single movie, Bill Robinson's *Harlem is Heaven,* and Micheaux not at all; and Addison Gayle's enduring compendium, *The Black Aesthetic* (1971), included not a line about movies. This meant that, at the height of a rage for Black material, the most often cited books were Peter Noble's out-of-print *The Negro in Films* (1947) and V. J. Jerome's pamphlet, *The Negro in Hollywood* (1951).

This meant that for the "pioneering" scholar there were no indexes of Black newspaper reviews or commentary, no clippings save for the Schomburg Center's vertical file and the Gumby Collection at Columbia, no accessible studio archives, few manuscripts (the NAACP records were still in process at the Library of Congress), no lists such as Phyllis Klotman's *Frame by Frame,* so that the simplest research foray was *sui generis.* I am not certain, but I believe my piece on the Black response to *The Birth of a Nation* in the *Historian* (1963) was a "first" in a scholarly journal, and another article on Hollywood and race after World War II in *Phylon* (1967), the journal founded by DuBois himself at Atlanta University, was a probable "second." In this context, book publishers were chary of risk, so that their books seemed compressed. Bogle's book lacked any scholarly apparatus at all; Leab's, we often heard, had been cut from two volumes down to one; and my footnotes were compressed to half their original length, with a probable loss of focus or clarity. Under these conditions, merely getting the story as straight as possible was a lofty ambition.

As to formulating a "Black aesthetic" independently of Hollywood movies, the almost universal model was one of connoisseurship: I liked it and therefore so should you. The hot book was Andrew Sarris's *The American Cinema* (1968), which he felt compelled to write, he said, because film history had stopped with Lewis Jacobs's *The Rise of the American Film* (1939), and the then current "sociologically oriented film historians" seemed drawn to film "less as an art form than as a mass medium."[8] As to theorists, few of the French or Germans whose jargon speckles so much current writing had migrated into English, so that of the two theoretical surveys of the day, Richard Dyer MacCann's anthology, *A Montage of Theories* (1966), cited them not at all, and J. Dudley Andrew's "introduction," *The Major Film Theories* (1976), offered a single essay on Christian Metz, in which Jacques Lacan, Julia Kristeva, and Louis Althusser are mentioned in passing in a single sentence, but no Derrida, Levi-Strauss, or Barthes. The result was an overwhelmingly personal approach to movie-watching, driven by an urge to attain a singular sense of "taste" expressed at its highest levels of urbane weeklies in the English-speaking realms. The last thing on a critic's mind would be a sense that there was a "universal" standard being practiced and that a "minority" aesthetic deviated from it in some way.

For their part, up to that time, African-American critics wavered between celebration and skepticism, between hope for a Black cinema and fear that it would never come. In the meantime, the existing Black cinema, including the work of Micheaux, faced this voice that swayed from praise to damnation. From time to time, when Hollywood outdid itself in reaching for a Black ambience in its movies, various African-American public figures praised the films for their long-overdue drawing of the Black "other" into the mainstream. Upon seeing King Vidor's *Hallelujah!* in 1929, for example, the lone Black congressman of the day, Oscar DePriest, hailed it as "the threshhold of civic and cultural emancipation."[9] Like other good "race men" of his day, DePriest grasped the event as a hopeful sign of an American medium on the verge of finding a place for Black ambition. In this sense, DePriest was like all Black publicists who took DuBois's path in finding "twoness" a haven in bad times and a fault in the good times. To miss this ebb and flow of hope is to miss much and to risk regarding ideology as a still pond rather than a lively fountain.

Thus it will be problematic to construct a Black aesthetic in which Micheaux will have an eternally unchallenged place. We may embrace his one-take methods, unevenly talented casts, and jangling glitches either as the predictable flaws arising from any shoestring operation, or we may find them to be such charming flaws that they seem a form of competence under pressure, as though making virtue of necessity. Perhaps this latter course is the way to truth of a sort. Certainly Green thinks so, if for no other reason than Micheaux's fluffs seemed as maturing "elements of style and texture" that at least marked off Black film from "criteria developed from the apartheid Hollywood industry." Unfortunately, the historian must turn to documents where no clear record survives that would suggest that either audiences or critics in Black circles caught this subtextual flooring under Micheaux's movies.

This is not to say some enterprising worker, perhaps even Green, will not uncover such sources. Certainly an impressive tool kit of critical methods stands ready to perform the task: Gregory Waller's efforts to "count the house" in the Black theatres of Lexington, Kentucky, and Mary Carbine's analysis of Black Chicago houses; Umberto Eco's (and others') "reader-response" criticism; the various hybrids of Marxism, particularly that of the Italian Antonio Gramsci whose ideas have been introduced into African-American issues by the Jamaican Marxist, Stuart Hall; applications to Micheaux's movies of Black folk tradition, much as Van Peebles delighted in portraying himself as an outlaw in the vein of Staggerlee or Br'er Rabbit; or James Snead's briefly sketched call for a "recoding" of Black in ways that affirm Blackness while challenging the image of Black as "other"; not to mention the various other sects of theorists drawn from Freud, Marx, and feminism.[10]

Micheaux's work, enclosed as it was in a baffling husk that made it often inaccessible to the audiences for which it was made, will not be an easy mark for those scholars who are finally getting around to it. Not only must the films be opened to inquiry, but new questions must be asked of them. How, for example, can we account for the evidence of Black disapproval and derision? How account for the uneven and often unfriendly Black press? Shall we take the glib way out and find Black moviegoers and critics guilty of Marxism's "false consciousness?" I hope we avoid this cant that blames the victim, particularly if we discover the victim to be Black and bourgeois, the 1960s version of "the enemy of the people."

Gramsci seems promising, in that his notes on Italy allow for class conflict to redefine political culture and, by extension, movie taste, without resort to the elusive proletarian revolution that never comes. Moreover, his openness to an organic leadership from within the group does not require a doctrinaire Leninist revolutionary cadre without which there can be no activism. Moreover, we can find Americanist parallels to Gramsci in John Kenneth Galbraith's notion of "countervailing powers," by which he defined an ever-constant arena in which no class wins but all classes bargain for enhanced status, much as Gramsci's radicals had done for renegotiated terms of "hegemony."

Particularly, we must insist on reaching beyond merely finding Micheaux a giant intellect who managed to make silk purses out of the sow's ear of poverty that he was given to work with. In what specific ways did he deviate from Hollywood practice, other than casting and rough edges? To what extent was this conscious? What do his surviving letters say that allow us to find him, as Green does, "deeply thoughtful?" How can we extend our reach into drawing inferences from unseen films that have left paper trails, without facing our colleagues' charges that inference by its nature is "ill-founded" or "not trustworthy?" If we are honestly reaching, why not reach beyond the limits? If we wish to find Micheaux's work outside of the conventions of Hollywood, how can we deal with his own conventions: the surprise switches in identity, the trick endings, the self-proclaimed and frequently assailed preference for light-skinned actors? How can we avoid the methodologically soft ground that might lead us to assert that Micheaux had invented specifically "Black" shots, cuts, framings, dissolves, and fades? Clearly the way to accomplish this task is to *do* it rather than ransack ancient footnotes for slippages that themselves were possibly induced by the socioeconomic context of *their* times. Errors creep into everything without specifically altering theses: I am certain, for example, that Professor Green did not intend to place Woodrow Wilson and Thomas Dixon together at Yale, rather than where they belonged—at Johns Hopkins.[11]

By now I hope my point is clear. Many years ago my generation tried to reveal Micheaux to a new audience, celebrate his doggedness, and make tentative sense of his work, all while facing scant scholarly resources— including roughly a half-dozen fewer Micheaux films than are extant at present. In the absence of his canon, we made use of Micheaux's own correspondence and that of his contemporaries, the columns of the few critics who paid him heed, and the moviegoers who remembered his work. Now we need to get on with it, neither raising more monuments nor living him down, but instead understanding him across the years in all his ambivalence and ambiguity.

Notes

1. Thomas Cripps, "The Films of Spencer Williams," *Black American Literature Forum,* XII (Lafayette: Indiana State University, Winter 1978), 132.

2. Thomas Cripps, "New Black American Cinema and Uses of the Past," in Gladstone L. Yearwood, ed, *Black Cinema Aesthetics: Issues in Independent Black Filmmaking* (Athens, Ohio: Ohio University, 1982), 22.

3. Donald Bogle, *Toms, Coons, Mulattoes, Mammies, & Bucks: An Interpretive History of Blacks in American Films* (Bantam Books: New York, 1973), 115; Daniel J. Leab, *From Sambo to Superspade: The Black Experience in Motion Pictures* (Boston, 1975), 81.

4. Braudel, *The Mediterranean and the World of Philip the Second* (New York: Harper Collins, 1949, 3rd ed., 1972), 272.

5. Mark Ellis, " 'Closing Ranks' and 'Seeking Honors': W. E. B. DuBois in World War I," *Journal of American History,* LXXIX (Bloomington, Indiana: Organization of American Historians, June 1992), 100.

6. Three illustrative incidents of Roosevelt's presidency are taken up in Willard B. Gatewood, Jr., *Theodore Roosevelt and the Art of Controversy: Episodes of the White House Years* (Baton Rouge: Louisiana State University Press, 1970), Chs. II–IV.

7. *Directors Guild of America: 1991 Directory of Members* (Los Angeles, 1991), 481–92.

8. Andrew Sarris, *The American Cinema: Directors and Directions, 1929–1968* (E.P. Dutton: New York, 1968), 15.

9. DePriest quoted in Thomas Cripps, *Slow Fade to Black: The Negro in American Film, 1900–1942* (Oxford University Press: New York, 1977), 251.

10. Gregory Waller, "Another Audience: Black Moviegoing, 1907–1916," *Cinema Journal,* XXXI (Champagne Urbana: University of Illinois Press, Winter 1992), 3–25; see also Mary Carbine, " 'The Finest Outside the Loop': Motion Picture Exhibition in Chicago's Black Metropolis, 1905–1928," *Camera Obscura,* No. 23 (Baltimore: Johns Hopkins University Press, 1991), 9–42; and on "recoding" see James A. Snead, "Recoding Blackness: The Visual Rhetoric of Black Independent Film," *Whitney Museum of American Art: The New American Filmmakers Series,* Program No. 23, 1–2.

11. Raymond Allen Cook, *Fire from the Flint: The Amazing Careers of Thomas Dixon* (Winston-Salem: J.F. Blair, 1968), 83, in which Dixon describes sitting in his first seminar in Hopkins next to Wilson.

5

The Black Writer in Hollywood, Circa 1930: The Casc of Wallace Thurman

Phyllis Klotman

On July 8, 1928, Warner Bros.'s first all-dialogue picture, *Lights of New York,* opened at the Mark Strand Theatre in New York: "The age of talkies had dawned."[1] Black writer Wallace Thurman, who was busy putting his imprint on the Harlem Renaissance, was in New York working on his play *Harlem* with his White collaborator William Jourdan Rapp. Perhaps he saw the landmark film with Rapp; they may even have met the director Bryan Foy. *Lights of New York,* a prohibition-age melodrama, which today is much less well known than *The Jazz Singer,* was important for several reasons. "First, it . . . demonstrated that a feature length talking picture [*The Jazz Singer* had music and a few ad-libbed lines by Al Jolson] could be made. But much more significantly, it . . . revealed to the astonished Warner Bros. and to the disturbed and even more dumbfounded movie industry as a whole that such a film could attract audiences. They looked, they listened, and sometimes they laughed in the wrong places—but they kept coming. And it was the talk, not the music, that brought them in droves to the Mark Strand Theatre."[2]

Lights of New York has some of the same implicit criticism of the city as the agent of corruption that we find in Thurman's play *Harlem,* but of course melodrama was a staple in the theater, as it became in the movies. During the mid-thirties Brian Foy was in charge of Warner's "B" picture unit. At what point he decided to establish his own production company and when he actually worked out a contractual arrangement with Thurman for at least the two films we can document, *Tomorrow's Children* and *High School Girl,* can only be conjectured. If his independent company fed Warner Bros.'s box office Moloch, he may well have been encouraged by them to turn out more movies for consumption. Thurman and Rapp certainly hoped for a filmed version of their play *Harlem,* and in 1929, Wallie (as he liked to be called) was "introduced around the studios." MGM apparently thought he could write something suitable for Nina Mae McKinney, the star of King Vidor's *Hallelujah!,* but no firm offer came because "they got cold feet and decided to do nothing until the box office returns on Halleluliah [sic] were known." He also interviewed at Fox and Pathe, where he was told he was too intellectual: "They had expected me to be like their Negro actors and were a little surprised at my line of talk. . . . I was told all around that all were eager to see a script of Harlem. They had had good reports but no approach [sic] from the producer or agent."[3] By August of 1929 he had received final "noes" from MGM, Pathe and Fox.

In spite of the rejection of *Harlem,* and Wallie's feeling that Hollywood was "more mad than Broadway," he was back on the West Coast in 1934. On April 14, 1934, the *Pittsburgh Courier* located him in Hollywood, "engaged by a motion picture company to write a film story at a stipend in excess of $250 a week, perhaps the highest salary paid a Negro in America." The *San Francisco Spokesman* on April 19, 1934, reported that "Wallace Thurman, young sepia author is going over big in Hollywood. From the movie city, come reports that his story, 'Sterilization' was accepted with such enthusiasm, that he was immediately signed up for a two year contract to write film stories." *Tomorrow's Children* was the title of the film to which the *Spokesman* referred. It was reviewed in *Motion Picture Herald* on May 29, 1934, as a "Topical Drama" by Bryan Foy Productions. Wallace Thurman is credited as author of the original story and as coauthor, with the director Crane Wilbur, of the screenplay. None of the credits is listed on the extant 16 millimeter print, except for Bryan Foy Productions—not even the cast. Nor has a copy of the original story or of the screenplay surfaced. The mystery is that a film about sterilization in which doctors actually explain the procedure for vasectomy, using the term, and salpingectomy or fallectomy, using neither term, would be produced in 1934. Even in the heyday of the "social problem" film, when exposés of poverty and corruption were grist for the mill of studios like Warner Bros. which "became known as the socially conscious studio,"[4] it is hard to conceive of the audience for a film which examines the morality of sterilization laws and deals with sophisticated medical terminology as though it were easily apprehended by the general public.

By 1934, as a recognized master of the low-budget film and a devotee of the "problem" film, Foy may have found the perfect writer to answer both his primary and secondary needs. Thurman's most recently published novel, *The Interne* (1932) with A. L. Furman, was the story of callous and even inhumane treatment of patients in a large New York hospital. Some of the most important scenes in *Tomorrow's Children* take place in a large metropolitan hospital run by the county which carries out court-ordered sterilizations, mainly of the poor, with little question and less conscience.

The plot devolves on seventeen-year-old Alice Mason, the sole support of her (Irish) parents and their feeble-minded, crippled, and criminal children. She is the victim of the social welfare system, which agrees to assist her family provided that she, her mother, and father will agree to be sterilized. The reviewer in *Motion Picture Herald* (cited above) described the film as: "Basically, . . . a topical study in eugenics, a matter currently being widely discussed. It is a frank presentation, from both a pro and anti standpoint, of human sterilization and its possibilities of improving or harming the human race." In fact, Thurman's arguments are heavily weighted against the idea of "human engineering," as the runner makes clear with its dateline Germany—"Newsflash! Hitler Decrees All Unfit to be Sterilized." What seems amazing today, some fifty years later, is the accuracy of the film's claim that twenty-seven states had put sterilization laws into practice (in two states it was voluntary), and how early in the century the first such law had been enacted: "Under these laws, the feeble-minded, the mentally ill, epileptics, and others may be subjected to investigation and examination to determine whether there is likelihood of similar defectiveness or disease being transmitted to their offspring, or whether there are other reasons why they should not be allowed to propagate."[5]

The first such law was enacted by Indiana in 1907; Georgia in 1937 was the last to establish such a policy before the 1940 Public Health Report was released. (California was among the 27, New York was not.) The analogy which the film's runner draws between legal sterilization in the United States and the heinous practices of the Nazis makes it abundantly clear that *Tomorrow's Children* intends to be an exposé, since "unfit" in Hitler's argot meant not only the physically and mentally handicapped but also Jews, Catholics, Slavs, "gypsies" (read people of color): the imperfect non-Aryan, that is, non-German. The problem is joined before the first frame since the question posed by the title is: Who will tomorrow's children be? Tomorrow's *White* children, since Blacks are not seen in the hospital or in the courts. In fact, it would probably have come as a great surprise to the audience to know that the original story was written by an African-American.

The roots of the thirties' message film can be traced back to the original film audience—the working class, which included many immigrants who barely understood English. The silent film was exciting, affordable entertainment. Once the initial excitement of seeing just any moving image was past, stories about themselves, with recognizable plot and setting, attracted large audiences, larger than early filmmakers had reason to expect. Hollywood filmmakers began to search other media to adapt to the screen—novels, plays. At the same time, the teens brought out muckrakers like Lincoln Steffens, whose exposés of corruption in government put him in the pantheon of investigative reporters yet unborn, and Upton Sinclair, whose revelations of exploitative practices by the meat packing industry (*The Jungle,* 1906) led to the establishment of the Food and Drug Administration. America may not have had its own Ibsen and therefore no home-grown *Ghosts,* but Sinclair also published, with the permission of the French playwright Eugene Brieux, a novelized version of Brieux's *Les Avaries* (*Damaged Goods,* 1913), a powerful appeal for enlightened education to stop the spread of venereal disease. The *New York Age* reported on June 21, 1917, that the Lafayette Players, the Black stock company which made an extraordinary reputation for itself from 1915 to 1932, performed *Damaged Goods* during that month at the Lafayette Theatre in Harlem. There was then a growing interest on the part of some American writers to bring to the stage and to the new movie medium realistic representations not only of the plight of the poor, who were the worst victims of the "robber barrons," but also issues of public policy, even when they involved sex.

Tomorrow's Children bears a strong resemblance to that earlier thesis drama, and to the filmed melodramas in which the poor triumph over the rich. In *Tomorrow's Children,* Dr. Brooks, the hero, faces a threat to his career if he refuses to operate on (sterilize) Alice Mason. Although Brooks is affluent and well-respected, it is his ethical and moral struggle that serves to dramatize the larger plight of the poor and powerless. The narrative's insistent linear structure keeps the central issue before the audience at all times. There are no flashbacks. The intercutting of relatively short parallel scenes is designed to keep the chronology straightforward and clear. Indeed, the opening sequences which introduce the principals exemplify this technique.

We first meet Alice Mason, the young heroine, with her boyfriend Jim, walking home from the laundry where they both work. They're in love and want to get married, but because she's the sole support of her family, she feels she can't desert them. Jim is very decent, clean-cut—he won't even kiss her in public; they're both neatly dressed but just short of shabby.

The parallel scene intercut at this point introduces Dr. Brooks, who has just brought Mrs. Mason (Alice's mother) home from the hospital in an ambulance. He attended her delivery of a stillborn infant in the charity ward, and out of concern, accompanies her in the ambulance. Mr. Mason, an out-of-work alcoholic, is seated at the kitchen table, which is covered with dirty dishes. The camera first shows him downing a glass of whiskey, his hand close to the almost-full bottle, which seems to be his main source of sustenance. Sullen, unmoved by the doctor's kindness, he sits surrounded by his crippled and feeble-minded children. They are all boys, and one, he says, "has the mind of a two-year-old," although he's 12. That child, who cowers on the floor next to an old chest, is playing with his only toys, his father's recently emptied whiskey bottles, in ironic imitation of adult behavior. The father is without sympathy or compassion for his children or his wife—"she can take it, she's been through it often enough"—so that the doctor's concern is all the more touching. When Alice enters the kitchen, having seen the ambulance parked outside her house, hero and heroine appear together in the same frame. The narrative requires our understanding of their inherent decency as well as our identification with them. Both are out of place in that closed environment: Dr. Brooks by his impeccable whites and his sensitivity, Alice by her normality and her loving devotion.

Seeing the extent of the burden Alice has assumed for the family's support, Dr. Brooks promises to get public assistance for them: "The city ought to be helping you. I'm going to report your case to the welfare board." What doesn't occur to him is that he will inadvertently set in motion the power of the state, which will then threaten the happiness of the young couple. The state decides that the entire family must be "sterilized" if they are to continue to receive financial aid. A city social worker and a policeman are sent to escort Alice to the hospital, forcefully, if necessary. Alice temporarily escapes her captors, but is shortly returned to police custody.

Before she is remanded to the hospital, however, Alice appeals the decision in her case with the help of Dr. Brooks and Jim. It is Thurman's opportunity to present the perspectives of various "candidates" for sterilization in a court that is clearly biased against the poor. The three cases presented to the judge before Alice's all involve men. Two are quickly dispatched by the judge; one is termed a "mental," the other a "criminal" case. They are obviously lower-class and are scarcely given more than a few minutes of the judge's time. These two cases are played out before the judge in the courtroom, but the next case originates in a chamber directly off the courtroom. It clearly points out the differential treatment given the rich and the poor. A prominent lawyer, now a senator, is readying his client for his imminent appearance. He's a well-dressed young man named Whitney who is attended by a nurse. The scene reeks of money and privilege. Whitney is made up to look like a sex fiend—heavy brows, dark Dracula-like circles under his eyes, diabolic leer. The question seems to be whether or not he'll be able to control himself long enough for the hearing to take place. And sure enough, the minute the lawyer's back is turned, Whitney rips the nurse's clothes off. The unctuous senator presents the case to the heretofore stern judge who becomes all compliant smiles when he sees the importance of lawyer and client: The senator produces two eminent doctors who testify that young Whitney's condition is just temporary, in spite of the findings of the state medical commission and the decision of the lower court. Of course, the appeal is granted and young Whitney is free to rape at will.

Alice Mason is the only female whose case is heard by the judge, unusual considering how sterilization statistics indicate that many more women were sterilized than men, even though the procedure of salpingectomy was more complicated than that of vasectomy.[6] Dr. Brooks insists that Alice is different from her family ("She's normal and has a good reputation"), she promises that she'll be "a good mother," and Jim implores the judge not to "tear her heart out . . . she's a good girl." The implication is clear—Alice and Jim are both highly moral, decent, honest (and probably patriotic)—all the middle-class virtues, even though they live at the poverty level. But the judge is indifferent to their suffering. No one can counter his hard line about the Mason family of unfit offspring: "Chances are her children will inherit the family taint. Three generations of unfit are enough." Their arguments are emotional, his decision rational. He has not a moment's hesitation in denying her appeal. This time we see an innocent, wide-eyed girl who is brutalized by the system of "justice" because she is poor and without influence. In this melodrama the villain wears robes and wields a gavel.

The narrative never allows the audience to evade the question of moral conscience; it is dramatized through the character of Dr. Brooks, who is next shown in his own tastefully decorated home complete with beautiful wife and child. The setting is in striking contrast to the coldness of the courtroom in the previous scene and to the mean surroundings of Alice Mason's home. His wife is not only beautiful (and blonde) but also sympathetic—she tries to assuage his guilt about what has happened to Alice, but he insists that she would not be at risk if he hadn't tried to get money for the family, which in turn precipitated the investigation by the social agency. To emphasize the point, the scene is shot in a sunlit room with Brooks' young daughter on his lap.

The narrative deserts Alice only when the sterilization issue becomes an illustrative study. As Dr. Brooks prepares the "criminal" Spike Howard for the operation, he gets out the illustrated charts, explains exactly what vasectomy is and the surgical procedure involved. He assures Spike that the whole process will probably take as long as a tooth extraction and be less painful. The scene becomes a lesson in physiology and sex education. With only a local anesthetic, Spike continues to be garrulous throughout the operation, which was touted in the runner as "The First Authentic Major Operation to Reach the Screen!" This scene may well have been the source of Foy's and *Tomorrow's Children*'s trouble with the censors. The Catholic Church included it on its 1934 "boycott" list.[7]

Although Brooks furnishes Spike Howard with detailed information about vasectomy, including references to the comparable operation for women—severing the fallopian tubes—he says nothing to Alice. There are no other women in the room to which she is confined, and it is the first time that bars at the windows are so prominently displayed. The mise-en-scène emphasizes the bareness of her surroundings—her isolation— and she implores Brooks for help. Yet she never loses sight of the issue: "Who gave them the authority to tell me I can't bring life into this world? Only God has that right."

The religious implications are not touched upon in the film until this moment, although the runner shows a clergyman in his pulpit making a pronouncement: "Sterilization must be abolished from the statutes of this country." It would not be surprising if Thurman's original story had omitted the religious issue altogether. In spite of his grandmother's teachings, Wallie never became a true believer. Indeed, one of his friends at the University of Southern California contended that Thurman was an atheist.[8] In the absence of the original story or the screenplay, there is no way of knowing whether or how the religious references originated. They seem perfectly natural in Alice's hospital bed plea to Brooks to get the operation postponed at least one day, and in her prayer: "Please, God, show him, won't you." The presence of the priest in one of the last scenes and his role in the climactic moments is somewhat surprising. Unless the audience is prone to accept the stereotype of the Irish Catholic household, where the father drinks but doesn't work and the children keep multiplying, there are no real indications that the Masons are Catholic until Father O'Brien arrives at their home with Jim. Jim has seen the failure of science and law and has evidently decided to put his faith in the church. Actually, the priest cannot convince Mrs. Mason, who is in her cups, to change her mind and sign the paper that will save Alice.

Movie melodrama wouldn't be complete without a buildup of tension leading to some kind of satisfying resolution. Having risked his future by pleading Alice's case with his chief, Dr. McIntosh—"Is science always right? Look at all the great men in the world who may be classified as having been insane or in some other way unfit. Look at Nietzche, Dostoevsky, Edgar Allen Poe. Suppose their parents had been sterilized? I thought you considered human values as well as scientific ones"—and then by refusing to be a party to her operation, Brooks is told by Dr. McIntosh either to come to his senses or resign. Then in a sudden gesture of magnanimity, McIntosh excuses Brooks as a "conscientious objector," leaving him free to respond to Jim's urgent call. The tension heightens as shots of Alice being wheeled into the operating room are cross-cut with shots of Brooks appropriating an ambulance and arriving in time to hear Mrs. Mason confess: "Alice ain't none of my daughter . . . her Ma brought

her here when she was just six months old. We've had her here ever since
and we don't know what happened to her real folks." The tension heightens
when shots of Alice in the anesthesiologist's stranglehold are cross-cut
with the rescuers confronting the judge in his courtroom. (In lieu of a
signed statement, he will accept Father O'Brien's priestly word.) If not
for the meticulous preparation for the operation, much antiseptic dressing,
washing of hands—perhaps Thurman's ironic play on sterilization—and
the added fillip of official observers from the medical commission, Alice
would never have escaped unscathed. The judge's call, of course, saves
her just as knife is put to flesh, but we don't know for sure until Jim utters
"Thank God" over Alice's inert body, and Father O'Brien says, "I told
you to have faith, my son."

The denouement takes place in the same hospital corridor where Jim
first sought Dr. Brooks and importuned him to help Alice in her appeal
against the sterilization order. No riding off into the sunset for doctors.
Duty calls again and Brooks disappears down the corridor as he is being
paged over the P.A. system—a samaritan in hospital whites who has
merely done the "right thing." The young couple are off to be married and
to live happily ever after in their three-roomed flat decorated at the five
and dime. Most of the ends are neatly tied, but the question raised by the
film remains moot. Alice is not the biological daughter of the Masons, a
fact which the audience learns early on. (This bit of dramatic irony
contributes to the emotional tension of the climactic scenes.) When the
Masons confer privately, after the social worker has issued her ultimatum,
Ma Mason expresses her unease about Alice because she is not their
daughter. Pa, on the other hand, doesn't want the information out because
he thinks Alice will then feel free to marry Jim and cease supporting them.
Ma Mason's convenient conscience allows her to rationalize that at least
Alice won't have to go through what she's gone through. On the other
hand, what if Alice had been their biological daughter? What about the
constitutional guarantees against the abridgement of civil rights? The
question of the constitutionality of sterilization laws is not raised by the
film, but it was in fact raised in the courts: one law was held valid by the
Supreme Court of the United States and seven others by the highest courts
of the respective states in which they were heard.

Eugenic sterilization statutes . . . were essentially unique, primarily
because they required, as a basis for judicial pronouncement, an evaluation of the science of eugenics. Moreover, while these laws required
a finding that certain persons were feeble-minded, insane, etc., which
element was present in commitment laws, they differed from commitment laws in that an erroneous adjudication once carried into effect
could not be rectified in the same measure as an error in committing

a person could be corrected. Also, while sterilization statutes were somewhat analogous, in legal aspects, to vaccination laws, these latter laws were aimed primarily toward prevention of disease and they did not, like sterilization enactments, seek to remove a biologic function; and they did not, as in the case of females surgically treated under sterilization laws, involve the risk of a major operation.[9]

The only indication in *Tomorrow's Children* that salpingectomy is categorically different from vasectomy is in the contrasting operating room sequences. Doctors have always known that there is greater risk to a patient when a general anaesthetic is required for a surgical procedure than when a local anaesthetic will suffice, and while Spike is clearly inconvenienced by the experience, he is fully conscious and able to talk. Alice, on the other hand, is incapable of uttering a sound once she is set upon by a heavy-handed anesthesiologist, who appears well schooled in the art of the headlock and to whom the camera returns at least three times during the tension-building climax. The fact that the operation itself deprives Alice of a voice emphasizes her status in society. When she speaks for herself, as she does to protest the sterilization order, no one listens to her. If she were a woman of privilege, like the social worker, she might have other allies to speak for her, but it is not at all certain that she would be allowed to make decisions on her own behalf. For the male world makes the decisions which she, as well as the social worker, is expected to follow. Even the doctor, who has Alice's interests at heart, decides to seek assistance for the family without consulting her. He tells her of his intention and she acquiesces. When her refusal to acquiesce to the court order brings down the wrath of the state, she is threatened by the officer of the court with force. Her protest to the judge goes unheard and her poignant appeal to Dr. Brooks when taken to the next layer of power goes unheeded. If not for the confession of Ma Mason, the only woman with the power of information, Alice would never have escaped the knife. It is, of course, the men who then ride to the rescue and, like the US cavalry, save the day.

Thurman's use of a female character to dramatize the sterilization issue is not surprising. His first novel, *The Blacker the Berry,* dramatized the issue of intraracial prejudice through a female protagonist and his second screenplay dealt with the problems of an adolescent girl. A cursory glance at *Variety*'s list of Warner film releases in 1934 reveals a number of films in which women figure in the central role, more in fact from a single company than one sees in the total annual output of the industry today.

1934 was the year that Universal released its three-handkerchief version of Fannie Hurst's *Imitation of Life,* according to Donald Bogle, "the first important 'black film' of the thirties," which became a real box office success.[10] A woman-centered melodrama, *Imitation of Life* is the story of two mothers trying to raise their daughters without husbands and with very little means. It also deals with the taboo subject of "passing" (across racial lines), which had rarely been touched upon in American films—the subplot of *Show Boat* (1936) had White actress Helen Morgan playing the role of Julie, the tragic mulatta whose "passing" is discovered. Although the issue of interracial sex is implicit in the film, and explicit in the novel, the racist attitudes which shape the tragedy of the mulatto are unchallenged. *Tomorrow's Children,* on the other hand, challenges the prevailing social attitudes about sterilization, as well as the legal ramifications.

Like *Imitation of Life,* it has its heartrending scenes but it does not allow the audience to separate itself from the issue. *Imitation of Life* allows a bifurcation. The Black mother's (Louise Beavers) loss of her daughter and her subsequent death from a "broken heart" is poignant, but the loss is mitigated by the White mother's (Claudette Colbert) success and happiness. Indeed the film reads as a negative criticism of passing—if Peola, the daughter, had been satisfied to stay within her race, the sad ending could have been averted. The White audience, while touched by the pathos, is distanced from the personal tragedy and also leaves the theater with a comfortable sense that the social order is still intact. Not so in *Tomorrow's Children.* Thurman insists on applying the sterilization issue to all levels of the society (with the glaring omission of African-Americans and other minorities) by giving at least some of the victims their moment of challenge to the victimizers or their minions: "How'd you like them to do it to you, doc?" Spike asks the surgeon during the operation. Other characters are also heard: one of the matrons delivering Alice to the hospital responds to the other with the acerbic line: "I'd like to hear the fuss you'd make if they were going to do it to you." Dr. Crosby, a strong supporter of sterilization, comments on Dr. Brooks's mood the day after his colleague's abortive attempt to help Alice fight the court order: "You look like they're going to do it to you." Brooks does indeed identify personally with the threat, in the idyllic scene with his wife and young daughter, when he says, "Think what we would have done if someone had stepped in and kept this happiness from us." The challenge is clearly to the audience: what would you do if you were faced with sterilization?

No records have yet surfaced which can answer the questions: Who saw *Tomorrow's Children?* How was it received at the box office? Therefore, we can only conjecture about its reception. *Variety* did not review it, nor did the New York *Times,* although both reviewed *High School Girl* the next year. The *Times* reviewer reports having seen *High School Girl* at the Astor in New York (review dated March 16, 1935) and the *Variety* reviewer indicates its opening the week of March 16th. The *Variety* review, dated March 20, 1935, is less than enthusiastic; it calls the film a "tiresome preachment on the facts of life and parental neglect." Another message film, *High School Girl* delivers its moral punch with a mailed fist. Babies having babies was not yet an everyday occurrence, but without recourse to legal abortion, coat hangers, suicides and parental guilt were not unusual in the case of unexpected and unwanted teenage pregnancies. The review in the *Times* did not find any redeeming value in the film, but *Variety* at least cites Crane Wilbur's acting if not his direction: "Story, direction and cast win no laurels with minor exceptions. One is Crane Wilbur, who impressively plays a biologist. He also directed but has done so in an ordinary manner." Like *Tomorrow's Children, High School Girl* makes a hero of the scientist. He is the "trail-breaker for modern enlightenment." Wilbur is the only actor who makes the transition from *Tomorrow's Children,* but that no doubt was as much for convenience as anything else, since he was also in charge of direction. The other cast members are relatively unknown, including Mildred Gover, a Black actress, who plays the maid in the "turbulent household" and who favorably impressed the *Variety* reviewer.

Thurman may well have been discouraged by the review of *Tomorrow's Children.* He never saw the reviews of *High School Girl* because he died before they were published. Bryan Foy may have decided that it would be cheaper to buy up his contract than to continue making films that either didn't get to the box office because of trouble with the censors, as *High School Girl* and *Tomorrow's Children* both had, or were not money-makers when they got there. Thurman was back in New York by May, perhaps before the shooting of *High School Girl* even started. His career as a screenwriter was shortlived, but it's clear that he intended to try to pry open the door to the big studios. On the first of July, 1934, he was in the hospital, ironically the same one he wrote about in *The Interne.* He didn't leave there alive.

Several other African-American writers, like Eulalie Spence, Langston Hughes, and Zora Neale Hurston, made overtures to or were wooed by Hollywood, but little came of it. Spence's only full length play, *The Whipping* (1932), was optioned by Paramount, but was never made into film.[11] The poet Langston Hughes, fellow writer, Harlemite, and long time friend of Thurman's, was "very eager to break into the film industry." According to biographer Arnold Rampersad, in 1934 Hughes sent his story "Rejuvenation Through Joy," a burlesque "based to some extent on Jean Toomer" to a Paramount executive. Despite the support of friends in the industry, "Rejuvenation Through Joy" suffered the same fate as Spence's *The Whipping.* However, Hughes continued to look for jobs in Hollywood. His only (qualified) success was *Way Down South* (1939), a collaboration with the Black actor-writer Clarence Muse for the producer Sol Lesser. Although it helped Hughes's perennial financial problems, it was the source of some embarrassment to him because of the compromises to his own integrity. *Way Down South,* with its stereotypical plantation setting and characters, was a vehicle for the White child actor Bobbie Breen. The best that probably can be said for the film is that it employed three hundred Black actors and gave Muse an opportunity to direct (with Bernard Vorhaus).[12]

Zora Neale Hurston arrived in Los Angeles in late spring of 1941—the last of the Harlem Renaissance writers to "go West." She actually went to work on her autobiography, and because a rich friend offered her a place to live. While she was there she served as a story consultant at Paramount, at the same time trying to convince the studio to adapt her novels to screen.[13] Apparently, nothing came of her efforts.

What Hughes and Thurman (and probably Hurston later) learned was that the "Negro" may have been in vogue in Hollywood in the thirties, but it was still the cardboard Negro, the Imitation-Judge Priest-Green Pastures-GWTW Negro. Certainly not the writer, director. Racist attitudes were as deeply entrenched in Hollywood as in any other institution in the United States. It was obvious in the studios' on- and off-screen treatment of Black professionals. Thurman's experience as a writer was in some ways unique. Although he was no more successful than his Renaissance friends in bringing his own version of African-American experience to the Hollywood screen, he was able to avoid racial stereotyping. The cost, it seems, was absence. If not for African-American independents like Oscar Micheaux, no alternative in Hollywood would have existed in the thirties. What amazing productions might have taken place had Micheaux been able or willing to collaborate with the African-American writers Hollywood found so easily expendable.

Notes

1. Harry Geduld, *The Birth of the Talkies* (Bloomington, Indiana: Indiana University Press, 1975), 201.

2. Ibid, 209.

3. Letter to William Jourdan Rapp from Wallace Thurman, May 7, 1929 (James Weldon Johnson Collection, Beineke Library, Yale University).

4. Peter Roffman and Jim Purdy, *The Hollywood Social Problem Film: Madness, Despair, and Politics from the Depression to the Fifties* (Bloomington, Indiana: Indiana University Press, 1981), 4.

5. James E. Hughes, *Eugenic Sterilization in the United States: A Comparative Summary of Statutes and Review of Court Decisions,* Supplement No. 162 to the Public Health Reports (Washington, D.C.: U.S. Government Printing Office, 1940), 1.

6. Statistics provided in the *Biennial Report of the Eugenics Board of North Carolina* from July 1, 1958, through June 30, 1968, show that the number of female sterilizations far surpassed those of male sterilizations: Male, 80; Female 2,075.

7. The *Hollywood Reporter* described *Tomorrow's Children* as "flanked by statements from health boards and objections from the Church." The *Motion Picture Herald* review stated that the subject of sterilization in the dialogue is "handled from an anti-sterilization viewpoint and very much in accordance with the tenets of the Catholic Church. . . . On the other hand, the action serves to demonstrate the scientific benefits of sterilization, with no regard for moral law wishes." (Brian Taves, American Film Institute catalogue research, April 17, 1990).

8. Letter from Thomas Reid to author, February 9, 1983. Reid was a fellow student of Thurman's at the University of Southern California. He was also business manager of *The Outlet*, a literary journal edited by Thurman and published in Los Angeles.

9. Hughes, 22.

10. Donald Bogle, *Toms, Coons, Mulattoes, Mammies and Bucks: An Interpretive History of Blacks in American Films* (New York: The Viking Press, 1973), 57.

11. Kathy A. Perkins, ed. *Black Female Playwrights: An Anthology of Plays before 1950* (Bloomington: Indiana University Press, 1989), 106.

12. Factual information and quotations in this paragraph from Arnold Rampersad's *The Life of Langston Hughes, Volume I: 1902–1941 I, Too, Sing America* (New York: Oxford University Press, 1986), 308–9, 367–9, 371.

13. Robert E. Hemenway, *Zora Neale Hurston, A Literary Biography* (Urbana: University of Illinois Press, 1977), 276.

6

Is *Car Wash* a Musical?

Richard Dyer

It would seem on the face of it odd not to consider *Car Wash* a musical. If, in John Russell Taylor's inclusive definition, a musical is "a film which . . . has its shape, its movement, its whole feeling dictated by music" (Taylor 1971: 10), then few films deserve the label as much as *Car Wash.* Both in terms of its relations of production and consumption, and as text, music is its determining raison d'être. Like *Top Hat, Easter Parade* or *Cabaret,* it was made to be sold on the strength of its songs and its singers, of "Car Wash," "You Gotta Believe," and "I Wanna Get Next to You," of Rose Royce and the Pointer Sisters. Like music videos, it was set up in part to sell the album of its numbers, and indeed a couple of years ago was rereleased (in Britain) as a music video. Equally, as text *Car Wash* is from start to finish organized by its music, with its narratives, characters and dialogues set to the tracks on the disco dance station KGYS.

Yet intuitively it also seems inaccurate to call *Car Wash* a musical. Lumping it together with *Top Hat* and others feels like one's missing something. If dubbing it a "Black musical" is problematic, since it implies that the Astaire/Rogers, MGM, Broadway adaptation line is a norm to which anything Black is deviant, still *Car Wash* certainly is not a White musical.

It is *not* not a White musical because most of its cast is Black—all-Black *Cabin in the Sky* and *Carmen Jones* are indisputably mainstream musicals (and in that sense White). Nor is it not so because it belongs musically to rock/soul as opposed to popular song à la Cole Porter and Rodgers and Hammerstein—*Jailhouse Rock* and *Purple Rain* are organized along lines that Porter and R & H would have been quite at home with. The lines of organisation are, however, the point. It is the nature of the relationship between musical numbers and narrative that distinguishes

93

Car Wash from White musicals, something it shares with many other Black-identified films from *St. Louis Blues* to *House Party.*

There is just one sequence in *Car Wash* that is like a White musical. The film depicts a day in the life of a car wash. At one point it is visited by a con-man preacher Daddy Rich and his entourage, the Wilson Sisters. Duane/Abdullah, the Black Power activist, ridicules Rich's fake religiosity, and Rich orders the Sisters to make him apologise. They do so by circling him, shaking tambourines and singing "You Gotta Believe (in something—why not believe in me?)" and as they do, musical accompaniment seeps in on the soundtrack, not courtesy of KGYS. Just as with Astaire and Rogers, or Garland and Kelly, a cue for a song is set up, taken, and people burst into singing and music comes in from nowhere in the diegesis. This is the only time this happens in *Car Wash.* Elsewhere a musical number is either clearly coming from a radio or else, on a couple of occasions, is performed by the characters: Floyd and Lloyd demonstrating, without accompaniment, their nightclub act to the others, Abdullah playing the sax by himself during the lunch break.

What decisively distinguishes *Car Wash* from White musicals, however, is not this matter of the numbers being diegetically motivated in the former. This after all is true of most backstage and bio-pic musicals, for instance, as well as *Meet Me in St. Louis,* with its use of party turns, music boxes, parlor ballads, people just singing the (eponymous) hit song of the day, and most characters able to play a musical instrument. Nor is it a matter of song content. *Car Wash* runs the usual Broadway/Hollywood gamut of love songs, happy songs, sad songs; in fact it is less broad in its range of what can be sung about than *Golddiggers of 1933* with "Remember My Forgotten Man," *South Pacific* with "You've Got to Be Taught," or *The Music Man* with "Ya Got Trouble" (with the exception of its one already alluded to, non-diegetic, more-like-White-musicals number, "You Gotta Believe"). What is different is what the numbers signify in the course of the narrative, and how they figure in the lives of the characters.

The difference may be indicated by taking a classic number from a classic white musical, *On the Town* (1949). At the natural history museum, Ann Miller tells Jules Munshin, whom she has just met, that she finds him attractive because he reminds her of a pithecanthropus erectus. Suddenly she starts singing to explain: "Modern man is not for me . . . Give me a prehistoric man." At the end of the singing, she, Munshin and the others (Betty Garrett, Gene Kelly, Frank Sinatra) start dancing. As they do, they take up various of the museum's exhibits, to play on or dress in; they move from one room to another; camera movement and editing expand the geography of the setting and dynamize the impact of their movements. In short, the number not only expresses Miller's libidinal delight, but also embodies a sense of release from the confinement of everyday space and time, a glorious escape from the restrictions of modern living.

My example is not chosen innocently or randomly. On the one hand, it is both one of my all-time favourites and a formally consummate example of the use of camera movement and editing in relation to body movement. On the other hand, the museum's artifacts, whose primitivism is so crucial to the number's construction of spontaneity and unrestrained energy, are, once past the model of the cave man, entirely drawn from Native American, African and Asian cultures. The museum becomes a microcosm of the imperialist playground, giving the White protagonists such splendidly taken opportunities for expansion and freedom. It is this dialectic of narrative and number, restraint and release, with the sense of there being terrain that would permit the latter, that is absent from musicals like *Car Wash.*

In the rest of this article I discuss the organisation of narrative and numbers in *Car Wash,* with some reference to other Black films, and consider the significance of their difference from White musicals.

In his article, "Repetition as a figure of black culture," James A. Snead argues that, while all cultures have necessarily to come to terms with recurrence and circularity, European-based culture tends to mask this by stressing linear development, whereas Black culture acknowledges it and makes room for it.

> In European culture, repetition must be seen to be not just circulation and flow but accumulation and growth. In black culture, the thing (the ritual, the dance, the beat) is "there for you to pick it up when you come back to get it" (Snead 1984: 67).

The latter is the principle that organizes *Car Wash.* The White musical does have highly foregrounded repetitions in the form of the reprise, but these are generally used either to mark the change that has occurred in the narrative (for instance, the promise of love become its fulfillment) or to signal the closure of the show (the major numbers repeated as the finale, overdeterminedly in *Hello Dolly!,* where the closure is the imminent marriage of the three central couples). Repetition in the tradition to which *Car Wash* belongs is much less heavily signalled and formalised, because it happens continually. It underpins the films in ways that present it as the feature of the culture they portray.

This idea may be illustrated by *St. Louis Blues* (1929),[1] not just in the fact that Bessie Smith sings the song twice (in a sixteen-minute-long film) as part of a narrative that suggests the endless cycle of men's abuse of women's love, but by the shifting spatial placing of the song in the film. She starts the song for the first time after her man, Jimmy (Jimmy Mordecai), goes off with another woman. She is slumped on the floor, a glass of gin in her hand. Through a cut (via a fade to black), the song carries over to her as she sits slumped at a bar, a glass of gin in hand. The camera then shows us a nightclub, with band accompanying the song and patrons joining in. She is at a working bar and does not face the patrons or apparently sing out to them—it is not clear whether she is the floor show or just a patron singing her sorrows, just as it is not clear whether she is Bessie or Bessie Smith. The song ends as Jimmy comes in; it must be at least days, probably months later; after a brief reunion, ending with him stealing from her and leaving, she takes up the song again in close-up with chorus over, and the film ends. The song is the thing that is always there, whether for Bessie (Smith) herself, for the chorus in the film, or for the viewers in the cinema. By dissolving clear space and time coordinates, the film constructs both the blues and Bessie-as-icon, and Black culture itself, in terms of recurrence and circularity rather than linear progression and completion.

The "thing" in *Car Wash* is KGYS, the disco dance radio station, an unending (though occasionally unheard) succession of repeated tracks and jive talk. JB, the first deejay we hear, even sets up the idea that the station is not just background music going on elsewhere but is in the listeners' heads:

> The JB is here, rappin' in your ear.
> The JB's not on your radio,
> Your radio's not really on.

Characters dip in and out of the thing in their ear, as does the narration of the film itself. The next two sections deal with each of these aspects of the film.

At one point *Car Wash* draws attention to the characters' dipping into the sound track. Mr. B, the White owner of the car wash, complains to Marsha, the White cashier, about the music: "You'd think just once they'd wanna hear Frank Sinatra, Perry Como." Marsha asks him why he doesn't put on what he likes. "I'll show you," he says and tunes the radio to a classical music station. After crying out in protest, the gang go into slow motion on the car they're working on. One of the ways they dip into the thing is to use it to work to; if the thing's not there, the work doesn't go so well.

The one sustained sequence showing the gang at work is done entirely to the "Car Wash" track. Everyone *moves* as they wash and clean. Floyd and Lloyd do their cabaret steps as they direct the steam guns; Hippo shakes his blubbery frame, and Lindy works his *fag ass,* as they bend into the car to vacuum; Geronimo boogies round the car with the duster. This energy and fun contrasts with the later sequence where Irwin, Mr. B's dope-smoking, Mao-reading son, stumbles into the empty wash, thinking he's starting work with the workers, and is covered with spray, which sends him into an ecstasy of "far out" exclamations. White joy is in a space freed from labor; Black fun dips into the thing to have a good time while working. The gang's musical approach to work is echoed in the end credit sequence, where the deejay introduces each of the characters as he would members of a music group, but substituting work instruments for musical ones:

> Dig the players on the session: blowing on steam guns, Floyd and Lloyd—Darrow Igus and De Wayne Jessie; sucking it up on the vacuum, Hippo—James Spinks—and Lindy—Antonio Fargas. . . .

Characters also dip into tracks to express more individual feelings, to themselves and to others. Marlene, the prostitute, calls a supposed boyfriend's number; as she dials, she mouths the words on the radio: "I'm gonna die, Baby, My whole world stops," anticipating what we have already been set up to be able to tell her, that when she gets through, it turns out that he's given her a false number. TC, the guy with the fantasy of being a Black superhero, the Fly, mouths the words of "I Wanna Get Next to You" to Mona, the waitress in the diner next to the car wash, giving her moony eyes. He is the most alert to the radio of all the gang, listening for the repeated name-the-tune contest that will get him tickets to the big concert, finally winning and persuading a resistant Mona to accompany him. He uses the *thing* to express his feelings and, more practically, to secure his date.

A recent, less elaborated, example of showing characters using the thing is *House Party* (1990), where what is available is the rap/house beat. All the young Black male central characters are able to improvise a rap when they need to, notably Kid (Christopher Reid) and Play (Christopher Martin), expressing friendship through rivalry at the party, and Kid using rap to keep his cellmates from raping him when he is briefly thrown in jail. This is different from White musicals, where characters do burst into song, but where this is not shown as continuous with the cultural life of the characters. In *House Party* rapping in friendship or defence is using what the kids listen and party to all the time. The film also makes use of sudden bites of house riffs, not physically located diegetically but clearly expressing the characters' feelings using their own cultural mode, once against drawing upon the resources of the thing that is always there.

Such dipping in and out of the always available music needs to be distinguished from the construction of Black musicality—the all-blacks-got-rhythm syndrome—of White cinema. That Black characters are liable to burst into song and dance at the drop of a hat is a commonplace even of nonmusicals: the Camerons showing Phil Stoneman round the plantation in *The Birth of a Nation* (1915) and stopping to enjoy the slaves' dancing; Harpo Marx drawn into the all-singing, all-dancing Black shacks behind the stables in *A Day at the Races* (1937); the Black woman passing for White who gives herself away when she can't resist the beat of the bongos in the British thriller *Sapphire* (1959).

In Hollywood's all-Black (before the camera) musicals too, Black musicality is similarly shown. *Hallelujah!* (1929) was entirely founded on a belief in the absolute pervasiveness of music in Southern Black "folk" culture, where work, love, and religion are intertwined and seamlessly expressed through song and dance. *Cabin in the Sky* (1942) and *Stormy Weather* (1943), though conforming to White conventions, still mobilize similar beliefs. The first time we see Petunia (Ethel Waters) singing is in church; the introduction of the title song follows Petunia telling Joe (Eddie Anderson) that she has heard angels' songs, Joe asking if they sing songs like hers, and saying he'd rather hear her sing. Here a notion of the pervasiveness of Black religiosity and spirituality naturalizes Petunia's propensity to burst into song, though the mise-en-scène still signals the transition from narrative to number as in other musicals (accompaniment comes in from nowhere), and some of the other numbers in the film have no such naturalization.[2] In *Stormy Weather,* when Bill (Bill Robinson) drops down on a cotton bale at the end of a day spent working on a steamboat, and complains, verbally and in body language, of how exhausted he is, the moment he hears the rhythm of a band off-screen, he taps off to join it and throws himself into an energetic routine.

What such presentations of Black musicality in musicals and nonmusicals alike imply is a perception of musical expressivity as an emanation of the Black personality, a given of the Black psyche. This is very different from the active *use* of music by characters in *Car Wash* and in much Black cinema.

Active use of music can even become a theme of these films. Gloria Gibson (1988) suggests that competing definitions of Black culture, as embodied in forms of music, structure Black independent films such as *The Blood of Jesus* (1941), where the righteous world, represented by spirituals, is contrasted to the unrighteous, represented by the blues. In the independent British film *The Passion of Remembrance* (1986), there is a sequence cross-cutting between two young women dressing to disco music to go out on the town and two older men in another room in the house moving to a calypso record—the men see their music as more authentic than the disco stuff, but the cross-cutting shows how both pairs use the music to similar funky ends. The possibility of a thematisation of music is hinted at in *Car Wash* itself, in the shot of Abdullah playing the sax. The fact that he is playing an instrument himself rather than using music supplied by the radio, and the cool jazz feel of his playing in contrast to the highly commercial beat of KGYS, are part of the construction of his character, as being in cultural political opposition to the attitudes of the others. His music, just as much as his words, his name change and the wearing of ANC colors, is part of his struggle with his community.

Such political thematization remains undeveloped in *Car Wash,* but is central to the structure of *Do the Right Thing* (1989). Here the contest of music is focused on Radio Raheem (Bill Nunn) and his ghetto blaster playing Public Enemy, returning again and again to pick up "Fight the Power." This is an alternative source of music to Mister Señor Love Daddy's radio show which functions, like KGYS in *Car Wash,* as a background available for use for the characters and a source of self-reflexivity for the narration. Love Daddy plays a wide range of current music and at one point lists many of the greats of Black music, encompassing Paul Robeson and Ella Fitzgerald along with contemporary chart artistes. In contrast, Radio Raheem is single-minded about the focused Black identification and insurrectionary politics of Public Enemy, using it to drown out the Latin sounds listened to by a group of Puerto Ricans and, finally, fatefully, refusing to turn it off in Sal's pizzeria. This precipitates the expression of Sal's territorialist anger (smashing the radio), Radio Raheem's death and the ransacking of the pizzeria. Radio Raheem dies for his music, for his promotion of his music, for what that music signifies for African-American identity and the struggle against racism.

Car Wash belongs to a tradition of Black films which show Black people using music, going back to it to pick it up when they need it, making it part of politics as well as, inseparably from, culture. It is, however, not just characters who do this, but the narration of the film itself.

In part this reinforces the feelings of the characters. The "Car Wash" sequence not only has characters moving to the music, but is overall cut to the Rose Royce track in a wonderfully, formally precise sound-image montage. The speed at which, for instance, the handles of the machinery are turned on or Marlene unzips her long boots, as well as the moment of each cut, all exactly match the beat and phrasing of the track. The sequence also draws together all the characters in and around the car wash, a bracketing effect used more selectively elsewhere to gather characters together in a shared mood. "I'm Gonna Die", mouthed by Marlene when calling Joe, is still playing over the scene of Loretta coming by and telling

Justin she's splitting up with him because he won't go back to school. The moody riffs of "Water" accompany three sequential narrative segments: the (late) arrival of Abdullah, taunted by the others for his Muslin name, snappily rejecting Lonnie's expression of concern; the taxi driver looking for Marlene, who has sneaked out of his cab without paying; Scruggs, one of the two White workers, worrying to Geronimo about having stayed out all night without telling Charlene, his girlfriend, and now having a burning in his penis. Similarly "I Wanna Get Next to You," used by TC to proposition Mona, carries over to Hippo gazing longingly at Marlene, and is picked up again towards the end of the film to embrace Charlene dumping off Scruggs's suitcase, and cashier Marsha making up for her date with smoothie customer Kenny.

The last example, however, points to the characteristic complexity of the film's narrational use of the sound track. All the characters connected to the number do indeed "wanna get next to" each other, but whereas TC and Mona do get together in the romantic spirit of the number, Hippo will have to pay to get next to Marlene, Charlene is rejecting Scruggs (as he has feared throughout the film) and the illusory quality of Kenny as a prospect for Marsha is only ambiguously offset by the sound of a car horn hooting as she leaves (we don't actually see her going off with him). The detail of the cutting of the image to the track in relation to Marlene and Hippo makes the interplay still more intricate. "Dreams of you and I go sailing by" accompanies voyeuristic shots of her legs from his point of view; she returns his gaze on "Whenever your eyes meet mine" before turning away contemptuously on "You're so good"; then as the song goes "And girl you make me feel so . . .", the camera zooms in on Hippo biting furiously into a hamburger on the beat after "so" (the actual word that follows is obscured by the sound of Calvin skateboarding by). Such cutting both does and does not reinforce the characters' feelings. It is at once literal (eyes meeting and hunger are visualised on cue), expressive (of the actual intensity of Hippo's desire), ironic (about the characteristic admixture of romanticism in a client-prostitute encounter) and in contradiction (her contempt registered against the song's adoration).

Such shifting and ironic interplay of sound and image occurs throughout the film. "Talk is Cheap," for example, brackets Hippo silently but expensively (he pays with his beloved radio) actually making it with Marlene, boss's son Irwin reading Mao out to unimpressed worker Lindy, and the confrontation between the latter and Abdullah, with Lindy saying, "Is the only thing you're good at shooting off your mouth?"—all variations on the cheapness of speech. "Zig Zag" is introduced as a song for "all you surfers out there . . . from Malibu to Newport Beach" but accompanies Calvin skateboarding. On the one hand, it's not real surfing; on the other, Calvin's superb skill is heightened by the pulse of the track and a climax in the music accentuates the drama of his falling off; and on yet another hand, he is seen from Irwin's amazed point of view, catching it in the latter's continuously mocked commitment to the far out. KGYS talk is also used to underscore the image. Sometimes this is quite unemphatic—Hippo arriving, huge on his little moped, as the deejay speaks of a low-calorie substitute. At other times it is more strongly pointed. When Native American Goody puts extra tabasco peppers in Hispanic Chuko's sandwich in revenge for his having played a trick on Marsha for which he, Goody, got the blame, his action follows the deejay introducing "Zig Zag" with "Let's see if this goodie is hot enough for you" (referring to both the tabasco and Goody's name). A news story about gay congressional aids ends with a congressman's opinion that he has nothing against gays as long as they stay in their place; on these words, we see Lindy going into the toilet marked "Ladies." It's a double gag: on the one hand, down among the women is where homophobic discourse places gay men; on the other, one place the very "out" Lindy clearly does not stay in is the closet.

For both the characters and the film's narration, KGYS is always there to go back to. This repetitional structure suggests a circularity that also characterises many of the narrative threads that interweave through the film.

For many of the characters—Lindy, Geronimo, Goody, Chuko—there is virtually no narrative thread to speak of, but where there is for other characters, things are most often substantially the same at the end of the film as they were at the beginning: Loretta, who wants Justin to go back to school, breaks off with him in the middle of the film but comes back for him at the end, when they agree to put off the matter once again until next week; Marlene the hooker, hoping for an escape route via her call to Joe, is left at the end waiting for her next trick; Irwin, so keen to identify with the workers, still goes off with his dad, the boss, at the end; Lonnie, the ex-con going straight, trusted by Mr. B with opening up and closing down the wash, goes to speak with Mr. B on behalf of Abdullah (whom Mr. B has fired) and is fobbed off with "Now is not the time," which, as Lonnie points out to him, is what Mr. B tells him every week. Where things are less clearly unchanging, they are generally unresolved (Will Floyd and Lloyd's audition be their big break? Will Kenny be there for Marsha?) or ambiguous: TC wins the spot-the-tune contest and Mona says she'll go out with him, but she's been out with him before, so why should this be any more permanent? Mr. B comes back to Lonnie and says he promises that they'll talk about the latter's ideas for the car wash tomorrow, they even shake on it, but why should one believe him? Where there really is change it is bad news: Hippo is without the radio that he took everywhere with him; Scruggs goes off alone with the suitcase Charlene has dumped angrily at his feet; Abdullah is fired, is foiled by Lonnie when he comes back to steal the takings and breaks down in tears, unconvincingly reassured by Lonnie saying that they will work it out together.

It has been argued that such narrative structures characterise African-American fiction. Writing in the context of literature, Blyden Jackson suggests that in "the typical Negro novel, after all the sound and fury dies, one finds things substantially as they were when all the commotion began" (Jackson 1972: 635). With qualifications, this is true of many black films beside *Car Wash*. *St. Louis Blues* implies that Bessie been there time and again with her man and will be there again. Kid in *House Party* makes a significant decision, choosing Sidney over Sharane, but the cycle of partying and being subsequently belted by his father for being out late has no immediate end in sight. While the ransacking of the pizzeria in *Do the Right Thing* is hardly an endlessly repeatable event, nonetheless the implied repetitionality of the groups and relationships shown in the film, the final sequence reprising the film's opening, the return to Mister Señor Love Daddy on the radio, the suggestion that it only needs another heat wave to trigger another act of revolt, the unresolved opposition of quotes from Martin Luther King and Malcolm X in the end titles, all these suggest a powerful undertow of circularity to the film's more obviously climactic organisation.

Such temporal circularity relates in turn, according to Jackson, to the spatial boundedness imagined in African-American narrative.

> All Negro fiction tends to conceive of its physical world as a sharp dichotomy, with the ghetto as its central figure and its symbolic truth, and with all else comprising a non-ghetto which throws into high relief the ghetto itself as the fundamental fact of life for Negroes as a group. (ibid: 630)

In other words, Black people don't get out of their situation, eventually or geographically.

Black characters do not move out the ghetto in the Black films discussed here. The parameters of the ghetto are marked by Sal, Pino and Vito in *Do the Right Thing,* who only go there to work and preserve a little enclave that they protect from the militancy of the ghetto represented by Radio Raheem. The fact that the middle-class and (to European eyes, at any rate) all-American streets of *House Party* are a ghetto is emphasised by the at once comic and sadistic, racist cop duo who patrol and keep the inhabitants in line. In *Car Wash,* we do see the characters who work at the wash leaving it, but we know that they will come back to it tomorrow; none will leave to go on elsewhere; even Abdullah will probably be reinstated thanks to Lonnie.

The customers in *Car Wash,* on the other hand, pass through the wash on their way from one place to another. With the exception of Daddy Rich and the Sisters, who have found a way out of the ghetto through a money-based religion, the customers are all White. There is, moreover, a sustained distinction drawn between Whites and people of color, having to do with bodily emissions.

Whites in the film cannot deal with and are victims of bodily emissions. Scruggs has a single one-night stand and instantly has a pain in his penis. "Miss Beverly Hills" drives up just in time to get her son out of the car before he pukes on it; she has it cleaned, making a fuss about a tiny mark left on the door, and drives off only to have the boy puke over her in the car. A man and his two children laugh at the workers' alarm at the barking Alsatian dog they've left in the car until the dog escapes and craps on the forecourt. Harold, a customer covered from top to toe in plaster, is offered by, presumably, his wife, a choice between Italian and Chinese food. The man TC and Hippo mistake for the mad pop bottle bomber reported on the radio turns out to be using the bottle to collect his urine sample—when in the excitement it smashes to the ground, one character after another says "Piss!" in amazement and Charlie says to Lonnie, "I just don't understand White folks".

People of color in the film take such matters, by and large, in their stride. Geronimo gives Scruggs worldly advice. Marlene, when Miss Beverly Hills remonstrates with her for leaving the toilet reeking of cheap perfume, says in amazement, "It's supposed to smell, lady, it's a toilet." The amused verbal scatology of the repeated "Piss!" echoes the exchange between TC and Lloyd, when the former is fantasising about being the Fly and the latter tells him he's "full of shit":

> TC: You wouldn't talk to me like that if I was the Fly.
>
> LLOYD: Oh yes I would. Because then you'd be full of fly shit. You know what else, man? There ain't nothin' lower than fly shit. Not kangaroo shit, elephant shit, or chicken shit. Ain't nothin' lower than fly shit.

This symbolic opposition between Black and White is a venerable one: Blacks in touch with their bodies, Whites uptight about theirs. Another way of putting it might be to say that, just as narrative structures and diegetic geography permit no escape from or transformation of Black living situations, so such symbolism does not allow Blacks to be anything other than their bodies. At the broad narrational and symbolic level, *Car Wash* suggests circularity and stasis as much as continuity and repetition.

Car Wash, by any sensible definition, is a musical. Equally, *Passion of Remembrance* and *Do the Right Thing* are obviously not. Yet *Car Wash* has more in common with them than with *Top Hat* or *The Sound of Music,* because for so much Black cinema, music is always there, not as background but as the thing that is there for the film to pick up. Yet *Car Wash* and *House Party,* at any rate, are just as single-mindedly committed to entertaining through conveying happiness as any White musical. What is at stake are different constructions of the nature and possibility of happiness.

Read by the conventions of White musicals, both the repetitionality and the circularity of *Car Wash* and others suggest spatial and temporal stasis, the impossibility of change for the happier in oneself or society. The musical numbers do not take the characters out of the moment, "transport" them, resolve their problems; the emotions and experience of the music do not lead to fundamental changes in their situation. The incredible elation of the moments in White musicals when we lift off from the vicissitudes of the story into the gorgeousness of the numbers is absent and unavailable to *St. Louis Blues, Car Wash* or *House Party;* also absent are the standard transformations of lonely hearts into husband and wife, chorus girl into star, failing business into success.

Yet there is a difference between repetitionality and the broader narrative circularity. At the level of the latter, there is an implication of being stuck where one is that is the antithesis of the vast majority of White musicals. In the latter there is nearly always change, both in terms of the fortunes of the characters and also the world they inhabit, whether they transform it (barn into theatre in *Summer Stock,* museum into dance space in *On the Town,* factory into dance space in *The Pajama Game,* a whole journey into self-expression in "Don't Rain on My Parade" in *Funny Girl)* or find new worlds to move into (*Naughty Marietta, Top Hat, Brigadoon, Oklahoma!*). White musicals are thus able to imagine the pleasure of changing oneself and the world, the utopia of transformation.

However, for most White musicals, such utopianism is generally understood to be *merely* that. If, in our best use of them, they keep open the gap between what is and what should be, and celebrate the desire for a better world, still they may also signal the inevitable "if only" of such desires, reinforcing a sense that, when we leave the cinema or turn off the video, we had better acquiesce to the way things are now. The transcendent utopianism of White musicals at one level offers a vision of change not found in Black films like *Car Wash,* but at another discounts such vision as a nice but impossible fantasy.

The other repetitionality in Black cinema, music as the thing that is always there, has implications different from its circular narratives. The latter imply the impossibility of change, whereas the repetitional use of music suggests that things are constantly changing, being made and remade. Everyone is able to use what's available to them, perform day-to-day bricolage; creativity is presented as a norm. In White musicals, the characters and/or their experiences of utopia in music are special and exceptional. In *St. Louis Blues, Car Wash, Passion of Remembrance, Do the Right Thing,* and *House Party* everyone (of color) can play with the music and clearly does so all the time. It's not a question of transforming ordinary life into a utopia, the longing behind White musicals, but of showing life as an ongoing matter of making and creating.

One could still regard this as conservative—it's making the best of circumstances without trying to change them, it's no more than a coping strategy to get you through the day. This is a conundrum of the cultures of other oppressed groups—I'm reminded of the arguments about camp, keeping gay men going but keeping us in our place too. As models for imagining happiness, there is perhaps not so much to choose between White musicals' transformative aspirations and impossibilism and Black films' set horizons and awareness of ordinary creativity.

In making this formal contrast and suggesting a political neutrality between them, I am only temporarily bracketing off questions of content in order to isolate implications of form. Such questions have to be taken on board. The formal differences are not by chance ethnically rooted; there are historical reasons for labelling them White and Black. The pleasure in expansiveness in White musicals (and other genres, especially the Western and other colonial adventure films) was imaginable because Whites were expanding into the world at other peoples' costs; the celebration of coping in Black musicals is necessary when even coping takes some doing in the face of racism. Equally, if we put gender into the equation we come up with another perspective. White musicals have often given women an active role in the utopian fantasy of transformation of self and society, whereas in the Black films discussed here women are at best (*Car Wash, House Party*) marginalised and are often the vehicle of misogynist fantasy (notably in *Mo' Better Blues*).[3] But content does not determine form, nor vice versa; formal devices are resources that can be used, though historical circumstances may prevent their appropriation by or appropriateness for a given social group. What I have wanted to do in these last paragraphs is to indicate the potential and limitations of two different constructions of happiness. One—which does not simply "happen" to be White but which does not always forever have to be—offers a form for enjoying the vision of change taking place; the other—in practice, but not in perpetuity, Black—offers a way of celebrating the recurrent human resources for survival and change.

Notes

1. For further discussion of *St. Louis Blues,* see Cripps 1978.
2. Jane Feuer (1985) discusses the importance of naturalization devices in White musicals with White characters, which serve to render the actual highly polished, professionalized and capital-intensive production of musicals in terms of "folk" values of spontaneity, authenticity, and the natural. In White discourses (emblematically in the notion of the "noble savage") such qualities are often nostalgically designated as lost to White people; the magic of White musicals is that they make those qualities compatible with White identity. Black people, in "benign" racial discourses the epitome of the noble savage, need no such devices.
3. Cf. the discussions of *Do the Right Thing* in hooks (1991) and Wallace (1990).

References

Cripps, Thomas (1978) *Black Film as Genre.* Bloomington: Indiana University Press.

Gibson, Gloria (1988) *The Cultural Significance of Music to the Black Independent Filmmaker.* Ann Arbor: UMI.

Feuer, Jane (1982) 'Hollywood Musicals: Mass Art as Folk Art'. In Peter Steven (ed) *Jump Cut: Hollywood, Politics and Counter Cinema.* Toronto: Between the Lines (52–63).

hooks, bell (1991) *Yearning.* Boston: South End Press.

Jackson, Blyden (1972) 'The Negro's Image of the Universe as Reflected in His Fiction'. In David G Bromley and Charles F Longino (eds) *White Racism and Black Americans.* Cambridge, Ma.: Schenhinum (628–636).

Snead, James A (1984) 'Repetition as a figure of black culture'. In Henry Louis Gates Jr (ed) *Black Literature and Literary Theory.* New York/London: Methuen (59–80).

Taylor, John Russell (1971) *The Hollywood Musical.* London: Secker & Warburg.

Wallace, Michele (1990) *Invisibility Blues.* London: Verso.

7

The Los Angeles School of Black Filmmakers

Ntongela Masilela

Only with the passage of time is it possible to reconstruct the conditions under which a Black independent filmmaking movement emerged in Los Angeles in the early 1970s. Founded at the University of California, Los Angeles, by African and African-American students, most of whom were completing a film degree in UCLA's Theater Arts Department, the movement had two distinct waves.[1] The first included Haile Gerima, Charles Burnett, Larry Clark, John Reir, Ben Caldwell, Pamela Jones, Abdosh Abdulhafiz, and Jama Fanaka; among those in the second were Bill Woodberry, Julie Dash, Alile Sharon Larkin, and Bernard Nichols. This essay solely concerns the first group, focusing on its structure and cultural configuration.

The arrival of Charles Burnett at UCLA in 1967, two years after the assassination of Malcolm X and the Watts Rebellion, and the arrival of Haile Gerima from Ethiopia, via Chicago, in 1968, the year of the assassination of Martin Luther King and the launching of the Tet Offensive in Vietnam, were generative events in the formation of the Black independent movement in Los Angeles, a school of filmmaking that would last approximately a decade. By 1978, when Teshome Gabriel, a distinguished scholar of African film and Third World Cinema, conducted a series of fascinating discussions with Brazilian film director Glauber Rocha at UCLA, the group had disbanded, as members moved in different directions even while remaining in close contact with one another.

The intellectual and cultural coordinates of this Black independent film movement are inseparable from the political and social struggles and convulsions of the 1960s. For these African and African-American filmmakers, imagination was inescapably wedded to political and cultural commitment.[2] The Civil Rights Movement, the Women's Movement, the anti-war movement, and activities in America in support of national liberation struggles in Africa, Asia, and Latin America informed the political consciousness of the members of the group. During this period, it is important to recall, the Third World was the cauldron of new Marxist ideologies: in Asia Maoism held sway; in Latin America Che Guevarism opened new political pathways, resurrecting the incomplete project of Simon Bolivar; and in Africa, as an Algerian revolution unfolded, Fanonists argued that only through revolutionary ideology could the people of this Black continent move forward.[3]

For African-American filmmakers, Fidel Castro's maxim that "the duty of a revolutionary is to make a revolution" prompted a concrete question: how might they establish an independent Black film enterprise that was true to their cultural roots and contested the falsification of African-American history by Hollywood. In 1971, Melvin Van Peebles's *Sweet Sweetback's Baadasssss Song* demonstrated that there was a huge market for Black films; as a result, Hollywood flooded the commercial film market with Black exploitation films in the 1970s. Independent filmmakers took inspiration from Van Peebles's accomplishment but also criticized the ideology of his film, searching for ways to demolish Hollywood's misrepresentation of Black culture. From Van Peebles's film, for example, one learned nothing of the revolutionary project of the Black Arts Movement of LeRoi Jones (later Amiri Baraka) and Larry Neal, work that had led James Baldwin to refuse an invitation from Hollywood to write a screenplay based on the autobiography of Malcolm X for fear that he would be participating "in the second assassination of Malcolm X." The challenge facing this generation of independent Black filmmakers was to find a film form unique to their historical situation and cultural experience, a form that could not be appropriated by Hollywood.

The search for such a form led them to the family dramas of Oscar Micheaux from the 1920s and '30s. The revolutionary breakthrough of the UCLA school was to draw on Micheaux's work, yet shift its social subject matter from a middle-class to a working-class milieu in which Black labor struggled against White capital. This shift was necessitated by the class warfare being waged against the African-American family, the terrible consequences of which had become apparent by the 1960s.

As an African, Haile Gerima confronted other historical issues. One of the most serious was voiced by Frantz Fanon in *Toward the African Revolution:* namely, that Africa tragically lacked an ideology, and thus in order to move forward, Africans needed to forge a new ideology or adapt a progressive one. In his voluminous writings, Amilcar Cabral likewise argued that, since European culture had been imposed upon Africa by colonialism and imperialism, the struggle for national liberation necessarily entailed the forging of a revolutionary, national culture. In achieving this, Africans would throw off the shackles of European history and rediscover an authentically African history. Gerima sought to contribute to such a process through his films; conceived of as both an art form and an intellectual project, his work would be inserted into and in dialogue with history. The formation of a Black independent film movement in Los Angeles made this goal seem possible.

Members of the film movement never subscribed to a single, hegemonic ideology. Different and sometimes diametrically opposed ideologies often were in conflict. For example, a dialectical tension between the cultural nationalism of the Black Arts Movement and the revolutionary nationalism of the Black Panther Party was central to the intellectual development of the members of the group, with Larry Caldwell and Ben Clark to a certain extent mediating these polar positions. Among African members of the group, moreover, the African Marxism of Fanon and Cabral (which had displaced the Pan-Africanism of Kwame Nkrumah and George Padmore in wake of the 1960 Congo crisis), was riven with tensions. Fanon's Marxism was predicated on the notion that the peasantry was a revolutionary class within colonized Africa; Cabral instead celebrated the African working class. Paradoxically, Ntongela Masilela, a native of the highly industrialized country of South Africa, leaned in the direction of Fanon, while Gerima, from the relatively feudal society of Ethiopia, was inspired more by Cabral.

Positions were never dogmatically held because robust ideological debate was valued; indeed, prolonged and intense discussions cemented the film movement together. Particular texts were considered of paramount value, enriching the political and artistic consciousness of the group. Fanon's *The Wretched of the Earth,* for example, was a central text, for it clarified the historical moment in which these filmmakers found themselves. Some of us emphasized Fanon's chapter on revolutionary violence, others the chapter on the emergence of national cultures at the moment of national liberation, and others Fanon's devastating critique of the African national bourgeoisie. Thus while the book was canonical, there was never a single, canonical reading of this great and complex work. Also prized was Ngugi wa Thiongo's *Homecoming,* which applied African Marxism, particularly that of Fanon, to African cultural struggles, and opened new considerations of the revolutionary possibilities of language. Richard Wright's *American Hunger,* published after twenty years of suppression, taught us the indissolvability of Pan-Africanism and Marxism. *The Autobiography of Malcolm X,* like the life of this great leader, proclaimed to us that anything was achievable if there was sufficient political will.

All these works, in addition to many others, spoke to us of the need to incorporate an international perspective in our work. Such a perspective was provided by new cinema of the period as well. The emergence of the Cuban national cinema—and more broadly, cinema from the Third World—was to have a lasting influence on the Los Angeles school. From the time of Tomas Guitterez Alea's *Memories of Underdevelopment* (1967) and Humberto Solas's *Lucia* (1968), through Alea's *Last Supper* (1977), the Cuban cinema was the preeminent film movement of the Third World, reappraising and interrogating its national goals anew as it assisted in the construction of a socialist society. What was exemplary about this national film movement was its ability to incorporate elements of other film movements into its own: the Soviet cinema of Dziga Vertov, the Italian Neorealism of Roberto Rossellini, and the French New Wave film form of Jean-Luc Godard. At the same time, the Cuban cinema developed a national film language consonant with the historical moment, a national language that was also one of the defining strands of the Third World cinema.[4] The importance of this project led Gabriel, Clark, Burnett, Masilela, Gerima, Caldwell, and others to organize the Third World Film Club, which from 1974 to 1976 screened Cuban and other Third World films at UCLA.[5] The club demanded that the university help fund the program, and after some struggle the university agreed. Through the club, independent Black filmmakers forged links with other progressive organizations to pressure the US government to rescind its ban on all forms of cultural exchange with Cuba, and one of the high points of the Black film movement was its success in assisting to break this boycott.

The Third World Film Club also explored the work of a wide range of progressive Latin America filmmakers, from Miguel Littin in Chile to Sanjines in Bolivia. As with films from Cuba, the importance of the Latin American Cinema for members of the Los Angeles film school resided in its uncompromising examination of the relationship between film and national culture. Sanjines's effort to place Bolivian Indians at the center of Bolivian national culture demonstrated that films must define or articulate Third World national cultures as *dialectical totalities* in which urban space was not privileged over rural space. The Brazilian Cinema Novo, whose films were frequently screened by the Third World Film Club, revealed a dynamic relationship among regionalism, national culture, history, and class struggle. Glauber Rocha's *Barravento, Black God White Devil,* and *Antonio des Mortes,* and the films of Nelson Pereira dos Santos, especially *Vidas Secas,* also focused on these same historical issues: Rocha through an exploration of religion and mythology, and Pereira through the asceticism of the novels of Remos.[6] The films of Ruy Guerra were engaged with this great national debate as well. Clearly, the Brazilian *Cinema Novo* taught us that film can be, should be, in fact must be, an intellectual enterprise.

This was illustrated convincingly by Octavio Getino and Fernando

Solanes's *The Hour of the Furnaces* (1968), from Argentina, and for us perhaps the premier example of the interaction of film form and revolutionary ideology in the Third World cinema. Quoting extensively from Fanon's *The Wretched of the Earth,* this film theorized the lived experience of Third World peoples against the historical backdrop of the Cuban Revolution. Examining the legacy of Peronism in Argentina, *The Hour of the Furnaces* clearly stated why Guevarism was the fundamental Latin American ideology of the 1960s. In its passion, political commitment, and intellectual brilliance, the film was on par with Regis Debray's *Revolution in the Revolution,* an ardent call for the liberation of Latin America which drew inspiration from the examples of Simon Bolivar and Jose Marti. Moreover, Rocha's attempt to articulate the premises of a "Cinema of Hunger," together with Julio Garcia Espinosa's treatise on "An Imperfect Cinema," represented the most ambitious efforts to theorize the aesthetic of Third World Cinema.[7] In seeking to define the cultural and historical contours of Latin American and Third World Cinema, the films of Sergio Giral and Pastor Vega likewise compelled the Black filmmakers of the Los Angeles school to ask themselves truly challenging questions. What was an African-American film or an authentic African-American cinema? What was an African film or an authentic African cinema?[8]

On the second question, the work of several established African filmmakers sheds light. A prefiguration of the new African cinema could be seen in Sembene Ousmane's *Black Girl* (1963), a study of the impact of French imperialism on Africans in France itself. The subsequent development of his work earned Sembene the right to be considered the "father" of the African cinema, and we had the opportunity to explore the prodigious range of his films in the fall of 1970, when the UCLA African Studies Center organized the first African film festival in North America. Seven leading African filmmakers—including Stephane Allisante from Niger, Oumarou Ganda from Cameroon, and Sembene himself—participated in the event. Major topics included the current lack of direction in the African cinema, the lack of adequate processing laboratories in Africa, the impact of European cultural imperialism, and the hardship of finding financing for our own films. The festival allowed members of the Los Angeles school to interact and exchange views with the leading lights of the African cinema. This author still remembers, for example, a long and animated discussion between Gabriel and Ganda.

The two outstanding figures of the first wave of the Los Angeles school of Black filmmakers are undoubtedly Haile Gerima and Charles Burnett. Their films reflect the preoccupation of the Los Angeles school with redefining the relationship of history to the structure of the family. History and family are the crucial strands of Gerima's *Bush Mama* (1974), Burnett's *Killer of Sheep* (1977) and *My Brother's Wedding* (1983), and Billy Woodbury's *Bless Their Little Hearts* (1984). Burnett worked at the intersection of this development: he photographed both *Bush Mama* and *Bless Their Little Hearts,* and wrote the screenplay for the latter film. The poetic realism of the early films of the Los Angeles school, reminiscent of the British documentary film movement of the 1930s (rather than French poetic realism in the same decade), is inseparable from the imagination of Burnett. The connection is not coincidental: Basil Wright, a leading figure in the British documentary movement, was one of Burnett's teachers at UCLA in the late 1960s, and persuaded Burnett to pursue film studies. Colonialism provided another point of contact with British documentary, but while Wright's *Song of Ceylon* (1938) was politically unaware of the colonialism in which it was enmeshed, the question of an internal colonialism in America was crucial to the Los Angeles filmmakers.

The influence of Fanon's *The Wretched of the Earth* on these filmmakers is more than apparent. While Gerima's films focus on politics and history, within which the family is situated and to which it must respond, Burnett is fascinated with the complex intricacies and mechanisms of the family structure itself. However, both were preoccupied with the politics of resistance within the family which emerged after the Watts rebellion of 1965. *Killer of Sheep,* a true classic of the Los Angeles school, is a paean to childhood. The film is structured around various forms of rituals: of the family, of childhood, of oppression, of resistance to oppression. Stan, the protagonist of *Killer of Sheep,* is involved in a series of complex rituals which hold his family together, triumphing through sheer will amidst the adverse and demoralizing conditions of working in a slaughterhouse and living in a ghetto, a territory occupied by the police. Yet his family exudes warmth and tenderness, especially his wife. There is no sentimentalizing of this lived experience, only a depiction of victory over hostile conditions. The film has many biblical allusions to damnation and redemption, but what makes it truly memorable are its poetic images, among the most remarkable in the history of African-American cinema.

While *Killer of Sheep* recalls the poetics of Italian Neorealism, *My Brother's Wedding* seems disconnected from the history of cinema. Perhaps the visual poetry of its middle-class setting and politics obviates an appeal to history. The focal point of the story is Pierce Mundy, caught in the uncertainties of young adulthood, and unable to decide whether to enter the middle-class world of his lawyer brother or align himself with the working-class world of his boyhood best friend, who has turned to crime. The bitterness attending Mundy's indecision propels *My Brother's Wedding,* a fallow moment before the storm of a major work of art, Burnett's *To Sleep with Anger* (1990).[9]

To Sleep with Anger is a penetrating exploration of the relationship between history (the past) and the family (the present), a metaphorical meditation on a central pattern in African-American history in the twentieth century: the Black migration from the South to the North. The central theme of the film is the dialectical conflict between the old history of the South and the new history of the North, and the impact of this unresolved tension on a particular lower-middle-class family in the Watts area of Los Angeles. The film concerns the transformation of the experience of rural sharecroppers (agricultural workers) into that of the proletariat (industrial workers). The tension between the old and the new has been a central preoccupation of African-American cultural historians in the twentieth century. The Harlem Renaissance, for example, was the result of this migration, as Houston A. Baker makes clear in *Modernism and the Harlem Renaissance.* The mutation of primitive blues into classical blues through the genius of Robert Johnson, as Amiri Baraka suggests in *Blues People,* was bound up in this social transformation, as was the Chicago blues of Muddy Waters. Richard Wright's novel, *Native Son,* likewise gives cultural expression to this historical experience. *To Sleep with Anger* is in keeping with this great heritage. Harry Manton, steeped in the tradition, superstition, and mythology of the Old South, sows discord and mistrust in the family of Gideon and Suzy, who are immersed in the new history of the North. This new history does not necessarily entail a rejection of the old history; rather Harry symbolizes the return of the repressed. *To Sleep with Anger* thus illustrates the central theme of Burnett's work: the impact of the discord of the past (of history) on the present.

Burnett's latest film, *America Becoming* (1991), is a documentary that records the discordant voices and historical experiences of new immigrants (mainly from Asia, Latin America, and the Caribbean) in the making of what may be a new America or, alternatively, the taming of these new peoples on behalf of an old and conservative America. Again, a dynamic between old and new structures the film. Burnett also situates his work within a legacy of African-American cultural history: the title of *America Becoming,* for example, is also that of a famous poem by Langston Hughes. The making of the film was contentious: its producers, the Ford Foundation, imposed a harmonious interpretation of this new immigrant experience on the work, whereas Burnett saw the experience as conflictual and crisis-ridden.[10] As a result, *America Becoming* least resembles the rest of Burnett's work.[11]

The strong vision of Charles Burnett fused with those of Haile Gerima and Billy Woodberry, respectively, in *Bush Mama* and *Bless Their Little Hearts.*[12] Together with *Killer of Sheep,* these films define the historical poetics of the Los Angeles school. But *Bush Mama* also opened up a new historical dimension through its emphasis on Third World feminism, in contradistinction to the male perspectives embodied in the other two films.

Focusing principally on the development of Bush Mama's consciousness about the oppressive conditions in which she lives, and her struggle to hold her family together, the film is very combative and "noisy." The sound track is simply extraordinary, as intensely pleasurable as that of Robert Altman's *Nashville,* a very different film. An urban acoustic space has rarely been conveyed more effectively than in Gerima's film.

At the center of *Bush Mama* is the intersection of three forms of oppression: class, gender, and racial. This multilayered texture constitutes the complexity and richness of the film. *Bush Mama* defines the situation of Black Americans as a form of internal colonialism comparable to Third World oppression, the great lesson Gerima learned from Fanon's *The Wretched of the Earth.* Developing historical consciousness, Bush Mama comes to understand that in order to overcome oppression in America she must assist in the emancipation of Africa from European colonial and imperial domination. Given this emphasis on the interconnectedness of struggle, and the historical experience of Africa, the transition from *Bush Mama* to *Harvest: 3,000 Years* (1976) was a logical progression.

Harvest was shot in Ethiopia a year after the Ethiopian Revolution in 1974. The revolution occasioned a critical reappraisal of Ethiopian history. Because of the longevity and lineages of that history, the history of Ethiopia is in large measure that of Africa. W. E. B. DuBois in *The World and Africa* situates Ethiopian history at the very center of African history, and Cheikh Anta Diop in *The African Origin of Civilization: Myth or Reality* shows the ways in which, at various times, the histories of Africa and Ethiopia are interchangeable. The Pan-African Movement and the Marcus Garvey Movement took this interpenetration of histories as self-evident.

Harvest, then, draws on a certain cultural heritage. But instead of emphasizing the continuity of Ethiopian history and its place within the imagination of the Black world, Gerima dissects a moment of discontinuity or break from the perspective of the peasantry. Gerima thus examines the class struggle within Ethiopian history. In contrast to revolutions in Algeria, Angola, and Mozambique, which countered the external forces of colonial and imperial domination, the Ethiopian revolution dealt with internal class contradictions; hence it was perhaps the most thorough revolution in twentieth century African history. *Harvest* defines the structure of the historical imperative of the peasant and working classes to overthrow the Ethiopian landed aristocracy, without moralizing the revolt. The impact of the change is shown from the perspective of a peasant family, in particular that of a very young woman. Like Sembene Ousmane's *Ceddo* (1977), *Harvest* situates female consciousness in a central position within African history.

With *Harvest: 3,000 Years,* the Los Angeles school demonstrated its internationalism. One of the best films to come out of Africa, *Harvest* defined what issues a Third World film should encompass from an African perspective. Anti-Hollywood in its narration, visual poetics, and theorizing of history, it occupies an important position in Third World cinema, on a par with the works of Rocha, Solas, Sanjines, Alea, and others.

A fundamental tenet of the Los Angeles school was an opposition to Hollywood. Yet even this view was not unanimously held. Despite the general tenor of the group, Jamaa Fanaka was very much fascinated with Hollywood and averse to the contentious ideological and artistic discussions that were fundamental to the formation of the school. Fanaka's work is a tangent from the movement's crucial project to develop an historically informed, authentic representation of Black and Third World peoples. While Fanaka in *Penitentiary* (1979) displays a solid grasp of film language, he ignores the disproportionate number of Blacks and other minorities in the prison population and the racism of the penal system that had been well documented in books such as *Soledad Brother* by George Jackson, *The Autobiography of Malcolm X,* and *Soul on Ice* by Eldridge Cleaver (however problematic the last author turned out to be). Additionally, Fanaka in *Emma Mae* (1976) seems oblivious to two historical events in the 1970s: the emergence of new African-American women writers (including Maya Angelou, Ntozake Shange, Toni Morrison, and later Alice Walker) and the emergence of African-American feminism. Nevertheless, Fanaka's works, including the recent *Street Wars* (1991), are an irreplaceable legacy of the school.[13]

Concerning other members of the group, little can be said because many of their recent projects are not yet complete. Attention should be called, however, to the work of Ben Caldwell. Caldwell's 1977 film, *I and I: An African Allegory,* is a mystical exploration of Black nationalism and African history, in which Caldwell argues that spiritualism is an essential component of the cultural profile of African-American people. The film aligns itself with an African cosmology, not only on the continent itself but as it has evolved in the diaspora, especially in Haiti, Cuba, and Brazil. A deep sense of religiosity also informs *Babylon is Falling: A Visual Ritual for Peace* (1983), a postmodern exploration of popular culture. A work Caldwell is presently completing at the California Institute of the Arts for the Watts Tower Art Center elaborates further on the theme of spiritualism. For Caldwell, African emancipation is not possible without spiritual liberation, a position that is unique among Black independent filmmakers of the Los Angeles school.

Since this essay is not a comprehensive inventory of films by the Los Angeles school, but rather recapitulates the intellectual and cultural conditions of its founding, some works by this generation of brilliant filmmakers have not been discussed. Nevertheless, several other films deserve mention. Larry Clark's *Passing Through* (1977) examines the relationship between a young and older musician, and celebrates (like the sound track to *Killer of Sheep*) the greatness of African-American music. Gerima's *Child of Resistance* (1972) was a foundational work of the Los Angeles school. One still remembers the tremendous stir it created at its first showing in the Melnitz Theater at UCLA and the challenge it posed to all students who became members of the movement. Gerima's *Ashes and Embers* (1982) is remarkable for its transposition of African oral narrative devices onto a different artistic medium, as the film tells a particular story from the Vietnam War as though it were an old African folktale. Gerima's *Wilmington Ten—U.S.A., 10,000* (1978) documents the oppression of Black people in America; and his *After Winter: Sterling Brown* (1985) is a tribute to a great poet of the Harlem Renaissance. These and other works await full historical appraisal.

Notes

1. Clyde Taylor, "The Birth of Black Cinema: Overview," in *Black International Cinema Berlin: 105 February 1989* (Berlin: Arsenal Cinema, 1989), 115–117. Also see the special issue of *The Black Scholar,* vol. 21, No. 2 (March–April–May 1990), on Black Cinema, particularly St. Clair Bourne, "The African-American Image in American Cinema," 12–19.

2. The notion that an ideological tendency is indispensible for artistic creativity is eloquently argued by Walter Benjamin in his remarkable essay, "The Author as Producer," reprinted in *Understanding Brecht* (London: New Left Books, 1976).

3. Fredric Jameson has sharply delineated the political contours and intellectual currents of this decade in "Periodizing the 1960s," *Ideologies of Theory, 1971–1986, Volume 2: Syntax of History* (Minneapolis: University of Minnesota Press, 1988), 12–19.

4. On the internationalism of national situations, see Fredric Jameson's "The State of the Subject (III)," in *Critical Quarterly,* vol. 29, No. 4 (1987), 15–25.

5. It should be mentioned that the Third World Film Club at UCLA also included other students from other Third World countries, particularly Iran and Brazil.

6. See the interview conducted by Teshome Gabrile and his students with dos Santos, "Cinema Novo and Beyond . . . A Discussion with Nelson Perira dos Santos," *Emergence 2* (Spring 1990), 49–82.

7. Fredric Jameson examines Espinosa's aesthetic of "An Imperfect Cinema" within the context of postmodernism in *Signatures of the Visible* (New York: Routledge, 1990), 218–219.

8. These questions were posed at a time when French filmmaker Jean-Luc Godard, from *La Chinoise* (1967) through *Tout va bien* (1972) had questioned the historical viability of cinema itself. Prophetically, in 1965, Louis Aragon titled a review of *Le Pierrot fou,* "What is Cinema Jean-Luc Godard." (See Jean Collet, ed., *Jean-Luc Godard* (New York: Crown, 1970). In *Wind from the East* (1969), a Marxist Western first shown in North America at UCLA, Godard asked Glauber Rocha to define Third World Cinema. Rocha had many interesting things to say. See James Roy MacBean, "Godard and Rocha at the Crossroads of *Vent d'est*," in *Film and Revolution* (Bloomington: University of Indiana Press, 1975), 116–138.

9. *To Sleep with Anger* was greeted with critical acclaim in practically all major American newspapers, including the *Los Angeles Times,* the *New York Times,* the *Village Voice,* and the *Los Angeles Weekly.* Georgia Brown, for example, writes: "Charles Burnett is our other world-class African-American filmmaker. The quiet one." ("The Trouble with Harry [and Henry]," *Village Voice,* 16 October, 1990, 59.) The other presumably is Spike Lee. The National Society of Film Critics gave its 1990 award for best screenplay to Burnett for *To Sleep with Anger.* The film also won best screenplay honors from the Independent Spirit Awards. But while the film has received much critical praise, it has had difficulty finding its proper audience, thus being shown largely to White audiences. (See Larry Rohter, "An All-Black Film (Except for the Audience," the *New York Times,* 19 November 1990, and Ann Thompson, "Anger Strikes Back: The Non-Marketing of Charles Burnett," *Los Angeles Weekly* 16–22 November 1990, 37.)

10. Burnett mentioned this interference to the author in several personal conversations in early 1990 while shooting *American Becoming,* and it was a constant refrain during our reminiscences with other members of the Los Angeles school. Also see the interesting article on the making of the film by Henry Chu, "Film on Monterey Park Conflict Reviewed," *Los Angeles Times* (25 October 1990), J1, J10.

11. After the showing of the film on April 13, 1991 at the American Film Institute Film Festival in Los Angeles, Burnett was questioned about certain omissions, particularly the absence of a Native American perspective in relation to the new wave of immigrants from non-European countries. Burnett described the limited options available to him during the making of the film. He expressed a wish to make a film in the near future on Native American cultures.

12. On the occasion of the 25th anniversary of the Watts Rebellion in August 1990, the Fanon Research and Development Center of the Charles R. Drew University of Medicine and Science, and the Los Angeles Library of Social Research, organized a tribute to the Los Angeles school of Black filmmakers, at which the work of Gerima, Burnett, and Woodberry was shown. In April 1989 UCLA held a Gerima retrospective, organized by Yemane Demissie, a young Ethiopian filmmaker. Among those attending were Burnett, Masilela, Gabriel and Caldwell.

13. A tribute to Fanaka organized for The American Film Institute Los Angeles Film Festival in April 1991 is in many ways a tribute to the Los Angeles school of Black filmmakers. The day after the premier of Fanaka's *Street Wars* at the festival, a symposium was held on "The African-American Filmmakers of Los Angeles: Is This a New Movement in American Cinema?" Participants included Charles Burnett, Bill Duke, Ruby Oliver, Jamma Fanaka, Ben Caldwell, Naema Barnette, Billy Woodbury, Roland Jefferson, Stephen P. Edwards, Hawthorne Jones, and George Hill. This is further evidence of recent recognition of the Los Angeles school as an important movement in American cultural history.

8

Reading the Signs, Empowering the Eye: *Daughters of the Dust* and the Black Independent Cinema Movement

Toni Cade Bambara

Cultural Work Ain't All Arts and Leisure

In 1971, Melvin Van Peebles dropped a bomb. *Sweet Sweetback's Baadassss Song* was not polite. It raged, it screamed, it provoked. Its reverberations were felt throughout the country. In the Black community it was both hailed and denounced for its sexual rawness, its macho hero, and its depiction of the community as downpressed and in need of rescue. Film buffs vigorously invented language to distinguish the film's avant-garde techniques and thematics from the retrograde ideology espoused. Was *Sweetback* a case of Stagolee Meets Fanon or Watermelon Man Plays Bigger Thomas?

Hollywood noted that Van Peebles' *Sweetback* was making millions and that the low-budget detective flick *Shaft* by Gordon Parks, Sr., also released that year, was cleaning up too. By 1972, headlines in the trade papers were echoing those from the twenties—"H'wood Promises the Negro a Better Break." I could wallpaper the bathroom with *Variety* headlines from the days of *Hallelujah!*, through the forties accord between DuBois/NAACP and Hollywood, through the "Blaxplo" era, to this summer's edition covering Cannes and the release of works by Lee, Rich, Vasquez, Duke, and Singleton and still ask the question: Never mind occasional trends, when is the policy going to change? Some fine works got produced despite the "Blaxplo" formula: revolution equals criminality, militants sell dope and women, the only triumph possible is in a throw-down with Mafia second-stringers and bad-apple cops on the take, the system is eternal.

Nowhere would the debate over *Sweetback* prove more fruitful to the development of the Black independent sphere than at the UCLA film school. By 1971, a decentering of Hollywood had already taken place there, courtesy of a group of Black students who recognized cinema as a site of struggle. A declaration of independence had been written in the overturning of the film school curriculum and in the formation of student-generated alternatives, such as the Ethnocommunications Program and off-campus study groups. The significance of the LA rebellion to the development of the multicultural film phenomena of recent years has been the subject of articles, lectures, interviews, program notes, and informal talks by Sylvia Morales, Rene Tajima, Charlie Burnett, Julie Dash, Monte-zuma Esparza, and most especially, most consistently, and most pointedly in connection with the development of Black independent film, by Clyde Taylor. Some of *Sweetback*'s techniques and procedures were acceptable to the insurgents, but its politics were not. The film, nonetheless, continued to exert an influence as late as 1983, as is observable in Gerima's *Ashes and Embers*, in which an embittered and haunted 'Nam vet is continually running, finding respite for a time with folks in the community. The film closes not with "The End," but "Second Coming," as in *Sweetback*.

The Black insurgents at UCLA had a perspective on film very much informed by the movements of the sixties (1954–1972) both in this country and on the Continent. Their views differed markedly with the school's orientation:

* accountability to the community takes precedence over training for an industry that maligns and exploits, trivializes and invisibilizes Black people;

* the community, not the classroom, is the appropriate training grounds for producing relevant work;

* it is the destiny of our people(s) that concerns us, not self-indulgent assignments about neurotic preoccupations;

* our task is to reconstruct cultural memory not slavishly imitate white models; our task leads us to our own suppressed bodies of litera-ture, lore, and history, not to the "classics" promoted by Eurocentric academia;

* students should have access to world film culture—African, Asian, and Latin America cinema—in addition to Hitchcock, Ford, and Renoir.

The off-campus study group, which included cadres from two periods—Charles Burnett, Hailie Gerima, Ben Caldwell, Alile Sharon Larkin, and Julie Dash—engaged in interrogating conventions of dominant cinema, screening films of socially conscious cinema, and discussing ways to alter previous significations as they relate to Black people. In short, they were committed to developing a film language to respectfully express cultural particularity and Black thought. The "Watts Films," as their output was called in the circles I moved in then, began with Gerima's 1972 *Child of Resistance*, in homage to Angela Davis, an instructor at UCLA before the state sent her on the run, and his 1974 feature *Bush Mama*. Both starred Barbara O (then Barbara O. Jones), an actress who hooked up with insurgents early on and has been with the independents since, working as performer, technician, and now as filmmaker (*Sweatin' a Dream*).

In 1977, the insurgents' thematic foci became discernible: family, women, history and folklore. Larry Clark's *Passing Through*, Charles Burnett's *Killer of Sheep*, and two shorts by Julie Dash, *Diary of an African Nun*, based on a short story by Alice Walker, and *Four Women* based on the musical composition of Nina Simone, made it a bumper-crop year. The edible metaphor is deliberate, and ironic. Proponents of "Third Cinema" around the world were working then, as now, to advance a cinema that would prove indigestible to the imperialist system that relentlessly promotes a consumerist ethic. And the works of the LA rebels reflected radical cultural/political theories of the day. The Black community-as-colony theorem, for example, informs Burnett's portrayal of both the protagonist's family and Watts. The omnipresence of sirens, cruisers, and cops define the neighborhood(s) as occupied territory. The family is portrayed as a potential liberation zone. In *Bush Mama*, the besieged Dorothy comes to consciousness through her daughter's questioning. While filming, Gerima's crew became the target of the LAPD, who equate Black men with expensive equipment with criminality; the attempted arrest was filmed, and the documented incident on screen in the fictional feature provides a compelling argument. This treatment of family and setting continued to inform the later films of Gerima, Burnett, and Billy Woodbury.

Alile Sharon Larkin's treatment of terrain in her 1982 *A Different Image* is the same. She uses the landscape (billboards and other ads that commercialize women's images), though, to highlight the impact sexist representations have on behavior in general (passers-by who regard the heroine as a sex object) and on intimate relationships in particular (the heroine's boyfriend fails to see the connection between racism and sexism). Larkin's film demonstrates the difficulty in and the necessity for smashing the code, transforming previous significations as they relate to Black women.

Three shorts by Julie Dash—*Diary of an African Nun*, *Four Women*, and the 1982 *Illusions*—are in line with this agenda. We note four things in them that will culminate in her more elaborate text of 1991, her feature *Daughters of the Dust*: women's perspective, women's validation of women, shared space rather than dominated space (Mignon Dupree in

Illusions presses for the inclusion of Native Americans in the movie industry, and she stands in solidarity with Ester, the hidden "voice" of the Euro-American movie star), and glamour/attention to female iconography.

In *Daughters of the Dust*, the thematics of colonized terrain, family as liberated zone, women as source of value, and history as interpreted by Black people are central. The Peazant family gather for a picnic reunion at Ibo Landing, an area they call "the secret isle." It is "secret" for two reasons, for the land is both bloody and blessed. A port of entry for the European slaving ships, the Carolina Sea Islands (Port Royal County) were where captured Africans were "seasoned" for servitude. Even after the trade was outlawed, traffickers used the dense and marshy area to hide forbidden cargo. But the difficult terrain was also a haven for both self-emancipated Africans and indigenous peoples, just as the Florida Everglades and the Louisiana Bayous were for Africans and Seminoles, and for the Filipinos conscripted by the French to fight proxy wars (French and Indian wars). Dash's Peazant family is imperiled by rape and lynch-mob murder (whites are ob-skene in *DD*), but during their reunion picnic they commandeer the space to create a danger-free zone. Music cues and resonating lines of dialogue in *DD* link the circumstances of the Peazants at the turn of the century to our circumstances today. Occupying the same geographical terrain are both the ghetto, where we are penned up in concentration-camp horror, and the community, wherein we enact daily rituals of group validation in a liberated zone—a global condition throughout the African diaspora, the view informs African cinema.

Daughters of the Dust capsulizes the stage of independent Black filmmaking ushered in by the LA rebellion in other ways as well. Spiritual and religious continuum, a particular theme of Ben Caldwell's, is central to the *DD* drama. Folklore, too, is key. Two further decisions Dash made highlight her strategy for grounding *DD* in the discourse of committed Black cinema. She drew her cast from films by her UCLA colleagues: Barbara O (as Yellow Mary) was in Gerima's *Child of Resistance* and *Bush Mama*, and in Dash's *Diary of an African Nun*; Adisa Anderson (as Eli) was in Alile Sharon Larkin's *A Different Image*; Cora Lee Day (as Nana) was in Gerima's *Bush Mama*; Kaycee Moore (as Haagar) was in Burnett's *Killer of Sheep* and Woodbury's *Bless Their Little Hearts*.

She also cast from films by other independents: Trula Hoosier (as Yellow Mary's woman friend) was in Charles Lane's *Sidewalk Stories*; Geraldine Dunston (one of Nana's daughters) was in Iverson White's *Dark Exodus*; Tommy Hicks (as Snead the photographer) was in Spike Lee's *She's Gotta Have It*; and Verta Mae Smart-Grovesnor (as one of Nana's daughters) was in Bill Gunn's video soap *Personal Problems*. She also drew from industry-backed films by Black filmmakers and from industry White-directed, Black-cast films: Alva Rogers (as Eula) was in Spike

Lee's *School Daze*, Tony King (as Eli's cousin) was in *Sparkle*. Note, too, that the presence of Barbara O links *DD* to other works by filmmakers, for she appears in Saundra Sharp's *Back Inside Herself* and Zeinabu Davis' in-progress *A Powerful Thang*.

The effects of intertextual echoes resulting from Dash's casting strategem are best discussed in screen demonstration, rather than in on-the-page discussions, but one example can perhaps illustrate the point. The presence of Dunston from White's lynching-migration film deepens the anti-lynching campaign theme in *DD* and underscores the difference between the White lynch mob's picnic (the dead man's sons find orange peels and other debris near the hanging tree) and the Black family reunion picnic. The existence of *DD* makes it easier than ever for someone to produce an anthology film on Black US history on the order of Kwati Ni Owoo and Kwesi Owusu's anthology film on African cinema, *Ouaga*, which combines film clips, interviews, and footage from FESPACO, the Pan-African film festival in Burkina Faso, and uses ideogrammed panels of cloth (event turned to story turned to punch line turned to proverb turned to ideograms woven in kente cloth) to segment the film's "chapters."

Dash's *Daughters of the Dust* is an historical marker. It not only promotes a back glance, it demands an appraisal of ground covered in the past twenty years, and in doing so helps clarify what we mean by "independent Black cinema." In its formal practices and thematics, *DD* is the maturation of the LA rebellion agenda. By centralizing the voice, experience, and culture of women, most particularly, it fulfills the promise of Afrafemcentrists who choose film as their instrument for self-expression. *DD* inaugurates a new stage.

> I'm trying to teach you how to track your own spirit. I'm trying to give you something to take north besides big dreams
>
> Nana

We meet the Peazants in a defining moment—a family council. Democratic decision-making, a right ripped from them by slavery and regained through emancipation, hallmarks the moment. The Peazants and guests gather on the island at Ibo Landing for a picnic at a critical juncture in history—they are one generation away from the Garvey and the New Negro movements, a decade short of the Niagara/NAACP merger. They are in the midst of rapid changes; Black people are on the move North, West, and back to Africa (the Oklahoma project, for instance). Setting the story amid oak groves, salt marshes, and a glorious beach is not for the purpose of presenting a nostalgic community in a pastoral setting. They are an imperiled group. The high tide of bloodletting has ebbed for a time, thanks to the activism of Ida B. Wells, but there were racist riots in 1902;

in New Orleans, for example, Black schools were the paramount target for torchings, maimings, and murder. Unknown hazards await the Peazants up North. The years ahead will require political, economic, social, and cultural lucidity. Nommo, from an older and more comprehensive belief system than meanings produced by the European traditions of rationalism and empiricism, may prove their salvation.

The Peazants, as the name suggests, are peasants. Their characterizations, however, are not built on a deficit model. It is the ethos of cultural resistance, not the ethos of rehabilitation, that informs their portraiture. They are not victims. Objectively, they are bound to the land as sharecroppers. Subjectively, they are bound to the land because it is an ancestral home. They tend the graves of relatives. Family memorabilia is the treasure they carry in their pockets and store in tins, not coins. They are accountable to the orishas, the ancestors, and each other, not to employers. *DD* is not, then, an economically determined drama in conventional terms, wherein spectators are encouraged to identify with feudal positions—the privileged overlord or the exploited victim, and then close the mind as though no alternative social modes exist or are possible. The Peazants are self-defining people. Unlike the static portraits of reactionary cinema—a Black woman is a maid and remains a maid even after becoming a "liberated woman" through the influence of a White feminist, and even after making a fortune with a pancake recipe (*Imitation of Life*), and a Black woman is prostitute and remains a prostitute in the teeth of other options (*Mona Lisa*)—the Peazants have a belief in their own ability to change and in their ability to transform the social relations of status quo.

While *DD* adheres to the unities of time, place, and action—the reunion takes place in one day in one locale scripted on an arrival-departure grid—the narrative is not "classical" in the Western-specific sense. It is classic in the African sense. There are digressions and meanderings—as we may be familiar with from African, Persian, Indian, and other cinemas that employ features of the oral tradition. *DD* employs a folktale in content and schema.

Instead of a "pidgin" effect, what the eye and ear have been conditioned to expect from the unlettered, the Ibo Landing characters use an imaginative and varied language—poetic, signifying, rhetorical, personal—in keeping with the productive artistry we're accustomed to outside Eurocentral institutions. In addition to affirming the culture, *DD* advances the idea that African culture can subvert the imposed one. Nana, the family elder, binds up the Bible with her mojo in a reverse order of syncretism. Continuum is the theme. The first voice we hear on the sound track is chanting in Ibo; the one discernible word is "remember."

A striking image greets us in the opening—a pair of hands, as in the laying on of hands, as in handed down. They're a working woman's hands.

Grandma's hands. They seem to be working up soil, as in cultivation, or maybe it's sand, certainly apropos for any presentation of an African worldview. And there's water, as in rivers. Then two voice-overs introduce the story. One belongs to Nana, the elder of the family, we will discover later: first, we see and hear her in sync during the film's present; later we see her in a flashback memory of bondage days, her hands sculling the dark steamy water of the dye vats then, together with other enslaved African women, wringing out yards of indigo-dyed cloth. The second voice is that of the Unborn Child; we will see her later on screen, too, as a visitor from that realm that supports the perceived world. The dual narration pulls together the past, present, and future—a fitting device for a film paying homage to African retention, to cultural continuum. The duet also prepares us for the film's multiple perspectives. Communalism is the major mode of the production. There's something else to notice about the dual voice-over narration. The storytelling mode is indabe my children and crik-crak, the African-derived communal, purposeful handing down of group lore and group values in a call-and-response circle.

The story opens with the arrival of two relatives, Yellow Mary and Viola, accompanied by Yellow Mary's woman friend from Nova Scotia and a photographer hired by Viola to document the reunion of the Geechee family, whose homestead is in Gullah country. The family already onshore is introduced by the thud-pound of mortar and pestle, as in the pounding of yam—an echo of the opening of Sembene's *Ceddo*, also a drama about cultural conversion and cultural resistance; in *Ceddo*, which portrays forced conversion, the daily routine of the village, as represented by the pounding of yam, will be disrupted, as signalled by the next shot, a cross mounted atop one of the buildings. The pounding and the drums in *DD* also evoke a Dash antecedent about imposed religious-cultural conflict. In *Diary of an African Nun* a convert to Christianity hears sounds from the village and can't see she can continue to teach her people to smother the drums, stifle the joy, and pray (she realizes) to an empty sky. Shrouded in white she chants, "I am the wife of Christ—barren and . . . I am the wife of Christ," as snow melts on the mountain revealing the rich, black, ancient earth.

Nana Peazant has called a family council because values are shifting. There's talk of migration. The ancestral home is being rejected on the grounds of limited educational and job opportunities. Haagar, one of Nana's daughters-in-law, is particularly fed up with the old-timey, backward values of the "salt-water Negroes" of the island. Her daughter, on the other hand, longs to stay; Ione's lover, a Native American in the area, has sent her a love letter in the hopes that she'll remain. Viola, the Christianized granddaughter, views her family in much the way Haagar does; Viola avers that it is her Christian duty to take the young heathen children in hand, which she does the minute she steps ashore. Nana struggles to keep intact that African-derived institution that has been relentlessly under attack through kidnap, enslavement, Christianization, peonage, forced labor gangs, smear campaigns, and mob murder—the family.

Nana and one of the male relatives of this multigenerational community do persuade several to stay, but realizing that breakup is imminent, that the lure of new places is great, Nana offers a combination of things for folks to take with them as protection on their journey, so that relocation away from the ancestral place will not spell cultural dispossession. As relatives wash the elder's feet, she assembles an amulet made up of bits and scraps. "My mother cut this from her hair before they sold her away from me," she says, winding the charm and binding twine around a Bible. Each member has a character-informed reaction to her request to kiss the amulet, the gesture a vow to struggle against amnesia, to resist the lures and bribes up North that may cause them to betray their individual and collective integrity. The double ritual performed, some Peazants depart and others remain.

Like many independent works of the African diaspora that conceptualize critical remembrance—Med Hondo's *West Indies*, the Sankofa Collective's *Passion of Remembrance*, Rachel Gerber/Beatriz de Nasciamento's *Ori*—DD's drama hinges on rituals of loss and recovery. The film, in fact, invites the spectator to undergo a triple process of recollecting the dismembered past, recognizing and reappraising cultural icons and codes, and recentering and revalidating the self. One of the values of its complexity and its recognition of Black complexity is to prompt us, anew, to consider our positions and our power in the USA.

While presenting the who o' we to ourselves, Dash also critiques basic tenets of both domination ideology and liberation ideology. An exchange illustrating the former occurs in a scene between Nana, the elder, and Eli, a young man fraught with doubt that his pregnant wife, Eula, may be carrying some White man's child. Their lines of dialogue don't mesh at first because each is caught up in her and his own distress—Nana is anxious lest Eli not be up to holding the family together in the North; Eli is too obsessed with doubt about the unborn child to be reasoned with. But then their speeches mesh.

"Call on the ancestors, Eli. We need to be strong again."
"It happened to my wife."
" 'My wife.' Eli, you don't own Eula. She *married* you."

Yellow Mary relates two stories that illustrate the latter point. Strolling along the beach with her friend and Eula, Yellow Mary recalls a box she once saw on the mainland, a music box. It was a bad time for her then, and she wanted that box to lock up her sorrow in the song. In the briefest of anecdotes, the process from sensation to perception to self-understanding to decision-is-mapped. Self-possession is a trait in Yellow Mary's unfolding of character; cultural autonomy is a motif in the entire *DD* enterprise. The allusion to both the sorrow-song and blues traditions in Yellow Mary's art-of-living anecdote sets the stage for a mini-essay on desire. Yellow Mary's walk, posture, and demeanor are in stark contrast to that of the Christianized cousin Viola. The careers of women blues singers in the twenties and thirties showed that Black women need not repress sexuality to be acceptable to the community. Unlike Yellow Mary, who must continually claim her sexuality, Viola has buried hers in Christian duty—that is, until perhaps, Snead the photographer, thrilled to be part of the family circle, in a moment of exuberance kisses her.

Yellow Mary's second story is about a time worse than bad, the death of her baby. Her arms were empty but her breasts were full. The White family she worked for used her to wet-nurse their children. "I wanted to come home, but they wouldn't let me. I tied up my breasts. They let me go." The allusion here is to Toni Morrison's 1987 novel *Beloved*. While Paul D is remembering the scourgings and humiliations of manhood, Sethe is caught up in the memory of gang rape in which the young White men of the plantation suckled her. "They took my milk," Sethe repeats throughout Paul D's cataloguing of atrocities. The yoking of Black women's sexuality and fertility to the capitalist system of exploitation was a theme in Dash's work prior to Morrison's *Beloved*, however. *Four Women*, based on the Simone text, relates the tragedy of three women in history— Saphronia, enslaved; Aunt Sarah, mammified; and Sweet Thing, lecherized. The fourth woman is Peaches, politicized: "I'm very bitter these days because my people were slaves—What do they call me? They call me Peee-Chezzz!"

The struggle for autonomy (or, how many forces do we have to combat to reclaim our body/mind/spirits and get our perspective and agenda respected?) is the concern of numerous Black women filmmakers—Camille Billops, Zeinabu Davis, Cheryl Chisholm, Ayoka Chenzira, Michelle Parkerson, Barbara McCullough, numerous others, and of course, Dash. What the Yellow Mary stories point to is the limitations of radical discourse that dichotomizes culture and politics, that engenders oppression and resistance as male, and that defines resistance as a numbered, organized, leader-led (male) action that is sweeping in process and effect. In tying up her breasts, Yellow Mary is a factory worker on strike.

Any ordinary day offers an opportunity to practice freedom, to create revolution internally, to rehearse for governance, the film promotes. A deepening of the message is achieved by having both Barbara O and Verta

Mae Smart-Grosvenor, author of *Thursday and Every Other Sunday Off*, on screen. O's personal act of resistance in *Bush Mama* carries over to *DD* through the actress playing Yellow Mary, a domestic and a prostitute. The perspective of domestics, who are in a better position than most workers to demystify White supremacy, as Smart-Grovesnor's book indicates, is a still-untapped resource for Black political theorists (including Afrafemcentrists). Likewise the prostitute's.

The thesis of daily resistance spreads from scene to scene. Eula's silence about the White rapist, for example, is a weapon; it shields Eli from highly probably violence. However, as a metaphor for cultural rape, silence must be overcome; the film *DD* is the voice. Speaking Gullah is also resistance; it combats assimilationist designs. Gullah is an Afrish first created by Mandinkas, Yorubas, Ibos, and others to facilitate intercontinental trade long before the African Holocaust. The bridge language on this side of the waters was recreolized with English. The authenticity of languages spoken by the Peazants, by Bilal, a Muslim on the island, by the indigo dyers and the Wallahs (met in flashbacks to slavery times) is one of the ways the film compels belief. The film's respectful attention to language, codes of conduct, food preparation, crafts, chair caning, hair sculptures, quilt making, and mural painting constitutes a praise song to the will and imagination of a diasporized and besieged people to forge a culture that can be sustained.

In the anticolonial wars and since, language has been the subject of hot debate in both diplomatic and cultural arenas. It is key to the issue of cultural-political autonomy, as in, for example, the development of national literatures and national cinemas. Which language shall a newly independent country adopt—that of the largest ethnic group within its colonialist-created borders, that in which the oldest literature is written, that in which the most compelling oral literature is transmitted, that which has been taught in the schools, namely the colonialists'? Kenyan writer N'gugi wa Thiong~o, Senegalese novelist and filmmaker Sembene Ousman, and Palestinian writer and theorist Ghassan Kanafani are a few stalwarts who have kept vibrant the arguments of Fanon, Cabral, and others concerning the imperatives of national culture. During the resistance struggles of the sixties in the US, writers in the various communities of color took up the vernacular-versus-vehicular debate and also opted in favor of languages in which their constituencies experience daily life; hence, literature written in Yorican, Black English, and Spanglais, for example, rather than "standard" or "literary" English. Ousman Sembene's use of Wolof in *Ceddo*, Euzhan Palcy's use of Martinican creole in *Sugar Cane Alley*, Trevor Rhone's use of Jamaican creole in *Smile Orange*, and Felix de Roy use of Papiamento, the creole in the Antilles, in *Eva and Gabriella* are examples of noncapitulation to strategies of containment by official and monied types who argue that vernacular is neither a dignified vehicle for presenting the culture nor a shrewd way to effect a crossover to cosmopolitan audiences who may enjoy your cuisine and appropriate your music but prefer that you speak in standard Europese.

It is not surprising to observe, further, that those filmmakers who argue for cultural authenticity also work to forge a diasporic hook-up. Sembene, for example, frequently links the Continent and Black USA; for example, through gospel music in *Ceddo* and with the Black GI in *Camp de Thieroy*. Palcy, in her screen adaptation of the Zobel novel, invents the character Medouze (who tells Jose about Africa) for the purpose of linking the Caribbean to the Continent; and for her second project, the Martinican filmmaker chose a South African work, *A Dry White Season*. Kwah Ansah's *Heritage Africa* is one of a host of efforts to revitalize in this decade the Pan-African connection. Three works by Haile Gerima make clear his position in this global agenda of cultural defense: *Harvest: 3,000 Years* set in Ethiopia, *The Wilmington Ten—U.S.A. 10,000*, about the Ben Chavis case in the USA, and *Nanu*, a work-in-progress set in the Caribbean. Two works by newcomer Zeinabu Davis demonstrate continuum. In an early short, *Crocodile Tears*, Davis makes a connection in content; the story is about an African-American woman of the US who goes to Cuba on the Venceramos Brigade, much to the consternation of her children. By the time Davis began work on her third short, *Cycles*, she had begun to fashion a deliberate diasporic aesthetic. *Cycles* speaks a Pan-African esperanto via altars, ve'ves, chants to the orishas, Haitian music, African music, and a speaking chorus whose individual accents blend US Northern-Southern-Midwestern with African and Caribbean.

Dash's *DD* evolved over a ten-year period in which independent Black filmmakers committed to socially conscious cinema were exchanging viewpoints with like-minded filmmakers throughout the diaspora, most especially in Britain and on the Continent. The diasporic links promoted in the sixties by St. Clair Bourne on the East Coast (editor of *Chamba Notes*, an international film newsletter) and Haile Gerima on the West Coast (organizer of first US delegation to FESPACO in Burkina Faso), continued into the eighties through the efforts of numerous programmers (for instance, Louis "Bilagi" Bailey, founder of the Atlanta Third World Film Festival, and Cheryl Chisholm who vastly expanded it) historians, curators, critics, supporters, and practitioners (Pearl Bowers serves to illustrate all known categories). Videographer Philip Mallory Jones's current three-channel installation, *Crossroads*, at the Smithsonian is emblematic of the diasporic connection. Dash's decision to set her feature and locate her production in the Carolina Sea Islands where African persistence is still discernible, and, further, to set the story at the turn of the century when retention was strong, enables her to situate the film in the ongoing history of the Pan-African film culture movement.

When Yellow Mary says, "You have to have a place to go where people know your name," she underscores what some people would call the DuBois double-consciousness theme, and what others would call the difference between true or primary consciousness and false or secondary consciousness. It is the Ibo tale which Dash employs in *DD* that keeps the question to the fore—Where is the soul's proper home? *DD*'s is an unabashedly Afrocentric thesis in the teeth of current-day criticisms of essentialism.

Nommo

Loss and recovery is established as a theme and an operation early on in *DD*. The operation begins with Dash's retrieval of a figure; that operation then leads us to a folktale. The landscape in the opening shots is hot, green, and sluggish. A boat glides into view. Embedded in the Black spectator's mind is *that* boat, *those* ships. As this boat cuts through the green, thick waters, we see a woman standing near the prow. She wears a veiled hat and a long, white dress. Embedded in the memory of millions is the European schoolmarm-adventuress-mercenary-disguised-as-missionary woman who helps sell the conquest of Africa as an heroic adventure. But this woman is not that woman. She's standing hipshot, chin cocked, one arm akimbo. The ebonics the message that this is not Brenda Joyce/Maureen O'Sullivan/Katherine Hepburn/Bo Derek/Jessica Lange/ Meryl Streep/Sigourney Weaver or any other White star venturing into Tarzan's heart of darkness to have a sultry affair with a pith-helmeted matinee idol, or with a scruffy, cigar-smoking cult figure, or with a male gorilla, in order to sell us imperialism as entertainment.

In this film, that hipshot posture says, Africans will not be seen scrambling in the dust for Bogie's tossed away stogie. Nor singing off-key as Hepburn plunks Anglican hymns on the piano. Nor fleeing a big, black, monstrous, white, nightmare only to be crushed underfoot. Nor being upstaged by scenery in a travelogue cruise down the Congo, part of a cluster of images that invite but don't commit. Nor being a mute and static backdrop for White folks' actions in the foreground, helping to make that passive/active metaphor of the international race-relations industry indelible. Nor being absent as cast members, ghosts merely in back-projected ethnographic footage purchased from a documentarist trained to go to people of color to study but not to learn from. Nor being absent altogether so as to make Banana Republic colonial-nostalgia clothing for a price clean-kill innocent.

The figure is claimed for an emancipatory purpose. The boat steers us away from the narrows of Hollywood towards salt-marshy waters that only look like the shallows. Bobbing near shore is a carving, the head and torso of an African rendered in wood. From the shape of it, we surmise that it was a "victory," a figure that rode the prow of a slaving ship. (In a later scene, Eli, husband of Eula, will baptize the "victory" and push it out into the depths.) The boat docks in an area richer still in meaning. A title comes onto the screen: "Ibo Landing, 1902." The date is important. The people whose stories will be told are one generation out of bondage. The date lingers on the screen six beats longer than the date in the 1985 Hollywood/Spielberg version of Alice Walker's *The Color Purple*, which is set in the same period.

In *Purple* "Winter, 1909" flashes over Celie bolting upright in bed in extreme foreground, screaming, in terror, in labor. The flash of the date fails to orient sufficiently. The spectator needs a moment to assemble the history: chains, branding irons, whips, rape, metal depressors on the tongue, bits in the mouth, iron gates on the face in the cane brakes that prevent one from eating the sweetness and prevent one from breathing in the sweltering blaze that scalds the mask that chars the flesh. The brutalized and brutalizing behaviors of *Purple*'s main characters have a source. That Spielberg did not appreciate the import of the date is our first clue that *Purple* will be hobbled in fundamental ways—the cartoon view of Africa, for example, which is in keeping with the little-bluebird journey of the flyer that covers the passage of years and announces that Shug Avery's hit town. *Purple*, nonetheless, was/is of critical importance to at least one sector of the community who draw strength from it—incest survivors, who need permission to speak of intracommunity violation.

The place name in *DD*, Ibo Landing, conjures up a story still told both in the Carolina Sea Islands and in the Caribbean. In Toni Morrison's 1981 cautionary tale, the novel *Tar Baby*, set in the Caribbean, it becomes the story of the hundred blind Africans who ride the hills. On deck, barely surviving the soul-killing crossing from the Tropic of Capricorn to the Horse Latitudes, the Africans took one look at the abomination on shore and were struck blind. They flung themselves over the side, swam to shore, climbed the rocks, and can be heard to this day thundering in the hills on wild horses. Haunting hoofbeats are a reminder to cherish the ancient properties and resist amnesia/assimilation/fragmentation. Paule Marshall also uses the tale to warn us not to bargain away wisdom for goods and "acceptance." The functioning of the Ibo tale in Marshall's 1984 novel *Praisesong For the Widow* is more precisely parallel to its role in *DD*.

Praisesong invites the reader to undergo a grounding ritual via Avey Johnson. A middle-aged widow living in White Plains, New York, Avey has all the trappings of success—stocks and bonds, wall-to-wall carpet, car, house, matching luggage. She's planning a trip to the Caribbean. She suffers, though, from a severe sense of loss. It registers as more than the loss of her husband. Like Jardine in the Morrison novel, Avey and Jay have been in flight; the fear of poverty and humiliation drove them to jettison cultural "baggage" for a fleeter, unencumbered, foot up the ladder. Avey receives visitations from her dead elder, Great Aunt Cuney, who directs her to *remember.* Avey's journey toward wholeness begins with remembering the story of the Ibos as handed down through generations in the Carolina Sea Islands where she spent her girlhood summers. In short, in order to move forward, Avey has to first go backwards.

The Ibos, brought ashore from the ships in a boat, stepped out on the land, saw what the Europeans had in store for them and turned right around and walked all the way home to the motherland. Once just a tale, fantastic in its account of people in irons walking thousands of miles on the water, the account of the Ibos' deep vision becomes an injunction to Avey. She must learn to see, to name, to reconnect. Great Aunt Cuney used to say of her grandmother, who handed down the tale, that her body might have been in Tatum, South Carolina but her mind was long gone with the Ibos. Avey finds strength in the tale and continues her journey; its success rests on her ability to read the signs that speak to the persistence of the ancient world(s) in the so-called New World. This practice of reading and naming releases nommo—that harmonizing energy that connects body/mind/spirit/self/community with the universe. Avey "crosses over" to her center, her authentic self, her real name, and her true work. As Avatara she assumes the task of warning others away from *eccentricity.* She stands watch in luxury high-rises for buppie types with a deracinated look. She collars them and tells her story.

In *DD*, the Ibo tale is both rejected and accepted by various characters. But the film's point of view is that it has protective power. In his nonlinear narrative *Ashes and Embers,* Gerima argued that folktales have healing power. The story of a 'Nam vet who has to come to grips with his positionalities as a Black man in the imperialistic US, *Ashes and Embers* moves back and forth between the past and present, and between the city and the countryside. Nate Charles Garnett (named for Nat C. Turner) is still haunted by the war eight years later. Wired ("like a ticking time bomb," a Korean vet he meets says of them both) and belligerent, he intentionally repels and attracts those who love him—his Gran, his lover Liza (played by Kathy Flewellan, a dark-skinned actress who plays a featured role, rare; a woman with independent radical politics, rarer; which she studies within a group and acts on in the community, most rare on screen. She's also the featured actress in Davis' "Cycles") and her son, and a neighborhood elder who runs a TV repair shop.

The drama gathers momentum when the elder tells Nate what his options are: "Keep running, go hide in the movies, lobotomize yourself with that escapist stuff or draw strength from the strong men. They're your models— DuBois—Robeson." The elder's speech on the strong men (as in the poem by Sterling Brown, subject of a 1985 film by Gerima and his students) propels Nate back to the ancestral place by train. Cross-cutting between Nate on the train and Gran by the fire with Liza, Gerima heightens the drama. Remembering the handed-down tale Gran used to tell him, Nate experiences from it the clarity and coherence necessary to "cross over." Gran is relating the very same tale to Liza, a tale passed down through the family since the Denmark Vesey uprising. "Listen to what I'm telling you and don't forget. Pass it on. Pass it on." It is a compelling account, passionately rendered, expertly paced.

"Crossing over," a term steeped in religion, as in crossing over into Jordan (Baptist and other), crossing over into sainthood (Sanctified, Pentecostal), crossing to or coming through religion (Country Baptist and AME Zion) crops up frequently in the speech of those on Ibo Island. Used by Haagar, the daughter-in-law eager to get her family off the island to more sophisticated environs, it suggests that she may fall victim to the worship of Mammon. Used by one of the men trying to persuade Eli, the distraught husband of Eula, to stay and be an anti-lynching activist, it equates responsibility with sacred work. The phrase "making the crossing," spoken by several characters, carries two meanings: being double-crossed, as in being rounded up for the Middle Passage; and being Ibo-like by sending the soul home to the original ancestral place, Africa.

"Crossing over" also calls to mind the contemporary phrase "crossover" as in "Whitening" a Black film project, or yoking a Black box office star to a White one in order to attract a wider, or Whiter, audience. *DD* is not a crossover project.

Empowering Signs

The TV experiment *All in the Family* proved that commercial success was/is in the offing for those who would pitch to a polarized national audience. White and other bigots were affirmed by the prime-time Archie Bunker show. White and other liberals read the comedy as an expose and applauded its creators for their wit. Black and other downpressed folks, eager for any sign of American Bunkerism being defanged, tuned in to crack.

There is no evidence in *DD* of trying to position a range of spectators, as many filmmakers find it expedient to do. *DD* demands some work on the part of the spectator whose ear and eye have been conditioned by habits of viewing industry fare that masks history and addicts us to voyeurism, fetishism, mystified notions of social relations, and freakish notions of intimate relations. Most spectators are used to performing work in the dark. But usually, after fixing inconsistencies in plot and character and rescripting to make incoherent texts work out, our reward is a mugging. *DD* asks that the spectator honor multiple perspectives rather than depend on the "official" story offered by a hero; it asks too that we note what particular compositions and framing mean in terms of human values. The reward is an empowered eye.

In *DD*, the theme of cultural resiliency determines composition, framing, music, and narrative. In conventional cinema, symbol, style, and thematics are subordinated to narrative drive; except, of course, that an ideological imperative overrides it all: to construct, reinforce, and "normalize" the domination discourse of status quo that posits people of color as less than ("minority," as they say).

Snead the photographer is a reminder of how ritualized a form of behavior taking pictures is, and that it need not be aggressive. His character changes in the course of the film. Initially bemused, curious about the backwoods folk Viola regards as heathens, he becomes the anthropologist who learns from "his photographic subjects." After interviewing people on the island, Snead discovers a more profound sense of his own self. The photographer character, the camera, the stereopticon, and kaleidoscope function in *DD* as cameras and video monitors do in *The Passion of Remembrance* by the Black British collective Sankofa. The film-within-a-film device, as Maggie Baptiste works in front of the monitor, accomplishes in the independent Black Brit film what shifting sight lines and the behavior of Snead do in *DD*—to call attention to the fact that in conventional films we're seduced by technique and fail to ask what's being filmed and in whose interest, and by failing to remain critical, become implicated in the reconstruction/reinforcement of an hierarchical ideology.

Dash not only expresses solidarity with international cadres whose interrogations have been throwing all codified certainties about film into crisis for the past twenty years, she also contracted as director of cinematography a filmmaker who questions even the 24-frames-per-second convention. In the early forties, when Dizzy Gillespie announced that 3/4 and 4/4 time signatures were not adequate for rendering the Black experience, Bebop was ushered in. It didn't arrive in a tux. It came to overhaul the tenets of Black improvisational music making and music listening. Arthur Jafa Fiedler, as his film shorts such as "P.F." indicate, is announcing no less.

Frame rates, the speed at which the sprocket-driven gears push film stock through the chamber of a camera, include, among others, 16 frames per second, 18, 24, 25, and so on. Of these technological possibilities—and even these are fairly arbitrary—24 has been the standard since the "talkies," not, apparently, because the synchronization of sound and visuals requires it, but because findings in the fields of kinesics and psycophysiology suggest that the 24-frame rate gives a pleasurable illusion of reality. In "P.F.," by orchestrating frame rates, Fiedler gives us something else; he multiplies the possibilities for multiple-channeled perception on the part of the spectator. For a project, namely *DD*, that asks the spectator to do as Avey did, read the signs, Fiedler is the perfect practitioner.

By the by: a number of Black psychologists and forensic lawyers are working in the combined field of kinesics and psychophysiology to explore the virulent and criminal impact of racist stressors (a sense of entitlement, belief in Black inferiority, a predisposittion to hog space, to break through a line, presume, engage in demonic-oriented Black/White discourse, complain about the music, set the pace) on Black individual and communal health.

One of the "signs" is signing, which the children do in games, and which Eli and several men do to talk across distances. The film poses the question asked of inventor Lewis Lattimore by Pan-African-minded folks at the turn of the century: How shall a diasporized people communicate? Answer: independent films. Trula Hoosier (Yellow Mary's woman friend) from Charles Lane's independent silent film *Sidewalk Stories* (mother of the little girl) has very few lines in *DD* but is in a great many scenes. Her silence is initially disconcerting but then seems functional, drawing attention to both the Gullah language and signing. In the woods where Eli (played by Adisa Anderson, the boyfriend from *A Different Image*) and his cousin (played by Tony King who, in *Sparkle*, beat up on Lonette McKee, who later starred in Dash's *Illusions*) silently performs an African martial art known in Afribrasilia as capoeira (the subject of a film by Warrington Hudlin, founder of the Black Filmmaker's Foundation which distributes, among other films, *A Different Image* and *Illusions*), cousin Peazant's reading of the signs of the time is what prompts him to speak, in order to persuade Eli to stay and be an activist. "They're opening up Seminole land," Cuz says, "for White settlers and Northern industrialists, not for we": a sure sign that there'll be an escalation of White-on-Black and White-on-Red crimes. Geraldine Dunston, who plays the mother of the christianized Viola, is an actress who appeared in Iverson White's independent film about lynching, resistance, and migration, *Dark Exodus*. Her presence adds weight to the anti-lynching campaign argument of Eli's cousin. The presence of a Native American in the cast, lover of one of the Peazant's granddaughters, drives home the multicultural solidarity theme, earlier sounded in Dash's *Illusions*.

There's a particularly breathtaking moment that occurs on the beach shortly after Nana has stressed the necessity of honoring the ancestors. It's a deep-focus shot. Close in the foreground are the grown-ups. They are facing our way. The men are in swallowtail coats. Some have on homburgs as well. Some are sitting, others standing. Two or three move across the picture plane, coattails buffeted by the breeze. They are talking about the importance of making right choices. Someone says that for the sake of the children they must. We see, across a stretch of sand glinting in the sun in midground, the children playing along the shore. Several of the grown-ups turn to look over their shoulders and in turning, form an open "door." The camera moves through, maintaining crisp focus, and approaches the children, except that the frame rate has slowed, just enough for us to register that the children are the future. For a split second, we seem to go beyond time to a realm where children are eternally valid, are eternally *the* reason for right action. The camera then pulls back, still maintaining crisp focus, as we backtrack across the sand, entering present time again as the grown-ups' conversation claims our attention again. Not virtuosity for virtuosity's sake, the past/present/future confluence is in keeping with film's motive impulse to celebrate continuum.

There are two things remarkable about the take. One, the camera is not stalking the children. I do not know how that usual predatory menace was avoided, but one contributing factor is that the camera is not looking down on them. Two, no blur occurs as is usual in conventional cinema. Throughout *DD*, no one is background scenery for foregrounded egos. The camera-work stresses the communal. Space is shared, and the space (capaciousness) is gorgeous. In conventional cinema, camera-work stresses hierarchy. Space is dominated by the hero, and shifts in the picture plane are most often occasioned by a blur, directing the spectator eye, controlling what we may and may not see, a practice that reinscribes the relationships of domination ideology.

When last we were on this Carolina Sea Island terrain in the movies, it was the 1974 Hollywood/Martin Ritt adaptation of *The Water Is Wide*, a nonfiction account by European-American Pat Conroy. In the film a blond, blue-eyed charmer (Jon Voight), come to rehabilitate Black youngsters, is pitted against a stern Black principal (Madge Sinclair) who won't let the children have any fun. The camera is in league with the ingenuous rascal who "teaches" the nine- and ten-year-olds how to brush their teeth. The camera joins the White man in the trees swinging his feet; in foreshortened perspective, it looks like he's penetrating their skulls. When the shots don't look like a mauling, they look like an auction-block frisking as teacher, made to look eight feet tall, looks down into the molars of the upturned, worshiping faces. With Voight as educational missionary in this colonial treatise, the history of forcible removal of children of color from their homes by agents of the European settler regimes in the US (Navajo most especially), Australia (Aborigine), and Africa, eager to indoctrinate them in White-run boarding schools, White foster homes, and White-run mission schools, respectively, is masked. My movie guide books refer to *Conrack* as "a gentle and moving story about a white teacher who goes to help culturally deprived youngsters on a South Carolina island."

There are wonderful moments of the children in Dash's *DD* that call to mind the children in Burnett's films. In *Killer of Sheep*, their ubiquity and vitality help keep the "bad luck" incidents, the cracking of the car engine, from being the flat tire on the family outing. The children try to coax Stan out of his job-benumbed state. His wife (Kaycee Moore, who plays Hagar in *DD*) tries to coax him into recognizing her needs. Dinah Washington sings "This Bitter Earth" as they dance. It's hopeless; actress Moore moves out of the frame, frustrated.

At the end of *DD*, Haagar (Kaycee Moore) is also frustrated. Her daughter hops from the boat to ride off into the sunset with her Cherokee lover. What a totally corny and thoroughly wonderful and historic moment it is (shades of Osceola). Though children in Burnett's more recent film *To Sleep With Anger* are not directed as well as previously (why couldn't the camera swivel and pivot rather than have the adult performers continually lift the children as though they were disabled?), there is that great moment on the roof when the young boy throws the pigeon into the air and coaxes it to fly, and the pigeon soars, circles, never leaving the shot, and comes right back. An operative metaphor for home; the home that in fact houses a tension, for the householders thought they had resolved the Southern culture-Northern culture contradiction, only to have Harry (the Danny Glover character) track in all the "hoodoo mess" Haagar of *DD* is eager to flee.

DD has a look of its own. I recall hearing that it was shot in 35mm and reduced to 16mm to reduce graininess. I don't think so. It feels in scope like a 70 mm or higher, encouraging the spectator's belief in limitless peripheral vision, for indeed a world is being presented. For all the long shots, neither a picture-book nor an unduly distanced feel results. The spaciousness in *DD* is closer to African cinema than to European and Euro-American cinema. People's circumstances are the focus in African cinema, rather than individual psychology. The emphasis placed on individual psychology in dominating cinema deflects our attention away from circumstance. Social inequities, systemic injustices, doctrines and policies of supremacy are reduced to personal antagonisms. Conflict, then, can be resolved by a shrink, a lawyer, a cop, or a bullet. Not, for example, by revolution.

By the time the unborn Peazant child will come of age in the twenties, the subversive potential of cinema will be in the process of being tapped in this country, by African-Americans in Philadelphia, Kansas, New York, and Texas, and by European-Americans in New York, Philadelphia, and California. By the time US cinema becomes industrialized in California, that potential will have been tamed, will have been brought into line with structures of domination and oppression. But the camera in the hands of Snead, a character who undergoes a transformation from estranged scientist to engaged humanist, and the other two pre-kinescope props, the stereopticon and the kaleidoscope, in the hands of the Peazant women, prompt us to envision what popular narrative, for example, might be like were dread, sin, and evil not consistently and perniciously signified in dominating cinema within a matrix of darkness, blackness, and femaleness. The props and their attachment to particular characters in *DD* keep central the distinctiveness of conscious Black cinematistes in opposition to commercial filmmakers, and in relation to independent Black filmmakers who regard the contemporary independent sphere as a training ground or stepping-stone to the industry, rather than as a space for contestation, a liberated zone in which to build a cinema for social change.

Two Spike Lee performers in key roles—Alvah Rogers as Eula, Tommy Hicks as Snead—are a reminder that Lee, who'd been a member of the Black Filmmakers Foundation alliance in the early eighties, opted for a route not taken by members of the conscious wing of the movement. In harnessing independent strategies with commercial strategies, Lee's been able to situate a range of spectators, often polarized spectators, thereby meeting the demand for social relevance, that is, the illustration of issues and the representation of Black people (without interrogations), and at the same time not letting go of a basically reactionary sensibility (homophobic/misogynistic/patriarchal) that audiences have been trained by the industry and its support institutions to accept as norm, as pleasureable, inevitable. There's a promo still from *DD* that shows an expanse of beach and sky. A solitary figure in a long dress strolls along the tidemark carrying a tattered parasol. A moist, romantic scene, it's reminiscent of a promo still from *Diva*, the 1982 Beineix film. African-American opera star Wilhelmina Wiggins, in a long dress, holds an umbrella in the dawn drizzle. There's an expanse of gray sidewalk grounded in fog. The solitary figure is surrounded by misty sky and air. End of comparison. *Diva* masks a theft-of-the-Third World shadow text with a mystery-thriller format cover. Although the young, White, French guy steals her voice and her concert gown, the Diva responds with warmth. Their inexplicable friendship is straight out of the international race-relations files that say we are flattered by rip-off (or, "Everything I Have Is Yours" in the key of F sharp). The happy-go-lucky, roller-skating Vietnamese girl who lives with the romantic White hero in the far-out loft is a character designed to mask French colonialism in Indochina in the past and the more recent terrors of the Vietnam War and Operation Babylift. At war's end, Saigon was like a burning building from which Vietnamese parents lowered their children to safety, never dreaming that those below would equate catching with owning, with having the right to fly them away, give them away, sell them away. "Like puppies," say those who are still petitioning the US government for the return of the stolen children. Many of the 1975–1977 petitioners wound up in the concentration camp at Fort Chaffee, Arkansas. Larry Clark's 1977 *Passing Through* addresses the issue of rip-off. He uses conventions of the action flick to protest cultural banditry. The kidnap-pursuit-shootout plot is driven by a communal sense of urgency: Black improvisational music must be rescued from the mob-controlled recording industry. *Passing* indicts status quo; *Passing* proposes a solution. An emancipatory impetus informs the ideology the independent film espouses.

The precinematic artifacts in the hands of Snead and the Peazant women, then, are like the mojo-bound Bible in the hands of the ancestral figure Nana. They speak to the power in our hands. As actress Smart-Grosvenor from the Bill Gunn work bends to kiss the amulet, we are reminded of Gunn's relationship to the independent sphere. Twice in the seventies Bill Gunn, contracted to produce Hollywood formulaic work, slipped the yoke and created instead two works of conscious cinema. His 1973 *Ganja and Hess*, which was supposed to outdo *Blacula*, a 1972 stylish horror film starring William Marshall, did explore the blood myth, and in the bargain fingered capitalism, Christianity, and colonialist Egypto/anthro/archaeo tamperings as the triple-hell horrors.

Gunn's 1975 *Stop!* was supposed to present a modernized Tarzan plot wherein foregrounded Whites undergo rites of passage against the backdrop of "Third World natives." The prototypic films—the Tarzan, Trader Horn, King Solomon's Mines adventures—did not acknowledge the circumstances of the indigenous peoples at all. Their literary sources, the empire literature of the Victorian period, did, but whether apologist (Kipling) or critical (Conrad), no revolutionary alternative was ever envisioned in the Eurocentric approach. In this era, when a revolutionary alternative cannot be denied, the turmoil is used to make dangerous the playing arena in which the White heroes find themselves—as in *In the Year of Living Dangerously*, for example. In *Under Fire*, Russell Price (Nick Nolte) pays no price for breaking an agreement and taking pictures of Sandanistas in the camp, nor for failing to guard the pictures from the murderous mercenary Oates (Ed Harris). Price's "innocence" feeds Oates; and hundreds of Nicaraguans are murdered so that Price can come to consciousness. In *Stop!* Gunn reverses the colonial-oriented relationship of empire dramas. Actual Puerto Rican independistas are foregrounded as the heroes of the text they determine. The White actors' characters and plot premises of the genre supply the motivations for moving around the island. Predictably, both films were placed under arrest, that is, shelved in the studio vaults. Fortunately Gunn kept the work print of *Ganja and Hess* and its screening over the years created a sufficient ground swell to buttress his suit against the studio. Shortly before his death, Gunn won full rights to *Ganja and Hess*. Shortly after his death, *Stop!* was released in time for a Whitney show.

As a performer, Gunn appeared in *Ganja and Hess*, and in Kathleen Collins' 1982 independent film *Losing Ground*. The film has two settings: Manhattan, where the main character, a philosophy professor, teaches; Nyack (where Gunn and Collins were neighbors, and where much of *Ganja and Hess* had been shot), where she lives with her husband, a painter (Gunn). A self-controlled woman who has cultivated a resolute rectilinearity in response to both her earthy mother and her Dionysian husband, the professor is looking for change, longs to get loose, find her ecstasy. She finds it when a student filmmaker persuades her to take on the role of a vamp in his version of *Frankie and Johnny*. The artist husband, meanwhile, is dancing it up with a Latina neighbor. There's a wonderful moment when the dancing couple hold still for an excruciating, suspenseful second before dropping into the downbeat of a doo-wop ten-watt blue-bulb yo-mama ain't-home basement-party memory of a git-down grind-'em-up: the kind of sho-nuff dancing Stan's wife (Kaycee Moore) was looking for in *Killer of Sheep*.

The late pioneer black woman filmmaker Kathy Collins Prettyman was a liberating sign. And the fact that a number of sisters have found their voices in film augers well for community mental health. The task now is to crash through the cultural embargo that separates those practitioners from both their immediate authenticating audiences and worldwide audiences.

Are Ee Es Pee Ee Cee Tee

Aretha

One of the highpoints in *DD* is a women's validation ceremony. Several characters in the drama need it. Two expressly seek it—Eula, "ruined," and Yellow Mary, despised. From the start, Nana and Eula welcome Yellow Mary into the circle. The other women relatives roll their eyes and mutter at the approach of Yellow Mary and her companion. Actress Verta Mae Smart-Grosvenor (author of the classic cookbook *Kitchen Vibrations: Travel Notes of a Geechee Girl* and librettoist of *Nyam: A Food Opera*; the presence of the culinary anthropologist gives authenticity to the Geechee Girl Productions project, not to mention the merciless preparation and presentation of food) delivers the line, "All that yalla wasted," which the others take up to shut their relative out. There are beautiful interactions between Nana and Yellow Mary, in the way they look at each other and touch. The two actresses appeared together fifteen years ago in Gerima's

Bush Mama. Dorothy, played by Barbara O, rattled by the noise of sirens, neighbors, social workers, and the police, found little comfort in the niggers-ain't-shit-talking neighbor played by Cora Lee Day. And there's a great moment between Yellow Mary and Haagar that comes straight out of Gerima's *Harvest: 3,000 Years*. One of the many memorable scenes in *Harvest* is the long-take walk of the peasant summoned from the fields by the landlord. The camera is at the top of a hill, to the right and slightly behind the murder-mouthing landlord. Without a cut, the peasant tramps across the fields, trudges over to the hill, scrambles up, grabbing at scrub brush, boosting himself on the rocks, and reaches the top, where he's tongue lashed by the landlord. In *DD*, Haagar stands arms akimbo at the top of a sand dune, giving Yellow Mary what-for. The take is not a long one, but the camera placement is the same as Gerima's. Yellow Mary comes up the dune while the older, married, mother of two, who outranks her in this age-respect society, mouths off. Just as Yellow Mary reaches the top, a hundred possibilities registering in her face (will she knock Haagar down, spit in her face, or what?), she gives Haagar a look and keeps on stepping. Hmph.

Eula initiates the validation ritual by chiding the relatives who were ready enough to seek Yellow Mary's help when a cousin needed bailing out of jail, but now slander her. "Say what you got to say," Eli interrupts, impatient. "We couldn't think of ourselves as pure women," Eula recounts, "knowing how our mothers were ruined. And maybe we think we don't deserve better, but we've got to change our way of thinking." Nana contributes wisdom about the scars of the past, then Eula continues, "We all good women." She presents Yellow Mary to the family circle and continues her appeal. "If you love yourself, then love Yellow Mary." Both women are embraced by the family. Then the wind comes up, rippling the water in the basin the elder's feet are being washed in, rippling the waters where the boat awaits for the departing Peazants.

Dash's sisters-seeing-eye-to-eye ritual has its antecedents in *Illusions*. Mignon Dupree (Lonette McKee) is a production executive in a Hollywood studio during the forties. Because of the draft and because she's mistaken for White, the Black woman has an opportunity to advance a self-interested career. That is not her agenda. She proposes that the studio, cranking out movies to boost the war being fought "to make the world safe for democracy," make movies about the Native American warrior clans in the US armed services. The studio heads's got no eyes for such a project. All attention is on a problem—the White, blonde bombshell star can't sing. A Black woman, Ester Jeeter (Roseanne Katon), is brought in as "the voice." Ester see Mignon and recognizes who she is. Mignon sees Ester and does not disacknowledge her. Ester is placed behind a screen, in the dark, in a booth, to become the singing voice of the larger-than-life, illuminated starlet on the silver screen. Mignon stands in solidarity with Ester. Unlike the other executives who see the Black woman as an instrument, a machine, a solution to a problem, Mignon openly acknowledges her personhood and their sisterhood.

The genre that Dash subverts in her indictment of an industry that projects false images (democracy, US fighting troops, the starlet) is the Hollywood story musical, specifically *Singin' in the Rain*, a comic treatment of the Hollywood careers ruined by the "talkies." In *Singin'* there is the obligatory ritual that informs the history of commercial cinema—the humiliation of a (White) woman. While the nonsinging star, played by Jean Hagen, is "singing" at a show biz benefit, the stage hands, who resent her fame and fortune, raise the curtain to reveal the singer, played by Debbie Reynolds. Does the Reynolds character stand in solidarity with the humiliated woman? Hell no, its her big career break. *Singin'* provides Dash with a cinematic trope. Victoria Spivey, Blue Lu Barker, Lena Horne and other musicians contracted by Hollywood for on-screen and off-screen work provide the actual historical trope, for the Reynolds character image is false too. Behind that image, in the dark, behind a screen, in a booth, was a Black woman. Dash's indictment, as well as her thesis about what cinema could be, carries over from *Illusions* to *DD*. The validation of Black women is a major factor in the emancipatory project of independent cinema.

As Zeinabu Davis often points out, a characteristic of African-American women filmmakers is tribute paid to womanish mentors and other women artists. Ayoka Chenzira, formerly a dancer, produced two shorts based on her training—the 1989 animation *Zajota and the Boogie Spirit* which chronicles the history of struggle and ends with an image, the drum disguised as a boom box, and the 1979 documentary *Syvilla: They Dance to Her Drum*, a tribute to her dance teacher Syvilla Fort. In 1975 Monica J. Freeman produced a documentary on sculptor Valerie Maynard. In 1976 Cheryl Fabio (of The Black FIlmmakers Hall of Fame in Oakland) produced a documentary on her mother, the poet Sarah Fabio. In 1977 Dash based two films on texts by Black women, Alice Walker and Nina Simone. In 1979 Carroll Parrot Blue produced a documentary on artist Varnette Honeywood. In 1981 Kathe Sandler produced a documentary on dance instructor Thelma Hill. In 1985 Michelle Parkerson produced documentaries on singer Betty Carter and on the Sweet Honey In the Rock music troup. In 1986 Debbie Robinson produced a documentary on four comediennes. In 1987 Davis produced a documentary on trumpeter Clora Bryant. In 1991 Dash collaborated with Jawole Willa Jo Zollar of the dancing/singing/acting performance art group Urban Bush Women to produce *Praise House*, in which the feminine principle is advanced as divine; one of several breathtaking moments involve dance lifts of sisters by sisters. All of these answer the question posed by Abbey Lincoln in the September 1966 issue of *Negro Digest:* "Who Will Revere the Black Woman?"

Roll Call:

Julie Dash, Ayoka Chenzira, Camille Billops, Carole Munday Lawrence, Jackie Shearer, Alile Sharon Larkin, the late Kathy Collins, Michelle Parkerson, Carroll Parrot Blue, Kathe Sandler, Jesse Maple, Pamela Jones, Yvonne Smith, Elena Featherstone, Zeinabu Davis, Barbara McCullough, Debbie Robinson, Ellen Sumter, Pearl Bowser, Nadine Patterson, Carmen Coustaut, Teresa Jackson, Omomola Iyabunmi, Cheryl Chisholm, Daresha Kyi, Funmilayo Makarah, Ada Mae Griffin, Sandra Sharp, Fronza Woods, Portia Marshall, Carmen Ashurst, Denise Oliver, Gay Abel-Bey, Monica Freeman, Cheryl Fabio, Helene Head, Malaika Adero, Jean Facey, Aarin Burche, Mary Ester, Pat Hilliard, Imam Hameen, Mary Naema Barnette, Shirikana Amia Gerima, Louise Fleming, Ileen Sands, Edie Lynch, Lisa Jones, Barbara O, Madeline Anderson, Yvette Mattern, Darnell Martin, Millicent Shelton, Denise Bird, Desiree Ortiz, Michelle Patton, Stephanie Minder, Claire Andrade Watkins, Annette Lawrence, Linda Gibson, Joy Shannon, Jacqueline Frazier, Sheila Malloy, Sharon Khadijah Williams, Dawn Suggs, Monona Wali, Demetria Royals, Gia'na Garel, Muriel Jackson, Nandi Bowe.

Julie Dash's *Daughters of the Dust* is an historical marker. It's suggestive of what will hallmark the next stage of development—a more pronounced diasporic and Afrafemcentric orientation. Another marker occurred in the period when *DD* was in the first stage of production—the September 1989 gathering of independents of the Native American, Latina/o-American, African-American, Asian-American, Pacific Islander-American, Middle Eastern-American, and European-American communities. "Show the Right Thing: A National Multicultural Conference on Film and Video Exhibition" was convened by a committee, predominantly women of color, for and about people of color in the independent sphere. Held at New York University, current base of filmmaker Chris Choy, the two-day series of panels on theoretical and practical concerns were presented by people of color practitioners, critics, and programmers from the US, the UK, Canada, and Mexico. In addition to panels and caucuses, hundreds of tapes of film and video were available for screening. The short subject has advanced greatly since the days of the "chasers," when theater managers used them to clear the house after the vaudeville show. Interactions among the all-American assembly at "Show" made clear that the conference title was a double injunction: internally, for responsible practice; externally, for a democratized media.

The "Show" conference, the first gathering of its size on record, was in contradistinction of state policy from the days of Cortez through the days of COINTELPRO to current-day cultural brokers manufacturing hype for the upcoming Quincentenary—keep these people separate and under White tutelage. Coming so soon on the heels of the Flaherty Seminar held in upstate New York that August—a predictably mad proceeding in which colonialist anthro-ethno types collided with "subject people" who've already reclaimed their image, history, and culture for culturally specific documentaries, animations, features, experimental videos, and critical theory (the program of lectures and screenings of works primarily drawn from the African diaspora was curated by Pearl Bowser; an unprecedented commandeering of the guest curator's program time was used to screen post-glasnost works from Eastern Europe, and the highlight of the usurping agenda was a screening of the spare-no-expense-to-restore Flaherty/Korda colonist work *Elephant Boy*)—"Show the Right Thing" was an opportunity for people of color and their supporters to recognize in each other the power to supplant "mainstream" with "multicultural" in the national consciousness, even as two dozen conglomerates escalate the purchase of the US mind by buying up television stations, radio stations, newspapers, textbook companies, magazines, publishing houses, and film studios that control major production funding, distribution, exhibition, at home and abroad, particularly in neocolonialist-controlled areas, and continue to exert a profound influence in universities where most filmmakers and critics are trained.

The next stage of development of new US cinema will most certainly be characterized by an increased pluralistic, transcultural, and international sense and by an amplified and indelible presence of women.

Brief Notes Re:
Programming with *Daughters of the Dust*

Progressive Representations of the Black Woman in Features

Haile Gerima's 1974 *Bush Mama* (Ethiopia/US)
Sharon Alile Larkin's 1982 *A Different Image* (US)
Menelik Shabazz's 1981 *Burning an Illusion* (UK)
Sankofa Collective's 1987 *The Passion of Remembrance* (UK)
(EuraAm) Lizzie Borden's 1983 *Born In Flames* (US)
Julie Dash's 1991 *DD* (US)

Mapping History from the Continent to Watts

Ousman Sembene's 1977 *Ceddo* (Senegal)
Sergio Giral's 1976 *The Other Francisco* (Cuba)
Med Hondo's 1982 *West Indies* (Mauretania/France)
Raquel Gerber's 1989 *Ori* (Brazil)
Ayoka Chenzira's 1989 *Zajota& the Boogie Spirit* (US)

Julie Dash's 1991 *DD* (US)
Charles Burnett's 1990 *To Sleep With Anger* (US)
Ancestral Figures: "An elder dying is a library burning down"-Fye
  Safi Fye's 1979 *Fad Jal* (Senegal)
  Med Hondo's 1982 *West Indies* (Mauritania/France)
  Euzhan Palcy's 1986 *Sugar Cane Alley* (Martinique/France)
  Larry Clark's 1977 *Passing Through* (US)
  Hailie Gerima's 1983 *Ashes and Embers* (Ethiopia/US)
  Julie Dash's 1991 *DD* (US)
Woman to Woman: 5 Documentaries and 3 Features
  Julie Dash's 1983 *Illusions* (US)
  Camille Billops' 1988 *Suzanne, Suzanne* (US)
  Cheryl Chisolm's/National Black Women's Health Project's 1986 *On Becoming a Woman* (US)
  Ngozi Onwurah's 1989 *Body Beautiful* (UK)
  Camille Billops' 1988 *Older Women Talking About Sex* (US)
  Michelle Parkerson's 1980 . . . *But then, she's Betty Carter* (US)
  Julie Dash's 1991 *Daughters of the Dust*
  Julie Dash's 1991 *Praise House*

Acknowledgments

Texts referred to:
  Toni Morrison's *Tar Baby*, New York: Knopf, 1981
  Paule Marshall's *Praisesong for the Widow*, New York: Dutton, 1984
  Toni Morrison's *Beloved*, New York: Knopf, 1987
  Abbey Lincoln's "Who Will Revere the Black Woman," *Negro Digest*, September, 1966: also in Toni Cade's *The Black Woman*, New American Library/Signet, 1970
Written Texts That Inform My Text:
  Zeinabu Davis' interview with Julie Dash in *Wide Angle*, Vol. 13, Nos. 3 & 4 (1991)
  Gregg Tate's interview with Julie Dash in *The Village Voice*, June, 1991 issue
  Pat Collin's *Black Feminist Thought: Knowledge, Consciousness and the Politics of Empowerment*, Boston: Unwin Hyman, Inc. 1990
  bell hooks' *Yearning: Race, Gender, and Cultural Politics*, Boston: South End Press, 1990
  Betinna Aptheker's *Tapestries of Life: Women's Work, Women's Consciousness, and the Meaning of Daily Experience*, Amherst: U of Mass Press, 1989
Spoken Texts by and Gab-fests with:
  Cheryl Chisholm on the empowered eye and on colonialist metaphors
  Francoise Pfaff on Tarzan and ethno footage
  Eleanor Traylor on the ancestral place motif in African American literature
  Zeinabu Davis on women paying tribute to women artists
  Clyde Taylor (talks, Whitney Museum Program Notes, articles in *Black Film Review* and elsewhere) on the LA Rebellion.
  A.J. Fiedler's lecture demonstration/screening at the Scribe Video Center's Producers Showcase program in Philly, 1991
  Ayida Tengeman Mthembe, who will be doing forums on the relationship between US policy toward Africa and the representation of Africa, Africans, and African Diasporic people on the commercial screen

9

Spike Lee at the Movies

Amiri Baraka

Writing about Spike Lee presented itself as an idea long ago, as a reaction to seeing the work and the ideas it carries. In this case, like many public people, his work is often linked to his public personality. Analysis would be less honest if both of those factors were not weighed, but usually one does confirm the other, except for those whose works are a mere reference for their personality.

Spike came on the scene as the bearer supposedly of the "experimental" and the innovative—not only the New York University film school, but more positively as a self-produced independent who reignited that ideal of a truly independent Black film presence, as has been struggled for by Greaves, Bourne, Gerima, Harris, and many others since Oscar Micheaux. From the beginning it was clear that Spike meant to do this even while utilizing the "major league" producers and distributors. (A few others have had limited or one shot deals with the majors, for instance, Ivan Dixon, Harry Belafonte, perhaps even recently, Eddie Murphy with his two fine films *Coming to America* and *Harlem Nights*.)

The general concept of an independent Black film practice coming out of an independent Black film movement leading to, hopefully, an independent Black film industry, has been, since Micheaux, the object of many tons of rhetoric and even a few tons of important work. What that would mean, finally, would be to have a completely independent (or *self-determining*) African-American film movement/industry.

"The problem of the 20th Century is the Color Line," said DuBois. This is a century which is, he also pointed out, the age of propaganda. It is part of the fundamental requirement for a Black democracy to have a broad and effective communication front: art, culture, media, journalism, film, and so on, expressing with maximum force and skill the beautiful (albeit tragic) and politically revolutionary (even though drenched in backward-ness) lives, history, and culture of the African-American people.

It is Art that strives to reflect life. What is, is always what's "heaviest." So that reality, its impact on us as *truth*, as stunning actuality, is delivered by art in varied ways: styles and forms. Art is the statement, the content, as a total expression of what is *true, objective*, no matter how fictional it may seem.

What exists is a statement. Its being can be counted and spelled. But unreality is also an actually existing category of being. That is, as an expression, even unreality becomes "a landscape" of its creator's world, as an idea, or a film. Wars are based on delusion.

The real lives we live are countable and spellable as well. And what we do, how we live, who we are, produce our ideas. What we create expresses objectively who we are as much as what we think. Also, in a class society, where and when we exist in terms of the ideology, the views we express, coincides with the dialectical objective world, or not, as an elaboration of real social life.

We do not exist singly, not even in our head. So we are part of many like lives, feelings, ideas, creations, and so on, existing elsewhere. We are voices speaking for the particularity of our registrations, but also products of particular classes. A class is as precise an indicator of a society and its social relations as it is of ourselves (specific to general).

Spike Lee expresses for me a recognizable type and trend in American society. He is the quintessential buppie, almost the spirit of the young, upwardly mobile, Black, petit bourgeois professional. Broadened, he is an American trend. Emerging as an indication of social and class motion, his development is expressed as a political economy, culture, and history.

But Spike has said he did not want to be concerned with history. So, in effect, what he claims as his art is confined to the contemporary moment. Yet who will deny the crushing immediacy as art and social expression of films made on the Middle Passage or Equiano or Douglass or Harriet Tubman? Is there anything "further removed" than Nat Turner's *Confession*? What we locate as "new" is an expression of how much we *knew* at the time!

The history of Black life in America is reflected as a jagged forward and backward, upward and downward, yet on further reflection, forward up in spite. After each revolutionary leap forward: the Black antislavery movement of the nineteenth century leading to the Civil War; the early twentieth century movement against lingering slavery and colonialism which brought Garvey, DuBois, Hughes, Hurston, McKay, The Harlem Renaissance; The 1950s to 1970s Civil Rights and Black Liberation Movement and Malcolm, Dr. King, the Panthers, Baldwin and Hansberry, Trane, Ornette, Cecil, and so on.

After each move upward there is a reaction, the most negative from the corrupt imperialist state and those institutions that were pushed in the superstructure (ideas and art as well as institutions are produced by an economic system fighting to survive).

So, daily, the revolutionary 1960s are attacked, belittled, covered, lied about as an institutional expression of the superstructure! The irony is that often the middle class who most directly benefited from the militant sixties, as far as the ending of legal American apartheid and the increased access to middle-management resources are concerned, not only take it for granted because they have not struggled for this advance, but believe it is Black people's fault that we have not made more progress.

There is a retrograde trend, to paraphrase Lenin after the failure of the 1905 revolution, describing "The Economists," which dismissed political struggle and declared instead that the economic struggle was principal. There is a whole successful school of Negro theater and film personalities whose fundamental identity is as caricaturists of the Black revolutionary politics and art of the 1960s, as if Black consciousness and political activism, and even the most historic and spontaneously creative aspects of the African and African-American culture, are merely Mantan Moreland cartoons.

In some ways I connect Spike with this school. Like Ellison and Ishmael Reed before him, they feel that only the Black middle class, including the "crafty" house slave, is *dignified*. We can, as Mao said, identify in art a class stand, an audience (for whom?), and also those whom the artist implicitly praises and condemns: what he has studied and what he does. Literature, Mao said, was an *ideological reflection of real life*.

She's Gotta Have It was tied to an ingenuous bourgeois feminism (its best "defense"). The reversal Nola practices, as an assertion of equality, is still not "correct," revenge, perhaps, but offered up in the film as an entitlement of her philosophical "freedom." Womanizing among men is negative and needs to be opposed. But manizing by "free" women is also normal conduct in bourgeois society.

And then there are the three men who revolved around Nola—Spike as the "chilly home boy" and young street blood, for whom *life* is apparently simply *a style*. Mars is not serious, for his "irresponsibility" is the character's essence: comic relief. The narcissistic actor Negro was a caricature in most ways, particularly the show window self-lust sex. Likewise, he is not a serious presence, class specific, not a person who escapes generic *type*. The worker who stages the balletic picnic for Nola and seems most nearly to touch on the concerns of real life cannot "hang," and in the end even rapes Nola as a chauvinistic monster. (The idea, " . . . serves her right! . . . " has already been spread through the film copiously. Even other women hated Nola, except the lesbian.)

My concern about the film turns upon the total statements the film makes. The three brothers squatting around a frantic bohemian Negress are who? Part of the chauvinism of most Black men is that they would not sit still for such. So what is the specific function of these guys? Ironically, the sexually freewheeling Black woman is not new; in fact, this echoes the basic slavemaster propaganda. So what are we left with? What is being said about Black women and Black men and the time and place where we live? What is being said is neither new nor progressive.

School Daze continues the "pop" cartoon approach to one segment of Black life. Nothing in the film *lives,* that is, proceeds from the actual connections the statements have to nature and real life. The film seems simply a construction, a composite of scenes to make something like a story, limiting the focus to *effects* so that the characters can remain anonymous and "remarked upon," rather than breathe and assert themselves.

The Mars character continues as much the same figure, now torn by class ambition and family loyalty, belonging to neither of the main social groups on campus, and giving an account of each that distorts and belittles both. The Militant is militant because he "hates light-skinned people." His girl secretly pines to be a "wannabe." In other words the "wannabes" wanna be White, the "Jigaboos" wanna be "wannabes"! So not only don't nobody wanna be Black, the Black community itself is alienated, even threatening to others. (The students only come in contact with the Black community in Kentucky Fried Chicken joints!) The light-skinned/dark-skinned conflict eschews actual class analysis. It is dealt with as "a number," a bit of music, ahistorical and cartoonish, reduced to the beat of a sorority competition.

Though both character development and theme are superficial, we see Mars (later, Mookie, then Giant) awarded this film's "Nola" as a ritual of his entrance into the middle class. Abruptly, the film ends abstractly calling for us to "Wake Up!" in what passes as a "militant" tag, intended to justify the author's confusion by attributing it to the audience (the people). But it's not a real wake-up; it's buppie on the way up.

In the same way, the film presents the Black college as a hipper (?), Blacker *Animal House* (R&B & copulation) while the Black community is shown as a set for *Hill Street Blues,* all animated with the vibes of NY pop art, NYU film school chic.

The drama in this worn-out genre comes through the recognition of topicality à la mode with character types confirming the conclusions of the superstructure, contending only for *their* place in the superstructure, carrying forward that special bourgeois nationalism that the petit bourgeois use for militance!

In *Do the Right Thing*, Mars has become Mookie, the name of a popular

Black ballplayer formerly with the NY Mets. The college student has become a messenger employed by the bourgeoisie, and thereby becomes seemingly the only active worker in the community. We know the artist also is a messenger, here for a "White institution," to convey the people's demand for democracy, belittled as it is by its representation as pictures in a pizza parlor. You have to have your own (pizza parlor?) to have democracy, is the message, confirming that only the owners, the bourgeoisie, can have democracy.

The militant is "bugged out," and the Black scholar is a spastic who annoys people by trying to sell photos of Malcolm and Dr. King. The mainstream political figure Da Mayor is a disillusioned alcoholic unable to understand or accept responsibility. His counsel to Mookie is, "Do the Right Thing." Its source seems to describe its seriousness.

We were told that the film would relate to the Howard Beach lynching. Yet nothing in the film bears witness to this except the rawest opportunism. The youth, Rahim, is murdered and the "riot" initiated because he is playing his radio too loud. But why, since this is not the cause of most poor, Black and Latino youths who are killed by the police? To depict the riot in this way is to assume the stance of the murderers, the State. Like Clifford Glover, Philip Patel, Yusef Hawkins, Emmett Till, and so on, who were murdered for playing their radios too loud. Like Malcolm and Dr. King—For playing their radios too loud!

Rahim is the lone Muslim name (described by Spike in some text as a "Knucklehead," bugged out too!). And Mookie chooses Jessie J. over Farrakhan. His sister warns against a relationship (?) with the White pizza parlor owner, evoking the name of Tawana Brawley, yet Nola is a description of what the State said about Tawana Brawley. The White pizza parlor owners have the only interior lives expressed. The rest are flat pop prototypes.

The killing of Rahim, attributed to the loud radio, trivializes the Black Liberation Movement in the same way that the bugged out movement for Black photos in the pizza parlor does.

Mookie's entrance into the struggle, with the brick, elaborates Spike's class stand with excruciating clarity!—Joining the struggle late and uncommitted yet becoming, de facto, its leader, its most militant force, yet alienated from the Black masses and acting "independently" of them, as some kind of petit bourgeois "leadership"!

Spike's repeated response is that he had no answers to state, that art was, by his definition, vague, general and noncommittal yet could utilize the saleable aspects of Black consciousness as an umbilical cord of social "relevance."

Mo' Better Blues is disappointing because of what it proposes to be about. Alice Coltrane stopped Spike from calling the film *A Love Supreme*, for it is not just about curse words. Alice knows that the music is still a live communicating being, that the world of its creators is a historical and fundamental subtext of Black life, American life, of history and struggle. The past become present—what is. The music is not background. It is "God" as much as anything else! It is being beings in worlds, testing the cosmic, motion as emotion! It is the record of every where and thing it has been. Black Music is the griot's tale, Pres' "story," learning the lyrics of the song, a specific "humanization"!

Like the failure to make the Howard Beach film, the refusal to make *A Love Supreme* as a living expansion of the music is likewise a decision to turn away from real history. Even some attention to the form of Black music would have provided the audience multiple avenues to the film.

Spike's scenes are ponderous and anecdotal. The camera is too passive as a narrative voice and entirely serial and blocked. To do *A Love Supreme*, the philosophy of Trane's music, and himself in relationship to it, would have to be the premise. The emotion in Trane's music is sperm and memory. Love is the highest emotion because it points to the evolving unity of the consciousness, from the base of that which it is the expression of. What is intellectual in Trane is the stance of openness to image and motion as an immediacy, feeling. Spike closes down Trane.

The worlds we carry, our creations, are advertisements of our real lives.

Dumas, Angelou, Baldwin, Hughes, Neal create a literature that uses the music as a probe of history and feeling. Consider the music's "information" alone, from all the different feelings expressed to the social life and history depicted. Consider the spectrum of the "where you at" of a song, its effective life, who and why it was sung, its ideas, the culture that created it, and what it keeps meaning, everyday.

Trane is so important because he carries us beyond "the given." The ideas in his music sear into us as rhythm-made emotion. The feelings are ideas, images, histories. The music itself is a world that must be paralleled both in the form and content of the film! Spike has tacked an anecdotal cautionary tale around the idea (not the spirit) of the music. The music is separate from the people. It is finally merely part of the "environment" of their melodrama, not itself the griot and creator.

The life of John Coltrane, in the simplest meaning of that, is more profound than "Bleek's." (Bleek? Wow! The name itself makes you wonder . . . is the life of music that grim to Spike L., or is it the street in the village that he makes reference to?) The fictional aspect of the film permits no overarching analogies, generalizations. It speaks only of the selfishness and ineffectuality of the artist and his art. The exploiter as nightclub owner, the chastisement as messing up the artist's lip.

The artist abandons his art for the *Black* woman . . . in case you miss

it, her name is Indigo, and that means we know Spike L. also digs (?) at
least Duke's titles (the light-skinned woman she just keeps on being
high Art, even her name ain't stereo-black). The abandoning of a style,
personified as "doing the right thing," exposes its superficial relationship
to real life, Black love, and art, by forcing the artist to abandon his art for
family. As if the two (and Spike L. has made some like comments) cannot
coexist. A bourgeois calumny, but why does Spike push it? The music is
made into a cloak for a bourgeois distortion of what art, what life is. Even
the relationships are skewed in the same way. Spike puts Miles Davis's
criticisms of Trane (that he played too long) in Bleek's mouth about
Shadow, but then he uses Shadow as the mouthpiece of ignorance, putting
Bleek (who is in no stretch of anyone's imagination a Trane-like figure)
down for being too inaccessible to the masses.

Does Spike think that Trane was inaccessible to the masses? Is that why
the most famous piece of music to come out of one of Spike L.'s Joints
is *Da Butt*? Is this why *My Favorite Things* was on the hit parade? What
was inaccessible to the masses was the high-priced nightclubs (owned by
the "Hackensacks" *and* the PaterSonnis) that the musicians are forced to
play in, usually in "White neighborhoods."

Trane was an innovator, pursuing one of the revolutionary modes of
struggle to transform society. Class struggle, the struggle for production, is
like a scientific experiment. Not all scientific experiments are immediately
understandable to the masses, even though what comes out of them might
be critically needed by them.

Trane was prying our music the rest of the way away from its Tin Pan
Alley lock-up. He was expressing that part of our Black-ass selves that is
not locked up and enslaved. That's why he generated such tremendous
controversy and power. But to drop, nay droop slyly the "inaccessible to
the masses" tip on Trane as an excuse for commerce and stale hops is jive.

I think this is one reason why the music is not taken on straight ahead,
and the great classics of African-American musical statement are used so
sparsely. The discography cited by the musicians playing in the film is
particularly chilling because it is so limited and parochial and "contemporary" in the sense of its temporal structure. Max Roach in the same
publication, of course, gives some sense of the entire classical scope of
the music.

That some commentators raised "anti-Semitism" because the aggressively negative club owners were Jewish is humorous and irritating. Now
Spike joins Farrakhan, Jesse J. and Mandela as enemies of humanity and
supporters of the Holocaust! It is an indication of the utter ruthlessness of
imperialism that it accuses its victims of being it!

What *Mo' Better* suffers from is a failure to understand the expression of the social that art is, and the emotional depth of real life. Tell the *Love Supreme* story in the context of "The Great Satan"! Tell how it is connected, yet objectively descriptive.

The essential centers of Spike's films are always in contradiction to the metaphor of his announced themes. *Mo' Better* tells us domestic life defies art and the music is an expendable environmental phenomenon—not the song of human history!

Mo' Better avoids open caricature, at least for the central characters forming the triangle (though the band is still cartoonish, ditto Spike's own returning trademark nigger nebbish . . . Giant? no shit . . . as in *Giant Steps*?), but uses a superficial narrative melodrama to disconnect art from human necessity. The musicians are a performance motif, abstract paradigms, who can be analyzed without understanding what they use their lives to create!

Bleek, as the flip side of Nola, says that his male chauvinism is "a dick thing." You can hear Nola saying that her chauvinism is "a pussy thing." But even that would have sounded like heavy theory in *She's Gotta Have It*! The conversation Bleek has with his father about sex and about father-and-son relationships is stunning, it is so sick. "Who taught you how to satisfy a woman?" says Pops, then later "who taught you to suck a sweet lucious juicy tender nipple . . . ?"

All the social relationships, if stitched together in paraphrase, are neurotic. And who is the nigger nebbish who returns and returns, this time as a pitiful excuse for those who think they need one for using White agents and business managers? "Giant" is another baleful comment on Black self-determination, as irresponsible as Mars and School Daze Dog; as mock important, yet *alienated* as Mookie (he is not an artist, he is the Negro version of the Hackensacks).

The opening and closing statements of the film (a little boy wanting to go out and play but forced to practice the horn) are Frank Capra-type cliches that draw immediate attention to the pedestrian "story" Spike drapes in front of the music. But what and whose story is Spike telling? Even the real "giant" whose hype had inspired (?) the film could not even remotely be the model, nor Diz, nor Monk, nor Duke, not even Miles or Bud.

There is some homage paid to the artist's "selfishness" once Bleek's lip is smashed and the light-skinned artist lady leaves for Shadow (!) who, Spike tells us, is more mass-oriented than Bleek, and so Bleek is forced to return to Indigo. So Shadow and the light-skinned lady get the art (together). Giant gets to be Moe and Joe Flatbush's doorman (the fate of Black enterprise?), and Bleek and Indigo have a baby Bleek all over again, rolling out with the Capra rerun.

So my continuing disappointment is that Spike has not appropriated the living anima of his "subjects." They are not "themes" because they do not reproduce themselves as ubiquitous summations of action. At best, Spike's films restate, often inaccurately, the place of our present. But Spike has never offered any new registrations or heightened understanding. It is all a simple acknowledgment of common popular reference, sometimes without the slightest penetration of the class disposition it reinforces.

The reason Sal gives Mookie his bread after the riot is because Mookie appears to confirm the injustice and the hurt done to Sal.

Racism is left as accident and misunderstanding. And who gives it succor, even as an object of benign sympathy, hides its reality, and conforms to its demands? Mookie is "classed off" from the rest of the wild, destructive, unemployed bloods, so he can return and explain the madness to Sal and the rest of us and even get paid for his concern. It is enough that we can dismiss it as a heat wave or the reaction of a hostile Black youth, his hands tatooed ("love and hate") like the murdering preacher Robert Mitchum plays in *The Night of the Hunter*. The dichotomy of Bleek's relationship with Indigo and Clarke is instructive. Clarke (male name, non-Afro name, light-skinned) is the artist, the independent; Indigo carries only her stylized Blackness as a lure to drag the Black artist away from his art, creating a polarity between her art and life as simple-minded as any bourgeois delusion.

We are always responsible for our own failure.

10
Spike Lee and the Commerce of Culture

Houston A. Baker, Jr.

"Brother Homer, wake up. The Black man has been sleeping for four hundred years." Zacharias Homer—a Black Brooklyn barber whose partner has recently been executed by gangsters—is, thus, summoned to a rendezvous with Nicholas Lovejoy. Lovejoy is both an ironic St. Nicholas, and a sinister Lovejoy, playing the broker/boss of the numbers trade in Bedford-Stuyvesant. He tells Homer that numbers are the poor man's stock market, a game that transforms dreams into reality.

In Spike Lee's award-winning student film *Joe's Bed-Stuy Barber Shop: We Cut Heads*, numbers have, indeed, financed the social work degree of Homer's wife Ruth and purchased a new organ for Bethel Church. The downside of the game, however, is that numbers have produced dreams and greed that bring about the execution of Homer's partner Joe. Even as we read the blue and red neon sign that opens *Joe's Bed-Stuy Barber Shop* on a rainy night in Brooklyn, Joe is about to disappear into the Hudson, dressed in the concrete mantle of a mob killing. This is film noir, as my colleague Manthia Diawara points out,[1] with a vengeance, setting up anxieties and expectations that betoken a Chester Himesian moralism.[2]

Lee's film, however, despite the implicit moral of Joe's death, is not a didactic lament filled with dark sobriety and improving maxims. *Joe's* funky humor manifests itself almost immediately, as the gangsters who force the barber into their car tune into New York's WBLS and fill the car with soul. As they prepare to kill Joe, he pleads: "Don't do this, man. How many times did I hook you up with a *great* cut?!" Music, humor, and medium, thus, combine to place us in the middle of a black, serio-comedic tale of culture and commerce.

The texture of the film is grainy, muffled, slightly unfocused, giving the "joint" (as Lee designates his productions) an air of both realism and low-budget independence. But any expectations of boredom or technical incompetence occasioned by this economical look are defeated by the film's perfect pacing, and rich cultural allusions and performances.

Before the first visual appears, we hear two Black male voices signifying—playing the dozens—sounding on each other's mothers and sisters. And when light comes up on Joe's shop, we hear the distinctive, low, musical signifying of the Black, southern, country blues. The blues give way to easy-listening jazz as the camera focuses on the shop's interior. First, a price list, then a poster of a nude Black woman appear before the camera pans to Joe. The urban, inner-city barbershop is, thus, quickly imbricated in a collage of Black music, sexuality, culture, commerce, and criminality.

As a traditional locale for Black male cosmetic and oratorical splendor, the barbershop has served the Afro-American community much as the baobab serves male elders in Africa. The barbershop, that is to say, is the source of Black male news, views, and revenues. And Joe has run his shop as—in the words of Lovejoy—"a valuable property." The sale of numbers has accounted for a very significant portion of his income, and Lovejoy has been the overseer of this commerce.

Zacharias Homer, however, who is Joe's survivor, is an idealist and a purist. Once he has placed a black wreath on his partner's barber chair with a banner that reads "We'll Miss You Joe," he is determined to run a clean shop. There will be no chemically processed hair, and no numbers. What Zach fails to reckon is that his idealism will also mean no customers. Day after day, he sits in the immaculate shop with nothing to do. His wife urges two courses of action. She first suggests that he do jerry curls in order, as she phrases it, to make "some of that curly green." Alternatively, she suggests that the two of them return to the South. She urges Atlanta as a place that will satisfy her own need for space in which to "stretch out." Ruth's ambivalent capitalism and nostalgia thus vie with Zach's Black urban idealism.

As a social worker, Ruth has had her fill of poor tenements and domestic impoverishment. Like other voices in *Joe's*, she doesn't believe that Bed-Stuy is "going to make it." Though Zach and Ruth share a passionate love scene, the idealistic barber is in a bind where his marriage is concerned. The wake-up call from Lovejoy comes at precisely the moment when his spirits and options are at their lowest. Entrepreneurship-in-blackface moves aggressively to the foreground as Zach is half-forced, half-delighted to accept Lovejoy's numbers proposition.

Joe's shop once again becomes a place of commerce, bringing droves of customers for cuts and numbers. Thadeous Powell, a delinquent whom Ruth has urged Zach to employ, oversees the numbers business at Joe's. Nicknamed "Teapot," he is a generational counterpoint to Zach. He possesses the wisdom and vocabulary of the streets, but also a desire to be a photographer.

When all the major characters have, thus, been introduced along with the film's major themes, we are positioned to encode *Joe's Bed-Stuy Barber Shop* with Black cultural and commercial significance. The drama that unfolds is set in a deteriorating, Black urban world that seems entirely removed from a dominant White culture. If White people have anything to do with the quotidian rituals of Bed-Stuy, we are not immediately aware of them. The world of the film is thus hermetic, taking on a parodic, nationalistic cast as Lovejoy proclaims the numbers a separate but equal version of Wall Street finance. Zach, in a similarly culturally separatist reading of American economics, aspires to the status of independent small businessman rendering a service that both relies upon and preserves a nonassimilationist look for Black America.

Zach and Lovejoy are undone, however, by a distinctively White American desire. For Lovejoy, as I have suggested, is a parody of both White capitalists and the White organized-crime boss. Rather than creating, shaping, and channeling the desires of the Black community, he merely provides an agency for temporarily sublimating them. And the community's principal desire remains commensurate with the White American dream. Further, Lovejoy's ability to provide even this sublimation depends, ultimately, upon the complicity of indigenous Black institutions such as the barber shop and the church. (Remember Bethel's new organ.)

That is to say, Lovejoy has no real property nor control in Bed-Stuy; he is merely the lightning-rod man for White materialistic desire in black-face. His commerce, then, is always a secondary agency, relying entirely upon what White America wants Black America to want.

Part of what White America desires, of course, is for Black America to believe "the hype" encoded in an ideology of Yankee ingenuity and bootstrap individualism. It is this ideology of independence and business-of-America-is-business entrepreneurship that Zach adopts as his ideal. He is—as a result—a somewhat deceived and naive man who strains viewer credibility. We are expected to believe, for example, that he is the only person in Bed-Stuy ignorant of his partner Joe's numbers transactions. Despite the bold signs advertising numbers that Zach himself puts up in the shop after he cuts a deal with Lovejoy, we are asked to believe that Joe's successor did not know how the barbershop was really financed.

And even if we are willing seriously to strain our belief, Zach still appears a somewhat improbably idealistic figure. He plays the role of a Black businessman who refuses to adapt his business practices (his style) to the changing desires of his customers or to adjust his social vision to comprehend the presence and implications of the numbers trade in Brooklyn.

In a word, Zach comes off as a stubborn, but somewhat stupid character whose consciousness seems always on the perimeter of the community in which he lives. He is the middleman of culture and commerce rather than the creative agent of either.

Who, then, operates the flow of Bed-Stuy life?

I believe that the posters of nude Black women that we see in Joe's shop provide some hint that the controlling agency lies in the province of desire. The posters are in the place of Black financial commerce, and they circulate as mere objects in the gaze of barbershop customers—and also, of course, in the gaze of theater audiences for Lee's film.

The posters seem to advertise the body of Black women as public spectacles for consumption by those who have the means to pay. As all poster art, these nudes are hyperbolical, super-idealized renditions of a peculiar form of "Black beauty." They are not renditions of "African princesses" (Lovejoy's designation for Ruth when he pays an unexpected visit to Zach's house). Rather, they are parodic imitations of White, pornographic poster art found in such public, traditionally male spaces as locker-rooms and service stations. They represent nothing tangibly Black and obtainable; they are merely an incorporation of Blackness into the sexual/consumption networks operated by a White visual economy. What you see is, thus, precisely what you can never get. What you see is, instead, what you are conditioned slavishly to desire.

In a very brief scene in *Joe's Bed-Stuy Barber Shop*, we see Teapot moving across an urban landscape that appears cleaner and more wholesome than the precincts of Joe's shop. Suddenly, the adolescent comes upon a Black male photographer and his Black woman model. The model takes off her coat and begins to assume various poses, her straightened hair and sheer dress blowing in the wind. The photographer shouts to the preening, mulatto model: "The American woman is going to love you."

It is at this decisive moment in the film that Teapot knows his life's work—he is going to become a photographer.

The scene with the model has, I would suggest, the quality of a primal scene of memory and desire. For clearly the "love" that the photographer has in mind is far more akin to consumption—the devouring—of nude, poster images through an economy of the gaze than to a spiritual *agape*. The photographer might just as well have said: "They are going to eat you up."

If Lovejoy is correct that ninety-nine percent of the American economy is comprised by consumers, then what Black folks consume is a secondary desire bought at a very high price, indeed. The price is, in fact, their very selves/bodies bequeathed to the consumptive maw of a spectatorial White economy. They seem self-willingly to exoticize themselves, becoming the other-who-is-not-wholly-other. Hence, they are willing to make themselves palatable for a White diet.

Thus, while Blacks busily move toward chemically processed hair and mulatto nudity, Whites rub their stomachs awaiting exotic morsels. What is implied is a veritable moveable feast of culture, commerce, and consumption. This feast is made explicit through the recounted dream/nightmare of one of Lee's characters. Silas relates his nightmare to a fellow barbershop occupant.

Silas says that he is the victim of a recurrent dream in which all the chocolate in the world has disappeared and all of the coffee as well. Moreover, he has become the only Black person left on earth. As he moves cautiously through Brooklyn streets, he is spotted by a mob of Whites. The mob gives chase, and Silas describes his flight through sections and boroughs of New York until, exhausted at last, he is trapped at Coney Island. He screams for mercy, but the mob is insistent, relentless. They move in and begin chewing him. "They just couldn't stand being without that chocolate," says Silas.

Here consumption and primal desire are rolled into a single frame. "See you later, Hershey Bar," says Silas's listener as the dream narrator rises to leave the shop. The listener might have parroted the Black male photographer encountered earlier and said: "Boy, America is going to eat you up!"

The great amusement-park game of the White mob is cultural, commercial, and sexual cannibalism of the other-who-is-not-wholly-other.

How does one resist such cannibalism in a Bed-Stuy context?

Well, the nude posters rather indicate that an archetypal, nativist response is to confront the gods of culture and commerce in the way that the women of Toni Morrison's *Sula* relate to the vengeful omnipresence in their lives: "They danced and screamed, not to protest God's will but to acknowledge it and confirm once more their conviction that the only way to avoid the Hand of God is to get in it."[3] To become a handmaiden of the lord is to buy into his schemes of exoticization—to make one's self over in the image of his desire.

To a very great extent, this is what "Lovejoy" (a perfect designation for the exoticized other!)—and, through Lovejoy's secondary agency, much of Bed-Stuy—has done. Lovejoy and his Bed-Stuy adherents have relinquished Southern blues and non-chemical hair in order to circulate profitably in easy-listening, slick, mulatto economies of the urban ghetto. They are *owned* colored folks blessed with plenty of nothing.

By contrast, the barber Zach who attempts to make it on his own is stymied by secondary Black desire in his very household, in the form of a wife who is, as I suggested earlier, culturally ambivalent. Ruth is the mulatto social worker who has earned a numbers-financed degree in order to serve the Black, urban community. But she is also the person who demands that Zach give up his idealism and make the "curly green."

Ruth is further complicated as a character by her desire to return to the

South and to Southern blues. It is finally a combination, it seems to me, of her desire for money *and* the South (in combination, of course, with Lovejoy's violent insistence) that forces Zach to give up his idealism and enter the numbers game.

And to enter the game is to lose. Zach is quickly driven to the same mentality as Joe. He attempts to abscond with Lovejoy's money in order to make an escape with Ruth to Atlanta. His attempt fails because Ruth reveals Zach's intentions to Lovejoy. Trapped like Silas in the secondary economies of Black America, Zach gives the money back to Lovejoy, passes one of the first-class tickets to Atlanta that he has purchased to Ruth, and sharpens the proverbial Black razor to resist any attempt by Lovejoy to compel him to turn over the barbershop's lease.

But if the foregrounded plot of secondary desire that I have just described is one of either failed or barely financed Black cultural idealism and resistance, there is another, more successful plot in the film. This plot relies upon a thematization of Black artistic/creative desire. When Zach is preparing to abscond, he shares some of Lovejoy's money with Teapot, telling the young boy to get out of town and lay low for a couple of weeks.

But when Zach's plans are foiled and he awakens on the day after Ruth's departure and Lovejoy's threats of violence to the barbership, he awakens to the sound of Teapot opening the shop. Around Teapot's neck is a sparkling, new, Nikon camera. He has purchased the camera, of course, with the money Zach gave him.

To his native rebelliousness and street wisdom, the formerly truant delinquent has added a fine imagistic instrumentality. He has obtained the means of production of the cultural image. And we know that Teapot fully understands the nature of White desire in relationship to image production and circulation.

Told by Zach that he may be in for violence if Lovejoy's goons invade the shop to intimidate or kill the barber, Teapot responds: "Then I'll just take a picture of your bullet-riddled body and sell it to the *Post*."

Zach looks up in appreciative amusement and says: "Make sure you give 'em a good shot for the front page."

Prior to this exchange, Zach has ordered Teapot to "take down all that shit," meaning the advertisements for the numbers, and, perhaps, the nude photos of Black women as well.

In any case, what is certain is that the tempest is now assuredly out of the teapot and empowered for cultural production. Earlier in the film, after the scene with the model, Teapot says: "I'm a real photographer," and Zach responds "That ain't no real camera."

And, truly, the nature of *reality* in Black, cultural terms is precisely what is imagistically at stake where the economies of desire are concerned in *Joe's Bed-Stuy Barber Shop*. The film seems, finally, to imply that imagistic control of the Black communal image has been seized by a younger generation that remains, nevertheless, connected with its older generational counterpart. At the conclusion of the film, Zach the barber and Teapot the image maker are in solid commerce within the valorized cultural space of the barbershop, engaged in one familiar cultural pastime of such shops—a game of checkers.

A full reading of the final scene of *Joe's* might suggest that it is only by exposing the secondariness of Black desire as a function of cannibalistic White economies, that one is able to create conditions of possibility for Black imagistic realism. The downside of this strong reading is that such Black *exposé* and achievement are patently at the expense of Black women as professionals, cultural workers, or marriage partners.

For the economies that rule at the end of *Joe's Bed-Stuy Barber Shop* are clearly ones of Black male bonding. They stress, as well, only a potential *Black male* control of imagistic, cultural production.

Ruth has returned to a reified South. The Black woman model seen in the film is scarcely in possession of her own image. She appears merely to be an object before the photographer's lens. She neither speaks nor reports.

Still, I would argue that the filmmaker of *Joe's Bed-Stuy Barber Shop* has managed to extrapolate, from the deteriorating, grainy, muffled landscapes of a Bed-Stuy that doesn't look like it is "going to make it," the possibility of a Black artistic reinstitutionalization of Black commerce and culture. To retrieve from Black urban blight the possibility of a *different* Black desire and its attendant creativity is, to be sure, an empowering reverie. And, in truth, the agency of the Black professional woman, Ruth—who does, after all, single Teapot out and force her husband to hire him—is paramount in this reverie.

Teapot is part of the emergent Black generation that is pictured jamming to the sounds of a powerful box in the lobby of the tenement building that Ruth visits. The adolescent is also the person who teaches a young, Black male friend how precisely to deliver self-defensive lines of street knowledge.

If Teapot's generation commits a purse-snatching assault on Ruth, it also seems bent on preserving certain Black cultural energies and possibilities of *imagistic control* in a Bed-Stuy where PS 142, Bethel Church, and even the barbershop itself are threatened with extinction.

To take control is to put real cameras in young, Black hands. The aim, then, is to alter the imagistic menu and diet of American culture. In a word, to tie into the politics of cultural consumption as a Black photographer, or filmmaker, in America is to change the joke and slip the yoke of White desire.

And changing the joke means, finally, to possess the ironic, creative detachment of a consumable "other" among aggressive chocoholics. In a sense, the goal is to possess a Black creative ability akin to the performance of Silas, the character who, of course, converts the nightmare of cannibalizing desire into an ironic, knowledgeable, self-defensive cultural narrative performance. *Joe's Bed-Stuy Barber Shop* suggests such ability from its first signifying to its concluding, cross-generational tableau. What Zach Homer awakens to is literally in the film's unfolding frames, Teapot with camera in hand—a *real* Black photographer bent on new images. Zach, one might say, awakens to the possibilities of his own Black culture reinstitutionalized.

And what more opportune site could exist for such reinstitutionalization than the posterized, public spectacle of the Black woman?

It seems incumbent for this woman to appear before an astutely more informed lens than any appearing in *Joe's* if the commerce of an authentically Black cultural order is to be successful.

The Black male awakening of *Joe's Bed-Stuy Barber Shop* seems both to forecast and demand its Black woman counterpart. And it can come as no surprise to theatergoers that Lee's second independent film opens with the awakening of a beautiful Black woman, divesting herself of bedcovers and assuring us that *she* has set the terms for her appearance before the camera. Hers is not the objectified presence of a barbershop poster, but a presence with an object—to set the record straight, in her own voice and image, of who precisely she is. This is Nola Darling. She represents Black woman's desire incarnate. Hers is a vision quest for the elusive "it" that provides human satisfaction. The film that brings her to us is *She's Gotta Have It*, the second effort produced by Lee's "Forty Acres and a Mule Filmworks."

The voices that we hear in advance of the visuals in *Joe's Bed-Stuy Barber Shop* constitute a field of allusion, gesturing toward a world of cultural meanings that the film seeks to explore or to gain a purchase upon. This Black male, culturally specific signifying is complemented at the beginning of *She's Gotta Have It* by the words and their implicitly Black woman's world of Zora Neale Hurston's novel *Their Eyes Were Watching God*[4]:

> Ships at a distance have every man's wish on board. For some they come in with the tide. For others they sail forever on the horizon, never out of sight, never landing until the Watcher turns his eyes away in resignation, his dreams mocked to death by Time. That is the life of men.
>
> Now, women forget all those things they don't want to remember, and remember everything they don't want to forget. The dream is the truth. Then they act and do things accordingly.

As an epigraph, Hurston's lines seem to announce the possibility of a filmic equivalent to *Their Eyes Were Watching God*, which is most adequately characterized, I think, as a Black woman's fictional autobiography. Hurston's protagonist, Janie Crawford, structures her account of her own living as a selective, autobiographical telling of a poetical dream life. Mining the unconscious economies of Black woman's desire, Janie manages to provide a self-portrait that has little to do with the public construction and "truth" of her life that circulates on the preeminently male porch of her second husband's store. As the teller of herself and her story, Janie comes out from under the covering narratives of others and takes both aural and visual control of a unique field of meanings. Presumably, Janie's course of cultural narration is what Spike Lee alludes—no, *aspires*—to for Nola Darling.

Before we actually see Nola in Lee's film, we are presented with black-and-white stills of inner-city life. The light of this landscape is sharp and clear, unlike the grainy shadows of *Joe's*. Life here is not realistically in motion. Instead, it has the formal definition of posed classicality. This is the world of the practiced photographer come of age, rather than the rough texture and predictable segues of the student filmmaker. A mature Teapot might enjoy being credited with such representation.

When Nola is finally before us, she says that she has consented to the film for one reason only—to clear herself of the charge "freak" (a sexually deviant and overly desirous person) levelled by others against her. She says, in fact, that she hates the very word "freak." Identifying the protagonist—and all other principal characters in the film—is a captioning name in bold letters set out by the filmmaker. These names and the bold black and white of the film print give the work the air of a documentary addressed specifically to us—the viewers. We, thus, become both chorus and jury in Lee's production, and I believe we are meant to place Nola at the center of our concern.

For she is, after all, the creator figure of the film. She is not only an autobiographer, but also an artist of collage. Like Romare Bearden, or like those countless generations of Black women quilt makers, Nola is able to create meaningful wholes out of fragments and patches. In her room, dominating the wall space of her apartment and immediately adjacent to her bed, is the huge collage entitled "May 19."

The date is both Nola's and Malcolm X's birthday, and the collage that bears it as a title is much like a Black woman's *Guernica*. The faces, mouths, and hands of the figures are exaggerated in the manner of Picasso's (and Bearden's) art, and the newspapers with their headlines that collage with these figures speak of disaster. The slaying of Blacks is the theme, and Nola's creation carries the scenic weight of a Black creative response to the deaths of Edmund Perry, Eleanor Bumpers, and Michael Griffiths.

It is Nola, then, who gives resonance to the unspeakable cannibalization of a White, dominant, indeed murderous, economy. Malcolm's birth/life understood and energetically and meaningfully collaged with present-day, creative understanding can produce a fruitful awakening.

Like Nola, we awaken in viewing the film to "May 19."

And perhaps it is because there is this energizing and self-created representation of Black understanding as tutelary spirit in her apartment that Nola says: "I can only do it in my own bed." The *place* of Nola Darling is clearly self-created, and her very own in its resonant creativity.

But like Hurston's Janie, Nola is in search of more than a solipsistic autobiography, a contemplative life, or a nationalistic art of collage. We see in a still shot of graffiti on a Bed-Stuy wall the message: "Bed-Stuy Party, Inc. Advocates that Brooklyn secede from Union, USA, America, Form own Republic Draw up New Constitution." It does not seem, however, to be a new political republic that Nola is after. In fact, much of the semantic weight of the movie hinges on Nola's not so much wanting any specific thing as *desiring* "it"—that nth variable that her therapist Dr. Jamison calls "love."

Hurston's Janie repudiates her first husband Logan Killicks because he is a grotesque of Black male ownership who secretly feels that Janie is too good for him. He therefore attempts to reduce her to the status of a mule. Her second and third husbands seek respectively to place Janie on a pedestal as a prized (mulatto) possession not unlike a poster, and to turn her into a playmate in a jealously Black male love game. Neither Joe Starks nor Vergible Woods ever quite comes to comprehend Janie or to acknowledge her creative independence.

Similarly, Jamie Overstreet, Mars Blackmon, and Greer Childs of *She's Gotta Have It* can provide only partial satisfaction for Nola's desire. Their shortcoming, like that of Huston's men, is their egocentric quest for total possession. They, in a very real sense, want to take over Nola's apartment, body, bed, and turn her into poster art that would, presumably, displace "May 19." Nola says to Mars: "How come every time I let a guy up here they want to move in?" And toward the close of the film, Nola is reflexively before us, concluding her own autobiographical tale as an exegete. She tells us that we have been privileged to hear of her life from people who "claim" to know what makes Nola tick. But, she qualifies these claims with the words "I think they might know parts of me."

Of course, this is precisely the rub: people know only *parts* of Nola. And unlike Nola herself, those who claim to *know* "parts" have not mastered the art of collage. Hence, each of her suitors seeks to impose his own image rather than to labor at the sparkling diversity and always excessive plurality of parts that make Nola "darling."

A woman who has "crawled backward" against the common grain of life until she learned to walk—a woman who in Sonny Darling's house went to sleep and arose to Black musical creativity—finds it intolerable to envision her magnificent excess frozen into a confining Black male image of possession. Though Nola is cast into self-doubt by her suitors' charges against her, she comes finally to realize that her *dreams*—and not men's *wishes*—are the genuine stuff of her being-in-the-world.

The interpretation that I have presented of Nola Darling's filmic autobiography can lead to the impression that the work is merely allegorical feminism. Again, my attention to Hurston's novel might imply that I wish to minimize Lee's originality by situating *She's Gotta Have It* in a web of novelistic anxiety and influence. But I do not wish either to take away from Lee's originality or to overallegorize his second film. Too much is missed by such an approach, not the least of which is that deft art of the comedic exposé present in Lee's oeuvre from the outset.

Always going beneath the covering sentimentality, and forever breaking the quiet silences of Black, middle-class respectability, Lee unmasks those truths that Black people know to be self-evident, but seldom have the courage to speak of—much less to trumpet in the outrageous manner of, say, Chaucer's "The Miller's Tale."

Lee is, it seems to me, an irreverent advocate of the desacralizing fart in church, or the pomposity-deflating belch in the face of royalty. He is—in the Black vernacular reading of the words—*nasty*, cold as ice, and a man (to quote Ice-T) whose lethal weapon is his mind.

In *She's Gotta Have It*, we are presented with marvelously funny cameos like the gallery of Black male sweet-mouthers who attempt to convince the Black woman to have sex with them. What we are presented with is a gallery of "originals," not unlike a rogues gallery from some eighteenth-century, picaresque novel. The men represent Nola's perception of "what is out there," so to speak, by way of Black manhood. This strikingly funny cameo concludes aurally with a pack of barking dogs. Lee calls it, in fact, his "Dog" jump-cut sequence. *Touché*, Spike Lee!

But the filmmaker is evenhanded in his art of the outrageous. Later in *She's Gotta Have It*, Nola has a dream/nightmare that is directly equivalent to the reverie of Silas. Three Black women burst into her apartment, calling her names and ranking her personality. "Homewrecker," "bitch," woman who only has sex with *their* men, corrupter of Black manhood—these are the charges the women level. Each woman is the significant "other other" (since Blackmon, Childs, and Overstreet are all supposed to be emotionally bonded to Nola) of her suitors.

What shall they do with Nola, they ask. "Let's set the bitch on fire!" is what they decide as Nola wakes up in a panic.

Neither men nor women in the Black community are capable of fruitfully collaging with Nola. She escapes their comprehension, eludes their possessiveness on, and provokes their wrath. The most unfocused and brutal assault on her comes, paradoxically, from Jamie Overstreet. I say "paradoxically" because Jamie is identified by Nola as the exception to the chorus of Black male dogs speaking lies. He is the romantic poet, the man who tells Nola that he will do whatever she wants and take her wherever she wants to go. But he is also in *She's Gotta Have It* the Black man as rapist.

When Nola summons Jamie to her house, saying that she needs him and that it is important that he come, the romantic is in bed with Ava, a dancer of his acquaintance. He has half given up on Nola as the fulfillment of his desires. Hence, he is confused, angry, and vengeful about the ability of Nola to make him agree to come to her bed, her place of exclusive ownership. He enters her apartment like a marauder and rapes her, fantasizing in the act the two other suitors and demanding from the pained woman an acknowledgement that her sex organs belong to him. He then concedes that he enjoyed *dogging* Nola. He, thus, plunges as thunderingly into the abyss of Black male caninity as the grossly offensive speakers seen in the earlier jump-cut.

What is wrong with Jamie?

He is, says Nola, a man driven by White-dominant fantasies from a Dick-and-Jane world of romantic love, the girl next door, monotheism and monogamy. All of these descriptors are "virtues" carved from a Western, materialistic necessity to keep every *thing* in the family. Jamie is an escaped rapist from the myth of romantic love. And he is doubly cursed, because the possessive arrangements of an ideology of romantic love were a bad, White male idea in the first instance. Circulated into the Black world, they become as lethal in their effects as the secondary desire of Black poster art in a Bed-Stuy barber shop. Mars Blackmon is essentially correct, then, when he is segued into a recitation by Jamie of one of his poems for Nola. Mars says: "That's the worst piece of shit I've ever heard . . . he ain't got no rap."

The Black male as street urchin and fly rapper is deconstructed in the person of Mars. Greer Childs is a stunning caricature of the "refined" Black man of yuppie predilections. He is Joe Starks without a pot to pee in, a man who has only his looks and his pretensions to buoy him up. When he spends tedious minutes folding his clothes into creased neatness while African rhythms pound ever more furiously and a nude Nola awaits his presence in bed, we are fully aware of Greer's ridiculousness.

But what of the other women in *She's Gotta Have It*? Clorinda Bradford and Opal Gilstrap are, respectively, a Black woman musician and a lesbian friend anxious to sleep with Nola. Clorinda has been Nola's roommate, but has been unable to comprehend her insatiable appetites. Opal wishes merely to initiate Nola into the rites of female love. Finally, neither of these women seems to have the "darling" qualities that make Nola an exception. It is Dr. Jamison, the therapist, who seems an intellectual and emotional match for Nola. Her Black woman's wisdom is that Nola's desire is not a pathological drive, but a healthy sexuality. It is Dr. Jamison who says that a full Black woman's "sexuality" is a desirable goal that can only be achieved by that most beautiful of "sex" organs—the mind. "Your beautiful sex organ is between your ears, not your legs," says Dr. Jamison.

Jamison's injunction can be narratively interpreted as: "To achieve a full Black woman's sexuality, you must be creatively in charge of your own narrative." In a word, the Black woman must bring her plurality out from under the covers and be an affective, intellectual, and, finally, political master of collage. Though she is beautifully incarnate desire in *She's Gotta Have It*, Nola allegorically signifies that elusive "it" that both creates and follows the dream defined as Black woman's territory. As a representation, she displaces the Black finance and entrepreneurship of *Joe's Bed-Stuy Barber Shop* with desire. Her story is the subtext made master code in the interpretation of the Black community. Lee, that is to say, finds his filmic subject in the subject of the Black woman climbing decisively out of the bed of everyone else's "freakish" fantasies, in order to recode what precisely her dreams signify in American economies of the gaze. Inverting the poet Margaret Walker's injunction, Lee seems to suggest that a race of women must now rise and take control. And certainly, Nola Darling's life, as she tells it, suggests a control of Black interests and images that is only vaguely present in the filmmaker's first effort.

Lee's first films are low-budget, minor masterpieces of cultural undercover work. They find the sleeping or silenced subject and deftly awaken him or her to consciousness of currents that run deep and signify expansively in Black America. Of course, the viewer—particularly the directly addressed viewer of *She's Gotta Have It*—is implicated in this process of awakening. The unspoken and unseen resonances of Black cultural life are often hilariously put before us as punchy one-liners such as Mars' quip to Greer Childs: "What do you know anyway? You're a Celtics fan." At times, the cultural signifying is as wide as a catalogue, like Zach's typology of heads including "log-head, rock-head, arrowhead, water-head, peanut-head, pudding-head, etc." This is a typology to which we could surely add Mars' derogatory "sixteen-piece chicken McNugget head" directed at a rival suitor.

We are assured by such in-group signifying that Lee is down with the Black cultural program. It is his larger thematizations, however, that enable us to rank him among the creative company of Black American artists and intellectuals who have dedicated themselves and their works to cultural

critique. Lee is not simply interested in displaying a dope cultural awareness, but also in awakening his audience to the hype, danger, and pitfalls
that accompany a complicitous Black silence before White, Western courts
of power and desire.

Now, it is not that Lee's films are devastatingly original, telling us
always things we do not know. What is striking about his work is that it
is, in fact, so thoroughly grounded in what we *all* know, but refuse to
acknowledge, speak, regret, or change.

The strong kernel of critique in his films removes him decisively, I
think, from the cult of art-for-art's-sake campness and the Afrocentric
posturings and Black filmic extravagance (or ennui) of neo-Black-Arts
cinematics. Serio-comedic realism combines with allegorical thematizations in his films to produce a cinematics of Black reveille.

The reveille becomes a clear filmic moment at the conclusion of Lee's
third film, *School Daze*, an effort that witnessed Lee's transition from
independent production to studio agency at Columbia Pictures. *School
Daze* was a much-heralded event for young, Black theatergoers, and the
fame of its giant dance scene in which the EU Band made "Da Butt" a
national dance ran far ahead of the film's general popularity. I remember
a Philadelphia deejay asking one of his call-ins to discuss Lee's movie.
All the young man could say was: "Did you check out that dance, man?
Did you see it? Da Butt is hip." Of course, the up-front intentionality of
School Daze has to do with Black institution-building in America. The
opening visuals of slave ships, coffles, one-roomed Southern shanties lead
into a photographic catalogue of Black leaders, intellectuals, and earnestly
well-scrubbed Black students and workers. The accompanying song for
these visuals is "I'm Going to Build Me a Home," sung Roland Hayes-
style. The institution that comes metonymically to stand for all Black
homebuilding is the Black college, called Mission College in Lee's film.

Now the idea of all of this is as appealing as Lee's previous mining of
Black cultural themes and institutions, but the actual execution of the
film seems to me an uneven admixture of brilliant cameos of cultural
signification and tedious pandering to weak clichés. What is most perplex-
ing to a viewer who has seen *She's Gotta Have It* is the almost complete
erasure from *School Daze* of even a hint of the creatively independent
Black woman. True, Lee is concerned in his third film with the Black,
bourgeois imitation of White fraternal and sororal conformity—the mindless subjugation of the body and soul to initiatory brutality in the name of
"brotherhood" or "sisterhood." That such conformity represents secondary
desire and a species of enervating lunacy is patently obvious and abundantly parodied in *School Daze*. The film also makes it clear that the
fraternity mentality in all of its imitative idiocy is emblematic of the Black
college tradition as a whole, a tradition that finds Black presidents and

members of boards of trustees terrified of offending their White overlords and benefactors. The homology seems to read: as Black Greeks are to White fraternities and sororities, so Black colleges as "home" institutions are to White cultural and economic capital. So far so good. There is even a counterimpulse to such slavish imitation present in the person of Vaughan Dunlap ("Dap") who represents a Black nationalist counterpart to a Zacharias Homer. "Dap" is the organizer of the antiapartheid forces at Mission, and as such, he plays against both the Phi Beta Kappa Keyed Virgil (student government president) and the Dean of the Gammite "Dean Big Brother Almighty."

But while the parallels that Lee stages and the cameo production numbers such as "Straight and Nappy" have a certain éclat, *School Daze* as a cultural project seems far less successful than either of the filmmaker's first two efforts. I think two factors account for the flatness of the third film. The first is the erasure of independent, Black womanhood that I have already mentioned. The second, I think, is the felt necessity of a young filmmaker to produce a box-office success, no matter what the cost. Hence, there are too many stylized musical slots (à la forties musical-interlude films that were always about soldiers on leave or classy tuxedoed White people suffering one sort of angst or another) and a lot of tired, wasted footage about college-student excess and cruelty. Finally, I think *School Daze* gives way to mere producer self-indulgence. Lee seems merely to be having a kind of mental brownout from the middle of the film to its stirring and unexpected close. The concluding lines of the work could well be reflexively directed at Lee himself: "Please wake up."

What one longs for at about the midway point of *School Daze* is the energy and creativity of Nola, or the humorously irreverent nasal tonalities of Mars Blackmon. Dap's high seriousness is severely compromised by his "time out" from Shantytown to make love to Rachel, who can only confess after their lovemaking that she is ready to capitulate to the enemy and join Delta Sigma Theta Sorority. Alas, it is just rather difficult to care at all.

From the previsual singing of "Lift Every Voice and Sing" (known as the "Negro National Anthem") to the final dedication of Lee's fourth film, we are wide awake. All of the reveillean trumpetings of his oeuvre are justified by the medium and fight-the-power message of *Do The Right Thing*. If Lee bugged far out in *School Daze*, he zooms back in like a timely stealth bomber in *Do The Right Thing*, a film that would surely satisfy the urgings of such geniuses of the Black urban vernacular as Langston Hughes.

Breaking again the silence of "Black respectability," and refusing to perpetuate stereotypes that maintain the White status quo, *Do The Right*

Thing, like Hughes' poetry, is a classic space of Black urban representation. Like Hughes's *Fine Clothes to the Jew*, Lee's film captures—in Black, classical form—the tonalities and images of one, synecdochic day in the life of urban Afro-America. (Says Lee, in his journal printed in the companion volume to the film: "Fellini's *Roma* is a good model for this film. I remember seeing it years ago. It's a day in the life of Rome. In *Do The Right Thing*, it's the hottest day of summer in Brooklyn, New York."⁵)

Neither "Blaxploitation" nor easy-laughter bawdiness, the energy of *Do The Right Thing* is intended sympathetically to portray a sector of Black urban life that is seldom positively represented. In the just mentioned companion volume to the movie, Lee writes:

> "In this script I want to show the Black working class. Contrary to popular belief, we work. No welfare rolls here, pal, just hardworking people trying to make a decent living." (p. 30)

In accordance with this creative intention, Lee's film tends to idealize the neighborhood and inhabitants who occupy the work's spaces of representation. There are no deteriorating buildings like those seen in *Joe's Bed-Stuy Barber Shop*, no sleazy criminals or vicious drug dealers, and apparently no necessity for a younger generation to learn the arch, defensive language of street knowledge. The absence of such naturalistic features on the filmscape does not, however, mean that the producer has given way to cinematic Black pastoralism. There is an ample stock of hard-grained, humorous, and brilliant allegorical realism invested in *Do The Right Thing*, and this stock simmers down to economical and deftly paced cultural commentary and critique.

Drawing on memories of his childhood in Bedford-Stuyvesant, and engaging his own astute ability to characterize (visually and aurally) present-day Black urban impulses and desires, Lee manages to give us the feel and texture of an actual neighborhood. He makes us suspend our disbelief through the magic of his serio-comedic realism. His film also manages to make us profoundly uncomfortable about the forces of racial division that hover in the air like murderous phantoms threatening the fragile stability of his imagined neighborhood. Everywhere, on the hottest day of the film's summer, there is racial tension, animosity, misunderstanding, discontent, anger, and frustration.

An air of apocalyptic energy and expectation is aroused at the very beginning of *Do The Right Thing* by the huge, blaring sound of Public Enemy's rap entitled "Fight the Power," which the group created specifically for Lee's film.

Volatile red light floods the screen. A bellicose-faced, tight-rhythmed Rosie Perez (who plays Tina in the movie) fills the screen with dance. She wears boxing gloves and looks for all the world as though she plans to take no prisoners. Thus we are scarcely in an atmosphere of James Bond silhouettes and sexy, progressive jazz.

We are in a rap universe where the boxer-shorted Perez means to fight the powers that keep her neighborhood unsafe for human habitation. Occupying the traditional male spaces of "the street," she is all energy.

There should, I think, be no misidentification of *Do The Right Thing*'s opening dancer with passive objects of the male gaze. She is, in fact, an androgynous and almost Amazonian representation of resistance.

And her resistance is Black cultural subversion par excellence. Rap, Black athleticism, and urban dance come together—or collage—against a backdrop of silhouetted neighborhood structures.

The scene is as stirring as the signifying moment when Bigger Thomas and his Black adolescent companion deconstruct White power on a cold Chicago street corner at the beginning of Richard Wright's *Native Son*. And, indeed, there is much to resist in the neighborhood presented by *Do The Right Thing*. First on the list is domestic colonialism—an economic and spatial domination of Black life represented by *Sal's Famous Pizzeria*.

Sal has been in Bed-Stuy for twenty-five years, and he is proud to say that people in the neighborhood have grown up on his food. Furthermore, he tells his son Pino that he is in Bed-Stuy "to stay."

There can be little doubt, however, that the role Lee creates for Sal is the role of a condescending, patronizing *owner* whose pizzeria's Wall of Fame contains pictures exclusively of Italian-Americans. Sal's handouts to Da Mayor (the self-ingratiating old wino of the piece played by Ossie Davis) are the only thing he offers without charge to the neighborhood— and even from Da Mayor he expects Uncle Tom servility and the menial labor of sweeping the pizzeria's sidewalk.

Before we see Sal and his sons drive up to the pizzeria to begin another day of profit-taking, however, we are greeted by the wake-up call of Mr. Senor Love Daddy, the strongman deejay of station WE-LOVE. Spilling forth a double-inversive patter, Love Daddy joins the Rosie Perez opening dance to set the pace and tone of one mode of Black resistance represented in Lee's film. We know from the outset, that is to say, that *Do The Right Thing* will move swiftly, musically, and aggressively. And both the Black dancer and the Black deejay are carriers and transmitters of a distinctive Black cultural style. *Do The Right Thing* makes clear, in fact, in its rapid-paced unfolding that what is acutely at issue in American urban spaces is precisely a conflict—virtually an almost uncontainable excess—of competing styles.

Essentialism, then, is not the moving force of Lee's film. For what, finally, is at issue are matters of style far more than of substance. And the most copious circulation in *Do The Right Thing* is enjoyed by Black style.

The cultural codes of Black America make their way through the rap of Public Enemy, the dance of Rosie Perez, and the deejay work of Love Daddy, as I have already indicated. They also flow energetically through the signifying of the Black three-man chorus on the corner, the hybridity of leadership strategies seen in Smiley's double bill of Martin and Malcolm, the "maxing out" and people-baiting of the Posse (Ahmad and Co.).

The deejay Love Daddy is both the acme of these myriad styles of the neighborhood (as signified by his multiple hats in the window of WE-LOVE) and the disseminator of Black style in its most efficacious form—"The Music."

The penultimate face-off in *Do The Right Thing* is between Sal and Radio Raheem—who, according to the Posse, even "walks in stereo." Sal and Raheem's final, violent encounter is foreshadowed early in the film when the young Black man enters the pizzeria with his box blasting a Public Enemy sound. Sal tells him that unless he turns off his box he will not be served. Thus when Radio returns to Sal's near the conclusion of the film in the "boycott Sal's" company of Buggin Out and Smiley, the ground of hostility has been already prepared.

To the demands of the boycotters and the noise of Raheem's rap sonics, Sal answers with biting epithets and hostile threats. Radio angrily intones "This is music—*my* music."

Reaching under the counter, Sal grabs a baseball bat and smashes Raheem's giant box.

An incredulous pause follows. Then all hell breaks loose in a melee of screams, fists, strangled oaths, and shattering pizzeria furnishings. The apocalypse is now, and it results in the death/murder of Raheem.

Of course, Raheem is far from blameless in the chaotic events that mark the ending of *Do The Right Thing*. He is an intimidating presence, standing taller and expanding broader than almost any other character in the film. Filming his presence in tight close-ups and at Chinese angles, Lee makes Radio always larger than life. He is also monotonic.

Confronting a group of Puerto Ricans who are assembled on a stoop drinking beer and listening—significantly—to the salsa dedication that Mookie has sent out to Tina, Raheem is a bully of rap style. He wins the radio throwdown only because his Puerto Rican adversary concedes: "You got it man."

Even the three-man Black chorus (ML, Sweet Dick Willie, and Coconut Ed) on the corner tell Radio to "Turn that shit down! Play some Bobby Blue Bland or something!"

But Radio insists that he doesn't like anything other than Public Enemy.

In his single-note domineering, Raheem actually seeks to colonize the spaces of audition of the neighborhood. His is the most audibly militant sound in the film, and the consequences of his stylistic aggression are somewhat overdetermined. For the colonizer (read: Sal) never occupies the colony with only mercantile personnel; the army/police are indispensable to his enterprise. And it is Gary, the mad White policeman, who murders Raheem.

Fortunately, Raheem represents only a single riff in the overall Black stylistic orchestrations of *Do The Right Thing*. The "honor roll" of Black artists that Love Daddy recites in the film is a powerfully diverse admixture of blues, soul, gospel, rhythm and blues, jazz, rock, funk, and other styles. And, indeed, the Black life that we witness in the neighborhood is as various as the altogether pluralistic demographics of today's Black inner cities.

Da Mayor and Mother Sister are a generation removed from the three-man Black chorus, which is at least two generations in advance of Jade and Mookie's cohort. Add Eddie, the Posse, little girls drawing on the sidewalk, Love Daddy himself, and you have a veritable microcosm of Black generations on one block. Moreover, when we factor in Mookie's interracial marriage to Tina, we even have an Afro-Hispanic convergence.

And out of this plurality come extraordinary congeries of strategies, proposals, and endorsements for what precisely constitutes the "right thing" to do in order to live a fruitful Black life in America. Though resistance is one strongly advocated element in Lee's film, there are also injunctions to "get a life," "get a job," "stay Black," and, of course, simply to "always, do the right thing."

Jade, Mookie's sister, is the most neutral of the Black characters; she is drawn to Sal in the same way that Ruth (of *Joe's* provenance) is drawn to the "curly green." Buggin Out is outrageously out of his mind. He is a Black nationalist manqué—an Air-Jordan, Black-machismo, fronting jiver. Smiley is the tragi-comic clown sacralized by his role as the purveyor of an image of now-dead Black leadership. The antenna of his cassette player is always up to attract the wisdom of the ancestors. It is Smiley— a stutterer and represented as the most inarticulate Black character in the film—who torches Sal's pizzeria, pinning, in the very conflagrational moment, one of his Malcolm/Martin pictures on the burning Wall of Fame. Thus, the colonial structure comes crashing down, not with a bang, but with a stutter.

The ambitiousness of *Do The Right Thing* lies in the film's rapid movement over so very many unspoken and underrepresented territories. For example, the jump-cut sequence of characters trading racial insults in a reprise of the "Dog" sequence in *She's Gotta Have It*, and the sisters' refusals of Half Pint's hustling in *School Daze*. But in Lee's fourth film the jump-cut works to illustrate the chilling, pandemic character of racism. The social content packed into the sequence is furious and alarming.

Similarly, the musical sequences of *Do The Right Thing* are not intended, as in previous Lee joints, to serve as cameos, or mere experimental juxtapositions. Instead, they are freighted with significance by the voice of Love Daddy; they assume monumental importance in their role as a thin, audible, and classically resistant line of Black survival energy in a "cold and cruel world."

At a macrolevel, *Do The Right Thing* seems politically to rewrite *Joe's Bed-Stuy Barber Shop* in sophisticated ways. For the malaise and distorting desire of Lee's first film are acted out essentially within the confining spaces of the barbershop and a half-light world of Black urban deterioration. The first film's analysis, as I have already demonstrated, centers on secondary desire, Black self-deprecation, and only the vague possibility of a creative refiguration of disabled landscapes.

One might say that in *Joe's Bed-Stuy Barber Shop*, the colonizing enemy remains implicit, manifesting itself only through the self's insatiable feelings of *lack*. In *Do The Right Thing*, by contrast, the artistic and social analysis is less self-centered, and anything but parochial. In Lee's fourth film, Bedford-Stuyvesant has been placed under intense sunlight, revealing not only the insufferable heat of racial animosity but also the behemoth of monied, colonial exploitation and denigration that is Sal's place.

Mookie is the character in *Do The Right Thing* who understands most clearly that the salvific course of action for the Black neighborhood in today's postmodern economies is not psychotherapy (à la Nola Darling). A mere laying bare of Black desire is not enough. "Getting paid" is what counts in *Do The Right Thing*. Economics—not psychology—dominate Mookie's life. From the introductory moment when we see him awaking to the task of counting his savings until his final scene with Sal, money is the channel of interaction for the young Black worker, who receives the double wage of $500 from his former boss at the end of the movie.

It seems significant to me that Mookie receives a double wage after he has, in fact, been the principal instigator of the direct violence against Sal's pizzeria. For he is, of course, the one who tosses a garbage can through the establishment's front window.

If Mookie has truly done the "right thing," then the movie seems to suggest that a violently aggressive Black energy of revolt can lead to Black economic empowerment.

Hence, the fantasy of *Do The Right Thing* is not as nostalgically limited as that of Lee's student effort, where the dream of independent ownership and a vaguely promised Black artistic potential are enough. In the *Do The Right Thing*, what seems called for and self-reflexively projected is an artistic license to overthrow the old silences and exclusions of a colonized artistic marketplace through an ironically violent extraction of capital from the colonizers themselves.

The grandfather in Ralph Ellison's novel *Invisible Man* talks about the Black man living with "his head in the lion's mouth" and acting as a "spy in the enemy's camp" in order to make a successful way out of noway in America. To a certain extent, Lee has worked this ironic position as the producer of a Universal Studios movie that allowed him to get "paid in full" for reporting decisively from the *inside* on the straight skinny of racism and White domestic colonialism in these United States.

The paradox of Lee's production as a filmmaker is that as it has become less "independent," it has also become more radically and politically Black. There is a vast distance between Teapot with his Nikon sitting in an independently owned Black barbershop and Mookie with a union film crew and Fruit of Islam Guards driving crack dealers out of a Black neighborhood and producing a highly financed critique of all ideological and economic forms of White, colonizing ownership.

From student production to oversight of a six-and-a-half million dollar budget (the sum for *Do The Right Thing*) is an almost intergalactic journey. And there are literally worlds of signifying distinction between Teapot's adolescent street knowledge and the astute, witty, brilliant critique of postmodern, urban hybridity seen in *Do The Right Thing*.

What I would suggest is that Lee has attained—in a short space—a brilliant understanding of the "commerce of culture" in a transnational era. And he has used this understanding to produce an original, cinematic critique capable of awakening us to subtle formations of colonialism's legacies as well as to self-reflexively revolutionary and creative strategies of Black cultural resistance.

Love Daddy urges the population of *Do The Right Thing*'s neighborhood (as well as filmgoers) to register to vote—and he clearly means to vote *against* Ed Koch, the former Mayor of New York. Entertainment as Black, political consciousness-raising, thus, manifests itself as a deft move of the head directly in the lion's mouth.

Yet, for all his political engagement and forceful Black cultural projections, Lee fails miserably in *Do The Right Thing* to heed the instructions that he jotted to himself while planning the film. In the companion volume to the work, he writes:

> I really must beef up the women's roles in this film. Not only Joie [Lee's sister who plays the character Jade] and Ruby Dee's characters, but the others as well. This is something I have to catch myself on. The women can't be secondary characters in this film. If I remind myself of this, it will be reflected in the work. (p. 62)

"Beefing up" is an unfortunate term for what, in any case, Lee forgot to do. *Do The Right Thing* fails to provide either visualizations or intelligent hearings of creative, culturally resistant Black women. The women's portrayals in the film do not go beyond stereotypes of the cantankerous shrew (Tina), the passive watcher-with-an-attitude and a gender-specific chip on her shoulder (Mother Sister), and those blandly neutral seekers after male company (Jade and Ella). At the moment of uprising against Sal's, women do not provide revolutionary counsel or energy; they only scream.

In our age of an advanced Black feminist critique—a critique that has translated into a mighty artistic and intellectual creativity—it seems a pity that Lee's revolution and resistance are confined almost exclusively to a Black male cast of characters. Surely Tina—even as bellicose dance—only carries filmgoers to the same limited, confrontational site occupied by Radio Raheem. Yvonne Smallwood and Eleanor Bumpers may join Edmund Perry, Michael Griffiths, and Michael Stewart in the film's memorial dedication, but the large, spirited, Blackwomanly resistance of such women does not find representation in *Do The Right Thing*.

Lee once thought of bringing Nola Darling over from *She's Gotta Have It* into his fourth film. It's a great pity that he did not follow his transportive instincts.

There are still manifold territories for Spike Lee to master (including a Black woman's critique), but it does seem to me that few Black artists, past or present—few, that is, who carry what the religion of conjuring calls "power"—would hesitate to welcome him into their energetic company. And in the manner of a true postmodern, Lee understands that his job is to get "paid in full" so that he can continue producing films of Black cultural resistance.

His mission is freedom—that monumental and elusive "it" that Black folks have always realized they gotta have.

Peace, Spike.

Notes

This essay has been expanded and revised from an article which originally appeared under the same title in *Black American Literature Forum*, vol. 25, No. 2 (Summer 1991), 237–252.

1. Professor Diawara is Professor of Comparative Literature at New York University. In 1989–90, he served as a Rockefeller Visiting Fellow in the Humanities at the University of Pennsylvania's Center for the Study of Black Literature and Culture, of which I am the director. His remarks on Lee were part of an informal conversation between us. Film Noir is mystery or detective cinema dealing with the half-light underworld of urban life.

2. Chester Himes was an Afro-American writer whose characters Gravedigger and Coffin-Ed energized detective novels of the first magnitude. The novels, which deal principally with Harlem's tempestuous and always morally deficient underworld, first appeared in a series *"noire"* issued by a French publisher.

3. New York: Alfred A. Knopf, 1974, 66.

4. Urbana, Illinois: University of Illinois Press, 1978, 9

5. Spike Lee (with Lisa Jones), *A Companion Volume to the Universal Pictures Film "Do The Right Thing"* (New York: Fireside, 1989), 28. All citations refer to this edition and are hereafter marked by page numbers in parentheses.

11

The Ironies of Palace-Subaltern Discourse

Clyde Taylor

The current crisis of knowledge and of criticism is just another circus spectacle unless it can be forced to deliver a more equitable redistribution of the power to represent in favor of the disenfranchised. After this crisis is exhaustively "clarified" by postmortems on modernity, what is needed, what I am searching for in this paper, is a technique or method, but nothing so tedious as a methodology, that can contribute to the practise of representational politics.

The elements of this practise are well known. Inescapable is the force and violence of the dominant paradigm of representation and interpretation, what Ralph Ellison allegorizes in *Invisible Man* as the Monoplated Light and Power Company. In opposition and resistance stands the excluded, the marginalized, the underrepresented.

From the outside, dominant Western discourse looks much like a crystal palace inside which legions of residents, having accepted the inheritance of the subject position from which knowledge is universally contemplated, narcissistically discuss "the world." The palace's many buildings rise in splendor from plains made barren by its levies of exorbitant tribute. Some of the tallest and most decorated structures are the towers of High Culture where the world's great art is housed, fetishized by guardians and hirelings who fabricate theories of aesthetics to lend credibility to the preservation and exaltation of these hieratic objects.

Huge batteries of light play across the facade of the palace, blinding those who approach it with unshielded eyes. At other moments the gigantic structures block out the sun. The surrounding plains have seen of late many bold and colorful structures rising from the marshes and weeds, only to be disassembled and erected elsewhere. These gypsy edifices are said to pose a nuisance to the palace residents, who claim that the noises rising from them disturb the classic air and damage property values. Whether because of arrogant missiles hurled by the envious or because of the mounting cost of repairs, the palace's pink magnificence has shown signs of recent decrepitude. At odd hours one can hear the tinkling of crashing crystal.

The existence of this city on the hill, its location at ground zero of every destination, forms the scene of the politics of representation. I propose to stage one version of this cultural politics as a dialectic of ironies, the ironies of domination. My starting premise is that cultural politics are played out on terms inordinately disadvantageous to the excluded when lodged in the terms of aesthetics, which once decoded turns out to be merely the palace rules of representation. Rhetoric, from which the useful trope of irony is drawn, offers a more promising grammar of action, even though compromised by its incubation within the palace.

In observing the ironies inseparable from the unequal contest over meaning that takes place between the monopolated light of the palace and the relatively hidden discourses of the disempowered, we can move toward a grammar of difference less diffuse and indeterminate than that in poststructuralist logic, and yet more agile and applicable to particular narratives than taxonomies of domination such as those of Frantz Fanon and Alberto Memmi.[1]

Allen Tate's definition installs a fairly broad, conventional concept of irony. He sees it as "that arrangement of experience, either premeditated by art or accidentally appearing in the affairs of men, which permits the spectator an insight superior to that of the actor."[2] The notion of symbolic conflict, where one party wins and another loses, surfaces in the idea of "superior insight." That notion need only be more fully developed in order for one form of irony to become an interpretive instrument in representational politics. In this usage, irony arises when a statement implies more, less, or something different when expressed or interpreted by participants located in different, opposing socio-political discourses.

Irony is inherently dialectical, but this character alone does not provide the necessary critical viewpoint. Richard H. Brown, following Kenneth Burke, has suggested *dialectical irony* as an alternative for positivistic sociological theory.[3] Brown's gestures toward a more "postmodern" sociological methodology, in which all positions, including the interpreter's, are viewed as specific and limited, doubtless carries some of the liberatory agency he finds in it. Though his search is for a "radical irony," it falls short of radicality by retaining in strategic places restricting legacies of the traditional western discourse on irony, such as the privileging of distance. He does not entirely fend off the observation of Hayden White that "as the basis of a world view, Irony tends to dissolve all belief in the possibility of positive political action."[4] Brown's advocacy of an interventionist dialectical irony that evokes the freedom that he finds in the ontology of art circumscribes its radical possibilities within a demobilizing aesthetic. The distance he urges as part of an ironic positioning devolves eventually into a Kantian aesthetic disinterestedness.

For the purposes I seek in the interpretation of ironies, to sharpen perception of the repressive as well as emancipatory elements in expression, the Western tradition of ironic analysis is ill suited. The limits of irony as seen from within the legitimate perimeter, even while proclaimed for its "freedom," are disclosed by Hugh Danziel Duncan. "Irony exists in one type of social bond, the bond of open, free, and informed discussion as a means to truth." Duncan views it as a form of expression that implies equality between the two speakers. The ironist in this situation "believes in critical intelligence created in free discourse among men who believe that such discourse creates and sustains social bonds." Despite Duncan's characterization of irony as open, it in fact resembles a closed rhetorical format, restricted to participants who are included in the dialogue as potential equals. The boundaries of Duncan's humanist ratio are announced when he adds: "When there are wide gaps between social classes, or when status groups become strange and mysterious to each other, irony fails."[5]

The polite curtain thrown over unseemly relations is stripped away by Walter Benjamin. "There is no document of civilization which is not at the same time a document of barbarism."[6] Benjamin's aphorism focuses the essential ground from which discursive irony blossoms, and simultaneously enlightens that moment of grotesque exchange where, for Duncan, irony fails. As John Brenkman elaborates Benjamin's gnomic phrasing, "The preserved and validated monuments of Western culture are not only the achieved expression of meanings and values and a resource of potential means of expression for civilization; they also carry the imprint of the violence and forced labor which has made their creation possible."[7]

Brenkman's paraphrase well serves Benjamin's meaning, but it also handily serves mine, were one to read "preserved and validated monuments" as *discourses*, the monologues of the palace. It is at this nexus of violence and violent suppression that dialectical irony takes on the character of discursive irony. This dimension of the ironic is understandably neglected to protect the "Noble Lie"[8] that preserves the presumed higher values of palatial wisdom from erosion.

Divergence of meaning on this level implies more than differences among citizens who share civic assumptions. It extends to differences between discourses and paradigmatic assumptions, which limit the possibilities of humorous or aesthetic reconciliations among the differing individuals who are to some degree their prisoners.

Writes LeRoi Jones:

> I look in my pocket; I have seventy cents. Possibly I can buy a beer.
> A quart of ale specifically. Then I will have twenty cents with which
> to annoy and seduce my fingers when they wearily search for gainful
> employment. I have no idea at this moment what that seventy cents
> will mean to my neighbor around the corner, a poor Puerto Rican man
> I have seen hopefully watching my plastic garbage can. But I am
> certain it cannot mean the same thing. Say to David Rockefeller, "I
> have money." and he will think you mean something entirely different.
> That is, if you also dress the part. He would not for a moment think,
> "Seventy cents." But then, neither would many New York painters.[9]

The need then is not to become an ironist mediating between competing positions or meanings, however helpful it might be to remind all parties of the truncation and contingency of their views.[10] A more radical practice would be to analyze the ironies sedimented in unequally weighted discourses to better understand the semiotic manipulations of power, and the rhetorical strategies available to the disempowered to improve the odds.

Liberal interpretations of irony associate it with a rhetoric of openness and freedom. Yet the limits of this freedom are disclosed in another liberal trope, that irony approximates the condition of art. But irony, like art, depends on framing and closure. The function of closure can be seen in a battle of wits where the first speaker tries to cut the dialogue at an embarrassing point for his victim. But the victim may likely reopen the play of meanings in order to close at another, victorious point. Change the frame and you change the game.

But the exchange between unequal discourses is always already ironic. The one most crucial advantage of dominant discourse is its ability to establish the frame of the dialogue (knowledge), according to the golden rule which says "them with the gold makes the rules."

Nevertheless, because of an inescapable false consciousness within official representation, namely the Noble Lie that the persuasiveness of its arguments has nothing to do with the weaponry at its disposal, the state terror that sustains it, or the acts of barbarism that installed it, it routinely speaks with a surplus of hollow grammar which from a disenchanted distance is already ironic, that is, incomplete, reversible, or deflatable.

Several genres of irony are already rooted in the positioning of speakers in relation to different discourses, and recur like leitmotifs of everyday literate speech. One of these, for example, might be identified as the irony of Enlightenment, of Monopolated Light and Power. A feature of utterances in this genre is appropriation of the posture of universality through the tactic of the repressed qualifier. To fish an example, we encroach upon the hallowed grounds and catch a snatch of the conversation within:

> The history of forms evidently reflects this process, by which the visual features of ritual, or those practises of imagery still functional in religious ceremonies, are secularized and reorganized into ends in themselves, in easel painting and new genres like landscape, then more openly in the perceptual revolution of the impressionists, with the autonomy of the visual finally triumphantly proclaimed in abstract expresionism.[11]

The rhetoric of this pronouncement embraces two ironies. The first lies in the disappearing act it imposes on all those whose formal histories are excluded. The second lies in the absurdity of the statement when viewed from the frame of perception of these excluded others—the marvel of such a universalized history channeling all its energies to end up in abstract expressionism.

The locutions of grand ellipsis, which are everywhere, speak Occidental in the name of aggregate humanity and further speak so comfortably that the exclusion of non-Western experience is achieved by the simple repression of a delimiting adjective. The discursive inequity is evidenced in the denial of this privilege by Western patriarchal discourse to all other discussants. Editors will insist that a book about the novel will include *African-American* or *Women's* in its title if the text bears limited reference to the work of White men.

Among other "noble" distortions of Enlightenment must be counted the appropriation of humanity in the name of *man*. Nor should we forget the repressed qualifiers in that characteristic Enlightenment document, the United States Constitution that spoke in the name of "we the people" but excluded women from the franchise and legitimated slavery. Still another classic site of this locution is Sir Kenneth Clark's book and television series *Civilization*, which includes only the art of the West.

The varieties of irony elude compilation within a grammar pretending to scientific precision. A rhetoric of irony falling short of a closed classification might be speculated, beginning with certain genres or discursive frames which tend to reproduce recognizable, recurring ironic postures. These postures reflect the dynamics of domination and resistance. The most absolutist form of irony that the powerful direct to those they subordinate under the most totalitarian conditions might be called despotic irony. The speaker calls attention to himself as a being superior to this despised other. Look at this thing which is a no-thing compared to myself, which is a preeminent something. As an example of despotic irony we might recall the practise of slaveowners in the United States giving their slaves such mock-heroic names as Cicero, Brutus, Caesar and the like. There is no need to explicate the irony involved. This slave-namer, to paraphrase Tate, permits himself and his witnesses an insight superior to that of the slave so named.

The great body of despotic representation in cinema lies in the legions of Sambo and other degraded caricatures of classical Hollywood movies. These are paralleled by stereotypic characterizations in literature, vaudeville, radio, advertising, and popular humor. The documentary film *Ethnic Notions* chronicles imagery saturated with despotic irony. One measure of despotic representations is that their victims have difficulty recognizing themselves or their humanity in them.

Two characteristics of despotic irony can be noted briefly. Despotic irony is rigorously Manichean. The ironist see the disparity between himself and his object as rooted in a binary order permanently fixing himself and his antithesis at opposite ends of the spectrum of existence. Then, because the distinction drawn rests on this cosmology of divided planes of existence, the ironist, like most speakers from the crystal palace, characteristically denies the existence of irony or intent to ironize in his utterance. He claims merely to be expressing the natural order. But this disavowal must often be read with a wink to the spectator included in the joke for having an insight superior to its object. Of course the need to ironize betrays an anxiety that demands self-confirmation.

Even during the era of slavery the despotic position was contested by a more liberal-modernist perspective toward domination. This posture has become increasingly influential as both modernization and liberation struggles have eroded or outdated the totalitarianism of despotic representation. This newer, more liberal hegemony buys heavily into the aesthetic, and those fusions of aesthetics and philosophies of history that read modern life and its functionally differentiated form of society as the fountain of alienation, and hope to find in the realm of the aesthetic a space of disengagement from this alienation.

> In the eighteenth and nineteenth centuries, conceptions of an autonomous aesthetic and philosophies of history repeatedly converge under the correct impression that their most fundamental and essential objective, to think the "other" of modern civilization, is identical.[12]

The self-deception of this liberal-modernist ideology has been in the appropriation of the non-Western "other," whether as savage, native, exotic, anthropological curiosity, as a manipulable object in its effort to think the "other" of modern alienation. Whereas the despotic subject represents this other as Caliban, the Ethiopic subject portrays it at best as Ariel.

This liberal mode of other-representation might suitably be called Ethiopic, recalling the tradition of nineteenth-century minstrels ironically naming themselves so. (I must reassure my Ethiopian friends that the term has nothing whatsoever to do with the Ethiopia of actuality.) The liberalism of minstrelsy must be understood as relative. The minstrel show of the last century formed a composite of imagery, including much of the most despotic formulae. At the same time, historians of minstrelsy see its practitioners as often liberal sympathizers with the Negro's plight. Its racial imagery was presented in a frame that mitigated the most totalitarian bite. Its liberalism is further attested by contrast to its more purely despotic counterpart in the representation of the other, the ritual drama of exorcism enacted in the lynching. Yet it justifies its self-interested distortions by relativizing them beside more absolute degradations.

The mode of representation of the nineteenth-century minstrel show typifies a principle characteristic of this ironic genre that persists in the increasingly liberalized regimes of later eras—the representation of a speculative self through the mask of the alien. Where the despotic ironist is motivated by a desire to exorcise all resemblance between himself and his Manichean double, the Ethiopic performer makes an exaggerated demonstration of liberality, and at the same time affects to shame, titillate or shock the more fundamentalist sectors of society by affecting "low" identity.

This mode of representation is also sedimented with recurring ironies, most of them ritually denied. The first is that the figure represented seldom bears much resemblance to the alien, at least in comparison to the presentation or representation the alien might make. And yet, the figure never discloses the self of the masker—which is the point of masks. Another irony is that those whose identities have been appropriated are expected to be grateful, both for the effete reformism sometimes involved in these portrayals and for the portrayals themselves, beside the alternative of being ghosted out of the script altogether.

The liberal reformism of the Ethiopic stance expresses itself in a posture of laterism—things will get better later, your day is coming—addressed to the claims of the appropriated, among those claims being the opportunity to represent their own unmediated identities. More, the Ethiopic performer adopts the mask of the repressed mainly to speak over their heads to the dominant majority. A subtext of patient stoicism is frequently included for the repressed to read as a message to themselves, but which also serves to restate conventional wisdom that the majority needs for consolation.

The Ethiopic mode reforms the despotic counters of dominant representation, using the image of the other as a form of convoluted special pleading for the cause of sectors momentarily squeezed by the regimens of modernity. Despite its ingenuity in aesthetisizing oppression, it preserves the subordination of the other to the script of structured power. Faced with the possibility of joining the outcasts in radical rebellion against a system that represses both, the Ethiopic artist retreats to comfortable distance within the zone of protection. Subscribing to the master narrative, Ethiopic portrayals reproduce the ironies of pastoralism, where a nether class expresses itself carnivalesquely but never in a way that challenges the guardians' right to rule.[13] Ethiopic representation generally views the possibilities of the repressed through a more pessimistic lens than they, from a different ideological posture, view themselves.

But another variety of ironies *is* struck when the repressed attempt to recover the meaning the world holds for them. One of these might be called Cyclopean after the moment when Cyclops calls to the gods, screaming that "Nobody has blinded me!" This position, which is rarely adopted in its purity, is reflected in the "minority" or subordinate creators who identify so ardently with the values and forms of their colonizers that they are ironically unable to recognize their contribution to their further subordination. They hold as valid expressions those that mimic the genres and traditions of their masters, and value no praise except that which comes from them.

Some writers of the nineteenth century who understandably surrendered to the lures of Cyclopeanism, sometimes described as "literary pets," also have their contemporary counterparts. They are often found among those who insist on being perceived as writers and film directors, not Black writers or women film directors. (An ambiguity must be respected. Some adopt this strategy to resist the impact of the suppressed modifier by claiming for themselves the universalized space marked out by the palace.) On the surface, their role in the politics of representation might be dismissed as minor, merely adding canon fodder to the bulk of received imagery. Actually, they play a useful role in providing comforting evidence to the crystal palace that its standards are fair. The Cyclopean performer also provides material for the Cyclopean consumer of culture, and helps to further confuse the subordinated spectator tempted to internalize the reigning spectacle.

A more complex mode is the Aesopian, in which the performer addresses the hazards of "minority discourse." A description of the Aesopian mode begins with the familiar sense of a speaker from a repressed community who inscribes one text for general (majority) consumption and another more subversive level of signification to be appreciated within the "freemasonry" of the subcultural group. The cycle of Brer Rabbit stories offer one distinguished body of Aesopian expression in Unitedstatesian culture.

More broadly, the Aesopian mode is the zone in which minority speakers approach the power of dominant discourse from a position of negotiation. The speaker in this position attempts to master a language understandable by the majority while also affirming the values and interests of the less powerful group. The question immediately confronting this position is: Which of two masters does the text most effectively serve? In Aesopian utterance, then, texts are precariously balanced so their ironies or registrations of semiotic difference typically fall on both sides of the discursive barrier between power and the lack of power, but may be calculated in retrospect to have served one better than the other. More typically a final flat judgment is hardly available, since the meanings remain mixed and, more importantly, the semiotic registers are often incompatible. For example, a certain ironic restitution of the power to speak is accomplished merely by the completion, publication or exhibition of the text. But how does this compute in the struggle over meaning beside the reinforcement of canonical knowledge the Aesopian text might confer upon received tradition?

Paradoxically, both "Ethiopic" and "Aesopian" are terms derived from the same root, *Ethiopia*, Aesop being the Greek designation of the famed storyteller they called "the Ethiopian." The kind of irony implied in each name carries a different tonality, yet the two modes share an entrenchment in doubleness. They both rely on masking, the one miming the "other," the second adopting masks in order to defend an unacknowledged self.

The temptation to deride the Aesopian performer out of hand as half-hearted or self-divided should be resisted. Almost by definition, every communicator outside the palace but within range of its networks is positioned at the crossroads of the Aesopian mode (not excluding this text). While we may celebrate more exclusively resistant texts and strategies, historically the impact of work done from an Aesopian standpoint has often brought results in a culturally democratizing direction, in dialectical relation to more insistently renovative work.

The more determined, singular ironies of resistance must be left for another discussion. Needless to say, among the strategies deployed there, frequently the import of the palace is reversed through rhetorical strategies of recoding or reframing, or by posing its irrelevance through potent communication that lies outside its cognitive map.

Some of these propositions may be put into play in a reading of the movie *A Soldier's Story*. This movie brought Charles Fuller's Pulitzer Prize drama *A Soldier's Play* to popular screens (directed by Norman Jewison and scripted by Fuller), and so offers the critical advantage of exhibiting an adaption from minority to majority expression. (The play, introduced by the Negro Ensemble Theater off Broadway, succeeded at first among small, largely Black audiences.) But further opportunity to query the meaning of adaptions lies in the fact that *A Soldier's Story* effects a paraphrase of Melville's classic tale "Billy Budd, Sailor: An Inside Narrative."

Adaptions are highly useful for the work of discursive analysis. When literary and filmic narratives employ adaptation they put two important facets of interpretation into highly visible motion. One is intertextuality— the by now axiomatic observation that all texts reverberate and dialogue with other texts and discourses. The other is the phenomenon of recoding: as texts reflect and bounce off each other, they also frequently recode the arguments and sentiments of existing works and traditions. When we accept the notion of intertextuality, we acknowledge that all texts are, in a broad, metaphorical sense, adaptions of previous expressions. Formal adaptions only do overtly and deliberately what other texts do inferentially.

When they cross cultural and power-patrolled lines of interpretation, adaptions can be particularly revealing of discursive ironies. By lining up an adapted text diachronically behind its model, we can clearly see the differences that, when read as discursive ironies, matter in the politics of representation. Lay viewers from repressed communities are right on target in decoding the politics of adaptation by indexing what was added, changed or left out in the transition between one telling and another.

The *Soldier's* narratives depart from "Billy Budd" by being remade in the popular genre of murder-mystery-suspense. Sarge Waters, a Black NCO, is murdered at a Southern army base during World War II. The base is further astonished when a Black captain, a rarity in the segregated army, is sent to investigate. At first both the Ku Klux Klan and White officers are suspected. But Captain Davenport's interrogation of the Black troops under Sarge's command uncovers a remarkably different story. Waters had been an intensely hated leader of an all-Black unit. Mean, contemptuous, seething with racial self-loathing, Waters brutalized his men for reminding him of a condition he could not escape. On Davenport's further investigation, Waters is seen persecuting a young soldier, C. J. Riley, to his death out of sheer metaphysical hatred for his gentle, easygoing, country ways. The surprising turn in this racial whodunit is that Waters (to give away the plot) was murdered not by racist Whites but by one of his own men, Peterson.

Discursive ironies arise in the translation from stage to screen, but others are situated in the play itself. But before we search out these divergent meanings we should place the social-discursive context of the time the play was written and first produced, November, 1981.

In 1980 the "backlash" against Black empowerment as represented by the Civil Rights Act of 1964 had given the Republican Party presidential victories in every election except 1976, and had brought Ronald Reagan into office on a highly ideological campaign to return the United States to pre-1960's values. African-American movement politics had gone into decline, replaced by Black electoral politics, largely ineffective against the conservative trend. Black men and a national "underclass" threatened to become synonymous, as Black male unemployment, especially among youths, rose to alarming heights. Crime by Black men, mostly against other Blacks, often in gang warfare, became a recurring sign for the deterioration of urban life. Black neo-conservative spokesmen rose to prominence by blaming these social disabilities on the adherence of Black populations to backward cultural traditions.

As though to balance this national assignment of Black guilt for Black pains, several cultural productions of the late 1970's portraying Blacks as honorable strugglers for their humanity won considerable success with crossover audiences. But one circumstance held in common by *Roots*, *Ragtime*, *A Place in the Heart*, and later *Cotton Club* and *The Color Purple* was their placement in an historical past. Some Black male writers complained during this period that their projects were ignored, if not censored. Perhaps more to the point, no works that foregrounded contemporary racism or economic exploitation won wide attention.

Fuller's earlier play, *Zooman and the Sign* (1978), framed an interesting moment in this discourse. An uncontrollable young Black tough, Zooman, accidentally kills the daughter of a struggling Black ghetto family with a stray bullet. The father, outraged by the fearful silence of his neighbors, erects a large sign across his house declaring the guilt through silence of his neighbors.

Zooman was a powerful dramatic work as played by the Negro Ensemble Theater. It upheld the call for internal criticism and group self-dependence to a Black community whose cohesive values seemed to be eroding. But for all its urgency it did not move on to Broadway, win a Pulitzer Prize or become a movie like *A Soldier's Play*. A few telling differences may explain their different receptions. *Zooman* held no significant roles through which White viewers could enter the drama and search for the comfort of centered subject position. It mainly exhibited a Black man making a lonely, courageous stand, whereas the gutsy actions of Black men in *A Soldier's Play* are rare and with one exception never in an honorable cause. Finally, *Zooman* was set in the historical present. It nevertheless carried a shock of outspoken Black self-criticism that would have overtones in Fuller's next play.

Though set in 1944, *A Soldier's Play*'s three Black male principals all carry resonance in the current national discourse on Black/White relations. Sarge carries overtones of the Black neo-cons who had come to attention in the 1970s ("You got to be like them!" he insists at one point). Except that in the intensity of his self-contempt and his Elizabethan guile and malice, as played by Adolph Caesar, Sarge is hardly recognizable as

anything but a fascinating metaphor. His neo-con identity is further complicated by the militance of his assimilationism, his contempt of the other
Black troops as Uncle Toms and his grudging respect for Peterson, who
stands up to him and fights back.

The crucial origin of Peterson's characterization lies in the historical
personality of Malcolm X. This affinity was furthered by casting Denzel
Washington who, as Peterson, physically resembles Malcolm. Washington
had in fact played Malcolm X in *The Conversation* at the Henry Street
Theater in New York, causing audiences to gasp at the resemblance. At
one point when he "cases" Waters, his rhetoric recalls specific, well-
known speeches of Malcolm: "White man gives them a little-ass job as
servant—close to the big house, and when the boss ain't lookin', old
copycat niggahs act like they the new owner!"[14]

The role of Captain Davenport is encircled by the national discourse
around affirmative action. Davenport may be located alongside the rise
of the buppie (Black Urban Professional), newly given a change for
"achievement" and social mobility by post-1964 legislative momentum,
on a parallel with tentative official moves towards desegregating the army
in 1944. Both the play and the movie make large investment in the question
of whether Davenport can hack it. This question is put bluntly in the play
(but dropped from the movie) by Captain Taylor, the White officer to
whom Davenport reports: "Look—how far can you get even if you succeed?" And even more bluntly raising the question of Black empowerment:
"I don't want to offend you, but I just cannot get used to it—the bars, the
uniform—being in charge just doesn't look right on Negroes."

Davenport is central to the issues the play and film choose to highlight.
He focuses that form of ambiguous composition necessary to minority
writers who must find a language that speaks simultaneously within dominant and dominated traditions. The White-identified spectator is offered
gratification in the form of an historical catharsis, in Davenport's being
given a chance to break down segregationist taboos in 1944 and open the
way to what many wanted to perceive as the color-blindness of contemporary society (a position asserted by Reagan). This spectator may be further
heartened by Davenport's demonstration that he can achieve by honoring
rather than short-circuiting the institutional rules of the game, whether
army, corporation or profession. That he upholds the institutional rules
even against errant members of his own tribe might confirm for the White-
identified viewer his loyalty to higher modern values.

Davenport enunciates for Black spectators parallel but different meanings. For them he might recall heroic endurance of heavy pressures while
contesting for small gains within racist US institutions. For Black viewers
the force of analogy might place fuller meaning on the contemporary
significance of his position. His success might hold comfort for a belea-

guered Black middle class, often annoyed that *its* story was being neglected in the media for tales of the underclass. In the years around the play's production a discussion arose about the struggles for credibility of Black executives in the corporate world, in which Davenport's example might prove an inspiring addition. That his success came in solving a *Black* crime may have aroused an uneasy respect for the "realism" dictated by the new "color-blind" ethos of the monoculture. The dual readability of the Davenport character signifies to his Aesopian positioning, since he is in every narrative circumstance the man in the middle. His centrality to the story also testifies to *its* immersion in Aesopian representation.

Set against the background of Melville's sea story, which it rewrites, the three principals of *A Soldier's Play*, Waters, Davenport, and Peterson, are reinscriptions of the pivotal figures in Melville's tale. Waters corresponds to Claggart, master-at-arms of the man-of-war *Bellipotent* "in whom was the mania of an evil nature," not from learned experience, but "innate," "a depravity according to nature."[15] The antecedent of Davenport is the ship's Captain Vere, a naval man of stoic rectitude beneath which is found a large, central humanity. Vere, like Davenport, must be taken as the trustable median between two extremes. The third member of this drama is Billy Budd, the handsome sailor over whose childlike, angelic innocence Melville waxes eloquent, whose impulsive blow kills Claggart after he had thrown the young sailor into moral confusion by accusing him of mutinous conspiracy.

The extrapolation of the doomed sailor-angel in Fuller's rewritten version is complex. This role is divided between the innocent, childlike, guitar-playing C. J. (Christ Jesus?), whose cultural simplicity inspires devious persecution in Waters, and Peterson, C. J.'s protector and avenger. How can we read these and other changes wrought on Melville's tale? We might first assure ourselves that arguments defending adaptive changes in the name of updatedness, dramatic convenience, or clarity are also motivated by ideology, by pressure of some socio-political rationales as opposed to others. "Billy Budd" and *A Soldier's Play* are both political dramas, enacted in military settings and in time of war. Billy was impressed as a seaman on the *Bellipotent* when the British navy was fighting the French *Directoire*, the government of revolutionary France circa 1797. During this period the maltreatment of His Majesty's sailors rose to the point of inciting mutiny despite the claims of patriotic duty. The comparable issues in Fuller's play are the backdrop of World War II and the more specific irritant of blatant racism in the US Army.

The most potent discursive ironies of the *Soldier's* play and film, heightened by contrast with Melville's story, collect around the ambiguous portrayal of Peterson. His psychology, his existentialist action would seem to invite close study. But his role is confined to two short scenes. He is seen thereafter only fleetingly, as narrated in a witness's words, killing Waters in not very gallant form, literally kicking him when he is down, drunk, and already beaten by White soldiers, before he shoots him. The necessities of the political narrative expressed in the play and movie dictate that the angelic killer Billy Budd must be split into two characters— the sweet victim isolated from the murderer—because Waters's murder cannot be condoned. The 1960s-style militance of Peterson is made to give way as an historical anachronism before Davenport's commitment to the rules—but not without a subtextual ambiguity.

Peterson and his existentialist act are confined as instruments to elicit Davenport's moral outrage (unlike Captain Vere, he is totally out of sympathy with the killer). The focus is placed on Davenport; and his upright, moral sleuthing answers with satisfaction the question that dominates Hollywood's discourse on Black Americans: to what extent shall we feel threatened by the empowerment of Black men?[16]

It is not surprising that in many narratives some characters become carriers or reflectors of discursive positions, nor is it trivial to view them *as* discourses, fighting, mating, mediating, and sometimes killing each other. Sarge Waters, for instance, functions as an *effect* of despotic representation and socialization who reverberates that despotism in the rhetoric and abuse he directs to the Black troops under him; Davenport inhabits and richly illustrates the ambiguous terrain where the negotiated self-representation of the Aesopian mode becomes the natural expression; while in Peterson we can see a position where the search for self-empowered resistance and expression is launched.

If we ask why Peterson's dilemma is not more fully probed, we are drawn to the discursive limits imposed here in order to highlight other meanings. Merely to suggest another narrative possibility, it is as though Dostoevsky had centered *Crime and Punishment* on the search for guilt of his psychological detective while placing Raskalnikov in a subordinate role as perpetrator. The parallel holds true for Billy Budd, whose consciousness is equally slighted. Billy's murder of Claggart begs interest as existentialist action, the gratuitous fatal act that later claims attention in European writing. Yet Melville restricts him within a characterization too innocent and childlike to open out these intuitions. "The glamorously daring but fatalistic sailor [of Melville's earlier fiction] has been politically castrated. Like the conception of the 'darky' in Shirley Temple movies, the good sailor is the child who lives cheerfully, zestfully and essentially mindlessly and gratefully under the care of the master."[17]

The innovation of Fuller's stage drama which made a Broadway run and a Pulitzer Prize possible was its occupancy of an Aesopian field of play circumscribed as "human" as opposed to the local, the ethnic. But we can more precisely note an intricate contrapuntal dance between these two sets of reference. Where the resulting Aesopian equations remain interestingly ambiguous in the play, they are resolved more Ethiopically in the movie. The Hollywood version runs true to form in making all adaptive changes as redistributions of symbolic honor to the advantage of the authorized version of history.

Some of the changes made by the movie are entirely predictable: illusory representation, diversified locales, and the infusion of harmonica/banjo music to signify "Negro environment." Other changes are more ideological but no less formulaic, like the enlarged role of Whites, all officers, in the movie. As predictable as a law of physics is the mediation of the original text toward the truisms of the master narrative.

The shift in the movie's treatment of Peterson is consistent with this law. In the play, Peterson's flight and capture are narrated as off-stage action. The movie orchestrates a confrontation between Davenport and Peterson in which Davenport's crafty detective work traps Peterson into admission of guilt. Davenport's righteous judgment imposes a more sharply defined closure on Peterson's moral risk-taking in the film than in the play. "Who gave you the right to judge? To decide who is *fit* to be a Negro and who is not?" This pronouncement, which passes easily in the formulaic moment reserved for such grand, crushing judgments, the moment of illumination for the crime text, is really an extraordinary non sequitur. It invokes a post-1960s discussion among African-Americans on the excesses of the Black identity movement but even that discussion would refer to verbal, not mortal interdictions. So understood, its resonance is to cower the militance celebrated in the sixties. This put-down of Black militance in the movie script echoes an obligatory representation in Black exploitation and other Hollywood movies, but ironically with a good deal more respect for the posture than the usual feckless caricature.

Peterson had not challenged Sarge's right to be Black but to be human. Even while refusing him sympathy, the play more than the movie inscribes motives by which a radical recoding of Peterson's actions and the play itself can gain a foothold among dissident viewers. Before he shoots Sarge, Peterson justifies himself to his companion. "Smalls—some people, man—If this was a German, would you kill it? If it was Hitler—or that fuckin' Tojo? Would you kill him?" By calling Sarge an "it" while negating his racial identity, Peterson is erasing Sarge's claims as human, not as Black. But through the strictures of the master narrative around the moral and cognitive potency of subalterns, Peterson's destiny coincides with the inevitable downfall of the rebellious Black, native, colonized, along with "The Emperor," Brutus Jones and many others. The portrayal of Peterson completes the inversion regularly exercised by the master narrative, that those whom the oppressed might consider as heroes of resistance are recoded and reinterpreted as villains.

The movie takes another ideological alteration in the closure of moral significance effected at the end of the narrative. The play ends with Davenport narrating Peterson's offstage flight and capture. As a kind of postscript, Davenport reports that through a foul-up, Waters was listed as killed in action and decorated posthumously as a hero. Further, the whole unit was wiped out in a German attack in the Ruhr Valley. Such a finale suggests ironically that the unit's struggles within military racism were futile, and that Peterson may have escaped death in combat by murdering Waters. The play ends, then, as an absurdist parable with Davenport summing up its significance in terms of futility. "For me? Two colored soldiers are dead—two on their way to prison. Four less men to fight with—and none of their reasons—nothing anyone *said* or *did*, would have been worth a life to men with larger hearts—men less split by the madness of racism in America." This postscript is scratched from the movie and replaced by a triumphal march of the unit through camp on its way toward the European front; triumphal because combat was regarded as a privilege for Black troops in World War II.

Interestingly, Melville's story also included a postscript. We are informed that after Billy's execution the *Bellipotent* distinguished itself in victorious combat against the French. Following Milton Stern's interpretation of the story as a product of Melville's late drift into classical conservatism—the flag is upheld by England, "the sole free conservative Power" against the French Revolution—this postscript throws a consoling aesthetic resolution over the victimized seaman's unjust fate. The harmony of the social order is maintained. By contrast, the postscript of *A Soldier's Story* seems even more complexly ironic and untraditional.

All three texts present mutinous actions if not mutiny as such. In "Billy Budd," the mutinous act, murder, is justified, or at least presented sympathetically. But in the *Soldier's* texts this sympathy is revoked; the mutinous action is framed as unjustified. We should ask ourselves when last we saw a movie about an unwarranted mutiny. Such would hardly be generic or, from a commercial standpoint, dramatic. The denial of justification is stronger in the movie. This normally unorthodox theme becomes digestible, popular entertainment for two reasons. One is that the repressed mutiny is by Blacks and hence metaphorical for Black rebellion or revolution. The other is that this non-canonical theme is palatably marginalized by the triumph of the affirmative action criminal investigator.

Broadly, a comparison of the three texts allows reflection on the possibilities of articulation within the three different discursive contexts. Melville clearly felt entitled to a level of metaphysical rhetoric, enveloping his tale in obscurantism, and linked to a dubious universalism, that nevertheless allowed him to approximate the tonalities of the great tradition. (Doubtless, his awareness of not writing for an immediate audience supported this license.) His themes have been summarized as "good versus evil; innocence versus experience; idealism versus expediency; morality versus necessity; the reality of history; and most of all, the problems of guilt, power and responsibility."[18] These themes are doubtless at work in *A Soldier's Play* too, though expressed on a humbler scale and more modestly invoked in critical responses. These themes might be thought of as being *smuggled* into the work.

My point is to note the allotment of grandeur, poetry, philosophy to which Melville is given license as an aspirant to the great tradition, the master narrative, compared to the confinements against which "minority literature" must contend. The contrast allows a discursive irony however since Melville's work can be read as an instance of clouding interesting questions of *social* justice, of class struggle and worker's rights, with the aestheticizations of the great tradition. Because a drama of pure good vs pure evil is hardly tolerable to audiences these days, and less so in an African-American setting, the *Soldier's* narratives necessarily psychologize the malignancy of Sarge and then make the morally astonishing actions of Melville's story more believable by splitting Billy Budd's role between C.J. and Peterson.

The interdiction of "minority expression" is felt in the limits discursively imposed on the play, but even more so in the context of popular cinema. The advertisements for *A Soldier's Story*, as for *The Color Purple,* insisted the drama offered was a human, not merely an ethnic one. Such claims testify to the persistence of such barriers that are putatively being crossed. But another reading of such a framing clue might be that by "human" is meant the ordering of values commensurate with that trans-ethnic realm of significance which, to this point, has been a prerogative of Occidental consciousness.

The *Soldier's* stories reflect the tension between the "human" drama favored by the palace, nicely enriched by epiphanies of individual, depoliticized psychology, and a collective historical and alternately human truth struggling to emerge. Coincidentally, Fuller wrote another play about Black "mutiny" some years ago. *The Brownsville Raid* is about an historical incident in Brownsville, Texas, when Black troops left base, shot up the town, and killed several people in revenge for the murder of some of theirs. That stirring play was less about meditative psychology and more about redemption of a moment of collective historical courage. The later *Soldier's Play* is an adaption, then, in which the earlier manifestation of collective subjectivity is pushed to the background, reimmersed into the shadowy ground of the problematical, the immanent.

Film director Paul Shrader discusses the double tier of signifying possibilities in a symposium on Spike Lee's *Do The Right Thing*. Shrader addresses the restraints imposed on a film like Lee's out of fear of its being incendiary.

> Its a truism that blacks have to outperform whites in similar situations. More is called for on the part of a black than a white. He cannot have the kind of personal controversy in his life that a white person has. The black is always, particularly in the position of power, held to a higher standard. Its interesting vis-a-vis Spike as a film maker, because I think the film is marked by extraordinary restraint and responsibility; that the temptation to vent must have been almost irrepressible. And yet he does hold back.
>
> I remember when I was young and very angry I wrote this movie *Taxi Driver*. Spike Lee does not have that privilege; he doesn't have the privilege to be angry. Society won't let him. It's too dangerous for a black person to be that psychopathically angry at whites, the way that white character in *Taxi Driver* was at blacks. It's just not allowed to him.
>
> Art doesn't need to be responsible. Art can be incendiary. Art can be inflammatory. Spike has been held to an extraordinary level of responsibility, and he has risen to it. Which was more than we should ever ask of any artist, and to his great credit that he did.[19]

Without overlooking the courage and fairness of these remarks, we must notice a slippage from the issue of the power to represent, to that of aesthetic performance. From the vantage of cultural politics, the significant double standard is one where less power of expression is accorded the Black filmmaker, not a higher standard of artistic accomplishment. Since art doesn't need to be responsible (another absurdity of the dogma of the aesthetic), Shrader is clearly not suggesting that *Taxi Driver* aimed at a lower artistic standard. Subtly and perhaps quite genuinely and naturally, Shrader's rhetoric places Spike Lee's dilemma within the same affirmative action category that Captain Davenport occupies, and draws closure around the same crucial point that drives Hollywood perception of Black males— the extent of the threat posed by them—by observing the decorum with which Lee handles the situation.

The point at issue for the project of liberatory cinema is the outcome of the negotiations imposed on repressed expression by these unequal levels of expressive possibility. These contradictions may be as sharply drawn as those between the master narrative and the slave narrative, or narrative of subordination. If the master narrative draws closure around the critical point for the maintenance of Occidental hegemony, whether within the grand texts of Christian eschatology, the inevitability of Western bourgeois progress over nature and less advanced societies, or the inevitable socialist triumph of the Western proletariat, it also conditions subordinate narrative frameworks for the possibilities of pagans, women, slaves, servants, the colonized, the non-Elect, the primitive, the backward, the non-Westerner, the others. However intricately elaborated, the decisive issue of these narrative possibilities is whether the representatives of such groups oppose the reigning symbolic order and consequently fall to defeat in futility and chaos, or whether they find sympathy and achievement (often sacrificially) by aligning themselves as apprentices of or dutiful converts and servants to the ways of the masters.

A *Soldier's Story* plays some arresting contrapuntal riffs on these alternative scales of conditioned social meaning. It places recollections of brutal oppressive circumstances in bygone military environments only to rise above them to a more refined set of issues surrounding the achievement of self-critical mastery by a representative of a new minority middle class. But the mastery achieved is firmly bounded by the criteria of orthodox mastery. Moreover the limited exploration of the "human" drama of this theme is exercised at the expense of another exploration of the human— that of Peterson's radical intervention. The irony within the text is that the dimension of Davenport's affirmative action narrative merely reaches the outskirts of human consciousness as defined by contemporary US ideology, while Peterson's story reaches a more genuinely open range of "human" contradictions.

The ceiling on discursive possibilities, particularly for Black male representation, is even more sharply identified in contrast with *Platoon*, the Vietnam war film made only a few years later. There the GI protagonist Chris serves under the fascistic Sergeant Barnes, who out of sheer hatred has killed another, humane NCO, Elias. After a fierce firefight with North Vietnamese troops, Chris and Barnes fight to a showdown. Finally, with Barnes unarmed, Chris coolly shoots him dead and returns to the States, his minor mutiny condoned by the narrative. Barnes and Sarge Waters are equally vicious characters, both fascists in temperament and style. The combat setting in which Chris kills Barnes perhaps extenuates his action more than the base-camp killing effected by Peterson. This proviso aside, we must ask what discursive alignments sanction one such killing and not another. The restraints accepted in the *Soldier's* narratives submit to a kind of sumptuary law for subaltern expression.

In these two interventions upon a classical narrative precedent one can read the difficulty of repressed discourse in turning the tables into a liberative ironic relation to the master text. Or, conversely, one can see the power of the grand narrative tradition, upheld from the crystal palace, to circumscribe meanings issued from silenced sectors. The manipulations of the murder mystery motif offer a case in point. The false leads in the *Soldier's* narrative are not the same as in, say, Fritz Lang's *You Only Live*

Once (1937). What is reversed is not only a murder solution but a solution to the discourse of racial disharmony as symptomized by a murder. The responsibility for the "crime" is flip-flopped halfway through so that it falls to internal Black dissension rather than to White racism. Can it be coincidental that the rhythm of this shift follows the neo-conservative shift in the national discussion of race?

These interventions demonstrate only some of many options for subaltern expression. They do not recode Melville's story so much as use it, perhaps, to establish an internal credibility. By dividing the character and actions of Billy into two personalities, the text gives greater expression, through Peterson, of the rebellion and conscious resistance that the younger Melville once found in his sailors. At the same time, it also isolates Peterson's actions for the moral reprobation that Billy escapes. The text manages to insert a pointed recollection of the past social abuse of a racially segregated military more poignant than Melville's aestheticized recollections of British naval maltreatment of common sailors. But these and other interventions amount, finally, less to a powerful resistance than to an accommodation, and in the movie a salute to the established order. Moreover, the subscription of the *Soldier's* narratives to this order entails the suppression of resistance energies to a subordinate level, one beneath that of works within the tradition like "Billy Budd" or *Platoon*. Despite some recalcitrant ambiguities and multivocal historical protests, the *Soldier's* texts make large concessions to the slave tale or narrative of subordination.

The premises of the Aesopian strategy of the *Soldier's* narratives rule out the possibility of radical resistance to dominant tradition, either by breaking out of its language and suppositions, or by reducing its legitimacy. This was guaranteed by the texts' offering of Davenport as point man for audience sympathy and identification. But given the premises of the story, Davenport's heroic quest will not be whether he can provide leadership to the underclass of Black men in the military. Rather it is whether he can prove himself symbolically within the terms laid out for him by a White military hierarchy, itself symbolic of White power structure. The last word, the punch line, in both play and movie, has Taylor saying: "I guess I'll have to get used to Negroes with bars on their shoulder, Davenport. You know. Being in charge." To which Davenport replies, "Oh, you'll get used to it Captain. You can bet your ass on that. You'll get used to it."

This affirmative action scenario bears an intertextual link with *In the Heat of the Night* (1967), also directed by Norman Jewison. Here, Sidney Poitier as a Philadelphia detective, trapped by accident into investigating a murder in a Southern town which is astonished by his presence in that capacity, also solves a murder with false leads. Here, too, he wins over the admiration of the official he reports to, the town sheriff, played by Rod Steiger, who is at first dubious and frightened of his competence.

The issue is important and the symbolic victory one that Black audiences too seldom have an opportunity to share, manipulative as it is. But it is achieved at a high price. The dearest cost is attached to the illusion furthered by the story of a Black middle-class salvation. As a glimpse of a future which is presumably close by for the audience, the idea of getting used to Black men in charge obscures the virtual powerlessness of the Black middle class. This is not a middle class in the sense of Western bourgeoisies that carry histories of successful economic development. It is more precisely the Black class in the middle. It has evolved as a symbolic middle class, manipulating itself as a symbol, of potential progress, and so on, and thereby mediating between the White elite class and the Black underclass.

Describing the alternative actions of this class in the middle toward the Black population, Toni Cade Bambara says, "Some take care and others domesticate." In the narrative situations we find Davenport, his function as a domesticator far exceeds his capacity as caretaker. It should be noted that, as representative of this class in the middle, Davenport achieves a success in interrogating Black troops and solving the crime that might have eluded a White investigator. An ironic distance stands between the discourse that is serviced by the model of an *individual* Black achiever helping the society work, and the discourse that is not serviced by the example of what this individual, as member of the class in the middle, might or might not do for the population he is identified with.

In this exchange with the grand narrative these variants are describable in terms of Allen Tate's definition of irony, wherein more than one meaning is produced, but one text is granted superior moral awareness and prestige than the other. The ironic distribution of knowledge falls out so that the subordinate is contained in a secondary position of knowing, or more importantly, of having its knowledge satisfyingly confirmed.

The strategies of interpretation put to work in this analysis give us a chance to read the dialectic of symbolic exchange at the moment of one fairly complex transaction. If the exchange of symbolic credit is in this case unequal, it reflects in part antecedent inequities that predicate it. Perhaps by continued readings of the discursive ironies involved in narrative representations, this mode of interpretation may mature into a method. Such readings are of course more productive when yielding fuller understanding of the politics of representation than ratings of individual works. A "conclusion" about the *Soldier's* texts would in itself resolve little. Immersed in a process of symbolic bartering in which we are all also implicated, it raises issues and other contending discourses which then open onto still more and different ones. And in each case, the individual interpreter places different weight on points of possible interpretation. The trail always opens as well onto other texts; this reading might easily explore more fully the problematics of Melville's tale, *Platoon*, or *In the Heat of the Night*, and from these onwards. Also the trail might, should, must lead to examinations of some of the issues as they come up in social reality as well as in representation.

This leads to a final point. The *Soldier's* narratives give us a chance to recognize that the Aesopian, no less than the Ethiopic text, relies on the credit it might claim for exposing the brutalities of oppression—in this case racism in the World War II military—to offset or efface the compromises it may make in bending the portrayal of the oppressed toward the comfort of hegemonic perspective. To return to the paradigmatic mask of minstrelsy, its ruling justification in the masking of the abused remains: *it's not as bad as lynching* and therefore ameliorative in the real world. This is a dilemma that demands careful, painstaking study. But no satisfying solution should include, I think, the perpetual postponement of the demand for more culturally democratic representation, the lack of which also makes a contribution to brutality.

Notes

1. Frantz Fanon, *Black Skin, White Masks* (New York: Grove Press, 1967); *The Wretched of the Earth*, (New York: Grove Press, 1966). Alberto Memmi, *The Colonizer and the Colonized*, (New York: Orion Press, 1965).

2. Quoted in Kenneth Burke, *A Grammar of Motives and a Rhetoric of Motives*, (Cleveland: World Publishing Co., 1968), 513–14.

3. Richard Harvey Brown, "Dialectical Irony, Literary Form and Sociological Theory." *Poetics Today*, Vol. 4, No. 3 (1983), 543–564.

4. Hayden White, *Metahistory: The Historical Imagination in Nineteenth Century Europe*, (Baltimore: Johns Hopkins University Press, 1973), 38.

5. *Symbols in Society*, (London: Oxford University Press, 1968), 226–27.

6. *Illuminations*, (New York: Schocken, 1969), 256.

7. *Culture and Domination*, (Ithaca: Cornell University Press, 1987), 4.

8. ". . .Plato's awareness that his Noble Lie, the myth of metals, would protect the stability of his Republic only so long as most people believed in it." Richard H. Brown, *op. cit.*, 554.

9. LeRoi Jones, *Home: Social Essays*, (New York: William Morrow, 1966), 167–68.

10. Again I want to distance myself from a certain modernist, aesthetic irony. "Given the unquestioned doctrine in dominant English criticism, which typically considers 'irony' to be the one universal feature of all imaginative literature, it is striking to see Gramsci's attack on 'irony' as the attitude of isolated intellectuals indicating the distance of the artist from the mental content of his own creation . . . a distancing related to a more or less dilletantish scepticism belonging to disillusionment, weariness and 'superuominismo.' " Timothy Brennan, "Liter-

ary Criticism and the Southern Question," *Cultural Critique* (Winter, 1988–89), 106.

11. Fredric Jameson, *The Political Unconscious: Narrative as a Socially Symbolic Act*, (Ithaca: Cornell University Press, 1981), 63.

12. Jochen Schulte-Sasse, "The Prestige of the Artist under Conditions of Modernity," *Cultural Critique* (Spring 1989), 90.

13. William Empson, *Some Versions of Pastoral*, (London: Chatto & Windus, 1935).

14. Charles Fuller, *A Soldier's Play*, (New York: Hill and Wang, 1981), 67.

15. Herman Melville, *Billy Budd, Sailor: An Inside Narrative*, edited with an introduction by Milton R. Stern (Indianapolis: Bobbs-Merrill, 1975), 61.

16.   Consider for instance the screen personae and careers of Paul Robeson and Sidney Poitier, or the persistent preference for Black male comics.

17. Milton Stern, *op. cit.*, xxix.

18. *Ibid.*, p. xi.

19. " 'Do the Right Thing': Issues and Images," *The New York Times* (July 9, 1989), A23.

12

Looking for Modernism

Henry Louis Gates, Jr.

The strictures of "representation" have had wide and varied permutations in the Black community. For as we know, the history of African-Americans is marked by its noble demands for political tolerance from the larger society, but also by its paradoxical tendency to censure its own. W. E. B. DuBois was rebuked by the NAACP for his nationalism in the 1930s and then again for his socialism a decade or so later. James Baldwin and Ralph Ellison were victims of the Black Arts Movement in the sixties, the former for his sexuality, the latter for his insistence upon individualism. Martin Luther King and Eartha Kitt, strange bedfellows at best, were roundly condemned for their early protests against the Vietnam War. Amiri Baraka repudiated a whole slew of writers in the sixties for being too "assimilationist," then invented a whole new canon of Black targets when he became a Marxist a few years later. Michele Wallace, Ntozake Shange, and Alice Walker have been called Black-male-bashers and accused of calculated complicity with White racists. Not surprisingly, many Black intellectuals are acutely aware of the hazards of falling out of favor with the thought-police, whether in whiteface or black.

In the case of artistic elites, the issues of representation arise with a vengeance. I want to talk a little bit about a revisioning of the Harlem Renaissance in which such issues become particularly acute—the film *Looking for Langston*, which was directed by Isaac Julien and produced by the Black British film collective Sankofa in 1989.

Distance and displacement have their benefits, as the literature of migrancy reminds us; so that it isn't altogether surprising that one of the most provocative and insightful reflections on the Harlem Renaissance and the cultural politics of Black America should come from across the Atlantic. I want to take a look at New York from the standpoint of Black

London; I want to examine the relationship between a New York-based cultural movement, such as it was, in the 1920s and one in London in the 1980s. Of course, the question of modernism has always also been one of a cultural vanguard or elite. And that means that the old "burden of representation" is always present. "The ordinary Negro never heard of the Harlem Renaissance," Langston Hughes remarked ruefully, "or if he did, it hadn't raised his wages any." Always, there is the question: what have you done for us?

But to see *Looking for Langston* as an act of historical reclamation, we might begin with the retheorizing of identity politics in Black British cultural studies, among such critics and theorists as Stuart Hall, Paul Gilroy, Hazel Carby, and Kobena Mercer.

Hall insists, rightly, on distinguishing between a conception of identity found in an archeology—in the sense of *res gestae*—and one produced by a narrative, even if an archaeological narrative. For him, that "partnership of past and present" is always an "imaginary reunification." But he also insists—something forgotten too quickily in the postmodernist urge to exalt indeterminacy—that "cultural identities come from somewhere, have histories." In a rather nice formulation, he writes that "identities are the names we give to the different ways we are positioned by, and position ourselves in, the narratives of the past." There's a certain reciprocity here that I want to hold on to. It says our social identities represent the way we participate in a historical narrative. Our histories may be irretrievable, but they invite imaginative reconstruction. In this spirit, diasporic feminist critics like Hazel Carby have made the call for a "usable past." This call for cultural retrieval—tempered with a sense of its lability, its contingency, its constructedness—has sponsored a remarkable time of Black creativity, or as we are bidden to call it, "cultural production." I'm talking, of course, about the work of recent Black British film collectives, which really can be seen to deepen and expand these arguments: this isn't a relation of mirroring, however, but of productive dialogue.

To talk about the way *Looking for Langston* sets in play history, identity, and desire, start with the fact that *Looking for Langston* is avowedly a meditation on the Harlem Renaissance. And let me emphasize that historical particularity is an essential part of the film's texture, rather splendidly realized, I think, by Derek Brown, the film's art director. Throughout the film, archival footage, including film extracts from Oscar Micheaux and period footage of Bessie Smith's "St. Louis Blues," is interspersed with Nina Kellgren's cinematography. What I want to argue is that its evocation of the historical Harlem Renaissance, is, among other things, a self-reflexive gesture: there's a relation, even a typology, established between Black British cinema of the 1980s and the cultural movement of the 1930s that we call the Harlem Renaissance. By its choice of subject, it brings out, in a very self-conscious way, the analogy between this contemporary ambit of Black creativity and a historical precursor.

We look for Langston, but we discover Isaac.

It's an association that's represented quite literally in one of the opening images of the film, where the film's director makes his sole appearance in front of the camera. He is the corpse in the casket. With six mourners presiding, Hughes's wake is a black-tie affair. And, of course, the film is also an act of mourning, in memorium to three men who died in 1987, Bruce Nugent, James Baldwin, and Joseph Beam ("This nut might kill us," we hear Essex Hemphill say in one sequence, reflecting on the AIDS epidemic; "This kiss could turn to stone.")

Visually, as I mentioned, there's a circulation of images between the filmic present and the archival past. Textually, something of the same interplay is enacted, with poetry and prose from Bruce Nugent ("Smoke, Lilies and Jade," which receives perhaps the most elaborate and affecting *tableau vivant* in the film), Langston Hughes (including selections from "The Negro Artist and the Racial Mountain," *The Big Sea, Montage of a Dream Deferred*, and other works), James Baldwin (from *The Price of the Ticket*), an essay by the critic and journalist Hilton Als, and six poems by Essex Hemphill. We hear an interchange of different voices, different inflections, different accents: including Stuart Hall reading expository prose of Hilton Als, Langston Hughes reading his own work, Toni Morrison reading Baldwin, and Erick Ray Evans reading Bruce Nugent. The credits identify Hall's as the "British voice," an interestingly ambiguous formulation. The result is an interlacement, an enmeshment of past and present, the blues, jazz, Motown, and contemporary dance music, London and New York: a transtemporal dialogue on the nature of identity and desire and history.

But the typology to which the film is devoted also enables another critique of the identity politics we've inherited from the Black nationalism of our youth, a critique that focuses on a malign sexual politics. Like the self-proclaimed "Aesthetic Movement" of England's yellow 1890s, chronicled by Arthur Symonds, parodied by Robert Hitchens, promulgated by such "born antinomians" as Oscar Wilde, Alfred Douglas, and Lionel Johnson, the Harlem Renaissance was in fact a handful of people. The usual roll call would invoke figures like Langston Hughes, Claude McKay, Alain Locke, Countee Cullen, Wallace Thruman, and Bruce Nugent; which is to say that it was surely as gay as it was Black, not that it was exclusively either of these things. Yet this, in view of its emblematic importance to later movements of Black creativity in this country, is what makes the powerful current of homophobia in Black letters a matter of particular interest and concern. If *Looking for Langston* is a meditation on the

Harlem Renaissance, it is equally an impassioned rebuttal to the virulent homophobia associated with the Black Power and Black Aesthetic Movements. On this topic, the perfervid tone that Eldridge Cleaver adopts toward Baldwin—to whom *Looking for Langston* is dedicated—indicates only a sense of what was perceived to be at stake in policing Black male sexuality. We see the same obsession running through the early works of Sonia Sanchez, and, of course, Amiri Baraka. "Most American White men are trained to be fags," he writes in the essay collection *Home*. "For this reason it is no wonder their faces are weak and blank, left without the hurt that reality makes. . . ." Amid the racial battlefield, a line is drawn, but it is drawn on the shifting sands of sexuality. To cross that line, Baraka told us, would be an act of betrayal. And it is worth noting that, at least in a literal sense, the film opens in the year 1967, with the death of Langston Hughes and the playing of a Riverside radio program in memorium.

It is difficult to read his words today: "without the hurt that reality makes." Baldwin once remarked that being attacked by White people only made him flare hotly into eloquence; being attacked by Black, he confessed, made him want to break down and cry. Baldwin hardly emerged from the efflorescence of his Black nationalism in the 1960s unscathed. Baldwin and Beam could both have told LeRoi Jones a great deal about the "hurt that reality makes," as could a lot of Black gay men in Harlem today who are tired of being used for batting practice. And in the wake of a rising epidemic of physical violence against gays, violence of the sort that Melvin Dixon has affectingly depicted in his new novel, *Vanishing Rooms*—it's difficult to say that we have progressed since LeRoi Jones.

That's not to say that the ideologues of Black nationalism in this country have any unique claim on homophobia. But it is an almost obsessive motif that runs through the major authors of the Black Aesthetic and the Black Power Movements. In short, national identity became sexualized in the sixties, in such a way as to engender a curious subterraneous connection between homophobia and nationalism. It's important to confront this head on to make sense of the ways *Looking for Langston* both fosters and transcends a kind of identity politics.

Surely one of the salient features of the work is its attitude toward the corporeal, the way in which the Black body is sexualized. Gloria Watkins has noted that Nina Kellgren's camera presents the Black male body as vulnerable, soft, even passive, in marked contrast to its usual representation in American film. It's a way of disrupting a visual order, a hardened convention of representation. There's a scene where we see slides of Robert Mapplethorpe photos projected on a backdrop while a White man walks through them. And I think there's a tacit contrast between those images, with their marmoreal surfaces and Primitivist evocations, and

Kellgren's own vision of masculinity unmasked. Indeed, this may be the film's most powerful assault on the well-policed arena of Black masculinity. *"And soft,"* Nugent writes of his character, Beauty, *"soft."*

In short, by insistently foregrounding—and then refiguring—issues of gender and desire, filmmakers like Reece Auguste, Maureen Blackwood, Isaac Julien, and others are engaged in an act of both cultural retrieval and reconstruction. And the historicity of that act—the way it takes form as a search for a usable past—is, as Hazel Carby and Houston Baker show, entirely characteristic of diasporic culture.

So the dialogue with the past, even a past figured as nonrecuperable, turns out to be a salient feature of what might be called the Black London Renaissance. The "partnership of past and present" is recast across the distances of exile, through territories of the imagination and of space.

A film like *Looking for Langston* is able to respond to the hurtfully exclusionary obsessions of the Black nationalist moment, and our own cultural moment as well, by constructing a counterhistory in which desire and mourning and identity can interact in their full complexity, but in a way that registers the violence of history. There are two reductive ways of viewing the film, therefore. The first is preoccupied with fixing the historical question about Hughes's sex life. The second says that the film is an imaginative meditation and "real" history is completely immaterial to it. On their own, both approaches are misguided. A more instructive approach is emblematized nicely by the Akan figure of "sankofa" itself (the word literally means "go back and retrieve it"), which refers to the figure of a bird with its head turned backward: again, the "partnership of past and present." Obviously the film isn't positivist history; and yet history, and the status of history, is its immediate concern. So we need to take seriously what Kobena Mercer calls the "artistic commitment to archaeological inquiry"[1] that's at work and at play here: and of course Stuart Hall's insistence that "cultural identities come from somewhere, have histories," is very much to the point.

While the film is not a simple exercise in identity politics, it cannot dispense with the moment of narcissism, of self-recognition. Hence the use of the mirror tableaux which thematize the film critic's concern with the dialectic of identification and spectatorship. A man in the club sees himself in the mirror and is caught up short. Water—ponds and puddles—is used as a reflecting surface. Indeed, toward the film's end, we are presented with a series of men who lie, Narcissus-like, with their face to a reflective surface. A belated version of the Lacanian mirror stage? Self-recognition? Or something else entirely? In the prose poem "The Disciple," Oscar Wilde writes:

When Narcissus died the pool of his pleasure changed from a cup of sweet waters into a cup of salt tears, and the Oreads came weeping through the woodland that they might sing to the pool and give it comfort.
. . . "We do not wonder that you should mourn in this manner for Narcissus, so beautiful was he."
"But was Narcissus beautiful?" said the pool. [. . .] "I loved Narcissus because, as he lay on my banks and looked down at me, in the mirror of his eyes I saw ever my own beauty mirrored."

The film, remember, is called *Looking for Langston*; it does not promise he will be found. In fact, I think that *Looking for Langston* leads us away from the ensolacement of identity politics, the simple exaltation of identity. We are to go behind the mirror, as Wilde urged. The film gives us angels— there are six of them, including the musician Jimmy Sommerville, with wings of netting and wire—but they are fallen angels, as Essex Hemphill tells us. There are moments of carnival—a club with spirited dancing amid the smashing of champagne glasses—but there are no utopias here. An angel holds a photograph of Langston Hughes, of James Baldwin, but history remains, in a phrase that Stuart Hall repeats, "the smiler with the knife." The carnival is disrupted by a group of men who are described indifferently by the credits as "thugs and police" and who represent both the authority of the state and the skinhead malevolence that is its funhouse reflection. In films like *Looking for Langston*, cultural studies becomes cultural work.

At the same time, controversy that surrounds the productions of Sankofa and Black Audio, the two most prominent collectives, leads to what has become *the* central problems for cultural criticism in our day. It's a theoretical terrain that can be taken either as a goldmine, or a minefield, depending on your point of view. I speak of the "new politics of representation," and the way this impinges on the normative self-image of the so-called oppositional intellectual.

To the extent that Black British Cinema is represented as an act of cultural politics, it then becomes vulnerable to a political reproach as elitist, Europeanized, overly highbrow; as a Black cultural product without a significant Black audience, its very "Blackness" becomes suspect.

This line of reproach ought to ring a bell: as I suggested at the start, it reprises one of the oldest debates in the history of Afro-American letters, which is usually framed as the Responsibilities of the Negro Artist. But the populist critique always operates in tandem as a statement about artists and critics.

The centrality of the issue is shown in the fact that a synoptic manifesto on the "new politics of representation" has been issued jointly by Isaac Julien and Kobena Mercer. Their argument follows Paul Gilroy, Pierre Bourdieu and Ernesto Laclau in linking the critique of essentialism to the critique of the paradigm of representation as delegation. That is, Julien and Mercer recast the ancient debate over "Black representation" by focussing on the tension "between representation as a practice of depicting and representation as a practice of delegation. Representational democracy, like the classic realist text, is premissed on an implicitly mimetic theory of representation as correspondence with 'real.' "[2]

It's been argued that we should supplant the vangardist paradigm of "representation" with the "articulation of interests." In such a way can we lighten the "burden of representation," even if we cannot dispense with it. But whose interest is being articulated?

Worrying that independent Black British cinema has become too estranged from the Black community, Paul Gilroy has recently proposed what he calls "populist modernism"—which some have decried as a highbrow version of the NAACP Image Awards. There are worries that normative proposals such as "populist modernism" can become techniques for policing artistic boundaries, for separating the collaborationist sheep from the oppositional goats, or perhaps the other way around. Gilroy cites Richard Wright's *The Outsider* as a model for Black art, but the poetic career of Langston Hughes might be an even more appropriate candidate for the category.

Perhaps more than any other African-American this century, Langston Hughes was elected popularly to serve as our "Representative Negro," the poet of his race; as we know, the burden of representation bore heavily upon him, profoundly shaping his career and preoccupations, propelling and restraining his own involvement with literary modernism. Nor is it surprising that his image should be, even in our own day, subject to censorship and restriction; Julien's difficulties with appropriating Hughes's texts reflect, in an ironic way, the central argument of his film.

How "modernist" is Julien's own technique? Manthia Diawara, a leading intellectual champion of Black British cinema, has observed that *Looking for Langston* has evident affinities with many avant-garde and experimental films of the 1970s. And yet, he argues, the film "appropriates the forms of avant-garde cinema not for mere inclusion in the genre, but in order to redefine it by changing its content, and re-ordering its formal disposition." In Julien's hands, he suggests, the techniques of the avant-garde are made to "reveal that which the genre itself represses."[3] Nor is it an uncritical act of reclamation. Diawara notes that "the dependency of artists and writers of the Renaissance upon their white patrons, and the links between the movement and Modernist Primitivism, are revealed in *Looking for Langston* as moments of ambiguity and ambivalence."[4]

Indeed, the importance of open-textured films like *Looking for Langston* is in presenting an aesthetics that can embrace ambiguity; perhaps it is not without its reverential moments, but neither is it a work of naive celebration. It presents an identitarian history as a locus of discontinuities and affinities, of shared pleasures and perils. Perhaps the real achievement of this film is not simply that it rewrites the history of Afro-American modernism, but that it compels its audience to participate in this rewriting.

Notes

1. Kobena Mercer, "Travelling Theory: The Cultural Politics of Race and Representation: an interview with Kobena Mercer," *Afterimage* Vol. 18, No. 2 (9–90).

2. Isaac Julien and Kobena Mercer, "Introduction—De Margin and De Centre," *Screen,* Vol. 29, No. 4 (Autumn 1988), 4.

3. Manthia Diawara, "The Absent One: The Avant-Garde and the Black Imaginary in *Looking for Langston,*" *Wide Angle,* Vol. 13, Nos. 3 & 4 (1991), 104.

4. Diawara, 108.

Black Spectatorship

13

Black Spectatorship: Problems of Identification and Resistance

Manthia Diawara

Whenever Blacks are represented in Hollywood, and sometimes when Hollywood omits Blacks from its films altogether, there are spectators who denounce the result and refuse to suspend their disbelief. The manner in which Black spectators may circumvent identification and resist the persuasive elements of Hollywood narrative and spectacle informs both a challenge to certain theories of spectatorship and the aesthetics of Afro-American independent cinema. In this article I posit the interchangeability of the terms "Black spectator" and "resisting spectator" as an heuristic device to imply that just as some Blacks identify with Hollywood's images of Blacks, some White spectators, too, resist the racial representations of dominant cinema. Furthermore, by exploring the notion of the resisting spectator my aim is to reassess some of the claims of certain theories of spectatorship which have not so far accounted for the experiences of Black spectators.

Since the midseventies much has been written on the subject of spectatorship. Early landmarks in the debate, such as articles like Christian Metz's on the Imaginary Signifier,[1] Laura Mulvey's on Visual Pleasure and Narrative Cinema[2] and Stephen Heath's on Difference,[3] with their recourse to Freud and Lacan, tended to concentrate the argument around gendered spectatorship. More recently, debates have begun to focus on issues of sexuality as well as gender, yet with one or two exceptions,[4] the prevailing approach has remained colorblind. The position of the spectator in the cinematic apparatus has been described by recourse to the psychoanalytic account of the mirror phase, suggesting that the metapsychology of identification (with the camera or point of enunciation) entails a narcissistic form of regression which leads to a state similar to the infant's illusion of a unified ego. But since spectators are socially and historically as well as psychically constituted, it is not clear whether the experiences of Black spectators are included in this analysis. Indeed, there are instances of film consumption which reveal the inadequacies of this approach and which implicitly question certain aspects of the prevailing problematic around spectatorship. To examine these instances, from the specific perspective of my own position as a Black male spectator, I want to suggest that the components of "difference" among elements of race, gender, and sexuality give rise to different readings of the same material. Specifically, as an African film scholar based in the North American context, I am interested in the way that Afro-American spectators may, at times, constitute a particular case of what I call resisting spectatorship. From the specificity and limitations of my own position as a Black male spectator the aim is to consider what insights this particular formation of spectatorship can bring to the analysis of Hollywood films.

To illustrate my argument I have chosen to begin with a sequence from *The Birth of a Nation* (directed by D. W. Griffith, 1915) to demonstrate how aspects of a dominant film can be read differently once the alternative readings of Afro-American spectators are taken into account, as the Black spectator's reluctance to identify with the dominant reading of this archetypical Hollywood text also underpins the protest elicited by a film as recent as *The Color Purple* (directed by Steven Spielberg, 1986). The five-minute sequence from *The Birth of a Nation* involves the pursuit of a young White girl by a Black man, often referred to as the "Gus chase" sequence. It takes place in the second part of the film, set in the period of Reconstruction in the South. Prior to this sequence, Senator Stoneman, one of the leading Northern White liberals, sends Silas Lynch, his mulatto protegé, to run for the seat of Lieutenant Governor in a Southern State. Silas conspires with "carpetbaggers" to deny Whites the right to vote and wins the election by means of the new Black vote. Soon, the new leaders of the South lift the ban on interracial marriages and the Whites, in response, form the Ku Klux Klan to protect themslaves from what they call "the new tyrants."

The "Gus chase" sequence begins with "Little Sister," from the plantocrat Confederate Cameron family, going to a secluded stream in the woods and ends with her death in her brother's arms. The sequence contains about 105 shots in six narrational units:

(1) Little Sister seen on her way to the stream/ Gus, the black man, following her unseen.

(2) Little Sister playing with a squirrel/ Gus watching her unseen.

(3) Gus confronting Little Sister and proposing to her/ Little Colonel looking for Little Sister.

(4) Gus chasing Little Sister/ Little Colonel coming towards the stream to look for his sister.

(5) Gus pursuing Little Sister to the top of the cliff where she jumps off/ Little Colonel approaching the scene.

(5) Gus, seeing Little Colonel, fleeing/ Little Colonel taking his dying sister in his arms.

The sequence is situated between two intertitles, one stating that Little Sister went into the woods despite her brother's warning, and the other that the gates of heaven will welcome her. Each alternated section is made up of several shots, some of which are repeated within the sequence. The rhythm of the editing is faster when Gus chases Little Sister and slower when Little Colonel takes her in his arms. Bright lights are cast on Little Sister and her brother while Gus is cast in dark shadows. Where Little Colonel wears a suit befitting his title and his sister wears a modest dress, Gus does not wear his captain's uniform and his broken English confirms his "inferiority" and otherness.

The dominant reading of this sequence supports a Manichaean worldview of race in which Gus represents absolute evil and Little Colonel and his sister embody absolute good. Editing, mise-en-scène, narrative content all combine to compel the spectator to regard Gus as the representation of danger and chaos; he is the alien, that which does not resemble oneself, that from which one needs protection. Whether Black or White, male or female, the spectator is supposed to identify with the Camerons and encouraged to hate Gus. Similarly, the popular Tarzan movies position all spectators, White and Black, to identify with the White hero; likewise, the Blaxploitation genre is intelligible to White spectators only if they suspend their critical judgment and identify with the Black heroes like Shaft in the film of that name (1971). What is at issue in this fragment from *The Birth of a Nation* is the contradiction between the rhetorical force of the story— the dominant reading compels the Black spectator to identify with the racist inscription of the Black character—and the resistance, on the part of Afro-American spectators, to this version of US history, on account of its Manichaean dualism.

In discussing the structure of myths, A. J. Griemas argues that at the basis of every story is a confrontation between *desire* and *law*.[5] The Oedipus myth provides a point of reference for certain theories of spectatorship which argue that each story fascinates the spectator to the extent that it retells the primordial Oedipus narrative, with its confrontation of desire and patriarchal order. But does this account for the positioning of the Black spectator of *The Birth of a Nation*? At the beginning of the story Gus enters the scene as the wrongdoer, and his punishment starts with the arrival of Little Colonel as part of a process to restore order and harmony in the South. Such an endeavor entails the resolution of the narrative fragment through Gus's punishment. The narrative thus proposes Little Colonel as the representative of the symbolic *White/Father* who will restore the law of patriarchal order by castrating the rebellious Black, Gus. It is Little Colonel who persuades the other Whites to form a Klan to terrorise and discipline the Blacks who threaten to destroy the social and symbolic order of the South. Thus Gus's desire for Little Sister is a transgression: the narrative of miscegenation links isomorphically with the Oedipal narrative of incestuous desire, an assault on the symbolic order of the Father which merits the most serious punishment—lynching. At the level of spectator identification, the narrative function summarised by the narrational sequence—"death of Little Sister"—is organised to position the spectator as the subject who desires to see, in the words of the intertitle, the "punishment and discipline of Gus and the Black race he symbolises."

The resisting spectator, however, refutes the representation of Little Colonel as an authoritative father figure and the narrative proposition that lynching is a means of restoring the racial and symbolic order of the South. By the time the film was made, the Civil War was understood by most Afro-Americans as a revolutionary war which emancipated the slaves and united the nation. The father figures and heroes of the story should, therefore, have come from the side of the victors, not that of the Klan, which symbolised resistance to the ideals of democracy. *The Birth of a Nation* appears to misread history for ideological reasons. Not only is Little Colonel a fake father and hero, but the Black experience is rendered absent in the text. The argument that Blacks in the South were docile and happy with their condition as slaves and that Black Northerners were only rebellious mulattoes aspiring to be White is totally unconvincing once it is compared to historical accounts of the Black American experience.[6]

It would be worthwhile to note how spectatorial resistance to the racist ideology encoded in *The Birth of a Nation* is expressed, often in "realist" terms, by invoking an alternative account based on Afro-American historical experience. This response has been recently echoed in certain reactions to *The Color Purple*. Pointing to the many racial stereotypes that it features, Rita Dandridge argues that, "Spielberg's credentials for producing *The Color Purple* are minimal. He is not a Southerner. He has no background in the black experience, and he seems to know little about feminism."[7] Bearing this point in mind I want to consider the image of the punished and disciplined Black man in contemporary films such as *Rocky II* (1979), *A Soldier's Story* (1984) and *Forty-Eight Hours* (1982), as well as *The Color Purple* itself.

It seems to me that the reinscription of the image of the "castrated" Black male in these contemporary Hollywood films can be illuminated by a perspective similar to that advanced by feminist criticism. Laura Mulvey argues that the classical Hollywood film is made for the pleasure of the male spectator. However, as a *Black* male spectator, I wish to argue, in addition, that the dominant cinema situates Black characters primarily for the pleasure of White spectators (male or female). To illustrate this point, one may note how Black male characters in contemporary Hollywood films are made less threatening to Whites either by White domestication of Black customs and culture—a process of deracination and isolation— or by stories in which Blacks are depicted playing by the rules of White society and losing.

In considering recent mainstream films, Eddie Murphy presents an interesting case for the analysis of the problematic "identification" between the Black (male) spectator and the image of the Black (male) character. Throughout the films in which Murphy has starred—*Trading Places* (1983), *Forty-Eight Hours*, and *Beverly Hills Cop I* and *II* (1984 and 1987)—his persona is that of the streetwise Afro-American dude, which might appear somewhat threatening. Yet in each narrative Murphy's character is deterritorialised from a Black milieu and transferred to a predominantly White world. As the *Beverly Hills Cop* he leaves Detroit for an assignment in Los Angeles, and in *Forty-Eight Hours* he leaves the prison (scene of punishment) to team up with the White policeman played by Nick Nolte. In this story, Murphy's character, Reggie Hammond, is a convict enlisted by the police to help track down two fellow prisoners who have escaped. Murphy's persona invokes the image of the criminalised Black male, and yet he is called upon to protect and enforce the law, given a gun, a police badge and handcuffs, all of which symbolise the same order that has punished and disciplined him. The two male protagonists are presented as antagonistic, but in the eyes of the Black/resisting spectator it is clear that he is only there to complement the White character as an authority figure. Nolte's character, Jack Cates, is tough, persevering and just, whereas Murphy's is exhibitionistic, inconsistent (swaying between good and evil) and inauthentic (he is to Nolte's character what Gus is to Little Colonel): Reggie Hammond transgresses the boundaries of the law established by Jack Cates as the representative of White authority. In one scene, which takes place in a redneck bar, Hammond asks Cates, the White policeman, to give him his gun and the badge temporarily, so that he can use them to obtain information from people in the bar. But Hammond cannot even get their attention until he starts an exhibition, shouting and screaming and throwing a glass which breaks on a mirror. It is interesting to compare this exhibitionist act to an earlier shot of a partially naked (White) female go-go dancer, the image of which frames the beginning and ending of this barroom sequence. Hammond takes the place of the woman as he becomes the object of the look of the men in the bar—and figure of the White spectator's fascination. In the fight between the two protagonists played by Nolte and Murphy, which takes place after the bar scene, Cates cannot get the desired information from Hammond, but on the other hand the fight is also motivated by the way that Hollywood requires that the Black character must be punished after he has behaved like a hero (albeit a comic one) and humiliated the White people in the bar. *Forty-Eight Hours* mixes genres (the police story and the comedy, the serious and the fake authority figures) and achieves a "balance" whereby the Black character is only good at subverting order, while the White character restores narrative order—in the end Hammond returns to jail. For the Afro-American audience, however, this racial tension and balance preempt any sense of direct identification with Murphy's character because ultimately his "transgressions" are subject to the same process of discipline and punishment—he is not the hero of the story, although he may be the star of the show. Black protagonists, such as Apollo Creed in *Rocky II*, receive a similar narrative treatment in which their defeat is necessary to establish the White male character, Rocky, as the hero. In both cases, the Afro-American spectator is denied the possibility of identification with Black characters as credible or plausible personalities. Thus, it cannot be assumed that Black (male or female) spectators share in the "pleasures" which such films are able to offer to White audiences.

Alongside the textual deracination or isolation of Blacks, the narrative pattern of Blacks playing by hegemonic rules and *losing* also denies the pleasure afforded by spectatorial identification. In terms of the Oedipal analogy in the structure of such narrative patterns, the Black male subject always appears to lose in the competition for the symbolic position of the father or authority figure. And at the level of spectatorship, the Black spectator, regardless of gender or sexuality, fails to enjoy the pleasures which are at least available to the White male heterosexual spectator positioned as the subject of the films' discourse. Moreover, the pleasures of narrative resolution—the final tying up of loose ends in the hermeneutic code of detection—is also an ambiguous experience for Black spectators. In *A Soldier's Story*, for example, Captain Davenport (Howard E. Rollins), a Black lawyer from Washington, comes to an army base in a small Southern town to investigate the murder of a Black sergeant. The dead sergeant had been hated by the enlisted Blacks because he blamed them for the problems caused by racism in the army. He was opposed to any expression of Black culture by the soldiers and is revealed at the end of the story of have been responsible for the death of Private C. J., who sang the blues, told folktales and played sports, thus asserting elements of Black culture. The Black soldiers resented the conflation of standard army behaviour with White culture and accused the sergeant of wanting to pass for White. Captain Davenport also represses his racial identity and idealises the US Army, yet while the sergeant displays his weakness through tears, uncontrollable laughter and alcoholism, the captain is cold, austere and businesslike. He rejects the probable but easy solution that the murder of the Black soldier was committed by the Klan, and embarks instead on a search for "the truth." The complex psychology of the two characters is not explored; the film simply idealises the army as a homogenous and just institution and ends with the arrest and punishment of a *Black* suspect, Pete (Denzel Washington). This surprise twist at the end of the narrative, which sacrifices one more Black man in order to show that justice exists, fails to satisfy the expectation, on the part of the Black spectator, to find the Klan or a White soldier responsible for the crime. The plot of *Soldier's Story*, with its predominantly Black cast, suggests a liberal reading of race in the American South; but by implicitly transferring villainy from the Klan to the Blacks, it denies the pleasure of resolution to the Afro-American spectator.

If we return to the sequence from *The Birth of a Nation*, it is possible to see the interaction of race and gender in two narrative situations which position the Black spectator in a similarly problematic relation to the film's ideological standpoint. The first is voyeuristic: Gus watches Little Sister as she innocently plays with a squirrel. Knowing that Gus has been following her, the spectator begins to fear for her safety. As the opening intertitle states, her brother warned her about the danger of being alone in the woods. Being watched unawares here connotes not the lures of voyeurism and exhibitionism, but danger, and equates Gus, intertextually, with the unseen danger that stalks the innocent in many thrillers and horror movies. The other situation concerns the chase itself. As Gus begins pursuing Little Sister, the parallel montage accelerates, encouraging the spectator to identify with the helpless condition of Little Sister. Only when Little Colonel appears does the spectator feel a moment of release, as she or he is repositioned to identify with the rescue of Little Sister. The long take of Little Colonel slowly raising his sister in his arms, and its subsequent repetition, is organised to make the spectator feel grief and desire vengeance against Gus. As I have argued, the Black spectator is placed in an impossible position—drawn by the narrative to identify with the White woman, yet resisting the racist reading of the Black man as a dangerous threat. It seems to me that a parallel dilemma is created in some scenes from *The Color Purple*, especially where Mister (Danny Glover) chases Nettie (Akosua Busia) on her way to school. This chase scenario is similar to that of the "Gus chase" sequence in many respects.

Both take place in the woods, outside "civilisation" and, in each case, a tall, menacing Black man chases an innocent girl with the intention of raping her. In each the girl epitomises innocence while the Black male connotes evil. The girls' activities—Little Sister playing with a squirrel, Nettie on her way to school to get a much needed education—encourage the sympathy of the spectator, while Gus and Mister symbolise a danger and brutality that solicits only antipathy on the part of the viewer. In *The Birth of a Nation*, evil and lust are attributed to the Black man and the Black woman alike, but in *The Color Purple* they are attributed to the Black male alone. Close-ups of Gus's nose and eyes appear to make him deformed, and telephoto lenses are used in *The Color Purple* to exaggerate Mister's features, as if to emphasise his inhumanity or bestial nature. Both films use parallel montage and fast rhythm to encourage the spectator to identify with the victims of the danger represented by Gus/Mister, and to desire lynching for Gus and punishment by death for Mister.

The pairing of these two "chase" sequences suggests another reading of the rhetoric of punishment. When Nettie hits Mister in the genitals her action can be seen as castrating, signifying the removal of the penis from an undeserving man; but in terms of narrative structure this can be read as a replay of the Gus chase sequence. The Manichaean figuration of Mister as evil (with its implicit judgement of Black males in general) is the main reason why some spectators—and Black men in particular—have resisted the dominant reading of *The Color Purple*. Its simplistic portrayal of the Black man as quintessentially evil prevents the film from dealing adequately with such complex issues as Black female and Black male relationships, White racism, sex, and religion that Alice Walker's original text addressed.

The treatment of the two shaving scenes also illustrates the film's denigration of the Black male. Here Celie replaces Little Colonel as the punishing agent or the father figure, just as Nettie does in the scene of the chase. Must the spectator adopt the dominant reading of these scenes, and be implicated thereby in the vengeance of Black women against Black men, or should this reading be resisted because it attempts to ally Black women with the symbolic White father in the castration of Black men? While the former reading is obvious in the first shaving scene, the latter reading is made possible through the montage of the second scene and the ideological positions of race and gender which it narrates. Because the first scene is preceded by a heartrending separation of the sisters imposed by Mister's cruelty, Celie's wish to kill him may be seen as a justified end to Black male tyranny and the liberation of the Black woman. But in repeating the same scene (note that *The Birth of a Nation* also repeats the vengeance-denoting shot of Little Colonel holding his sister), its message is unmistakable. The Black man's place of origin, Africa, it is implied, is' the source of his essential evil and cruelty. By intercutting violent shots of ritualistic scarring and other initiation ceremonies with shots of Celie and Mister, the film might be read as suggesting that sexism is fundamental to Black male and female relationships and that its locus is Africa. For the resisting spectator, the problem with this interpretation is that such juxtapositions might equally be read by a White male spectator as not only exonerating the White man from sexism, but more importantly, calling for the punishment of the Black man as the inevitable resolution to the conflict. Throughout this article I have argued for an analysis of resistant spectatorship, but the question of how some Black spectators identify with the representation of Blacks in dominant cinema—through an act of disavowal?—remains to be explored. On a more positive note, however, resisting spectators are transforming the problem of passive identification into active criticism which both informs and interrelates with contemporary oppositional filmmaking. The development of black independent productions has sharpened the Afro-American spectator's critical attitude towards Hollywood films. Black directors such as Charles Burnett, Billie Woodberry and Warrington Hudlin practice a "cinema of the real" in which there is no manipulation of the look to bring the spectator to a passive state of uncritical identification. The films show a world which does not position the spectator for cathartic purposes, but one which constructs a critical position for him or her in relation to the "real" and its representation. Other directors such as Larry Clark, Julie Dash, Haile Gerima and Alile Sharon Larkin use a mixed form of fiction and documentary in which the documentary element serves to deconstruct the illusion created by the fiction and makes the spectator question the representation of "reality" through the different modes. Clyde Taylor describes Clark's *Passing Through* (1977) as an attempt to "subvert the Hollywood action genre, riffing its search, confrontation, chase and vengeance formulas with unruly notes from the underground."[8] Women filmmakers like Larkin and Dash practice the mixed form, to counter dominant sexist and racist perceptions of Black women.

As more audiences discover such independent Black films, spectatorial resistance to Hollywood's figuration of Blacks will become increasingly focused and sharpened. In the influential Third Cinema film, *The Hour of the Furnaces* (1968), Frantz Fanon is quoted as saying that "every spectator is a coward or a traitor," a comment which resonates in independent film practices that question the passive role of the spectator in the dominant film culture. One of the roles of Black independent cinema, therefore, must be to increase spectator awareness of the impossibility of an uncritical acceptance of Hollywood products.

Notes

This essay was originally written in French in 1986 for inclusion in a special issue of *CinémAction* entitled "Le cinema noir Americain." It appeared in English for the first time in the *Screen* special issue, "The Last 'Special' Issue on Race," Vol. 29, No. 4 (Winter 1988). First of all, I wish to thank these journals for their kind permission to reprint this version of my article here. Second, I wish to acknowledge the criticism by several colleagues of my essentialist position in the article. Clearly, I am glad I wrote it, because it expressed my deeply felt sentiment about the representation of Blacks in the classical cinema. Feminist psychoanalytic theory was then the best instrument to articulate this sentiment. The article was also important for starting a debate in Black film criticism about race, class, gender, and sexuality. As I reread it today, I smile, and wonder about some of the totalizing claims I made. For a womanist critique of the article, see Cheryl Butler, *"The Color Purple* Controversy: black Woman Spectatorship," in *Wide Angle*, vol. 13, Nos. 3 & 4 (1991).

1. Christian Metz, "The Imaginary Signifier," *Screen,* Summer 1975, Vol. 16, No. 2., 14–76.

2. Laura Mulvey, "Visual Pleasure and Narrative Cinema," *Screen,* Autumn 1975, Vol. 16 No. 3, 6–18.

3. Stephen Heath, "Difference," *Screen,* Autumn 1978, Vol. 19 No. 3, 51–112.

4. Homi K. Bhabha, "The Other Question," *Screen,* November–December 1983, Vol. 24 No. 6, 18–36.

5. A.J. Greimas, *Sémantique Structurale*, Paris, Larousse, 1966, 213.

6. Reactions to *Birth of a Nation* and its place in Hollywood's history of racial representation are discussed in Donald Bogle, *Toms, Coons, Mammies, Mulattoes and Bucks*, New York, Bantam, 1974; Daniel Leab, *From Sambo to Superspade*, New York, Houghton Mifflin, 1976; Thomas Cripps, *Slow Fade to Black*, New York, Oxford University Press, 1977.

7. Rita Dandridge, "The Little Book (and Film) that Started the Big War," *Black Film Review*, Vol. 2, No. 2, 1986, 28.

8. Clyde Taylor, "The LA Rebellion: New Spirit in American Film," *Black Film Review*, Vol. 2, No. 2, 1986, 11.

14

The Harlem Theater: Black Film Exhibition In Austin, Texas: 1920–1973

Dan Streible

When we think of the history of the traditional, American, moviegoing experience, a number of images come to mind: the mighty Wurlitzer organ accompanying a movie palace's silent-era feature, the iconic searchlights proclaiming a Golden Age Hollywood premiere, teenagers cruising at the local drive-in, an audience of otherwise sensibly attired adults wearing cardboard 3-D glasses, and more recently, young adults carrying five-dollar bills to the cineplex at the end of the mall in order to see the latest sequel. But while these iconic, even stereotypical, images suggest something of the truth behind the American movie theater's history, they also omit much of the social reality that has coexisted along with these instances of the mainstream filmgoing experience. While Hollywood features and first-run urban theaters may have greater single importance than any other mode of exhibition, a number of other important alternatives have fleshed out audiences' encounters with film.

One such alternative, with a fascinating yet understudied history all its own, was the Black movie house circuit that existed in the United States from (at least) 1907 until the 1970s.[1] With the project in mind of examining the cultural, social, and economic history of Black film theaters, I will discuss in this essay the development of Black film theaters in Austin, Texas, focusing especially on that city's longest standing and most prominent "show," the Harlem Theater.

Although movies came to the Texas capital before the turn of the century, and all-movie theaters began to proliferate there during America's post-1905 nickelodeon boom, the first recorded "colored" film theater—the Dixie-Dale—opened in Austin in 1920 under the management of Joseph Trammell. I found no other details about Trammel or the Dixie-Dale, but it is recorded that after two years the theater was renamed the

Lincoln and managed by A. C. Lawson until it closed in 1928 or '29. Austin also supported a second Black movie house in the 1920s. The Lyric, which opened in 1922, just one block east of the downtown Lincoln, was owned and operated by Dr. Everett H. Givens, a practicing dentist (with an office next door) who would become Austin's most prominent Black civic leader from the 1930s until his death in 1962. For reasons unclear at this point, Dr. Givens's Lyric, which changed its name to the Dunbar when A. C. Lawson took over its management in 1929, survived the Lincoln by a few years, closing in 1931. Whether the first Black film theaters in Austin closed due to the Depression, the cost of converting to sound, or some other reason, is impossible to judge given the paucity of data available about these enterprises.

However, placing the existence of the Lincoln and the Lyric in the contexts of both African-American life in Austin and the concurrent national Black film theater scene enhances a historical understanding of these two houses both as businesses and as entertainment venues. From a national perspective, we know that the motion picture theater, with its roots in the Jim Crow era, had always been subject to racial segregation. Sometimes Black patrons were restricted to balconies or other special sections of the theater, but Black-only theaters were common in the United States from at least 1910, a year when a Black newspaper in Washington wrote matter-of-factly that "there are separate motion picture theaters among the whites and blacks in this country."[2] Although at the turn of the century "there was hardly a theater for colored people in the entire United States,"[3] by 1925, there were at least 425 Black theaters (of all types), virtually all of which offered films "in whole or part." Of these, nearly half were, like the Lyric and possibly the Lincoln, Black-owned.[4]

But ownership of Black movie houses, in contrast to the first-run, White theaters of the day, was not done by regional or national chains, nor by affiliated circuits; because houses operated independently, the dynamics of local conditions affected theaters like the Lincoln as much as national structures did. Historically, social and economic conditions changed greatly for Austin's Black community when its first Black movie houses appeared. During and after Reconstruction, Black neighborhoods had existed in several locations around Austin: Clarksville in west Austin, Kincheonville to the south, Gregoryville in East Austin, Masontown in the southeast, Horse's Pasture and Wheatville to the north, and so on.[5] Compared to other towns of the time, particularly in the South, race relations were fairly calm, albeit within the practice of institutionalized racism. The town boasted "three colleges and institutions for colored people,"[6] maintained some neighborhoods (such as Masontown) that were racially integrated among Blacks, Whites, Hispanics, and Asians, and in general obtained a reputation as a town without the major problems of racial violence that plagued most American communities. But during the teens segregation patterns began to develop.[7] In 1919 a White representative of the young NAACP was beaten by a White mob in the middle of downtown, and in the 1920s "the city of Austin created a 'Negro district' in East Austin . . . induc[ing] blacks to move there" by implementing tough zoning laws elsewhere.[8] So it was that the majority of Austin's African-American population (which has consistently remained at just below twenty percent of Austin's total) became concentrated in an area east of downtown and between 12th Street to the north and 7th Street to the south.

Not surprisingly, then, both of Austin's silent-era Black theaters were built on East 6th Street, near the racial dividing line of East Avenue, within the only downtown shopping and dining district that served Black patrons,[9] yet away from the White theater district on the city's main thoroughfare of Congress Avenue. I could uncover little information, however, that would indicate the nature or reception of these early movie houses. Longtime Austin resident L. C. Jones recalled visiting the Lincoln as a child, where he remembers a piano player accompanying the motion picture entertainment. Lonnie Bell, who wrote for the Black press in Austin for fifty years, indicates that in the 1920s both the Lyric and the "Lawson Lincoln Theatre" were among the very few venues for Black entertainment in the city and so "did well before the Great Depression in '29."[10] Other information about Everett Givens also indicates that he made the Lyric/ Dunbar into a focal point for the Black community, viewing the theater as a civic improvement project as much as a business investment.[11] That these two movie houses were well received and supported by the Black community can also be inferred from the fact that a 1940 account of Austin history prepared by students at Tillotson College (a Black institution) referred to the era of 1905 to 1929 as a time when "privately owned amusement centers were developed" by Blacks—even though no other Black amusements of record were instituted during this period.[12]

As I mentioned earlier, the cause for these theaters' demise cannot be established absolutely, but several factors undoubtedly offer reasonable explanations. Bell's assertion that it was the economic devastation of the Depression that closed the Lincoln and Dunbar makes logical economic sense. Black theater owners, like even the big-time operators, would have been hit hard as the US economy collapsed. Moreover, inasmuch as movie tickets are purchased with "disposable" income, Black patrons would have been especially likely to curtail their moviegoing since even before the Depression Blacks in Austin earned only one-half the wage of White workers.[13] More specifically, both houses in Austin would have found it even more difficult to cope with the hard times if they attempted to make the costly transition to sound technology in the late twenties or early thirties. The Dallas Film Board of Trade's statistics on Texas theaters indicate that many theaters, especially independently operated ones, closed in the early thirties, having no sound. (In Austin, two of the five White houses, the Crescent and Star, also went out of business in 1929 to 1931.) Furthermore, one-third of Texas' thirty "colored theaters" were listed as "closed, no sound" by the mid–1930s.[14] Other factors may have led to the closure of the Lincoln and Dunbar, but, given the theaters' dependence on the patronage of a small, economically marginalized population, in the midst of a severe depression their failure is not surprising.

But the history of Black film theaters in Austin did not end with the closing of the Dunbar in 1931. In that same year, real estate was purchased and construction begun on a new movie house that would serve as the hub of Black filmgoing in Austin for the next forty years. The Harlem Theater, which opened on October 5, 1935,[15] distinguished itself from the earlier theaters—and all subsequent ones—by being located in the heart of East Austin, at 1800 E. 12th Street, where it could better attract Black movie-goers.

However, before discussing the reasons for the Harlem's longevity, I point out that although it was Austin's only exclusively Black theater, it was not without its competitor for Black audiences. All accounts of Austin in the 1930s and forties agree that the Ritz Theater was the only other house that admitted Black patrons on a regular basis, though customers there were limited to balcony seating and made to use a separate entrance. The Ritz, located on the same block of East 6th Street where the Lincoln operated, opened in 1930 under White management, showing a variety of second-run Hollywood films. Manager J. J. Hegman (and his son after him) maintained the segregated seating policy until the Ritz's closing in the early 1960s. More prominent Austin houses, such as those first-run members of the prestigious Interstate Theater circuit (the Paramount, Texas, State, and Queen), advertised "colored midnight shows" from time to time as part of the chain's overall marketing scheme.[16] Thus, while there was some competition for the Black filmgoing audience, segregated, White-managed theaters did not attempt to offer African-Americans the filmgoing experience and environment of an all-Black house like the Harlem; however, the Ritz balcony and special events at other White movie establishments did continue to cultivate and maintain Black filmgoing in the Depression, when no Black Austin theaters were open.

When the Harlem opened in the midst of America's depression in late 1935, the theater soon established itself as one of Austin's most visible and stable Black-owned businesses. In film industry terms, the Harlem's success was small. With only 14,000 African-American residents in 1936, Austin's marketplace for Black films was extremely limited, and the theater never expanded nor led to a chain of others. But, through a combination of strategic location, product differentiation, managerial conservatism and diversification, the Harlem Theater was able to become a profitable local business in the midst of an industry whose structure tended to favor national giants.

Like the Lyric before it, the Harlem was established by a middle-class, Black Austin native who had been educated at Tillotson College and operated successfully in other local business before embarking on a risky career in the amusement industry. But George F. Jones, who was already in his forties when he opened the Harlem,[17] had also had some experience in programming films for Black audiences. His older brother Evie had purchased an Edison projector in the teens and traveled to tent shows in the South and Black churches in Philadelphia showing "church movies" (that is, filmed passion plays) to all-Black audiences.[18] After college, five years as a postal clerk, and ten years as a bookkeeper, George F. Jones himself had worked as the head of Prairie View, Texas's Auditorium (a film theater) while employed as a clerk at Prairie View State College (1925–1935).[19] With his wife, Sadie, a Prairie View graduate and educator, Jones was active in the Austin real estate market[20] and their "co-partnership" became known for "accumulating valuable real estate holdings."[21] For the last two decades of his life Jones devoted most of his efforts to managing the Harlem, setting up residence next door to the corner theater upon his return to Austin from Prairie View. While his establishment may not have been unique for its time (there were more than three or four hundred Black theaters in the country), the Harlem was remarkable for being only one of seven US theaters owned and operated by Blacks.[22]

As an experienced theater manager, real estate buyer, and member of Austin's African-American community, George Jones no doubt realized the importance of the theater's strategic location in determining its success at attracting moviegoers. East 12th Street was essentially the Main Street of East Austin.[23] The area around the Harlem represented a microcosm of African-American life: it was both a quiet neighborhood of residences, churches, grocers, drug stores, beauty shops, and cafés, and a place to be "going up on the cuts"—a street where the action and entertainment were, in the form of taverns, beer joints, and (a block away) the Cotton Club and Paradise Inn for music and dancing.[24] The Harlem was also part of "The End," that area around 12th and Chicon Streets (one block away) where Austin's streetcars, until their cessation in 1940, stopped and turned back toward downtown.[25] In essence, those factors which determined that White theaters were centrally located along Congress Avenue—transportation proximity, pedestrian traffic, shopping convenience, high visibility—similarly made East 12th the choice location for a successful Black movie house.

In terms of architecture and facilities, the Harlem was much like smaller, second-run houses found in towns across the country. The green, two-story, art deco exterior featured a neon marquee topped by the letters of the theater's name in lights. A small walk-up ticket window was flanked on either side by double doors and permanent lobby card and one-sheet poster displays. Inside, a small carpeted lobby led to the air-cooled auditorium, where chairs were divided into three sections by two aisles. Restrooms were on either side of the smallish movie screen, with a stage in front and dressing rooms hidden behind. Double wide "necking seats" were conspicuous at the ends of every other row on the center aisle. Upstairs there was no balcony, but small screening rooms were situated on both sides of the main projection booth, where two 35mm projectors were installed. The manager's office was maintained just off the right-hand side of the lobby.

The seating capacity of the Harlem is a matter of some confusion. Various printed sources put the number of seats variously at 685, 500, 480, and even as low as 250. Obviously the number probably changed slightly over time. George Jones made some renovations in the 1940s, and in the fifties a wider screen was installed. But judging from employees' oral accounts and photographic evidence, the higher numbers seem more accurate. Those numbers also indicate that the Harlem was of average house size, both for Black theaters and for second-run theaters in general.

But while the Harlem building may have been unexceptional, its programming in the 1930s and forties often set it apart from the other theaters in Austin. The basic format that Jones followed often mimicked the usual bill of movie fare found elsewhere: Saturday matinees, midnight shows, Fox Movietone newsreels, action serials, double features of Republic "B" Westerns and Hollywood "A" films, with occasional cartoons, and so on. In this respect, Black audiences got and enjoyed the same films and film stars as White audiences across the country. The Harlem programming during this period was difficult to identify in specific detail, but some of the features advertised included *Tropic Holiday* (1938, Dorothy Lamour), *Charlie Chan's Murder Cruise* (1940), *Too Hot to Handle* (1938, Clark Gable), and later, *Within These Walls* (1945, Thomas Mitchell), *Firebrands of Arizona* (1944, Republic), *A Tree Grows in Brooklyn* (1945, Elia Kazan), and *Sealed Verdict* (1948, Ray Milland). But, as George F. Jones' nephew and Harlem employee, L. C. Jones reported, Black theaters were usually considered last-run possibilities for the major Hollywood studios' product. Big star vehicles usually took a year or more to reach the Harlem, and prestige pictures sometimes never made it. The Harlem playbill for August 23–27, 1940 confirms this account: a recent Charlie Chan release was playing the same weekend as *Tropic Holiday* and *Too Hot to Handle*, both of which had been released two years earlier.[26]

But the Harlem distinguished itself in a more important way by offering the only Austin outlet for the all-Black productions made outside of the Hollywood studios. Again specific programming instances were difficult to identify, since newspapers did not list the Harlem's showtimes, but several sources confirm that the theater attempted to run Black productions when they were available. Horace Marion, a thirty-year employee, recalled that during Jones' tenure the Harlem featured a number of all-Black movies, especially Westerns starring Herb Jeffrey and some Black gangster pictures. In addition, Jay Knowles, an Austin film collector, owns a number of posters which had originally hung in the Harlem; they advertize such films as *Killer Diller* (1948, starring Butterfly McQueen and Nat King Cole), *She's Too Mean for Me* and *Up Jumps the Devil* (starring Black comic actor Mantan Moreland.)[27] It should be added, however, that although there was a major distributorship for Black films in Dallas (Sack Amusement Enterprises), the Hollywood distributors and White exhibitors conspired to keep Black productions marginalized. First, it was stipulated that Black productions would only be circulated in theaters having seventy-five percent or more Black patronage. Secondly, they "attempted to set low rental rates for colored cast plays," making the business of all-Black productions hardly profitable.[28] Thus, it remains uncertain whether the Harlem showed mostly regular movie fare because the Hollywood oligopoly offered little else, or because the management and audience actually preferred Roy Rogers to Herb Jeffrey.

As with White movie houses of the era, the Harlem of the 1930s and forties also supplemented its film programming with live entertainment and other attractions. Musicians, touring circuit shows of Black dance/variety groups, or individual performers such as the local favorite "Cherokee Bill" (a trickshooter and stunt artist) would appear on weekends and late-night bills. And Tuesday nights featured drawings for prizes donated by local merchants ("bicycles, watches, and groceries").[29]

Similarly, just as all-Black entertainments (both live and filmed) constituted a product Austinites could never or seldom find at the Ritz, the Black staff at the Harlem provided filmgoers with an environment that was surely more appealing to most than the segregated trappings of the downtown movie houses. While the Interstate theaters employed Black porters and maids (and *all* of their porters and maids were Black) the ticket girls, ushers, managers, and concessionaires were white.[30] However, all positions at the Harlem were filled by Black employees—with the single exception of the projectionists. Jones hired only union projectionists, and the local IATSE/MPMO was not integrated until the 1960s.[31]

But for a small neighborhood theater like the Harlem, any sort of product differentiation—whether it was with films, live acts, or "ambience"— would have failed to produce enough box office for the theater's survival. As with any theater, the bulk of the profit came not from fifteen and twenty-five cent admissions, but from concessions. On this count, the Harlem again distinguished itself as unique among Austin theaters. In addition to the usual popcorn, candy and soft drink sales, the Harlem operated a confectionery. L. C. Jones recalled that he was hired by his uncle George to run the Harlem Confectionery (it was sometimes listed as a separate business in the city directory) at the theater. This concession stand served moviegoers at a counter inside the lobby and also sold to walk-up customers on the street through a screened window that opened onto the Salina Street side of the building. The confectionary sold not only popcorn, candy, and drinks, but also ice cream, pickles, and chili burgers. On the opposite side of the theater, in the lot between the Jones residence and the Harlem, an outdoor "watermelon garden" featured umbrella-protected picnic tables where film and food customers could sit. By diversifying his movie house with such supplementary services, Jones created a popular neighborhood establishment with broad appeal, much as the drive-in operators of the 1950s or the picture palace entrepreneurs of the 1920s did.

Within the structures of a segregated society and economy, the Harlem capitalized on the possibilities of a movie house supported only by Black patrons, but its growth was necessarily limited by market size. Rather than attempt to expand into other theater holdings, Mr. and Mrs. Jones used such profits as they made to invest in real estate and maintained the Harlem in its original form until Mr. Jones's death in 1951.

But a transition to White ownership of the Harlem had already begun a few years before. According to several interviewees, Texas film business-men named Frank Lucchese and Jack Adams had purchased a half interest (possibly the silent partner Mr. Fry's share) in the Harlem during the late 1940s. When George F. Jones died, his widow sold the remaining share of the business to Lucchese as well. Then, in 1952, Frank Lucchese turned the Harlem over to his brother Sam, who managed the theater under the same policies as Jones until 1960.

The background to the Lucchese's involvement with the Black theater business is of some interest here, as it serves to illustrate the long and intricate tradition that ethnic film theaters possess.[32] The Lucchese family's interest in film theaters dates back to the first Sam Lucchese (1867–1929), an Italian immigrant and Texas bootmaker who bought a small San Antonio film theater which expanded into a chain of local houses (including the Nacional and Zaragosa) playing only Mexican/Spanish-language films. Son Frank managed the lucrative theaters until selling out in the 1930s. Then, in 1945, two Dallas film distributors, Jack Adams and Bob Warner, banded with Sam Lucchese, Jr., to form the Triad Amusement Company, which purchased two of Dallas' Black theaters, the Century and the State. For various reasons, a deal was struck in which Frank Lucchese left Austin in order to take over the Dallas Theaters, while his brother Sam moved from Dallas in order to take over management of the Harlem *and* of the Cactus Theater.[33] The latter, opened in 1939, was a White theater on East 6th which had been doing poor business but was somehow forced into the deal that enabled the Luccheses to acquire the Harlem.

With the arrival of Sam Lucchese, then, the Austin Black film theater entered into a new phase of its history: several changes were eventually made at the Harlem, and a new Black theater, the Carver, was opened where the Cactus had been. At both theaters, Lucchese continued to hire only Black employees (with the exception of himself and his son). Programming policies at the two theaters were basically identical, but strategies were put in place that differed slightly from those practiced by George Jones.

Second-run Hollywood movies still made up most of the programming, but Lucchese, either because of his distributor connections or his race, was able to secure more desireable film product and do it more quickly than Jones had been able to do. Six-month clearances were still common for the Harlem, but the theater was able to book prestige films like *The Ten Commandments* and the reissued *Gone With the Wind*. Very few all-Black productions were booked, but whenever Hollywood vehicles for Black stars of the 1950s (Dorothy Dandridge, Sidney Poitier, Harry Belafonte, and so on) became available they met with success at both shows, particularly at the Harlem.

A more significant policy shift, however, was Lucchese's successful attempt to program Hollywood genres which were, according to the "conventional wisdom," supposed to be most appealing to ethnic audiences: horror films and action films. Action/adventure films, Westerns, and gangster pictures usually did well at any time, Sam Lucchese III recalled from his days working for his father at the Harlem. Revivals of *Dracula*, *Bride of Frankenstein*, and the like made for successful midnight shows, which by the 1950s attracted mostly teenage audiences. As the Harlem's teen audience increased, rock and roll movies, from *Blackboard Jungle* (1955) on, also proved more popular than the usual run of films.

Live shows featuring touring Black variety groups continued to be popular, but were hired with less frequency as the decade wore on. A particularly popular act was a group known as the Brown Skin Models, who appeared several times at the Harlem for midnight weekend performances. But as professional touring groups began to dwindle on the film circuit, they were replaced at the Harlem by talent shows. Local performers would compete, on a weekly or monthly basis, for prizes given by area businesses.

In addition to continuing the Harlem's tradition of a film theater for the African-American community, Lucchese also attempted to keep a sagging box office up by competing more vigorously for the audience's ticket money. Like George F. Jones, he almost never took out advertising space in either the White or Black newspapers, but he did expand the Harlem's advertising practices. Flyers hyping the coming week's films were printed weekly and left in stacks at grocery stores, druggists, liquor stores, and restaurants around East Austin. Secondly, permanent one-sheet displays were installed in fifteen to twenty locations throughout the East End, and posters advertising the Harlem movies were changed twice each week. Finally, the Lucchese management attempted to offer Harlem patrons more appealing movie technology. Bids for 3-D installation were taken, but decided against. However, sometime around 1956 to 1957, Cinemascope equipment was purchased and a new, wider screen was built.

Although the success of the Harlem was limited in this era of falling movie attendance, the Carver—which Lucchese had never wanted to operate anyway—had an even slimmer profit margin. The theater was much smaller (only two hundred and fifty seats) and suffered from the competition offered by the Ritz and later the Yank, which programmed similar second-run films and some Spanish-language films. Although Lucchese tried to promote the Carver's opening by inviting Black civic leaders to the premiere, even that evening's crowd failed to fill the theater.[34] The theater's downtown location was no longer a desirable characteristic, as Austinites moved further and further away from the small area between the state Capitol building and the Colorado River. Ticket sales at the Carver in the late 1950s were sometimes as little as ten dollars a day. The second Black film theater remained a liability for the Lucchese operation. Within a year of Sam Lucchese's death in December 1960,[35] the Carver Theater closed. During the next ten years it reopened under four different names: The Carlos (1964–65), The Capri (operated by Paul Mathieson, 1965–1973), The Vagabond (1974) and The Sun (1975). Billed as an "art theater," the dollar-house fluctuated between programming X-rated skin flicks and revival/repertory films. Although its features occasionally had a Black or ethnic orientation (a documentary series about Black musicians, a horror triple feature),[36] the East 6th Street theater always played to integrated audiences after 1961.

The Harlem, however, remained a Black film theater throughout the 1960s. While the new management never had to turn away White customers (as Sam Lucchese had done on a number of occasions earlier in his tenure), the business attempted to continue to program for Black audiences. Little is known about how the Harlem was run by its second White owner, Vernon L. Smith, from 1962 on. Sam Lucchese's son recalled that Smith was from Dallas, and probably had a background with a distribution firm there. Josephine Ramey, who sold tickets at the Harlem for Smith, recalled only that as a film programmer he "didn't have the pull" of the previous owners, and business fell off considerably before Smith sold the Harlem (to Andy Majek) some time around 1970.

But the real reason that the Harlem went into decline in the 1960s was not so much related to management styles or to the quality of films, as it was to the changing social conditions in Austin and the nation. Up through even the late 1950s the White Interstate theaters had a written policy which instructed employees to inform customers that "this theater does not cater to Negro patronage at this time."[37] In December 1960, when University of Texas's Students for Direct Action began to demand desegregation by marching in front of the Texas and Varsity theaters,[38] Interstate attempted to discredit the protestors.[39] But the incident-plagued trend toward public integration persisted throughout the decade. As African-Americans generally became accustomed to using what had been White-only facilities— such as movie theaters—the ability of the Harlem to compete for the Black audience lessened. With the potential for African-American citizens to attend any theater or drive-in in town, the need for an exclusive Black theater became more and more irrelevant to many residents of East Austin.

Nevertheless, in July 1973, the Harlem, after having been closed for six months, reopened under the interracial management team of John Hutkin (a local sound engineer), Dennis Baum (an investment counselor), and Willie Winn (who had held various jobs in East Austin). The renovated theater, it was announced would institute a new, "Black-oriented screen policy," "designed to serve its community."[40] For the remainder of the year, the Harlem showed three features a week, with matinees and midnight shows on weekends. The specifics of its programming can be traced accurately, since for the first time in its forty-year history the theater began to advertise in the local newspaper. In 1973 the Harlem played most of the wave of "blaxploitation" films that were being shown at the other Austin theaters as well—*Superfly TNT*, *Hit Man*, *Trick Baby*, *Blacula*, *Black Caesar*, *Death Master*, and *Trouble Man*. The new owners showed an occasional non-Black film with the traditional action/horror appeal (*Soylent Green*, *For a Few Bullets More*), but preferred Black music films (*Wattstax*) and Hollywood movies by African-American directors and/or with Black subjects (*The Great White Hope*, *Across 110th Street*, *Buck and the Preacher*). It is difficult to assess how well the theater was doing financially during this brief period, or in what way its clientele had changed, but such concerns became irrelevant on December 30, 1973, when the Harlem Theater burned to the ground.[41]

But had fire not destroyed the East Austin institution, it is doubtful that the Harlem could have survived much longer as a Black movie theater. Although the East 12th Street neighborhood remains predominantly African-American, the establishment of a Black theater remains predicated on the assumption that there is a need in the community for services denied in White businesses.[42] The Harlem, like other East Austin businesses of its day, was a creation of segregation; one needed a Black movie house because African-Americans were excluded from all other movie houses. It was created in an era when, under the advice of conservative leaders like Booker T. Washington and Dr. Everett H. Givens, African-Americans were encouraged to make the most of their separate lot rather than insist on integration. "There are better five-cent theaters conducted by colored Americans than any controlled by the Whites, and why do you insist on going where you are not wanted?" the "Negro press" of 1910 told movie patrons.[43] With a philosophy of an integrated economy replacing one of a separate African-American economy, by the 1960s the days of the exclusively Black film theater were numbered.

Notes

1. In researching this paper the earliest reference I found to a particular Black movie house was 1910, but Greg Waller has presented evidence of a Black-run nickelodeon that opened in 1907. "Black Moviegoing and Film Exhibition in Lexington, Kentucky, 1906–1927." Paper presented at the Society for Cinema Studies Conference, Washington, D.C., May 27, 1990.

2. *Washington Bee*, July 9, 1910, 4.

3. *Negro Yearbook*, 1912, 24.

4. *Negro Yearbook*, 1931–32, 379.

5. "The Early Days in East Austin," *Austin American-Statesman*, March 2, 1986, D41.

6. *Austin City Directory*, 1903–04, 4. The schools were Tillotson College, Samuel Huston College, and the Texas Colored Deaf, Dumb, and Blind Institute in northwest Austin.

7. Freeman, Martha Doty. *East Austin: An Architectural Survey*. MS, 1980.

8. "The Early Days in East Austin," D41.

9. Longtime member of Austin's Black press, Lonnie Bell, wrote that East 6th Street was "the only place blacks" could eat, drink, shop for clothes, etc. See "A Look at Austin Black History from World War I to 1983," *East Austin Times*, February 11, 1983, 6. L. C. Jones, who came to Austin in the 1920s and later worked on East 6th in the clothing business, confirmed this in our interview.

10. Bell, 6.

11. Flachmeier, Jeanette H. "Pioneer Austin Notables," vol. II, 1980, 32. Givens reportedly arranged for children who did not have ticket money to earn passes by doing work.

12. Brewer, J. Mason, ed. *An Historical Outline of the Negro in Travis County*, 1940, 34.

13. Ibid.

14. *1936 Texas Theater Guide*.

15. Green, Le Verne. "Flames Engulf an Era, Black Celluloid Heroes," *Austin American-Statesman*, January 20, 1974, II, 9.

16. *1942 Yearbook: A round-up of showmanship ideas for every month of the year.* Interstate Theaters. Hoblitzelle Collections, HRC, University of Texas at Austin.

17. The Harlem property was also invested in by a silent partner, a Mr. and Mrs. Fry, according to both L. C. Jones and Travis County courthouse deeds for 1931.

18. As reported by L. C. Jones and his sister Evelyn Hamilton.

19. Brewer, J. Mason. *A pictorial and historical souvenir of Negro life in Austin, Texas, 1950–51,* 7. The notes also seem to indicate that George Jones had also done some type of film programming while working at the "DB&O," Austin's school for deaf and blind orphans.

20. Ibid. Travis County courthouse records also confirm this.

21. Ibid.

22. *Negro Handbook 1942,* 37. The other Black movie houses were in Paris, Texas; Washington, D.C.; Arkansas, Virginia, and Ohio (two).

23. "The Early Days in East Austin," D42.

24. Ibid. Also, confirmed by the L. C. Jones interview, November 30, 1988.

25. Dr. Everett Givens's dental practice had also moved to this area (1203 Chicon), further indicating the location's importance to the Black community.

26. *The Austin Informer,* August 24, 1940, 5.

27. The latter two films were released by Ted Toddy, a White Atlanta producer who "made black pictures with black casts" in the forties and also distributed the films of Black producer Oscar Micheaux. From an interview of David F. Friedman by David Chute. "Wages of Sin," *Film Comment* August 1986, 38.

28. *Negro Handbook 1943,* 261–262.

29. Green, 1974 (cited above).

30. From employee records in the Hoblitzelle Theatre Arts Collection, Harry Ransom Humanities Research Center, University of Texas at Austin.

31. This, according to Jim Malloy, former head of Austin's projectionists' union, who worked at the Harlem occasionally. This was not the case nationwide, however. In 1930 one hundred of the union's 2,600 motion picture operators were Black, though they were limited to work in the "colored belt" and could not vote in or attend regular union meetings. For a short time the twelve operators in Harlem had split off from IATSE and formed their own union, United Association of Colored Motion Picture Operators. See *Negro Membership in American Labor Unions.* Department of Research and Investigations/National Urban League, 1930, 96–97.

32. This material taken from interviews with Sam Lucchese, November 28, 1988, and from biographical files in the Barker Texas History Center, University of Texas at Austin.

33. This Cactus was owned by Austin's veteran theater entrepreneur, Richard S. "Skinny" Pryor, whose son "Cactus" not only worked at his namesake theater, but later went on to fame as an entertainer in radio, television, newspapers, and films.

34. Josephine Ramey, who worked at the Harlem as ticket salesperson for many years, worked at the Carver on its opening night. Interviewed December 1, 1988.

35. Lucchese was killed by a seventeen-year-old employee while leaving the Harlem late one night. "Trio Charged in Gun Death," *Austin American-Statesman,* December

7, 1960, 15; "Lucchese, 52, owner of Harlem and Carver shot in head," *Austin American-Statesman*, December 14, 1960.

36. Richardson, C. A. "Capri Theater Aids Hopper Movie," n.d. Clipping in Austin History Center file, AF-M8300 (21).

37. Interoffice communications from Interstate General Office, Dallas, to all city managers. June 10, 1954 and June 7, 1956. In the Hoblitzelle Theatre Arts Collection.

38. "Racial Fuss Closes Door to Theatre," *Austin American-Statesman*, December 10, 1960. "Integration Group Mills at Theatres," December 11, 1960.

39. Jim Malloy maintained that the local Interstate manager commissioned him to install a hidden camera (!) in front of the Varsity so that protesters could be recorded on film by the ticket seller. Malloy built in the hidden camera and set up a screening of the final product for several Interstate managers who met at the Austin Hotel. He was not privy to their secret meeting, but he assumed that they were looking for political undesirables among the group, in order to smear their cause.

40. "Harlem Theater Re-Opens," *Austin American-Statesman*, July 16, 1973, 59.

41. Green, 1974. Today the property where the Harlem was built remains an empty lot. However, the memory and legacy of the theater's role in the East Austin community were paid tribute in 1989 when students from Austin Community College painted a colorful mural replica of the Harlem. On the facade of the closed Elks Lodge building, just a few blocks from where the theater originally stood, a life-sized representation of the deco building is now on public display (complete with three-dimensional marquee reproducing the Harlem's cutout letters).

42. See Kinzer, Robert H. and Edward Sagarin. *The Negro in American Business: The Conflict Between Separation and Integration.* New York: Greenberg, 1950.

43. *Washington Bee*, June 4, 1910, 1.

Archives Consulted

Austin Texas History Center, Austin Public Library, Austin, Texas.

Barker Texas History Center, University of Texas at Austin.

Hoblitzelle Collection, Theater Arts Collection, Harry Ransom Humanities Research Center, University of Texas at Austin.

Travis County Courthouse, Deeds and Records, Austin, Texas.

Interviews

Hamilton, Evelyn. Santa Monica, California (via telephone). November 30, 1988.

Jones, L. C. Former employee of the Harlem and Carver Theaters: nephew of the Harlem's original builder/owner. Austin, Texas. November 30, 1988.

Jones, Alice. Former employee of the Harlem and Carver Theaters. Austin, Texas. November 30, 1988.

Knowles, Jay. Private Collector; Harlem patron. Austin, Texas. October 27, 1988.

Lucchese, Sam. Former employee of Harlem and Carver Theaters; son of the second owner of the Harlem. Austin, Texas. November 28, 1988.

Malloy, Jim. Motion Picture Operator. IATSE. Austin, Texas. December 1 and 2, 1988.
Ramey, Josephine. Ticket salesperson at the Harlem. Austin, Texas. December 1, 1988.

Other Sources Consulted

1936 Texas Theater Almanac. Dallas: Dallas Film Board of Trade, 1936.

1938 Texas Theater Guide, 14 edition. Dallas: Dallas Film Board of Trade, 1939.

1942 Yearbook: A Round-Up of Showmanship Ideas for Every Month of the Year. Dallas: Interstate Theatres, 1942.

1955 Texas Theater Guide.

1956–57 Texas Theater Guide.

1960 Texas Theater Guide.

Abajian, James de T. *Blacks in Selected Newspapers, Censuses, and Other Sources,* 198?

The Afro-American Texans. University of Texas at San Antonio, Institute of Texan Cultures, 1975.

Austin American-Statesman.

Austin City Directory.

Austin History Center, clippings file.

Barker Texas History Center. Biography files: J. J. Hegman, Sam Lucchese, Dr. Everett H. Givens.

Bell, Lonnie. "A Look at Austin Black History from World War I to 1983." *East Austin Times,* February 11, 1983, 6.

Bell, William K. *A Business Primer for Negroes.* New York, 1948.

Bogle, Donald. *Blacks in American Films and Television: An Encyclopedia.* New York: Garland, 1988.

———. *Toms, Coons, Mulattoes, Mammies and Bucks.* New York: Von Nostrand Reinhold, 1972.

Brewer, J. Mason. *An Historical Outline of the Negro in Travis County.* Austin: Sam Huston College, 1940.

———. *A Pictorial and Historical Souvenir of Negro Life in Austin, Texas: 1950–51.*

Capital City Argus.

Chute, David. "Wages of Sin," Film Comment, August 1986, 32–48.

Cripps, Thomas. *Black Film as Genre.* Bloomington: Indiana University Press, 1978.

———. *Slow Fade to Black:* The Negro in American Film. Oxford: Oxford University Press, 1977.

The Crisis: A Record of the Darker Races. NAACP journal, 1910–

East Austin Times.

Fachmeier, Jeanette Hastedt, *Pioneer Austin Notables,* vol. 2. Austin, 1980, 29–33.

Freeman, Martha Doty. *East Austin: An Architectural Survey.* Unpublished MS. 1980.

Fuller, M. A. B. comp. *Historical booklet of religious, business and professional men and women.* 1948. Austin Texas History Center, A 920 Fu.

Guzman, Jessie Parkhurst, ed. *Negro Yearbook 1952*. New York: William H. Wise & Co., 1952.

Hall, Bruce H. "The Negro and His Pleasures." *Opportunity*, May 1937, 138, 156.

The Illustrated News (Austin).

Kinzer, Robert H. and Edward Sagarin. *The Negro in American Business: The Conflict between Separation and Integration*. New York: Greenberg, 1950.

Klotman, Phyllis Rauch. *Frame by Frame—A Black Filmography*. Bloomington: Indiana University Press, 1979.

Murray, Flo, ed. *The Negro Handbook*. New York: Wendell Malliet & Co., 1942–1949.

Murray, James. *To Find an Image: Black Films from Uncle Tom to Superfly*, Indianapolis: Bobbs-Merrill, 1973.

Negro Digest.

Negro Membership in American Labor Unions. Department of Research and Investigations, National Urban League. New York: Negro U.S. Press, 1930.

Operation Impact: Working Papers on East 11th & 12th Street Area. MS February 16, 1988.

Simons, Ada, ed. *Delta Sigma Phi Present the Black Heritage Exhibit: A Pictorial History of Austin, Travis County, Texas' Black Community, 1839–1920*. n.d.

The Voice (Austin).

Work, Monroe N., ed. *Negro Year Book 1912–1938*. Tuskegee: Negro Yearbook Publishing Co.

15

The Black Image in Protective Custody: Hollywood's Biracial Buddy Films of the Eighties

Ed Guerrero

Since the collapse of the early to mid-seventies Black movie boom and the Blaxploitation genre, the terms of Black representation in dominant, narrative cinema have drastically shifted and regressed in a number of significant ways. Besides the resurfacing of the crude and obvious stereotyping of Blacks in such films as *Caddyshack* (1980) or *Weird Science* (1985), or the reemergence of moments of blackface and a sustained representational style amounting to "neo-minstrelsy"[1] in such films as *The Blues Brothers* (1980) or *Soul Man* (1986), Hollywood has deployed a variety of narrative and visual "strategies of containment"[2] that subordinate the Black image and subtly reaffirm dominant society's traditional racial order. There has been much protest and critical writing, for example, about Black energy and talent being confined to expression in mostly comic roles and vehicles, in complete disproportion to the paucity of dramatic features exploring the range and complexity of Black life and culture in America. Certainly this issue tends to be illustrated by the screen personas and career trajectories of superstars Bill Cosby, Richard Pryor and Eddie Murphy, in contrast to a deficit of dramatic stars, male or female, of similar stature.

Another all-too-common industry strategy for containing the range and potentialities of Black filmic talent is that of giving a Black star top billing in a film in which he or she is completely isolated from other Blacks or any referent to the Black world. In this situation, what there is of Black culture is embodied in an individual Black star surrounded and appropriated by a White context and narrative for the pleasure of a dominant, consumer audience. Perhaps one of the most unambiguous expressions of this convention is the frank celebration of militarism and patriarchy *An Officer and a Gentleman* (1982), in which Louis Gossett Jr. is reduced to a deracinated zero, culturally differentiated only by the color of his skin. Moreover, Whoopi Goldberg's two comedy/action vehicles *Jumpin' Jack Flash* (1986) and *Burglar* (1987), while giving her the cultural latitude of two brilliant vignettes, in which she impersonates a disgruntled Black maid and parodies one of the Supremes, confine her in the isolation of playing to White sensibilities.

Additionally though, when it has come to the representation of Black romance or sexuality on the screen, Hollywood has almost entirely avoided or repressed the former and, to this day, has depicted the latter in the most distorted and perverse terms and images, from the romantically sanitized star vehicles of Sidney Poitier to the Black woman's routine construction as the sign of the whore, to the depiction of Black men as sex criminals from Gus in *The Birth of a Nation* (1915) to Mister in *The Color Purple* (1985). And overall, it has been argued, extending the ideas in Laura Mulvey's work exploring the cinematic objectification of the female body, that, in the broadest sense, all of these narrative strategies and modes of Black representation and subordination construct the Black body as the object of "the look" for the pleasure of the dominant spectator. Perhaps Gladstone Yearwood maps the terms of this understanding best when he observes that when it comes to Blacks on the commercial screen, dominant spectator pleasure

> . . . centers around the acquisition of the black body through symbolic domination and control, and involves (a) the constitution of the specta-tor in relation to the film, (b) the specific presentation of the black body within the narrative diegesis and (c) the ideological area which surrounds the development of cinematic languages and pictorial tech-nology in the ways that camera and lighting, for example, function to attach semes of inferiority, fear or suspense to blackness. Hence, traditional cinema produces a structure of seeing within which the black body is constituted as the object of the look, thus reproducing traditional relations in society.[3]

While keeping the often overlapping lines of these various conventions of Black representation in mind, for the purposes of this essay, I wish to discuss what has come to be the predominant narrative and marketing strategy for constructing and containing the cinematic image of Blacks in the eighties, the biracial "buddy formula." The buddy movie has been a Hollywood staple for some time and has made biracial statements going back to *The Defiant Ones* (1958) and *In The Heat of the Night* (1967). Moreover, the present cycle of biracial buddy vehicles was preceded by a seventies cycle of White, male buddy movies initiated in 1969 with the release of such influential films as *Easy Rider, Butch Cassidy and the*

Sundance Kid and *Midnight Cowboy.* During the seventies many critics were quick to observe that the White, male buddy films of this period were most obviously a reaction, transcoded into cinematic terms, to the then-emergent Women's Movement. According to critic Robin Wood, the buddy films of the seventies mediated a number of shared qualities, including the all-important marginalization or erasure of women from the narrative, the absence of a home and the narrative articulation of a journey. Wood also notes that, while these films were commercially successful, they had all but disappeared by the early eighties.[4]

However, to extend Wood's argument, what has happened is that the White, male buddy movie of the seventies has mutated into the biracial buddy formula of the eighties. And as a result of this racial transposition one must add one overarching characteristic to those already posited. It seems that in a decade most easily identified by the tenure of the Reagan Presidency, the rise of an ideologically conservative cycle of Hollywood films variously known as the "cinema of recuperation" or "Reaganite Entertainment,"[5] and the return of big-budget films of "blockbuster" economics, Hollywood has put what is left of the Black presence on the screen in the protective custody, so to speak, of a White lead or co-star, and therefore in conformity with dominant, White sensibilities and expectations of what Blacks should be like. Perhaps Black filmmaker Robert Townsend best describes the film industry's paranoid perception of Blacks in the eighties when he observes that "Hollywood is afraid that if you have more than one black person in a movie you have a black movie."[6] Because Hollywood is intent on bringing in the broadest box office possible with the installation of crossover thematics and the recognition of a few token Black stars, first Richard Pryor, and since the mid-part of this decade, Eddie Murphy, dominant cinema has been reluctant to cast Black leads without a White buddy as cultural and ideological chaperone or without a space or point of identification structured into the diegesis for the dominant spectator. Noted variations on this latter strategy consists of seeing Black social struggle through White eyes, as when the comparatively petty travails of reporter Donald Woods marginalize the historical struggle of his Black "buddy" Steve Biko, in *Cry Freedom* (1987). Or consider one of the infrequent White buddy vehicles of the eighties, *Mississippi Burning* (1989), which reduces Blacks to passive objects of their own history when a key event in the insurgence of a sixties, activist, Black, political consciousness is told through the experiences and emotions of two White FBI agents.

Film industry attempts at depicting the Black world in any degree of social intricacy or psychological depth, or as understood from a Black point of view, as few and far between as they were, quickly became casualties of the eighties implementation of the biracial buddy formula.

Moreover, Black critics Warrington Hudlin and Donald Bogle astutely observe that contemporary biracial buddy films present the audience with escapist fantasy narratives and resolutions, which in some instances articulate allegorical or metaphorical dimensions that mediate America's very real and intractable racial problems.[7] For instance, weigh the social tensions and fears transcoded into the sci-fi buddy feature *Alien Nation* (1988) when a spaceship carrying escaped alien slaves lands in California and quickly establishes an expanding community in LA that is patrolled by a bispecies buddy team of undercover cops. Because its complex imbrication of politicized and racially coded meanings allude to all non-White racial minorities, the film's narrative is allegory for the present wave of Latino, Asian and West Indian immigration to this country, while it also evokes the nation's repressed, historical relationship to Blacks and chattel slavery.[8] Thus one can discern that the popularity and number of these films is due, in part, to their ability to transcode, even into terms of fantasy, social unease over rising racial tensions of a recently pluralized society with an expanding non-White population to accommodate and a shrinking reserve of economic opportunities. Moreover when one considers that by the mid-eighties the average cost of a film was twelve to fifteen million dollars, and three times that amount had to be recovered to make a profit,[9] in the final instance, for the film industry, the primary appeal of the biracial buddy movie is material. Hollywood well understands that the biracial buddy film represents a proven formula for meeting first its material but also ideological needs. For the buddy formula is able to attract the demographically broadest possible audience while negotiating, containing and fantastically resolving the tangled and socially charged issue of race relations on the screen.

Perhaps one can best understand the results of the overdetermining pressure of the biracial buddy formula and crossover marketing on Black filmic representation by examining the schizophrenic trajectory of Richard Pryor's, and to a lesser degree Eddie Murphy's, films. In the case of Pryor, his films seem to pull in two distinct directions. One current of Pryor's work consists of his Black-oriented vehicles, which employ a variety of Black actors and actresses, and which position him as the main protagonist negotiating politicized narratives focused on the social complexities of the Black world, or Black and White race and class relations. This current is best exemplified by such films as *Which Way Is Up?* (1977), *Blue Collar* (1978), or *Bustin' Loose* (1981), Pryor's brilliant concert film *Richard Pryor Live in Concert* (1979), and his autobiographical *Jo Jo Dancer Your Life Is Calling* (1986). The second current in Pryor's work, represented by such films as *Silver Streak* (1976), *Stir Crazy* (1980), *Brewster's Millions* (1987), and *Hear No Evil, See No Evil* (1989) which feature him as lead or co-star in a series of crossover buddy vehicle comedies that isolate and subordinate him in a dominant cultural context, and limit his talents to playing the comic foil or to scene stealing. Moreover, moments in some of these vehicles come embarrassingly close to regurgitating, in updated forms, putrid stereotypes of Hollywood's frankly racist past. In *The Toy* (1983) Pryor plays a contemporary slave, chattel brought home and kept for the entertainment of a rich man's son. In *Silver Streak* Gene Wilder dons blackface, gaudy clothes and follows Pryor's instructions on how to act stereotypically Black in order to evade pursuing villains. A milder variation on this theme is played out in *Stir Crazy,* when Pryor shows Wilder how to avoid mistreatment in prison by acting "bad," which turns out to be a comic interpretation of Black urban toughness and cool. Notably, one could not imagine either of these scenes surviving without protest if it were not for Pryor's star power or negotiating presence in them.

Most revealing though, is the fact that this latter current of crossover buddy films is by far the more commercially successful and popularly accepted direction in his work. Pryor's attempts at Black focused narratives, dramatic or otherwise, with the exception of Pryor's live concert productions, were by comparison to his buddy movies, box office duds. The moviegoing audience has refused to recognize Pryor on his own self-defined cinematic terms, which have always involved an exploration and articulation of the intricacies and ironies of Black life in America. Rather, when it comes to narrative commercial cinema, the dominant audience has mostly supported Pryor as a meek clown in the protective cultural custody of a White buddy or co-star. And as some critics have sadly noted, as the decade has worn on Pryor's formulaic comedies have become ever more ossified and clichéd, reflecting "an almost obsessive yet futile desire to please the white moviegoing public."[10]

To a lesser but still recognizable degree one can discern this same social, dichotomizing pressure in the filmic work of Eddie Murphy. Notably, his comedy-adventure *The Golden Child* (1986), and his Black-focused comedies *Coming to America* (1987) and *Harlem Nights* (1989), all of which situated Murphy in Third World or Black environments and supported him with non-White or Black casts, came nowhere near the box office earnings of his buddy movies. Murphy's buddy vehicles, *48 Hours* (1982), *Trading Places* (1983) and *Beverly Hills Cop I* and *II* (1984 & '87) were tremendous box office hits that propelled Murphy to the position of top entertainer in America by the mid-eighties.[11] As for *48 Hours,* the film that launched Murphy's superstar career, it literalizes the metaphor of the Black image as held in protective custody, for Murphy plays a convict who is temporarily paroled to a tough inner-city cop (Nick Nolte) to assist in solving a series of crimes. Paralleling the relationship between Sidney Poitier and Rod Steiger in *In the Heat of the Night* (1967), Murphy and Nolte are trapped in circumstances where they must form an uneasy alliance to resolve a disruptive criminal situation for the benefit of the dominant social order. And much like *In the Heat* the two protagonists come to respect each other, and function in the narrative as biracial buddies. In another narrative detail that compares to the actions of Poitier's character in *The Defiant Ones* (1958), Murphy's character, Reggie Hammond, reveals himself as no militant by choosing not to escape when he has the chance. He prefers instead to remain unfree in order to help solve the problems of the system which has confined and punished him. It would seem that Hudlin and Bogle's observation—that biracial buddy films in many instances are metaphor or allegory for race relations in America— is relevant to all three of these films, *48 Hours, In the Heat,* and *The Defiant Ones,* in that they all depict Blacks and Whites caught in situations that they would have rather avoided, and in which they are interdependent and ultimately must come to understand each other to solve the poisonous problem of racial conflict in order to keep the society intact. Of course the limitations of this reading are obvious, for dominant cinema either proscribes or eradicates the Black point of view in these narratives; invariably it is the Black man who makes a sacrifice to solve the White man's problems.

However, the cinematic terms of Black subordination run much deeper than merely volunteering Black energy to solve the problems of the dominant social order. And to better understand these terms one must explore, the by far most analyzed, written-about and impressive scene in *48 Hours,* which occurs when Reggie Hammond (Murphy), as a criminal impersonating a cop, violently crashes and proceeds to interrogate an entire redneck country and western bar. This scene clearly draws upon Gene Hackman's memorable, racially reversed but similar rousting of a "ghetto" bar in *The French Connection* (1971). However, Murphy's bar scene is deceptive, in that it seemingly depicts an overturning of Black/ White power relations. The scene thus appears to contradict the racial order of a narrative which inscribes Whites in the superordinate position. Under more thoughtful analysis, though, it becomes clear that the bar scene makes the subtle argument that if Blacks were to attain social authority and leverage, and by implication full equality, they would behave as brutally towards Whites as they have been historically treated by them. So in the spectacularly violent and visual logic of dominant commercial cinema, there occurs in this scene a sort of masochistic, titillating pleasure for the dominant spectator, which consists of seeing his or her "worst nightmare"—as Hammond puts it in the diegesis—played out, while at the same time Reggie Hammond as "the return of the repressed"[12] is safely distanced and contained in the illusionistic zone of the movie screen.

Murphy has been able to guarantee his position as one of the eighties' top box office commodities with the outstanding successes of *Beverly Hills Cop I* and *II*, both of which were the top grossing films in their respective years, '84 and '87. As further material evidence of his popularity, Murphy's films have earned over $685 million for Paramount in the past five years, and he has signed an exclusive, six-picture contract with the studio that will earn him twenty-five million dollars.[13] Moreover, because of his tremendous crossover appeal, Murphy has been able, as were Poitier and Cosby, to modify to a degree the terms and conventions of Black cinematic containment. In *Beverly Hills Cop,* which was an enormously popular hit, earing $64.5 million in its first twenty-three days of release, ranking ninth among the top fifty money-making films of all time,[14] as well as in *Cop II,* Murphy is able to use star power accumulated from previous hits to moderate the terms of the buddy formula, and place himself in the superordinate position in the narrative, using his supporting White, buddy cops as foils or straight men for his irreverent, streetwise humor. Yet as the names of both films indicate, one he leaves Detroit, Murphy is situated in an all-White locale and all-White narratives.

The recurring central gag or comic motif, played to endless variation in all of Murphy's hit, buddy vehicles is predicated upon the Black penetration of clearly demarcated White cultural, social or physical space. Moreover the expression of this penetration is tinted with class concerns and tensions. Clearly the most powerful instance of this motif in *48 Hours* is its bar scene. Moreover, in *Trading Places* the entire narrative turns on Murphy's transposition from Black pauper/hustler to stockbroker. And in *Beverly Hills Cop I* and *II*, Murphy's intrusiveness takes the form of a Black, streetwise cop from Detroit, dressed casually in a high-school letterman's jacket for undercover effect, dissembling and using various ruses to penetrate the exclusive, all-white socialite dominions and clubs of Beverly Hills. In some manner all of these films are driven by the disruptive effects of Murphy's irreverent and cocky interpretations of Blackness on the dominant White social order. And of further significance, because of the duality of racial perception in American culture, with Whiteness constructed as the "norm" and Blackness as its absolute polar "other,"[15] the cultural contrast, social tension and irony exploding within these scenes energizes a comedy that can be enjoyed from a number of spectating positions on the racial-cultural continuum, from dominant to resistant to liminal and so on.

Therefore, without discounting Murphy's considerable talents or unique gift for comic improvisation, it is clear that the source of energy and tension in all of Murphy's buddy movies is race, and to a lesser degree class, deriving from Murphy's Blackness challenging White exclusion, but not domination or privilege, as he crashes bars, parties (most notably Hugh Hefner's), private supper clubs and spas, while he appropriates cars, mansions and so on to move the plot. Yet, importantly, the problem with the challenge of such an interpretation of Blackness is that it is that of an isolated Black individual relentlessly contained by a White environment. And while Murphy gets the upper hand in almost all filmic encounters and confrontations, the ultimate result of such a challenge is integration and acceptance on White terms in these film's plots and resolutions. After winning the grudging acceptance of a White street cop, at the end of *48 Hours* Murphy is returned to prison. In *Trading Places* he is integrated into the capital class, and by the film's closure he has fully internalized its values. And in the two *Beverly Hills Cop* movies, Murphy leaves his responsibilities in Black Detroit to diligently solve the problems of a city whose very name is emblematic for ostentatious displays of wealth and privilege, as well as its racial/social exclusivity.

However, to say all of this is not to entirely dismiss Murphy's films or talent. For the problems raised by his screen persona, characters, and films stem as much from the terms of fetishization and social confinement, which to some degree all stars must endure, overlaid with dominant cinema's ceaseless containment of the Black image, more than they do from any predilection on his part. In the final instance, the biracial buddy formula and Murphy's star power are overdetermined by the needs of the social and economic moment. For the power and appeal of his comedy lie in his paradoxical positioning at the top of the entertainment business, while he raises and rationalizes the contradictions of America's ongoing, mostly repressed, or masked discourse on race. But also, as discussed, much like Richard Pryor before him, he has used his star power to attempt to break out of the confinement of Hollywood's formulas. Through his association with the "Black Pack" Murphy has used his considerable leverage to place more emerging Black filmmakers into production situations in the industry.[16]

What is more, to interrogate the biracial buddy formula in all of its intricate expressions as an instrument of domination is not to overlook those few films that hold out the possibility of a more humane and less ulteriorly manipulated representation of biracial buddies. Two industry attempts at varying the formula and depicting Black and White buddies with more social honesty than is usual for Hollywood are *Lethal Weapon,* starring Danny Glover and Mel Gibson, and *Gardens of Stone,* starring James Caan and James Earl Jones, both released in 1987. *Lethal Weapon,* while trapped in the staid conventions of the action/cop/buddy movie, proves interesting in that it contrasts the wise restraint of an older Black cop, (Glover) with the risk-taking, violent actions of his younger White partner (Gibson). Moreover, in exception to buddy thematics, the Black cop has a family and home, and his relationship to them is explored. Thus his character is broadened and humanized beyond Hollywood convention, which is something that Glover says initially attracted him to the script.

Gardens of Stone explores the relationship between two career army sergeants, Caan and Jones, who are attached to a stateside, ceremonial burial detail at the height of the Vietnam War. The film depicts the interracial social life of these buddies with a degree of intimacy and normalcy almost always absent from commercial productions. And as with such eighties films as *Reds* and *Ragtime*, both released in 1981, *Gardens*'s ideological spin runs counter to the dominant politics of its moment of production. For the military funerals that the sergeants oversee graphically reveal the real costs of war repressed in the militaristic fantasies of "Reaganite entertainment." Sadly though, the sequel to *Lethal Weapon*, the *II* movie, rearticulates many of the codes of domination/devaluation that the original production worked to undo. One of the most memorable subordinations in this film is the sight of Danny Glover trapped in the business position on a toilet that is about to explode.

All in all, one must expect biracial buddy films to persist in their many variations as long as they are profitable, as long as the politics of the dominant "norm" are held in place, and as long as the racial interdependencies and tensions that these films transcode remain with us. And given the strong approval the putrid fantasy on race relations and buddy movie, *Driving Miss Daisy* (1989), received from the Academy Awards, that could be a while yet. However, because by the year 2000 most Americans will be of non-European descent and because the film industry is a profit driven system, the convention of placing non-White buddies in the protective cultural custody of the White "norm" must inevitably erode and open up to new combinations and possibilities.

Regarding future paradigm shifts in the buddy formula, two films, both of which are parodies of the buddy detective adventure, come to mind that suggest innovative new directions. Wayne Wang's *Chan is Missing* (1981), deploys an Asian-American cabbie and his buddy nephew to deconstruct the cinematic myth of the Chinese detective, while Keenen Ivory Wayans' *I'm Gonna Git You Sucka* (1988) deploys African-American buddies to spoof Hollywood's Blaxploitation genre. But in the future, perhaps the most important factor in broadening and equalizing the representation of all non-White peoples on the commercial screen will be the dialectical pressure exerted on Hollywood by the humanized, culturally complex, self-fashioned images of people of color in their emergent and independent cinema practices, as exemplified by such eighties films as Spike Lee's *She's Gotta Have It* and *Do The Right Thing*, Wayne Wang's *Dim Sum*, Luis Valdez's *La Bamba* and Steven Okazaki's *Living on Tokyo Time*.

Notes

1. James A. Miller. "From Sweetback to Celie: Blacks on Film into the 80's." *The Year Left 2, Toward A Rainbow Socialism, Essays on Race, Ethnicity, Class and Gender.* Mike Davis, Manning Marable, Fred Pfeil, and Michael Sprinker eds. London: Verso,

1987, 140–41. Gladstone Yearwood. "The Hero in Black Film." *Wide Angle,* Vol. 5, No. 2 (1983).

2. Fredric Jameson. *The Political Unconscious.* New York: Cornell University Press, 1981, 52–53. William C. Dowling. *Jameson, Althusser, Marx.* New York: Cornell University Press, 1984, 77–78.

3. Gladstone Yearwood, *op. cit.*

4. Robin Wood. *Hollywood from Vietnam to Reagan.* New York: Columbia U. Press, 1986, 227–30.

5. Robert Philip Kolker. *A Cinema of Loneliness, Penn, Kubrick, Scorsese, Spielberg, Altman.* New York: Oxford U. Press, 1988, 237–65. Andrew Britton. "Blissing Out: The Politics of Reaganite Entertainment." *Movie* 31/32 (Winter 1986).

6. Richard Gold. "Hiring Of Black Talent A Gray Area." *Variety* (25 March, 1987), 36.

7. Michael E. Ross. "Black and White Buddies: How Sincere Is the Harmony?" *The New York Times* (14 June, 1987), 27.

8. Ed Guerrero. "The slavery motif in contemporary film: *The Color Purple* and *The Brother From Another Planet.*" *Jump Cut* No. 33 (Feb 1988), 52–59. Here the author explores some of the many ways that the repressed historical experience of slavery is sedimented as allegory and metaphor into the representations and codes of popular cinema.

9. Andrew Britton, *op. cit.*

10. Peter Roffman and Bev Simpson. "Black Images on White Screens." *Cineaste* 13 N3 (1984), 17. Christopher Atwell. "Pryor: A Look Back to Anger." *The City Sun* (8–14 March, 1989), 17, 20.

11. David Ansen, David Friendly, and Katherine Ames. "Revival of Black Movies?" *Newsweek* (7 January 1985), 50.

12. Robin Wood. *Hollywood from Vietnam to Reagan.* New York: Columbia U. Press, 1986, 77–80. Michael Paul Rogin. *Ronald Reagan, the Movie, and other Episodes in Political Demonology.* Berkeley: U. of California Press, 1987, 237. The authors cited here agree that what is constructed as nightmarish or monstrous in horror films specifically, and to a degree in all films, is nothing less than the return of the symbolically cloaked, politically or socially repressed. Reggie Hammond senses this Freudian mechanism when he argues that White people's worst nightmare is a Black man with a badge and a gun.

13. Gail Buchalter. "The New Black Clout in Hollywood." *Los Angeles Times Magazine* Vol., IV No. 8 (28 February 1988), 8. Gene Lyons, Peter McAlevey. "Crazy Eddie." *Newsweek* (7 January 1985), 48.

14. Richard Corliss. "Street Smart Cop, Box-Office Champ." *Time* (7 Jan. 1985), 103.

15. Richard Dyer. "White." *Screen* Vol. 29, No. 4 (Autumn 1988). Sylvia Winter. "Sambos and Minstrels." *Social Text* Vol. 1 (1979), 152. Here, Winter eloquently describes the social construction of the *norm* and *other.* "First of all the system produced the imaginary social signification of the Place of the Norm. The Place of the Norm is constituted by and through the definition of certain desired attributes. The sign that pointed to one's possession of this attribute was whiteness of skin. The sign that pointed to its nonpossession was blackness of skin, which revealed non-human being."

16. Gail Buchalter. "Eddie Murphy and the Black Pack." *Los Angeles Times Magazine* Vol. IV, No. 8 (28 February 1988).

16

The Construction of Black Sexuality

Jacquie Jones

Sexuality must not be described as a stubborn drive, by nature alien
and of necessity disobedient to a power which exhausts itself trying
to subdue it and often fails to control it entirely. It appears rather as
an especially dense transfer point for relations of power: between
men and women . . . an administration and a population. Sexuality is
not the most intractable element in power relations, but rather one of
those endowed with the greatest instrumentality: useful for the greatest number of maneuvers and capable of serving as a point of support,
as a linchpin, for the most varied strategies.

Michel Foucault,
The History of Sexuality

The imaging of Black sexuality in mainstream film, particularly Black
male heterosexuality, continues to be the most denormalizing factor in the
definition of the Black screen character. By sabotaging the ability to create
or maintain primary ties to other individuals through intimate contact, the
Black male character calls into question not only his ability to function as
a legitimate, full—in other words, normal—member of film culture, but
also cancels the ability to be perceived as capable of complete humanity.
Without reconstructing the sexuality of the Black character it is impossible
to enter into the more general discourse of identity.

Although Black male heterosexuality is generally treated as the dominating context in which Black feminist and Black gay and lesbian critical
theories are situated, I submit that Black male heterosexuality itself is
also a repressed discourse currently characterized by powerlessness and
reaction in the mainstream cinema. To deemphasize the importance of
male dominance and to reconstruct Black sexuality in cinema, one must

begin to look to Black independent cinema for new models of "normalcy" which include self-directed sexuality.

I have generally confined this argument to representation of heterosexual behavior in film culture, with a specific emphasis on Black male heterosexuality, because these issues dominate the current crisis in imaging. This is not done to diminish the existence or importance of Black gay and lesbian representation and misrepresentation. In fact, I suggest that Black gay independent film has produced the most valuable model for reconstructing Black heterosexuality.

Although Black independent film continues to challenge the status quo of power in film culture, this argument is focused on mainstream film because the chief concern here is the impact these representations have in establishing roles and behaviors in the broad film culture. For example, of the over four thousand films commercially distributed to general audiences from 1980 to 1988, only thirty warranted listing in Donald Bogle's comprehensive encyclopedia, *Blacks in American Films and Television*.[1] Of those, only five were independently produced.

With well over half of moviegoers under the age of eighteen (and African-American youth represented disproportionately in that number), the motion picture industry is now arguably the chief socializing agent of this society, often preempting the power of schools, churches, even families to prescribe behavior, establish values, and impart grave societal information. In fact, as motion pictures become increasingly comprised of violence (motion pictures today can average as many as two hundred acts of violence per hour), the motion picture industry has inscribed into the film culture sexual intimacy as the only legitimate humanizing contact.[2] Furthermore, the mainstream film industry as the dominant agent of popular culture is naturally more charged with the custody of the gender and racial status quo that sustains it and gives it power. One need only look to the scores of movies released in recent years in which women who are deemed promiscuous are systematically stalked and killed by deranged men. Their behavior evidences a desire to self-direct and control their bodies, and thus challenges the male-centered power dynamic at the foundation of this society. And this, the media has decreed, is unacceptable.

For the past decade, examination of the media has focused on multicultural participation and representation without sufficient debate as to the level and nature of issues of sexuality. Furthermore, extensive critical debate has surrounded every major Black-cast film distributed to mainstream audiences—films that account for less than one percent of American films released—while action adventure and other popular mainstream products have quietly been incorporated into the collective consciousness of contemporary culture. Deemed politically insignificant, these films, which are the most widely viewed by the general audience, delineate and assign behaviors that ultimately maintain and promote stereotypic assignment of the Black character, despite a degree of cosmetic inclusion into the main action of contemporary mainstream film.

The 1988 Dennis Hopper release *Colors* speaks volumes on Hollywood's assignment of intimacy between African-Americans. While the film's headliner, Sean Penn, a typical young cop with a chip on his shoulder, runs roughshod over his East LA beat, his love scenes are softly shot and nuanced, prefaced with the traditional rituals of courtship.

By contrast, as Penn and his partner stalk a killer, they surprise the suspect at his "girlfriend's" house. Before they even enter the house, the shrieks emitting from the "girlfriend," and the sounds of the headboard of the bed hitting the wall, can be heard—much to the amusement of the attending police officers. As the officers enter, the audience immediately sees the entirely nude back and buttocks of the Black criminal (as opposed to the modest waist up shots of Penn earlier) in an act that looks almost brutal. Once the presence of the police is known by the couple, the man is shot and killed as he reaches for his pants while the still-naked "girlfriend" looks on. (To make matters worse, although the woman concerned is the "girlfriend" of the suspect as thought, the man killed is not the suspect at all but a friend of the suspect's.)

There is no misreading such a juxtaposition of sexual imagery. While the on-screen presence of White men has always been peculiarly modest, Black men have traditionally been on display, depicted as overly developed and animal forms. This is not to suggest that White men have not and do not appear nude in motion pictures. Yet, categorically, just as the inconsistencies between the exposure of the male and female bodies in the cinema are related to the classic objectification of women in the society in general, the racial inconsistencies of the exposure and depiction of the bodies of men is clearly tied to the inherent dehumanization of the Black man in the society.

From the inception of moving pictures as entertainment, the intended audience has been the White population of this country, with particular emphasis on the White male, being the only segment of the population with true disposable income, and with the power to influence and shape public thought and policy. However, given the changes in the demographics of the moviegoing audience in terms of gender and race, the young Black male is now significantly represented in the target audience of such motion pictures as *Colors,* which deals with gang violence within the Black and Latino communities of Los Angeles. Inasmuch, the constructs of White male sexual distance, that is the on-screen White male sexual figure as an almost invisible conduit for the exposure of the White female for the vicarious pleasures of other White males, has new social significance.

The almost demure aspect of the on-screen White sexual lead has come to represent the antithesis of Black male sexuality. The White male is responsive and interactive. His goal, in this sense, is to maintain primary contact with women, although this usually translates into pursuing a sexual connection. In the rare film portrayals of White men as abusive to White women, the men have already been defined within the context of the film as outside prescribed societal norms, as in the film *9½ Weeks,* in which Mickey Rourke is a game-playing sadist who systematically enslaves a willing masochist.

On the other hand, the Black male character in mainstream film, when allowed to be overtly sexual, is never seen in such light. Instead, he is always the oversexed caddish character of Eddie Murphy in the 1982 film *48 Hours.* Seemingly, this character's only mission as a sexual being is to engage in the act itself, with whomever is available, and never to establish more than the most carnal relationships with Black women. His sexual behavior functions instead as an indictment of his feral nature, spiritual deficiency and lack of allegiance to the group, the society, by failing to create or maintain primary ties with other individuals.

Clearly, the frequency with which these themes are played out is not incidental. They suggest that there are fundamental differences in the sexual behavior of Black males and White males and are ultimately indicative of the psychic inferiority of the Black male. Further, by removing the Black male's capacity for intimacy in this society, the audience is never able to conceive of the Black male character as completely human, even beyond the temporal film reality.

Most dangerously, by depriving the Black on-screen male of a connection to the society through any type of humanizing relationship, mainstream motion pictures offer only models of violence and other forms of antisocial behaviors. While these behaviors also exist among White men on-screen, they are given a societal framework in which one is a part of a unit, man and woman, and for which one engages in behaviors necessary to preserve that unit. Imperfect as the latter scheme may be presented in the general cinema, it does provide a context for the otherwise pointless and undirected violence which has become the mainstay of the medium.

Here there is an essential struggle for self-definition or differentiation which these characters seek to assert in mainstream film. However, because the Black male character is only able to differentiate himself in a subjective relationship to women, he remains incomplete. In other words, the Black male character, as defined through his sexual behavior, is not able to overcome the problematic of domination which begins with a denial of dependency. Instead, the Black male character can only define himself through violent separateness.

The emergence of the "buddy picture," those films that team White heros with Black sidekicks, has firmly established the idea of violent differentiation as privilege for the Black male character in popular film culture. The buddy picture has also translated into the appearance of the most significant numbers of Black actors in American films since the Blaxploitation era, and, so, has defined the Black male screen presence of the eighties and early nineties.

In these films, Black male sexuality is constructed in one of two ways. In the first construction, the sex act itself for the Black character is manifested through the violent action of the film, which substitutes as climax for Black male heterosexualism, while the remaining sexual action (that part of sexual definition disengaged from the act itself) is manifested through roles the Black buddy accepts which have been traditionally assigned to the White female: roles like comforter, nurturer, and partner in the main action of the film. Love and loyalty of the Black male are focused on the White hero. In this way, mainstream film can either blatantly ignore and substitute the sexuality of the Black male character, or confuse it with issues of gender representations. Either way, the power dynamic of White male-Black male is obscured by the less clear issues of social membership and gender roles, and the sexuality of the Black male is realized through individualized physical dominance rather than sex itself, when realized at all.

One strange twist on this idea was the film *Beverly Hills Cop*. In a reversed situation, Eddie Murphy is the hero Axel Foley, with a White sidekick. In this film, the formula—hero, buddy, hero's love interest, versus bad guys—is never completed. Novelist Trey Ellis writes: "As Foley, Murphy is a Black hero in a commercial White film, and because of this, a completely banal comedy-adventure film becomes a bizarre fable of interracial homosexual love. Hollywood was so afraid of giving Murphy a love interest that an ordinary American adventure film became the colored Cage Aux Folles." (16).

In the conventional buddy film, the White female romantic figure does function as the outlet for *real* sexual desire, although she is obviously devalued, since the shared responsibilities and activities essential to true intimacy are assumed by the Black buddy. In this way, the *purity* of the White male lead's heterosexuality is preserved, as is the gender hierarchy. This also functions to illegitimize homosexuality by eliminating the possibility of same-sex erotic contact, and to completely eliminate the Black female character. However, in *Beverly Hills Cop,* that did not happen. Instead, sexuality was represented only in the form of homosexual innuendo and ambiguous statements of love between male characters. Although the assumption that homosexuality is aberrant and emasculating, inherent in the model as well as this film, is itself problematic, the film clearly sets out to emasculate the hero and render him powerless in a personal sense, though he may triumph physically.

The second construction of Black male sexuality differs, in that it is relative not to White male sexuality but to Black female sexuality. In an effort to establish differentiation here, the Black male character must assert his separateness by assuming the role of the White male. Further in assuming this role without context, his separateness is achieved in a necessarily more violent manner. Perhaps this is best stated in this study of male domination by Jessica Benjamin in her essay "Master and Slave":

> [M]ale domination is rooted in a struggle for recognition between men in which women are mere objects or tokens: the prize. In terms of psychological development, the relationship of domination is not only based on the pre-Oedipal drama of mother-child, but it is also perpetuated in the Oedipal triad. In the Oedipal conflict, the father enforces the separation of the boy from his mother, demanding not merely that he relinquish her as a love object, but also as a subject with whom to identify. The father's aggression or interference, which the boy internalizes or identifies with, is reenacted in the repudiation and objectification of the mother and asserting his own boundaries is inspired by the powerful and *different* father (italics mine). Seeking recognition from this father, the boy is aspiring not to be nurtured but to gain prestige. He gains it by repudiating the mother as visibly, as violently, as possible. (289)

Clearly, in this scenario, the Black male assumes the role of the boy; the Black woman, the mother; and, of course, the White male, the father. This should not be a shocking metaphor, since mainstream motion pictures function simply as the most immediate form of culture transmission and as such are a natural forum of the pronouncements of the society at large. An example is the film *48 Hours,* mentioned above. In it, Eddie Murphy achieves differentiation by devaluing and rendering powerless his counterpart as sexual being. Murphy's character assumes all power in defining their relationship, establishing the parameters and limiting the contact. The woman functions only to fulfill his wishes. Again, the Black male is unable to conceive of the female as like or necessary and can acknowledge her only through domination.

When a Black "hero" *is,* rarely, situated in a "normal" personal structure (as a husband and father, for example) in which there is an assumption that he has accepted the notion of interdependency and need not differentiate violently, as in the 1986 film *Lethal Weapon,* the character is routinely sanitized beyond recognition. Robbed of all traces of ethnicity or real sexuality, Danny Glover's character in that film holds all the appeal of a fast-food job for an inner-city youth faced with the prospects of drug peddling. While Mel Gibson, the headliner of the film, wins and woos "the girl," Glover is seen as one-dimensional and unexciting by comparison. In a final, revealing scene in *Lethal Weapon,* Glover's teenager daughter develops a crush on Gibson, obviously reestablishing the intended audience for the film. Through the division and segmentation of Black on-screen sexuality, popular film culture is able to define the context of desire as well as the realization of sexuality between characters. Given the absence of a Black male figure other than Glover, this attraction can be seen as "normal," in that it adheres to the rules of heterosexuality. Moreover, given the dynamic of the White male lead as physically and ethically supreme, the young girl's attraction to Gibson functions as hegemonic wish-fulfillment. No woman is able to resist the brave, White protector.

Yet, there is another, more subtle, aspect of this crush that has its roots in American history: that is, the rationalization of the historic sexual abuse and exploitation of the Black woman in America by White men, which has ultimately controlled the imaging of Black women in American film from its inception. The Black temptress, by initiating sexual contact with White male, relinquishes all rights to or claims for protection and, at the same time, alienates the Black male. Although Black women classically are not diminished in the same fashion as Black men by the media (they are allowed, for example, far more emotional complexity than Black males), they are likewise devalued on the grounds of moral inadequacy.

When sexually present in American film of the last decade, the Black female character generally appears as the link between the profane and the supernatural (except, of course, in the occasional Black-cast or independently-produced Black film to get mainstream distribution). The historical precedent is clearly articulated by historian Richard Hofstadter:

> Naked and libidinous: for the white man's preoccupation with Negro sexuality was there at the very beginning, an outcome not only of his own guilt at sexual exploitation—his easy access to the black woman was immediately blamed on *her* lasciviousness—but also of his envious suspicion that some extraordinary potency and ecstatic experience was associated with primitive lust. (108)

In the 1987 film *Angel Heart,* Mickey Rourke's figurative descent into hell is marked by his sexual liaison with Lisa Bonet as a blood-drinking voodoo priestess. Through this type of thematic device, the power of the Black female to self-direct is eliminated, as it is clear that she is directed by higher forces. Similarly, the White men are, in effect, let off the hook with regards to Black women, as they too are overcome by supreme other-world energy.

Abusive and inhumane acts are never directed toward Black women by White men unless the Black woman is shown as sexually permissive or deviant, as in the British released *Mona Lisa.*

In that film, Cathy Tyson stars as a Black whore befriended by a small-time hood played by Bob Hoskins. She confides all types of abuses to Hoskins throughout the film, but her own abusiveness of the villainous character played by Michael Caine, formerly her pimp, is never separated from the fact that she is a prostitute and continues to be a prostitute even after other alternatives exist for her. In the final scenes, Tyson betrays her friendship with Hoskins, and reveals a sexual love for a teenage, White prostitute, obviously jeopardizing any sympathies the audience may have accumulated for her.

As in other films involving the issue of prostitution, the sexually and economically oppressive structures allowing for this type of exploitation of women are not adequately delineated and, therefore, allow for only the most condescending of compassion from any audience. Further, by making Tyson's character Black and a lesbian shown engaging in sex with men, the film plays on the theme of sexual insatiability and, in the end, leaves the viewer judging if not blaming Tyson.

To discuss the sexual dynamic in the occasional film by Black male directors to get mainstream distribution of recent years, it is necessary to return to the definition of male domination put forth by Benjamin. To say that the Black female character is devalued along traditional mainstream lines, that is, much in the same way as White women are devalued in relationship to White men in American film, is too simplistic. In fact, women are so brutally relegated to the status of "prize" as to suggest an overidentification with White maleness and the systems of sexual oppression in the society at large.

Most prominent of these films are, of course, those of Spike Lee. Even Nola Darling, the "heroine" in Lee's first feature *She's Gotta Have It,* who was widely hailed as a liberated, postmodern, Black woman, was only allowed to be viewed through the attitudes of the three clearly deficient men—a narcissist, a dullard and a social retard—who ultimately defined her existence. The Black women in Lee's other feature work similarly embody traditional "female" concerns, monogamy and physical appearance, for example, in stark contrast to the *real* issues faced by the men in these films. In *School Daze,* Lee's second film, the women struggled with skin-color dynamics while the men battled in the arenas of physical and psychic control, and world issues such as apartheid. In *Do the Right Thing,* it is the men who initiate and sustain all action relevant to the plot, while the women function as commentators. In *Mo' Better Blues,* Lee's latest feature, the characters of Clarke Betancourt (Cynda Williams) and Indigo Downes (Joie Lee) are completely incidental to the melodramatic portrait of the self-absorbed jazz trumpeter Bleek Gilliam (Denzel Washington) struggling with his own issues of self-direction. Furthermore, laced through the action of *Mo' Better Blues* is the stand-up comedy routine of the late Robin Harris, which inundates the audience with the most low and vicious misogynist rhetoric.

In all four of these films, the central female characters are powerless and, in one way or another, abused. The abusiveness of the treatment itself removes the women in Spike Lee's films from the status of participant, and relegates them to that of victim. By rendering women powerless, sexual activity in the films functions as a kind of symbolic rape rather than cooperative process. Mookie (Spike Lee), for example, in *Do the Right Thing* has power only through sex, and in the climactic violent action of the film (which he only initiates rather than completes) he only achieves dominance through sex. Obviously, this type of portrayal does not enhance the capacity of the characterization of either Black male or female for intimacy, or even the expression of true sexual desire. Instead, as in White-directed mainstream film, the sexuality of the Black male character can be seen as the struggle for power-over, as the only means of gaining recognition and prestige.

Benjamin writes,

> The importance currently assumed by violent fantasy can in part be attributed to the increasingly rational, individualistic character of our culture, to the increasing deprivation of nurturance and recognition in ordinary human intercourse. (282)

Inasmuch, the challenge in reconstructing Black sexuality in cinema is not that of creating perfect balances of power and sexuality on screen, but rather that of integrating the sexual with the political and social.

Black independent cinema has often succeeded in normalizing sexuality by integrating sexual themes directly into the main action. For example, in Charles Burnett's independent classic, *Killer of Sheep,* the protagonist wrestles with personal power. A primary manifest of his powerlessness is his inability to be sexual with his wife. The conflict does not center around physical impotence, but a more pervasive inability to isolate and control his desire. The importance of the theme within the narrative illustrates the primacy of this relationship in the film's more general text of power.

To return to Benjamin here, the current crisis in the imaging of Black sexuality in mainstream film stems, in general, from "the increased aesthet-icized and eroticized violence in our media [which] suggests the fallacy in our ordinary understanding of control and self-control." (296) Yet, by extending the boundaries of self-control into the realm of the sexual, and integrating that into the narrative, Burnett resists the mandate to self-define through violent separateness. By allowing the film to encompass both the protagonist and his wife as like but distinct, in *Killer of Sheep,* their sexuality is constructed in a normal space.

Still, the most valuable and explicit model for normalizing the Black heterosexual construct comes from a recent experimental exploration of Black gay identity, Marlon Riggs' *Tongues Untied,* possibly the most powerful examination of Black sexual identity ever produced. The film integrates on all levels, structurally and thematically, and ultimately delineates the immediacy of situating the sexual at the core of self-definition by equalizing it with the political and social imperatives of Blackness. Through mass-media excerpts, autobiography, and illustration, the manipulation of Black sexuality by society, of which cinema is the most powerful mechanism, is presented dramatically. Intrinsic here is the awesome power to control desire and definition through limiting, segmenting, and devaluing Black sexual identity.

Finally, I do not suggest the reconstruction of Black sexuality as a prescription for mainstream film, but rather as an imperative for a revision in the critical evaluation of power relationships in film culture to fully include sexuality. The hysterization of Black sexuality has historically been fundamental to the hegemony in popular film. The failure of criticism to address the denormalization of Black characterization through the manipulation of sexuality leaves open not only the danger of recycling the same dsyfunctions in Black film, as has been the case in the films of Spike Lee, but also the likelihood of critics to define based on these relationships. The inclusionary politicization of sexuality, as in *Killer of Sheep* and *Tongues Untied,* on the other hand, allows for the normalization of the Black character by valuing sexuality and rooting it in humanism.

Notes

1. Averaged from figures obtained from the Motion Picture Academy of America
2. According to the National Coalition on TV Violence

Works Cited

Benjamin, Jessica. "Master and Slave." *Powers of Desire: The Politics of Sexuality.* Ed. Ann Snitow, Christine Stansell and Sharon Thompson. New York: Monthly Review Press, 1983. 280–299.

Ellis, Trey. "The Gay Subtext in Beverly Hills Cop." *Black Film Review* 3 (Spring 1987), 15–17.

Foucault, Michel. *The History of Sexuality.* New York: Vintage Books, 1980.

Hofstadter, Richard. *America at 1750: A Social Portrait.* New York: Vintage Books, 1973.

17

Race, Gender and Psychoanalysis in Forties Film: Lost Boundaries, Home of the Brave and The Quiet One

Michele Wallace

To be human is to be subjected to a law which decentres and divides: sexuality is created in a division, the subject is split; but an ideological world conceals this from the conscious subject who is supposed to feel whole and certain of a sexual identity. Psychoanalysis should aim at a destruction of this concealment and at a reconstruction of the subject's construction in all its splits.

Juliet Mitchell,
Introduction I to *Feminine Sexuality:*
Jacques Lacan and the ecole freudienne, 1982.

It is not entirely true that no one from the world I knew had yet made an appearance on the American screen: there were, for example, Stepin Fetchit and Willie Best and Mantan Moreland, all of whom, rightly or wrongly, I loathed. It seemed to me that they lied about the world I knew, and debased it, and certainly I did not know anybody like them—as far as I could tell; for it is also possible that their comic, bug-eyed terror contained the truth concerning a terror by which I hoped never to be engulfed.

James Baldwin,
The Devil Finds Work: An Essay, 1976[1]

Whereas oral representations of Afro-American culture,[2] as epitomized by Black participation in the record industry and in some aspects of popular theatre, demonstrate a cycle of invention, appropriation and reinvention,[3] in the realm of visual representations of Blacks, it often appears as though only one predatory kind of figuration dominated. That figuration can be summed up as what Botkin calls the Sambo figure.[4] His first appearance occurs on the theatre stage in the minstrel dramas that manufactured White supremacist versions of Black culture, in which White actors played all the roles in blackface. This figure was quickly adapted to a set of conventional stereotypes in illustrations, photography and advertising. The filmic counterparts were in evidence most strikingly in the early film *The Birth of A Nation,* which set the racial agenda for the film industry.[5]

But there is mounting evidence that film has been a chief player in race relations, or the lack there of, since the release of *The Birth of A Nation.* Up until the release of *Guess Who's Coming To Dinner?,* there is an interesting correlation between national governmental policies regarding "race," and film portrayals of racial subjects, especially in regard to the military, for instance.[6] While there was a period of about a decade, after the Blaxploitation era, during which characterizations of Blacks were virtually nonexistent in American films, since 1986 and the release of *The Color Purple,* film has gradually emerged as the principle arena in which the problem of the visual in Afro-American culture is being interrogated and reformulated. Regrettably, in both cases—that is, in the case of Civil Rights interventions in the Hollywood film industry in the forties, fifties and sixties, and in the case of the recent emergence of Black films—the construction of gender relations has been sadly predictable, conventional and even retrograde.[7]

Gender is as important as "race" to understanding how "invisibility" has worked historically in all fields of visual production.[8] A great deal of important work has been done on how constructions of gender have impacted on visual media. In particular in film studies, there has been an impressive outpouring of academic feminist film criticism in the US. Grounded in what I will call a post-marxist preoccupation with the subversive capabilities of cultural practice (also called cultural studies), much of this film criticism has also been heavily influenced by the cross-fertilization of psychoanalysis and semiotics. The content generally circulates around questions of female spectatorship and/or whether or not the gaze is "male."[9] Most such debates stem from the influence of Laura Mulvey's ground-breaking article "Visual Pleasure and Narrative Cinema," first published in *Screen* in 1975.[10]

Lately, however, when posed in psychoanalytic terms in which the formation of the subject is not historicized, the problem of the "gaze" has become a source of irritation to those who wish to propose alternative subjectivities on the grounds of "race," ethnicity, sexuality or class. While various practitioners of feminist psychoanalytic film criticism are attempting to incorporate this challenge into their methodologies, much of their earlier work, which relies so heavily on Lacan, makes it all too clear that sexual difference has absolute priority as the bedrock of the formation of subjectivity.

Alternatively, the question of spectatorship, when detached from its psychoanalytic moorings, has shown itself more adaptable to other approaches, most prominently one in which an ethnographic focus on audience reception is substituted for the psychoanalytic reading of how subjectivity is challenged and/or reconstituted by a particular filmic practice.[11] Unfortunately, however, I think such approaches, while useful, also serve to reconsolidate the present consensus regarding the raceless ahistoricity of sexual difference and the unconscious. In the end, you're still left with the impression that you have to be middle-class, White and American or European in order to have experienced gender differentiation as a crisis of signification and in order to have an unconscious.[12] I regard this as a potentially dangerous idea.

First, the exclusion of the Black subject from discussions of psychoanalysis, as well as other prominent academic discourses, has meant that "race" has been largely excluded from consideration in many of the various fields of the humanities. As such patterns of exclusion quite naturally carry over into the interdisciplinary fields of postmodernism, critical theory, cultural studies, and women's studies, it has meant that theoretical formulations in these fields don't ever have to encompass or account for women of color or Black women. Even emergent analyses of new identities and/or subjectivities of postcoloniality, "race," and sexualities don't have to add up in terms of providing a better understanding of the subjectivity of women of color, particularly minority or Black woman in the US.[13] Rather, the result of adding all these debates and discourses together is quite the opposite: the subjectivity of the woman of color or the minority woman is placed under further erasure.

My delineation of the cultural phenomenon of "invisibility," both racial and gendered, in the case of the Black woman, and my forays into the various realms of the problem of the visual in Afro-American culture are attempts to find out why this is so and whether or not anything can be done to reverse this trend. My intention is, first, if possible to theorize *this* problem as the *real* problem of the problem of the visual. Second, failing to adequately theorize this problem (which seems almost inevitable in any individual attempt), my goal is rather to open a space or an aporia in which such theorization (or practice) will ultimately have to take place. While the practice of such theorization is not confined to the biological woman of color—I am not a vulgar essentialist—women of color should feel welcome to engage in such theorization and/or practice.[14] "The difficult I'll do right now," as Billy Holiday use to sing and my mother always likes to remind me, "but the impossible will take a little while."

My emerging convictions regarding these matters has led me to adapt a radically deconstructive posture vis-à-vis the problem of a corrective interpretation. The purpose of the deconstruction is neither nihilistic nor aimless (although I enjoy thinking of myself as an anarchist) but the pursuit of an inexorable third term or third category in which both "race" and gender can be taken into account.

In the following essay—my first in-depth essay on film—my intention is to engage in a preliminary examination into conjunctions of "race" and gender in feminist film theory and criticism. First, I will discuss some of the basic characteristics of "race" in classic film history as they have been delineated by Afro-American film historians. Then, moving on to a discussion of forties classic films, I will focus on suggesting how this conception of "race" might be considered in relationship to gender concerns in feminist psychoanalytic film criticism. In the discussion of the "problem" films of the 1940s—*Lost Boundaries, Home of The Brave,* and *The Quiet One*—I will take on issues bearing upon the psychoanalysis of "race." Unfortunately, such discussion will remain introductory and rudimentary because of space.

According to Donald Bogle, there were five basic stereotypes essential to the characterization of Blacks in American films from the very beginning. The first four were drawn from the case of Black characters in Harriet Beecher Stowe's *Uncle Tom's Cabin* (which was made into film on several occasions): Toms, coons, mulattoes and mammies.[15] The last and most marginal of the stereotypes, "the big black buck," dates back only to the appearance of D.W. Griffith's *The Birth of A Nation* in 1915. In this film seeking to justify the birth of the Ku Klux Klan, in which Blacks are all portrayed by Whites in blackface, brutal Black bucks assault White men and rape White women in scenes pretending to recreate Reconstruction's impact on the South.

The Birth of a Nation detailed the South-should-have-won-the-war positions which would dominate representations of Blacks in a wide range of fields (politics, history, literature, film, popular illustrations, ephemera, and advertisments), for the better part of the century. But Bogle says the film's most important contribution was epitomized in the figure of the brutal Black buck, who provides a kind of key to the subsequent concerns in Black film. He credits *The Birth of The Nation* with having made the screen appearance of violent, sexual Black men so controversial that for a long time Blacks were cast "almost exclusively in comic roles."[16] While he explains that typecasting plagued all minorities in US films, "no minority was so relentlessly or fiercely typed as the black man." The subsequent appearance of the bad Black man on screen is interpreted as a strategic triumph. "Not until more than a half a century later," after *The Birth of A Nation,* "when Melvin Van Peebles' *Sweet Sweetback's Baadasssss Song* (1971) appeared, did sexually assertive black males make their way back to the screen," Bogle writes.[17]

The fantastically mysogynistic *Sweet Sweetback's Baadasssss Song* is still being celebrated by young Black filmmakers and hailed as the father-work of Black independent film.[18] It goes without saying, however, that practices of resistance are always deeply compromised by their willingness to make major concessions to other hegemonic conventions. Also *Sweet Sweetback's* canonization seems an explicit call for some manner of psychological reading of its scenario. It might be a good idea to begin with the failed Oedipal scene which begins the film, in which director Melvin Van Peebles's son, Mario, is shown nestled between the thighs of a full-grown Black woman (old enough to be his mother) having sexual intercourse, her legs spread eagle as she cries "sweet sweetback!"

Although Bogle doesn't really focus on sexual difference, it is clear within his system which stereotypes are male and which are female. Mammies and tragic mulattoes are female. Mammies are generally "over-weight, middle-aged, and so dark, so thoroughly black, that it is preposterous even to suggest that she be a sex object." Whereas the tragic mulattoes are the forebears of "the part black woman—the light skinned Negress" who is "given a chance at lead parts and" is "graced with a modicum of sex appeal."[19] Coons can be female, as in the case of Topsy—a female child coon—but gender in coons is viewed as arbitrary and insignificant. Of course, bucks are always male and highly sexed.

Thomas Cripps also emphasizes the centrality of *The Birth of A Nation,* not as a source of Black stereotypes but as a focal point for racial responses to Hollywood practices, among which he includes the "struggles of a weak minority for a protective censorship . . . a century long campaign to affect Hollywood movies at their source, and finally, a parallel line of race movies."[20]

It was *The Birth of a Nation,* more than any other cultural event, Cripps says, which propelled Blacks to unite in coalition with other ethnic groups, and galvanized the membership of the NAACP to protest Hollywood practices. Blacks lobbied for laws banning racial slander and made direct appeals to Griffith, who insisted right up until his death that his film was not racist. Finally, various factions, including the NAACP, Booker T. Washington, Elaine Sterne, Carl Laemmle, Julius Rosenwald, vice president of Sears and Roebuck, vaudeville promoters and stockbrokers organized to make their own rebuttal film called *Birth of a Race.* The film, unlike *The Birth of a Nation,* did poorly at the box office. It featured an odd assortment of racially uplifting scenes—"Simon the Cyrene helping Jesus to bear the cross, head shots of the races of the world, Lincoln and emancipation." In the last reel, Cripps says, "a black and white farmer are working their field when they hear the nation's call to arms, whereupon they dissolve from overalls into military uniforms and march off toward the camera and out of the frame."[21] Consistent with most subsequent attempts in independent Black films or in a White-dominated Hollywood film industry, *Birth of The Race* focused on producing "positive" corrective images of Black men. Often what such efforts did, in the process, was further corroborate dominant perceptions regarding gender and gender/ race conjunctions.

In Hollywood in the forties, this drama was played out on a larger scale than ever before. The demands of World War II coincided with the peak of the film industry's influence in the US. The war itself had a profound impact on women's roles and on perceptions of the status of "race" in general, and Blacks in particular. The film industry was a full participant in the dissemination of these issues.

During the war, while the men were abroad in the military, women were encouraged to work in factories and to replace men on the job in general. One of the results in the film industry was the consolidation of the importance of the "women's film." There had always been films in which female characters dominated. In the forties, gender became a field of polarization in film, as though in response to a rising anxiety over sexual difference. The conventions of sexual difference were concretized precisely in a system in which there were predominantly films about men and then a smaller numbers of films about women aimed at female audiences.

After the war such conventions were further problematized by the appearance of a series of interesting filmic effects later called "film noir" in the sixties. In such films, the polarization of gender was often accompanied by an implicit racial polarization. For instance, in *Mildred Pierce,* as in many of the women's films and/or in the films noir, the cast is lily-white. The presence of the Black Butterfly McQueen as a comedic assistant cook, waitress, and finally maid (her downward mobility is part of her hegemonic appeal) only serves to pepper the stew, to further coroborate the unquestionable Whiteness of Mildred's and Vida's world. When Butterfly first comments upon Joan Crawford's obvious industry and ambition, "I don't know how you get up so early in the mornin'. I sleeps till noon," she identifies herself as consistent with a long line of coon characters.

From the vantage point of individual talent or from the perspective of the limitations of the "star" system, despite the obvious stereotyping, Butterfly McQueen obviously made a unique contribution to American film. In fact, she belonged, as well, to a complex tradition which deserves further study, of feisty maids and housekeepers (most of them White working-class types) in film noir.

But I would also argue that in McQueen's scenes with Joan Crawford, Butterfly provides a "study in black and white." A recurrent feature of visual racial stereotypes, this "study in black and white" provides not only the shadow/light visual juxtaposition so effective in Manet's *Olympia,* but also from the perspective of genre, the bumbling, lazy, Black, asexual, and childlike female provides further emphasis on the sexual appeal, businesslike maturity, and competence of the White female by her structural location as a binary opposition. Interestingly enough, some feminist film critics have pointed out how the fetishization of the female figure in classical Hollywood film, because it doesn't function to further the plot, may threaten to subvert the dominance of a phallocentric narrative and, as such, the status quo. In this context, Butterfly's role might be interpreted as further generic means of minimizing such dangers or, on the other hand, as a further incorporation of fetishization. Both Butterfly's lines and her visualization are decorative aspects of mise-en-scène. She has even less to do with the plot than the various settings of lower-middle-class home, waterfront cafe, roadside restaurant, beach house and fabulous mansion. It is possible to describe the film in many ways without ever including her, as I would imagine feminist film criticism has repeatedly done.

In such a context, how does one introduce questions of identification and female spectatorship in regard to the Black female viewer? I am proposing that it is important to do so in thinking about dominant film practices in the forties, because Blacks formed substantial audiences for such films. According to Jacqueline Bobo, by 1942, there were four hundred thirty Black movie theaters (ninety percent white-owned or managed) in thirty-one states, and about two hundred more White theaters with Black sections. By 1943, blacks were spending about one hundred fifty million dollars annually on movies.[22]

In the fifties, I grew up in Harlem as a member of a family that had lived in Harlem for three generations. There were still large movie theaters in and around Harlem then. My mother and my grandmother constantly took my sister and me to the movies downtown as well as uptown. Radio City Music Hall at Rockefeller Plaza (along with the Central Public Library on 42nd Street and the Museum of Modern Art on 53rd Street) were cultural fixtures in my growing up, institutions to which we repeatedly returned for pleasure, as well as confirmation of our understanding of the status quo. My mother and my grandmother often laughed about how my sister and I had been taken to see *The Wizard of Oz* at Radio City Music Hall when we were two and three (1955) and had ended up under the seats because we were so frightened of the dazzling lights and sound.

Much as it was for the women and gays in Manuel Puig's novels (*Betrayed by Rita Hayworth, Heartbreak Tango, Kiss of The Spider Woman*), the "stories" and "stars" (their costumes, hairstyles and affectations) of the Hollywood films of the thirties, forties, and fifties formed an intensely important cultural currency between the women in my family. As such movies as *The Maltese Falcon* (1941), *Double Indemnity* (1944), *Laura* (1944), *Mildred Pierce* (1945), *The Dark Mirror* (1946), *Gilda*

(1946), *The Postman Always Rings Twice* (1946), *Caught* (1949), *Sunset Boulevard* (1950), and *The Big Heat* (1953) were shown and reshown on television, my grandmother and mother taught me to know and love Lana Turner, Rita Hayworth, Gloria Swanson, Joan Crawford, Ingrid Bergman, Gloria Grahame, Barbara Bel Geddes, and Barbara Stanwyck, not because they were "white" but because they were "stars."

It was always said among Black women that Joan Crawford was part Black, and as I watch these films again today, looking at Rita Hayworth in *Gilda* or Lana Turner in *The Postman Always Rings Twice,* I keep thinking "she's so beautiful, she looks black." Such a statement makes no sense in current feminist film criticism. What I am trying to suggest is that there was a way in which these films were possessed by Black female viewers. The process may have been about problematizing and expanding one's racial identity instead of abandoning it. It seems crucial here to view spectatorship not only as potentially bisexual but also multiracial and multiethnic. Even as the "Law of the Father" may impose its premature closure on the filmic "gaze" in the coordination of suture and classic narrative, disparate factions in the audience, not all equally well indoctrinated in the dominant discourse, may have their way, now and then, with interpretation.

But the question remains of how Black female viewers regarded the Butterfly McQueens and the Hattie McDaniels that occasionally and awkwardly (veritable flies in the buttermilk) appeared in these films. As a child, I suppose I rebelled against identification with McDaniels and McQueen, but as an adult I came to know Butterfly McQueen as a woman who owned a brownstone on Convent Avenue in Harlem, along the route I took to City College every day when I was an undergraduate there. I learned that her career had been greatly diminished by her unwillingness to continue to play such roles as she had as Prissy in *Gone With The Wind* (1939).

Later, I also learned that Hattie McDaniels was the first Black person to win an Oscar (and the only Black woman until Whoopie Goldberg in 1991) for Best Supporting Actress in *Gone With The Wind.* Given the narrow restrictions on the roles that Black actresses could play in the thirties and forties (either maids or entertainers), McDaniels excelled at her craft. She was so perversely commanding in the "Mammy" role that Jamaica Kincaid was moved to write in *The Village Voice* in 1977 that she had always wanted a Mammy.

As an adult, as a woman, as a Black woman and a feminist, I strongly identify with both the restrictions McDaniels and McQueen faced, and their efforts to surmount them. I've seen such little improvement in the film roles for Black women (especially dark-skinned Black women) in my lifetime. As a desiring subject, my coterminous and simultaneous identification with Joan Crawford *and* Hattie McDaniels in *Mildred Pierce* helped to form the complicated and multifaceted "me" that "I" have become. This process of identification, I would submit, has never had a comfortable resting place, given dominant film practices, so, as I've grown older and wiser, it is ever more constantly in motion.

Yet I find myself irresistably drawn to many of the concerns that psychoanalytic feminist film criticism raises. When Kaja Silverman writes in a description of how suture works to corroborate sexual difference, "The spectacle of classic cinema promotes a constant re-enactment of the primal 'discovery' of the female subject's lack,"[23] this strikes me as an apt way to describe one of the agendas of *Mildred Pierce.* But it is also important to remember that this conception of "the female subject's lack" has a particular history and socio-economic trajectory, and that within that system of "lack," there is also inscribed a racial hierarchy in which White women are privileged. It boils down to the following: White feminists have a hard time imagining themselves as agents of racism but feminists of color don't have a hard time with this at all.

As for other kinds of Black participation in the films of the forties, what Cripps calls "race" films had all but died out by 1941. Whereas the production of what Bobo calls "independent Black-cast films," many of which were financed by Whites, reached their third and last peak in the mid-1940s.[24] Often mirroring Hollywood generic conventions, some of the actors who specialized in stereotypical roles in White films, such as Mantan Moreland, Stepin Fetchit, and Bill Robinson, also starred in Black-cast films such a *Tall, Tan, and Terrific* (1946—Moreland), *Big Timers* (1946—Stepin Fetchit) and *Harlem is Heaven* (1947—Robinson).[25]

Also in forties Hollywood films, there were often a lot of Black entertainers singing, dancing, or playing instruments in musical interludes that functioned as self-contained segments. Bogle calls this "the Negro Entertainment Syndrome" which was designed to use Blacks in films without having to integrate them into the plot. These segments could be cut out of the film when showing it in the South.[26] The performances of both Hazel Scott and Lena Horne were circumscribed by such conventions. Scott, a child prodigy and a concert pianist, refused to appear in films as anybody but herself seated at the piano. As she told Ebony in 1944, "black women were too often cast as whores or maids."[27]

Like Scott clinging to her piano, Lena Horne clung to her role as a chanteuse in "a long line of movies where she was pasted to a pillar." Bogle quotes Horne as saying, "They didn't make me into a maid, but they didn't make me anything else either. I became a butterfly pinned to a column singing away in Movieland."[28] Where she probably got to stretch out the most was in the Black-cast musicals *Cabin in The Sky* (1942) and in *Stormy Weather* (1943). But in both, Horne's roles conform to well

266 / Race, Gender, and Psychoanalysis

established Hollywood gender stereotypes of femmes fatales. Interestingly, neither film did that well at the fox office.[29]

What did do well at the box office, however, were the "problem" films of 1949. *Home of The Brave, Lost Boundaries* and *Pinky,* Bobo tells us, were the highest-grossing films of 1949 for their respective studios: United Artists, Film Classics and Twentieth Century Fox.[30] Both *Pinky,* directed by Elia Kazan, and *Lost Boundaries,* directed by Alfred Werker, tell stories about passing. In *Pinky,* Jeanne Crain, a White actress who plays the daughter of Ethel Waters, revisits her mother in the South after having passed for White in the North. (Not having been able to locate a print of this film yet, I must leave discussion of it to some other time.)

Lost Boundaries is about a Black male doctor, Scott Carter, and his wife Marcia (played by White actors Mel Ferrer and Beatrice Pearson) who pass for White in a small New Hampshire town called Keenham and raise two children, a boy, Howard and a girl, Shelley, (also played by White actors—Richard Hylton and Susan Douglas) without telling them that they have Black blood. When World War II begins, the fierce patriotism of father and son forces both to enlist. Dr. Carter is given a post as a doctor and an officer in the navy until his Black blood is discovered. The navy then rejects him entirely.

In the film's climax, Dr. Carter tells Howard that he has Black blood. Howard is driven half mad by the realization that he is a "Negro." He runs off to Harlem (which includes a close-up of a street sign for 135th Street and Lenox Avenue as well as documentary-type footage of Harlem street scenes) to find out what it means to be Black. In a dingy rooming house, while he sleeps, tossing and turning, over his head we watch images of his father, mother and sister dissolve into visibly Black images.

In a dark hallway of a rooming house he gets drawn into a fight. When the police come, he is found standing over a dead body with a knife in his hand. He is arrested and interrogated by a friendly Black police lieutenant played by Canada Lee, who explains why his father didn't want him to be Black. If you can be "white," why would you ever want to be "black," all the visibly Black characters say, again and again, in the film. In the end, he is happily reunited with his father, and they with the town, in a final scene in church in which the minister delivers a sermon preaching racial tolerance.

In this film, "passing" as a psychological dilemma is gendered male. The parallel scene of the mother telling the daughter is never shown. All the evidence would suggest that the daughter took the news rather calmly. In fact, the *Reader's Digest* story upon which this "true story" was based completely focuses upon the psychological traumas of the son, which were much more complicated than in the film. In *Reader's Digest,* Howard (named Albert Johnston), who already had a close Black friend at college, thinks of himself as a liberal and seems pleased when he first learns that he is Black.

But then his grades begin to fall, he contemplates suicide, and his father sends him to a "well-known Negro psychiatrist." While in the navy, he is sent to a mental hospital. After discharge from the navy, he begins to travel around the country looking up relatives, trying to figure out which way is up. The tale goes on and on, with a series of interesting ethnographic details about Negro society and "passing" in the forties.[31]

In *Home of The Brave* (directed by Mark Robson), a Black soldier (James Edwards) named Peter Moss suffers from paralysis because his best friend, a White man (Llyod Bridges), begins to call him a nigger and then gets killed immediately afterwards. Under the supervision of a psychiatrist, who becomes the tiresome superego of the narrative, we are told that Peter is paralyzed because he feels responsible for his friend's death; he wanted his friend to die. His psychiatrist says he wanted his friend to die, not because he called Peter a nigger, but because everybody in battle wants the person next to him to die instead of himself.

Your problem has nothing to do with being a Negro, the psychiatrist yells at Peter. You have to get this chip off your shoulder and realize you're like everybody else! A cured Peter, able to walk again, ends up going off with a White one-armed soldier named Mingo, to start a restaurant.

In *The Devil Finds Work,* a book he wrote on film in 1976, James Baldwin says of this scenario.

> But why is the price of what should, after all, be a simple human connection so high? Is it really necessary to lose a woman, an arm, or one's mind, in order to say hello? . . . A man can fall in love with a man: incarceration, torture, fire, and death, and still more, the threat of these, have not been able to prevent it, and never will. It became a grave, a tragic matter, on the North American continent, where white power became indistinguishable from the question of sexual dominance. But the question of sexual dominance can exist only in the nightmare of that soul which has armed itself, totally, against the possibility of the changing notion of conquest and surrender, which is love.[32]

Two documentaries, *The Quiet One* (1948), written by James Agee and directed by Sidney Meyers, and *Let There Be Light* (1946), directed by John Huston, both focussed on a universal male psyche from a psychiatric point of view, both of which also suggest that racial categories simply don't exist. These two documentaries help to further clarify the nature of the dilemma Baldwin elucidates. In *Let There Be Light,* three Black soldiers are included among a random sample of psychologically impaired World War II veterans. Although one Black soldier says, in a group therapy session, that he didn't speak until he was seven and another—who has repeated crying spells—says he was raised to look down on children whose families had less, race is never mentioned in the highly psychoanalytic narration of the voice-over. Sponsored by the military, *Let There Be Light* was never actually released because of its transgressive honesty regarding the extent of psychological problems (about twenty percent of casualties) among World War II veterans.

In *The Quiet One,* a little Black boy who has been abandoned by his parents, and now lives in The Wiltwyck School for Boys in upstate New York, must deal with his feelings of self-hatred and alienation. Scripted by James Agee, *The Quiet One* juxtaposes documentary footage and staged dramatic scenes with a psychiatrist narrator. In flashbacks, we see the little boy's environment of poverty and deprivation as he is beaten and tormented by a mean old grandmother in the ghetto.

The unfolding drama, which never allows him to speak in his own voice (rather the psychiatrist paraphrases his remarks from their psychoanalytic sessions), shows him learning to negotiate his feelings of love for a Black male counselor. Again, throughout this film, "race" is never mentioned.

Even a brief perusal of these materials suggests to me how specifically calibrated were issues of "race," especially "race" in relation to gender, in films made in the forties. In the aftermath of the Jewish Holocaust, Hiroshima, Nagasaki, the Japanese internment, the integration of the military, and in the early stages of the McCarthy era and the Cold War, the particular political environment of the late forties made the range of safe discussions of such topics a narrow one.

What is fascinating to me, and deserves more examination, is the question of how the increasing prominence of a psychiatric and/or psychoanalytic discourse impacted on definitions and criteria of "race" as a national "problem" within dominant film practices. Obviously, none of these films is really about women. There are no women at all in *Home of The Brave.* In *Lost Boundaries,* the women are among the most conventional and limp I've ever seen in film. The positive-images mandate means these women have to be dreadfully dull. In *The Quiet One,* the women are nothing more than lifeless shadows. But what fascinates me about all of these films is the superimposition of a narrowly psychoanalytic Oedipal drama upon the otherwise reckless vagaries of "race."

The institutionalization in the forties of a psychoanalytic/psychiatric discourse in the US was central to the formation of conventional notions of masculinity, sexual difference, family, and personality in dominant film practice.[33] What is more, the ways in which these conventions were translated into plot, suture and mise-en-scène, continue to inform contemporary perceptions of film that is pleasurable to watch. Particularly suggestive here is that further examination of these matters might reveal unanticipated insight into the gendering of "race," the problem of the visual in Afro-American culture, and "the changing motion of conquest and surrender."

Notes

1. Juliet Mitchell, Introduction I to *Feminine Sexuality* by Jacque Lacan, New York: Norton, 1982, 26; James Baldwin, *The Devil Finds Work,* New York: The Dial Press, 1976, 19–20.

2. I realize that the problem of defining Afro-American culture in any cohesive way is insuperable. See Paul Gilroy in "It Ain't Where You're From, It's Where You're At: The Dialectics of Diasporic Identification," *Third Text,* London, England, No. 13, Winter 1990/91, 3–16. By the term I don't mean anything more heady than whenever and wherever Blacks attempt to grapple with issues of identity and self-representation. The agent might be considered anybody, from a lone Black actor working in a project entirely produced by Whites (such as Courtney Vance in John Guare's Lincoln Center production of *Six Degrees of Separation*) to an institutional framework such as Spike Lee and Forty Acres and A Mule.

3. LeRoi Jones, *Blues People: Negro Music in White America,* New York: Morrow, 1963; Charles Keil, *Urban Blues,* Chicago: Univ of Chicago, 1966; Lawrence Levine, *Black Culture and Black Consciousness: Afro-American Folk Thought from Slavery to Freedom,* New York: Oxford UP, 1977; Robert Palmer, *Deep Blues,* New York: Viking, 1981; Nelson George, *The Death of Rhythm and Blues,* New York: Pantheon, 1988.

4. Joseph Boskin, *Sambo: The Rise & Demise of an American Jester,* New York: Oxford UP, 1986, 13. Boskin suggests that this figure, who was widespread in Britain (perhaps even conceived there) as well as in the US, was usually male, and perhaps constitutionally "male" in gender. See my "De-Facing History," *Art-in-America,* December 1990, for further details on how Sambo images functioned in the visual arts in the nineteenth and early twentieth centuries.

5. Donald Bogle, *Toms, Coons, Mulattoes, Mammies, & Bucks: An Interpretive History of Blacks in American Films,* New York: Viking, 1973; Thomas Cripps, *Slow Fade to Black: The Negro in American Film, 1900–1942,* New York: Oxford UP, 1977.

6. Thomas Cripps, "Film" Chapter in *Split Image: African Americans in The Mass Media,* eds. Jannette L. Dates and William Barlow, Washington D.C.: Howard UP, 1990, 125–172.

7. Karen Grigsby Bates, " 'They've Gotta Have Us': Hollywood's Black Directors," *The New York Times Magazine,* Sunday, July 14, 1991, 14–19, 38–40, 44, including cover.

8. I take my concept of "invisibility" from Ralph Ellison's use of the term to describe the condition of Blacks in the US mid-twentieth century in relation to historiography and the production of culture in *Invisible Man.* References to "invisibility" range over most of the essays in *Invisibility Blues: From Pop To Theory,* Verso/Routledge, 1990. In my earlier *Black Macho and The Myth of The Superwoman* (reissued by Verso/Routledge in 1990 with a critical introduction), I suggested that gender was as important as "race" to understanding the plight of the woman of color.

9. There are important exceptions to these generalizations about feminist film theory. For instance, in *Camera Obscura*'s issue on "The Spectatrix" (John Hopkins UP, 1989, 20–21), Constance Penley describes herself as having "studiously avoided or even resisted the idea of the female spectator" in favor of a more heterogeneous concept of identification. Also, in regard to the constant problematization of these issues, see the range of essays in *Women in Film Noir,* ed. E. Ann Kaplan, London: British Film Institute, 1978; *Psychoanalysis & Cinema,* ed. E. Ann Kaplan, New York: Routledge, 1990; and *Fabrications: Costume and the Female Body,* eds. Jane Gaines & Charlotte Herzog, New York: Routledge, 1990.

10. *Screen,* Vol. 6, No. 3, 6–18, 11. There are many examples. Some notable ones are: Jacqueline Bobo, "*The Color Purple*. Black Women as Cultural Readers," in *Female Spectators Looking at Film and Television,* eds. E. Deidre Pribram, New York: Verso/Routledge, 1988, 90–109; Manthia Diawara, "The Nature of Mother in *Dreaming Rivers,*" *Third Text,* 13 (Winter 1991), 73–84; Trinh Minh-ha *When The Moon Waxes Red: Representation, Gender and Cultural Politics,* Routledge, forthcoming 1991; Jackie Byars, *All That Hollywood Allows: Re-Reading Gender in 1950s Melodrama,* UP Chapel Hill, 1991; Bell Hooks, "Is Paris Burning?" *Zeta Mazazine,* June 1991, 60–64; Jane Gaines, "White Privilege and Looking Relations: Race and Gender in Feminist Film Theory," *Screen,* 29:4 (Autumn 1988), 12–27.

11. Janice Radway (in *Reading the Romance: Women, Patriarchy, and Popular Literature,* Chapel Hill: Univ of NC Press, 1984), and Stuart Hall in ("Encoding/Decoding" in *Culture, Media, Language: Working Papers in Cultural Studies, 1972–79,* (London: Hutchinson, 1981), have been highly influential in this context. Good examples of this approach abound, for instance, most of the essays in the Pribram anthology cited above, and the essays in the "Popular Culture and Reception Studies" issue of *Camera Obscura,* 23, May 1990.

12. See my essay on "Multiculturalism and Oppositionality" in forthcoming *AfterImage,* 1991.

13. Happily, there are wonderful exceptions to this generalization in the work of Hazel Carby, bell hooks, Gayatri Spivak, Trinh Minh-ha, and Kobena Mercer.

14. See my "Modernism, Postmodernism and The Problem of The Visual in Afro-American Culture," eds. Russell Ferguson et al., *Out There: Marginalization and Contemporary Cultures,* New York: The New Museum, 1991, 39–50; "De-Facing History," *Art-In-America,* December 1990, 121–128, 184–186; "Multiculturalism and Oppositionality," forthcoming in *AfterImage,* 1991. Also, my work on this topic included in 1991 unpublished papers on "Gender and The Problem of The Visual in Afro-American Literary Criticism" (delivered at the CUNY Graduate Center in New York and Beyond Baroque in Venice, CA); "Race, Gender and Advertising" (delivered at the Cooper Hewitt in New York, Princeton Univ and the Walker Art Center in Minneapolis), and "Modernism, Postmodernism and The Problem of The Visual in Afro-American Art—II" (delivered at the Randolph Street Gallery in Chicago, the San Francisco Institute of Art and the California Art Institute in Valencia).

15. Bogle, *op. cit.*

16. Bogle, p. 16.

17. Bogle, pp. 16–17.

18. *New York Times,* Sunday, March 31, 1991, 9.

19. Bogle, pp. 14–15.

20. Cripps article, p. 131.

21. Cripps article, pp. 134–136. Also, see Manthia Diawara's "Black Spectatorship: Problems of Identification and Resistance," in *Screen,* 29:4 (Autumn 1988), 66–76,

for a sensitive reading of crucial "Gus chase" sequence in *The Birth of A Nation*, which takes into account contemporary issues in psychoanalytic film interpretation.

22. Jacqueline Bobo, "'The Subject is Money': Reconsidering The Black Film Audience as a Theoretical Paradigm," *Black American Literature Forum*, Volume 25, Number 2 (Summer 1991), 424.

23. Kaja Silverman, *The Subject of Semiotics*, New York: Oxford UP, 223.

24. Cripps article, p. 145; Bobo article, p. 423. Bobo defines independent Black-cast films as "films made by Black people or white-backed organizations which featured Black actors and actresses."

25. Bogle, p. 108.

26. Bogle, p. 121.

27. Bogle, p. 122. Scott appeared in *Something to Shout About* (1943), *I Dood It* (1943), *The Heat's On* (1943), *Broadway Rhythm* (1944), *Rhapsody in Blue* (1945).

28. Bogle, p. 127.

29. Lena Horne, *the* Black female film star of the forties (the first Black woman ever to appear on the cover of a film magazine), was closely aligned with Walter White of the NAACP and Paul Robeson, and was extremely political. In fact, her political positions led to her being blacklisted and banned from film roles. Horne was listed in *Red Channels* in June of 1950 for her support of the Hollywood Independent Citizens Committee, the Joint Anti-Fascist Committee, and W. E. B. Dubois and Paul Robeson's Council on African Affairs. Gail Lumet Buckley, *The Hornes: An American Family*, New York: Knopf, 1986, 203–213.

30. Bobo article, p. 424.

31. W. L. White, "Lost Boundaries," *The Reader's Digest*, December 1947, 135–154.

32. James Baldwin, p. 68.

33. Krin Gabbard & Glen O. Gabbard, *Psychiatry and The Cinema*, Chicago: Univ of Chicago Press, 1987, xv. While recent discussions of Frantz Fanon (*Black Skins, White Masks*, New York: Grove Press, 1967) are relevant here, they are beyond the scope of this present article. Also, I plan to refer to them at length in an article in progress on the relevance of "film noir" to contemporary Afro-American film production (for an anthology edited by Joan Kopjec and Mike Davis for Verso). Briefly, however, it seems to me that Fanon is not especially useful to a Black feminist film criticism because of the way in which he succumbs to, and/or conflates, the confusion of the "woman" and the "primitive" or the "uncivilized" (not White) in Freud. Nor do I completely agree with how Jane Gaines reframes the issues.

18
Reading Through the Text: The Black Woman as Audience

Jacqueline Bobo

The novel *The Color Purple* (1982) is a critical component of a tradition of Black women's literature. It continues an effort by Black women writers to give Black women an empowering view of themselves. The central problem with the film *The Color Purple* (1985) is that the empowering aspects of the strong Black women are neutralized and the full dimensions of patriarchal domination are obliterated. In the Steven Spielberg production the Black woman as protagonist has been displaced as the center of the story, which becomes a chronicle of an abusive Black man's journey toward self-understanding. The film changes him from an evil person into one who is perplexed and confused. The film grants the male protagonist salvation because he has arranged for a happy ending for the woman he misused throughout the film. This is the antithesis of the ending of the novel, which revolves around an abused Black woman beginning to appreciate herself and becoming economically independent.

Although the film shifted the emphasis of the story from that of a Black woman and replaced it with a Black man's angst, there is increasing evidence that many Black women generated a positive reading of the film. In an earlier study I examined the heated debates surrounding the film, as well as Black women's seemingly overwhelming favorable response to it. I researched Black women's reactions through watching and listening to television and radio talk shows, and through reading newspaper and magazine articles. Additionally, Black women's responses were gauged through informal conversations and formally, through several sets of unstructured interviews. I determined that a significant number of Black women had a favorable reaction to the film and that it was meaningful in their lives.[1]

This analysis addresses the way in which Black women gave an empathetic reading to a film that appeared, on the surface, to be presenting a Black woman's story, but which contained a vastly different subtext. The film, as structured by Spielberg, harkens back to earlier negative depictions of Black women in creative works. I will examine the film from the perspective of its ideological construction of Black women and its formal structure as developed by Steven Spielberg. Black women's favorable reaction to the film will then be assessed. The aim is to account for the way in which a significant number of Black women "read through the text"[2] to reconstruct satisfactory meanings from a mainstream cultural product created by a White male filmmaker.

Ideological Construction

The Ideological project of Black women writers throughout the history of their creative endeavors was to effect a cultural transformation by presenting a different version of Black women's social and cultural history. The ideological intent of media representations of Black women's lives is to maintain the status quo by resurrecting previously demeaning images of them. The process has a history in media depictions of Black people in general. Michael Winston, in "Racial Consciousness and the Evolution of Mass Communications in the United States," traces the evolution of media codes about racial representations. These were set views that presented a social reality that was understood to be unreal. The codes became firmly established during Reconstruction as a legitimation of the social, legal, institutional, and economic forces that were used to deny Black people full entry as free people into a world their labor had enriched. The racial codes were refined and sustained to support legal segregation that minimized contact between Black and White people. As a result, this mass-mediated social (un)reality was reproduced in later cultural forms; thus, media images of Black people were continually reconstructed from previous media representations: first print, then radio, film and television.[3]

The codes served a specific function; that were used to generate a "commonsense" understanding of those who could possibly threaten the established order. Anything that could be seen as an ideological corrective had to be neutralized and contained. As part of a continuum of novels by Black women writers which attempt to repudiate long-standing negative ideologies, *The Color Purple* was especially subversive.[4] As an example, the images of the young Celie being treated as a slavelike object and sexually abused are similar to ones presented in earlier Black women's literature. Harriet Wilson's *Our Nig* (1859), Harriet Jacobs/Linda Brent's *Incidents in the Life of a Slave Girl* (1861), and Margaret Walker's contemporary slave narrative *Jubilee* (1966), all portray Black women who were sexually exploited and abused by the slaveowners. These works written from a Black woman's perspective were a strong counter to the pervasive depictions of the sexually promiscuous Black woman. Negative constructions of Black women's sexuality have been the cornerstone of many oppressive ideologies that are used to mask capitalist, racist and sexist motives. As a consequence, Black women writers at the turn of the century were constrained in their explorations of Black women's sexuality. Later writers were not as reticent. As Shug and Sofia openly discuss their sexual feelings in *The Color Purple,* other writers attempted to illustrate the full range of Black women's sexuality. Barbara Christian observes that contemporary Black women writers have developed Black women's sexuality as a source of empowerment, for its suppression is another form of Black women's oppression.[5] Examples are present in Nella Larsen's *Passing* (1929), Zora Neale Hurston's *Their Eyes Were Watching God* (1937), and Toni Morrison's *Sula* (1973).

Another instance where *The Color Purple* draws on images from past works and imbues them with power is in its presentation of the "ordinary" young Black girl who struggles against society's notions that because she is dark with nappy hair she is not to be appreciated. This is exemplied by Celie's character in *The Color Purple* and in previous Black women's novels: Gwendolyn Brooks' novella *Maud Martha* (1953) and Morrison's *The Bluest Eye* (1970).

In these works, although there are poignant depictions of abuse and oppression, there are also times when the protagonists resist their imposed social conditions. In *Our Nig* Frado stops Mrs. Bellmont from beating her; Harriet Jacobs/Linda Brent devotes her life to resisting enslavement. She writes: "The war of my life had begun; and though one of God's most powerless creatures, I resolved never to be conquered."[6] In *Jubilee,* Sis Hetta's daugher Vyry wages a quiet struggle to preserve her family during slavery and the postbellum period. And, in Hurston's novel, Janie Crawford endures two abusive marriages; in defense of her life, she ends the last.

The film version of *The Color Purple* presents a view of Black women that is in direct opposition to these earlier works. The stories told in Black women's novels were a product of a conscious effort to portray multidimensional characters who attempted to attain some measure of control over their lives. In the film, the strong Black women are replaced by the standard negative images. Sofia, a model of strength and resistance, becomes the overbearing matriarchal figure. Rather than someone who resists the domination of her husband Harpo, Sofia seems to have him henpecked.

The Shug Avery of the film is presented as a victim of her insatiable sexual appetite rather than as a women who exercises the same privileges as men, including acting out her desire to sleep with whomever she chooses. As a corollary, Shug is disempowered as she longs for her preacher father's approval. Shug's father as a preacher is a character who was invented for the film. In it, Shug is seen as someone who regrets the life she has lived and who assents to others' view of her that she is a loose woman. Her constant quest for absolution from her father takes away her central source of power in the novel: that she does what she wants, and has the economic means to do so.

The depictions of Celie in the film are intended to show her as an unloved waif. What the film neglects, however, is a clear picture of why she is this way. Celie is a victim of racism, sexism, and patriarchal privilege. In the film Celie's dismal condition is the result of a quirk of fate, but this is the extent of her oppression. Celie does not represent the Black women who share her repressed state. She is presented as an individual who suffers hardships but who eventually ascends to fortune's favor. As Celie and Shug represent the extremes of hopelessness and strength in the novel, the following section will examine how their impact is diminished in the film.

Shug

The film character Shug values her preacher father's opinion of her more than she needs her "hedonistic" lifestyle. Rather than a secure Black woman who lives her life according to the dictates of her value system (as she is presented in the novel) the film version of Shug is obsessed with winning her father's approval. In the novel, when Celie is bathing Shug as she is recovering from her illness, Celie asks her if she misses her children. Shug replies that she doesn't miss anything.

In the film, as Celie is bathing Shug, she asks her if she has any kids. Shug is lying in the tub and the scene is shot so that what we see is the back of Shug's head and her hands waving around holding a bottle of liquor and a cigarette. We see Celie straight on. Shug answers Celie's question that her children are with her Ma and Pa. There is a cut to Shug lying in the tub. She looks wretched and sad. She says, "never knowed a child to come out right unless there's a man around." There is a cut to a reaction shot of Celie who is busy mixing the bath oils to pour in the tub. Celie looks at Shug innocently. As we cut back to her Shug moans, "children gots to have a pa." Shug then sits up in the tub and asks Celie, "Yo Pa love you? My Pa love me." She says this last proudly. "My Pa still love me," she says, then starts crying. "He still love me. 'Cept he don't know it. He don't know it." At this point she is overcome and starts crying harder.

"My Pa still love me," Shug says, in spite of the fact that she has not been living up to his moral standards, as the film implies. In case the point is missed, later in the film Old Mister comes to visit while Shug is recuperating from her illness. Old Mister walks up to the house and we see the back of him in a long shot as Albert (Mister) emerges from the house. They stare at each other and walk around each other in a circle in front of the porch swing. All the while the two are looking at each other they say nothing. Albert smiles at his father and sits down on the swing. There is a cut to a close up of Old Mister's foot between Albert's legs. We see Albert over Old Mister's shoulder as Old Mister leans down to talk to him. Old Mister says that Albert couldn't rest until he got Shug in his house. There is a cut back to Old Mister's foot between Albert's legs; Old Mister pushes the swing with his foot. Old Mister asks Albert: "What is it with this Shug Avery? She black as tar. Nappy headed. Got legs like baseball bats." Celie is in the house getting Old Mister a glass of water. She watches the two of them through the window. In a voice over Celie says: "Old Mister talking trash about Shug. Folks don't like nobody being too proud or too free."

Old Mister is still talking under the voice over. He says of Shug that she is a juke-joint jezebel, and that she isn't even clean, "I hear she's got that nasty women's disease." At this point Celie spits in Old Mister's glass of water. There is a cut to Albert as he tells Old Mister that he hasn't got it in him to understand why he loves Shug. Albert says that he has always loved her and always will, "I should have married her when I had the chance." Old Mister replies that Albert would have thrown his life away along with a good portion of Old Mister's money. Old Mister says that all Shug's children have different daddies. Albert replies that he can vouch for Shug's kids all having the same father. Old Mister counters, in an passage that is different from the novel, "You can vouch for nothing. Shug Avery done set the population of Hotwell County a new high. You just one of the rusters, boy." Albert says nothing; he is looking as if he wants to say something but is afraid to do so. When Celie comes out on the porch with the glass of water, Old Mister tells her: "Celie, you has my sympathy. Ain't many womens low they husbands 'ho to lay up in they house."

In the film Shug is not presented as someone with a normal sexual lifestyle, but as a lascivious and hot-blooded woman. The dialogue that was added to the story, when Old Mister says of Shug that she is a "juke-joint jezebel" and someone who sleeps with many of the men in the town, exemplifies this. Another instance is shown when Shug comes to visit Mister and Celie after her marriage to Grady. The two men are discussing Shug, while we see her listening in another room. Mister tells Grady that they both had her in their own way, "but we had her." Shug is listening to this conversation with a pleased smile on her face as if she does not mind being talked about as someone who has been passed from one man to the other.

In the novel Shug has a carefully thought-out system of values. She lives her life according to her standards and is free to do so because she is not dependent on anyone emotionally or economically. In the film she is controlled by all the men connected to her: Mister, her father, Grady. She is not the self-possessed woman in the novel, but someone who is pulled by the strings of her sexuality and her insecurity about the way she lives her life. The film casts a moral judgment on Shug and the result is one that implies that those who follow Shug's example may not be as lucky as she. In the film, when Shug goes to her father's church singing a song of repentance, he finally accepts her. She says to him, "See daddy, sinners have soul too," and he embraces her in an act of absolution.

As the film character Shug is not a powerful presence, her relationship with Celie dissolves into one that is constructed as typical female pettiness. Her treatment of Celie, seen at first in the comment "You sho is ugly," and the way she orders her around by telling Albert "git that thang to fix me something to eat," become harsher and meaner than they were in the novel. Her insipid actions in the bath tub as Celie is bathing her are incongruent with what she represents to both Mister and Celie. Because Shug is presented as a weak woman with questionable morals, the significance of Celie's struggle to value herself is undermined. In the novel, Celie represents those who are never acknowledged as important. They are insignificant, poor, dark-skinned Black girls. It is not until Celie realizes her true worth, gained through the examples of the women around her, that she has the ability to throw off the mechanisms of her oppression: her image of herself, Mister's omnipresent abuse, and her inability to support herself economically. Because Shug is powerful in the novel, Celie becomes powerful. Because Shug is presented as a petty jealous woman in the film, Celie is seen as the unloved, ugly-duckling stepsister. What she represents is a specific individual with a specific problem rather than many Black women who toil under similar circumstances.

Celie

In two of the least realized depictions of the subjugation of women in the film we see the young Celie used as a packhorse: first, when the stepfather gives her to Mister and the two of them travel to Mister's farm. Mister is riding the horse and Celie is trudging along behind. She is loaded down with her belongings, ostensibly symbolizing a mule, in the sense that Zora Neale Hurston wrote of the status of Black women. This same portrait of Celie the packhorse is given when Shug leaves to go touring with her band. Mister and Shug are shown walking with their arms around each other toward the band members waiting in the car. Celie is walking behind them, again lugging everything that no one else wants to carry. The symbol of Black women as mules does not only mean that they were beasts of burden, it means that they were without exercisable options in life. They were given as little thought and consideration as dumb animals. That the same scene is reenacted with Shug as the perpetrator neutralizes the first instance because Celie is seen as a helpless victim of life's unfair circumstances rather than as someone who does not see a way out from under Mister's domination.

Steven Spielberg's inability to understand the historical conditions that resulted in Alice Walker's themes and characters produced not only a simplistic exploration of a Black woman's life, but one that in fact undermines the revisionist efforts by previous Black women writers. The film bypasses the process that started with the slave narratives and their chronicle of the lives of Black women used as breeders, chattel, and sexual repositories. It ignores the period where the Black woman's perceived sexuality was redefined. The film overlooks the transitional moment where the average Black girl was given a place of importance. The writers within the Black woman's writing tradition reconstructed the perception of the Black woman as a figure in culture and in history. Their efforts are sabotaged in the film version of *The Color Purple*. As constructed by Steven Spielberg, the film resurrects previous characters from mainstream media and gives them a modern-day gloss. Shug becomes the licentious cabaret singer, Sofia the castrating Amazon, and Celie becomes an orphan Annie.

Formal Structure

Steven Spielberg is the most successful director in Hollywood's history. His three biggest films, *Jaws* (1975), *E.T.* (1982), and *Indiana Jones and the Temple of Doom* (1984) have combined to gross almost a billion dollars.

Spielberg revealed that he directed *The Color Purple* because he had long wanted to do a different kind of film, one that was not "stereotypically a Spielberg movie." He wanted to do a film that involved character rather than one that relied heavily on special effects: "I wanted to work in the same arena as directors like Sidney Lumet and Sydney Pollack—and Paddy Chayefsky, in terms of what he had done as a playwright and writer."[7] Spielberg agreed with those who said that his track record of being a successful director helped get the financial backing to make the film: "I think only because of who I am today with my past successes added up, that the studio would say yes, do whatever you like. Do the telephone book if you'd like.[8]

The film *The Color Purple* has been manufactured in line with Steven Spielberg's experiences, cultural background, and social and political worldview. Stuart Hall writes of "hegemonic politics" wherein cultural producers consistently inscribe hegemonically preferred meanings in their creative works.[9] A director as successful as Spielberg would seem to have the freedom to structure his film in whatever manner he chose. But Spielberg's sensibilities have been shaped by forces different from those which produced the novel. This is the primary reason he made the film as he did. He tapped into his consciousness and experiences, and produced a work that reflected his general outlook. It is for this reason that Spielberg could say of Walker's novel that it was not about race, that if the novel had been about racial conflict, "I wouldn't have been the right director for the project and I would not have done the movie."[10]

Spielberg's view of the novel, that race was not its predominant feature, raises the question of how he envisioned it. He saw the story as that of a young girl who is unloved and alone and as "Dickensian."[11] This is an important consideration, because it reveals much about the film's structure, subtle racist overtones, and overall mood. Spielberg's reference to Charles Dickens (and perhaps film versions of his novels) shows why the film was made within the genre of melodrama, as were the works of Dickens, why the center of the story shifted from a female perspective to that of a male subjectivity, and why many of the characters' actions were acted out in a stereotypically racist manner.

A melodramatic technique allows an artist to establish a connection with an audience by following a familiar pattern and establishing a recognizable code for interpretation. It emphasizes drastic shifts in mood, vastly different tempos, and a mixture of styles. According to Thomas Elsaesser in "Tales of Sound and Fury: Observations on the Family Melodrama," the novels of Charles Dickens in the nineteenth century featured discontinuity and sudden switches from horror to bliss to emphasize the social contradictions in England's moral fabric.[12]

The structure of *The Color Purple* is a conventionalized melodrama of heightened emotionalism induced by music and heart-tugging moments. The film is two hours and thirty-four minutes long and contains almost two hours of music. The parts of the film that are not accompanied by music have previously recorded natural sounds, such as birds chirping, frogs croaking, and wind whistling through the cornstalks.

A potentially powerful scene is always juxtaposed with a comic routine. The transitions occur abruptly because the film cuts from scene to scene rather than using dissolves. The transitional overlaps are those using sound: voices, music, or in some instances train wheels and hands clapping. It is this aspect of the design of the film that gives it an ambivalent quality. At times it seems to maintain the tone of the novel, as when Mister's harsh treatment of the young Celie is graphically presented. The moment is lost, however, when there is an abrupt cut to buffoonery, most of which comes from the character Harpo. The character's comic antics and their strategic placement lessen the power of the subversive moments, such as instances of Mister's abuse of Celie, and moments that show her loneliness and isolation. Two sequences in particular stand out.

The first occurs during the shaving scene with the young Celie and Mister. This sequence comes right after Mister has forced Nettie to leave his farm. As she leaves she points her finger, and says that nothing but death can keep her from writing to Celie. Celie is standing at the fence crying and calling Nettie's name. There is a cut to an empty chair on the porch. We hear the sound of Celie's footsteps approach the chair. She enters from the right of the screen, Mister enters from the left. As Celie begins to shave Mister he grabs her arm, telling her that is she cuts him he will kill her. Celie is scared to death. While shaving Mister, Celie nicks him, he jumps up, and raises his arm prepared to strike her. We hear the sound of the mailman approach, and Mister runs to the mailbox. Celie goes into the house and leans on the sink, taking deep breaths. She knows she has had a narrow escape, for if the mailman had not arrived Mister would have struck her.

After Mister reads that Shug is not coming, he yells to Harpo to saddle his horse, and enters the house where Celie is cowering. She asks if she can see if a letter has come from Nettie. This is a medium shot of Celie and Mister. Celie has her back to the camera. This set-up makes her look very vulnerable and small, as Mister appears much larger and older. Mister tells Celie that he never wants to see her at the mailbox, that he has fixed it so he can tell if it has been "messed with." All during this tirade he is jabbing his finger at Celie, pushing her backward. He yells at her, "You understand!" The sequence is one of sheer terror for Celie and we get a sense of Mister's brutality. Imediately, there is an abrupt cut to Harpo trying to saddle the horse, and the full impact of the action with Celie is lost.

Another example of the awkward structure of the film that conveys a mixed message of anger and comedy again involves a moment with Celie that is disrupted by Harpo's antics. After a comic interlude of the adult Celie helping Mister get dressed for the arrival of Shug, he leaves and she begins cleaning the house. She finds the scrap of paper with the word "sky" written on it. It brings back memories of Nettie teaching her how to read. Celie stands at the window in close-up, looking out with the piece of paper clutched in her hand. In the voice over she says: "she say she write, but she never write. She say only death can keep her from it. Maybe she dead." The moment is held as Celie begins to cry. It is an impressive portrayal of the depth of Celie's loss, shattered with the next shift to the arrival of Harpo and Sofia walking down the road to the house to meet with Mister.

The sudden changes to Harpo not only undermine the force of the scenes that come before his actions, but are stereotypically racist. More than falling through the roof repeatedly, the subtle shifts in Harpo's language recall caricatures of Black people from past racist works. When he attempts to saddle the horse for the first time, he misses the horse completely and says "I'm gitting to it, I'm gitting to it." The viewer has been prepared for the language of the characters and in many cases some of the words are said differently from the way they are used in the book. For example the word "mammy" is used sparingly. In the novel the stepfather, Fonso, uses the word mammy several times. In the film he says "mama" rather than "mammy." That he does so indicates Spielberg's partial effort to use as few commonly perceived negative words as possible. The shift in Harpo's words then can only be seen as intentional. When the grown-up Harpo saddles the horse he says "Yessah Pa, yessah. I'se gitting to it. I'se gitting to it." Nowhere in the novel is that kind of language used. Alice Walker carefully uses what she categorizes as Black "folk language" to show how Black people at a particular time and in a specific setting talked, and still talk in many instances. She never resorts to the stereotypical words and phrases of the Joel Chandler Harris type, yet in the film, the characters, especially Sofia, Shug, and Harpo, occasionally slip into these phrases. This is particularly true of Harpo. When Mister brings Shug home in the wagon Harpo asks repeatedly "Who dis, Pa. Pa, who dis?" In the novel he merely says "Who this?"

Spielberg's attempt to emulate the melodramatic conventions of Charles Dickens not only created a disruptive structure, but displaced Celie as the central focus of the story. Spielberg constructed three scenes to show the connection with Dickens, and the result was that Mister became the central character in the film. The scenes involve Celie and/or Nettie and the Dickens novel *Oliver Twist* (1837).

The first scene sets up the connection with the novel. In it Nettie is teaching Celie how to read. The book they are reading is *Oliver Twist*. The sequence begins with a medium shot of Celie and Nettie standing in a swing. We see only their shoes. Celie is hesitantly reading from the book, stumbling many times over the words. When she gets to the word "systematic," she asks Nettie what it means. Nettie explains in a way that Celie can relate it to something she does in her life. Nettie says it's "like when you have a way of doing stuff and you do it the same way every time." She tells Celie it is similar to how they hang the sheets first so they can (here Celie joins in with her and they say simultaneously) "put the socks in the cracks."

The next scene occurs as Mister is pursuing Nettie on the horse as she is on her way to school. As the sequence begins there is a sound overlap that is the transition from the previous scene where Celie and Nettie are playing their hand-clapping game. As they clap faster and faster, there is a cut to Nettie walking with her schoolbooks in her hand. The sound of the claps blends into the sound of the horse's hooves as it trots faster and faster to catch up with Nettie. She turns around to see Mister on the horse approaching her, as she walks faster and faster down an incline. The camera moves up into a crane shot so that what we see is Nettie hurrying away from Mister on the horse. The feeling in watching the scene is that she is vulnerable and helpless. There is a cut to Mister on the horse riding beside Nettie and she fearfully watches to see what he will do. Mister goes through a series of playful routines. As the perspective shifts from Nettie's point of view to that of the viewer, there is a cut to the horse with an empty saddle. Nettie stops, looks, then Mister walks out in front of her. He takes off his hat and there are purple flower petals on top of his head. Mister grabs Nettie's hands and begins a playful dance. As she attempts to pull away Mister dances her into the bushes. There is a cut to a shot of the horse grazing, and the shound of a sharp hit. Mister groans loudly, the horse jumps, and Nettie comes out of the bushes screaming and swinging her books wildly. As she does so, the books fly out of her hand, and there is a close-up of the book *Oliver Twist*. There is a cut to Nettie running away in the distance, then Mister falls into the frame holding his groin. Mister rolls over and says, "I'll git 'cha. I'll git 'cha."

The surface intent of this sequence is to lead the viewer into an association with the Dickens' novel. The underlying message conveys something else. It emphasizes who Spielberg considers to be the central character in the film. At the moment most women would consider to be a nightmare becoming a reality, what is privileged is the sound of Mister being hit in the groin, an image of the horse jumping, and as Nettie runs away, Mister falling into the frame with his hands between his legs. Each of the three times that I saw the film in the theatre, most of the audience reacted more to Mister's discomfort than to the scene that had been acted out, that of a young girl almost raped.

The scene is similar to the one at the beginning of the film after Celie has been hit with the rock, and Mister is having sex with her. The scene begins with a shot of belts hanging on a headboard. The camera slowly tilts down past a picture of Shug on the stand into a close-up of Celie lying in the bed with her head wrapped in a bloodied bandage. There is the familiar rhythmic sound amplified by the belts banging against the headboard. As we look at Celie, there is the sound of Mister's grunt, and Celie is pulled upward. Mister's arm enters the frame, hits the headboard, travels down Celie's face past her lips. Celie's voice is heard in the voice-over:

> I don't cry. I lay there thinking about Nettie while he on top of me. And wonder if she safe. And then I think about that pretty woman in the picture. I know what he doing to me he done to her. And maybe she like it.

The camera pans over the picture of Shug, moves back down to a close-up of Celie, holds on her, then Mister falls into the frame saying "Jesus" as an indication of his physical state at the completion of intercourse with Celie.

What should have been an image of repulsion becomes one that emphasizes Mister's gratification. Both of these scenes described above are ones of insensate cruelty that are neutralized by their representation and privileging of Mister's reactions rather than that of the victims.

The third *Oliver Twist* scene is the transition sequence where the young Celie becomes the older one. This scene comes on the heels of the one involving the young Harpo saddling the horse. Mister yells out to Celie that he wants his supper when he comes back. We see Celie in a close-up while she responds pitifully, "Yes suh." In the background there is the shadow of a chair. Celie turns around, walks to the chair, we see her shadow on the wall as she picks up the book, sits down and begins to read from the Dickens novel. In the voice-over we hear her reading while there are shots of a purple flyer blowing across the fields, the mailbox, porches, and the tops of houses. It finally becomes attached to a door, face up. The flyer announces the expected arrival of Shug. There is a cut to the older Celie confidently reading the passage from the book. She reads so that the audience will understand the symbolism that has been presented, that her life is not a good one and fate has dealt her an unfair hand. She reads:

> For the next eight or ten months Oliver was the victim of a systematic course of treachery and deception. He was brought up by hand. The hungry and destitute situation of the infant orphan . . . (her voice blends into the current action at this point).

Spielberg's sense of the novel *The Color Purple*, that the life of a young Black girl growing up in a world in which she has no access to power until she empowers herself is equivalent to the life of Oliver as chronicled by Dickens (or rendered in the film versions of his novels), reveals much about the overall mood of the film. It is one of "sweetness and light" rather than of horror and evil; it is stylized and stagey, and it plays too much to the comic elements of life rather than dealing substantially with emotional issues. Some observers make the same judgment about Dickens, that he appeared to be showing the ordinary life of the Victorian environment, but it was a facade of realism that emphasized the comic and contained stagey aspects of melodramatic conventions.[13]

The film is frustrating to watch at times, as it moves from scenes that are emotionally wrenching to ones that are incomprehensible. This is a shortcoming not only of the film, but of the genre of melodrama as well. According to Ellen Seiter in "The Promise of Melodrama: Recent Women's Films and Soap Opera," melodrama introduces injustice, evil and chaos into its dramatic world, but does not resolve the issues it portrays except by a "kind of narrative sleight-of-hand." Seiter observes:

> Melodrama not only represents a troubled world; its message is itself troubling. In exposing evil and treating the subject of suffering, it raises contradictions which it cannot resolve in a consistent and sensible way.[14]

Seiter submits that a critical question regarding the genre of melodrama is whether it will be subversive in its effect on an audience, prompting its members "to recognize oppression and social injustice," or if it merely functions as a means of escape.

Because Spielberg structured the film melodramatically, this both draws an audience into the story while it camouflages its inadequate and confusing portraits of the three central Black women: Shug, Celie, and Sofia. The moments of humor in the film provide comic relief, but the abrupt cut from the dramatic to the comic neutralizes its moments of power. The ubiquitous music under the emotional scenes is intrusive in many instances, but serves to move many viewers in spite of themselves. As a consequence, Spielberg's use of melodrama both enhances the film and makes its message slippery to comprehend. This is especially true of the way in which the women are presented.

Black Women's Response

The literary scholar Deborah McDowell submits that Alice Walker deliberately and consciously wrote to an audience of Black women. McDowell offers as support the structure and plot of the novel, which has two Black sisters writing to each other.[15] McDowell also feels that Alice Walker's novel emphasizes, through its choice of subjects and images, that earlier Black women writers had written without an audience "capable of accepting and appreciating that the full, raw, unmediated range of the Black woman's story could be appropriate subject matter for art."

According to McDowell, Alice Walker is able to accomplish her "revisionist mission" in *The Color Purple* because of "the social realities and literary circumstances of her place and time."[16] In other words, at the time that *The Color Purple* was published there were other Black women actively working to reclaim the Black woman's image and to alter substantially the oppressive conditions of Black women's lives.

The preoccupations and concerns of Black women activists and writers resonate with the lives of many Black women. As such, the issues they addressed can be seen as constituting a reservoir of background knowledge that Black women used as a discursive strategy for meaning construction of the film *The Color Purple*. This does not mean that the women who engaged positively with the film were aware of this heritage of Black women's activism. It means that the issues that these women considered to be important were pervasive ones in Black women's lives; thus, the women could be interpellated, or hailed, by a creative work in which these elements were present.[17]

Paradoxically, the film *The Color Purple* was constructed according to mainstream values; the meanings embedded in the film are ones that are deeply ingrained in this culture. The struggle to resist the pull of the film, and to extract progressive meanings, is the same struggle needed to resist domination and oppression in everyday life. This battle is not a new one for Black women. Their cultural competency (the repertoir of discursive strategies brought to bear on interpreting a text) stems from growing up Black and female in a society which places little value on their situation.

Toni Morrison writes at the end of *The Bluest Eye* about Claudia and Frieda MacTeer's memories of the battle against a societal image of them as unimportant:

> Or maybe we didn't remember; we just knew. We had defended ourselves since memory against everything and everybody, considered all speech a code to be broken by us, and all gestures subject to careful analysis; we had become headstrong, devious and arrogant. Nobody paid us any attention, so we paid very good attention to ourselves.[18]

In paying good attention to a film in which aspects of their histories were depicted, Black women were able to extract images of power and relate them to their lives. In the best of all possible worlds, Black women would be able to see themselves represented in films that are directed by Black women. Unfortunately, there are no Black women who are allowed (meaning financed) to mount the kind of production as that given *The Color Purple*.

The Spielberg film exists; this cannot be changed. Other films about Black people and Black women that are produced by mainstream artists will continue to be made.[19] The critical issue then becomes one of how to affect the reception to the works so that they are not seen in isolation but in relationship to the total lives of Black people. Those creative works that are blatantly and irretrievably racist should be protested for the harm that is done. Those that are well-intentioned but patronizing and negative should also be criticized. However, a work which gathers to it an audience who embrace it and use it productively should be analyzed and assessed for the benefits that can be derived from it. Critics and scholars as well as media activists should intervene in the message of the film in such a way that an audience can use the cultural product as a tool for change in other aspects of their lives.

Notes

1. See Jacqueline Bob, *"The Color Purple*: Black Women as Cultural Readers," *Female Spectators Looking at Film and Television,* ed. E. Deidre Pribram (London and New York: Verso, 1988), 90–109; and, "Sifting Through the Controversy: Reading *The Color Purple,"* *Callaloo: A Journal of Afro-American and African Arts and Letters* 12: 2 (Spring 1989), 332–242.

2. The notion that media audiences can make meanings from mainstream texts separate from the intentions of the filmmakers is discussed in Ellen Seiter et al., eds., *Remote Control: Television, Audiences and Cultural Power* (New York: Routledge, 1989).

3. Michael R. Winston, "Racial Consciousness and the Evolution of Mass Communications in the United States," *Daedalus: Journal of the Academy of Arts and Sciences* 3: 4 (Fall 1982), 171–182.

4. For a more detailed examination of the heritage of Black women writing see Barbara Christian's *Black Women Novelists* (1980), Mary Helen Washington's *Invented Lives* (1987), and Hazel Carby's *Reconstructing Womanhood* (1987).

5. Barbara Christian, "From the Inside Out: Afro-American Women's Literary Tradition and the State," *Center for Humanistic Studies Occasional Papers,* eds. Wlad Godzich, Nancy Kobrin, and Dayna Anderson, 21 vols. (Minneapolis: University of Minnesota, 1987), 16.

6. Harriet Jacobs [Linda Brent], *Incidents in the Life of a Slave Girl, Written by Herself,* ed. L. Maria Child (Boston: privately printed, 1861), introduction and ed. Jean Fagan Yellin (Cambridge: Harvard University Press, 1987), 19.

7. Glenn Collins, "Spielberg Films 'The Color Purple'," *The New York Times* (15 December 1985), Section 2, 23.

8. *Alice Walker and "The Color Purple",* videocassette, dir. Samira Osman, narr. Susannah York, BBC, 1986.

9. Discussed in Lawrence Grossberg, "History, Politics and Postmodernism: Stuart Hall and Cultural Studies," *Journal of Communication Inquiry* 10: 2 (1986), 61–75.

10. BBC Documentary, *Alice Walker and "The Color Purple"* 1986.

11. Glenn Collins, "Spielberg Films 'The Color Purple'," Section 2, 23.

12. Thomas Elsaessar, "Tales of Sound and Fury: Observations on the Family Melodrama," *Movies and Methods* Vol. II, ed. Bill Nichols (Berkeley: University of California Press, 1985), 170.

13. M.H. Abrams, et al., eds. *The Norton Anthology of English Literature* Vol. II (New York: W.W. Norton & Company, 1968), 744.

14. Ellen Seiter, "The Promise of Melodrama: Recent Women's Films and Soap Opera," diss., Northwestern University, 1981, 9.

15. Deborah E. McDowell, " 'The Changing Same': Generational Connections and Black Women Novelists," *New Literary History* 18: 2 (1987), 297.

16. McDowell, " 'The Changing Same'," 296.

17. There is a complex process of negotiation that occurs when viewers watch a film or television program. Viewers will interpret a text based upon elements in their background that prompt them to dismiss what is being presented, to accept it, or to travel the continuum between the two. For a discussion of this process see David Morley, "Texts, Readers, Subjects," in *Culture, Media, Language,* Stuart Hall, et al., eds. (London: Hutchinson, 1980), 163–173.

18. Toni Morrison, *The Bluest Eye* (New York: Holt, Rinehart and Winston, Inc., 1970; reprinted New York: Simon & Schuster, Inc., 1972), 149. The reference is from the 1972 edition.

19. This particular issue is becoming hotly contested as more works by Black writers are being adapted to film and television. Several writers are insisting that their works be directed by Black people as other directors have not demonstrated the ability to translate the specifics of Black culture. The Black playwright August Wilson explains his desire for a Black director for the film adaptation of his play *Fences* in *Spin* 6:7 (October 1990), 70–71. The Black playwright Lorraine Hansberry had similar reservations about allowing her play *A Raisin in the Sun* to be adapted to film, and she was able to write the screenplay herself. For her views on the subject see Hansberry, "What Could Happen Didn't," *New York Herald Tribune* (March 26, 1961), 8.

19

The Oppositional Gaze: Black Female Spectators

bell hooks

Thinking about Black female spectators, I remembered being punished as a child for staring, for those hard, intense, direct looks children would give grown-ups, looks that were seen as confrontational, as gestures of resistance, challenging authority. The "gaze" has always been political in my life. Imagine the terror felt by the child who has come to understand through repeated punishments that one's gaze can be dangerous. The child who has learned so well to look the other way when necessary. Yet, when punished, the child is told by parents, "look at me when I talk to you"— only, the child is afraid to look. Afraid to look but fascinated by the gaze. There is power in looking.

Amazed the first time I read in history classes that White slaveowners, men, women, and children, punished enslaved Black people for looking, I wondered how this traumatic relationship to the gaze had informed Black parenting, Black spectatorship. The politics of slavery, of racialized power relations, were such that the slaves were denied their right to gaze. Connecting this strategy of domination to that used by grown folks in Southern, Black, rural communities of my growing up, I was pained to think that there was no absolute difference between White who had oppressed Black people and ourselves. Years later, reading Michel Faucault, I thought again about these connections, about the ways power as domination reproduces itself in different locations employing similar apparatuses, strategies, mechanisms of control.

Since I knew as a child that the dominating power adults exercised over me and over my gaze was never so absolute that I did not dare to look, to sneak a peep, to stare dangerously, I knew that the slaves had looked. That all attempts to repress our/Black people's right to gaze had produced in us an overwhelming longing to look, a rebellious desire, an oppositional gaze. By courageously looking, we defiantly declared: "Not only will I stare. I want my look to change reality." Even in the worse circumstances of domination, the ability to manipulate one's gaze in the face of structures of domination that would contain it, opens up the possibility of agency. In much of this work Michel Foucault insists on describing domination in terms of "relations of power" as part of an effort to challenge the assumption that "power is a system of domination which controls everything and which leaves no room for freedom." Emphatically stating that in all relations of power "there is necessarily the possibility of resistance," he invites the critical thinker to search those margins, gaps, locations on and through the body, where agency can be found.

Stuart Hall calls for recognition of our agency as Black spectators in his essay "Cultural Identity and Cinematic Representation." Speaking against the construction of White representations of Blackness as totalizing, Hall says of White presence:

> The error is not to conceptualize this "presence" in terms of power, but to locate that power as wholly external to us—as extrinsic force, whose influence can be thrown off like the serpent sheds its skin. What Frantz Fanon reminds us, in *Black Skin, White Masks,* is how its power is inside as well as outside: "the movements, the attitudes, the glances of the other fixed me there, in the sense in which a chemical solution is fixed by a dye. I was indignant; I demanded an explanation. Nothing happened. I burst apart. Now the fragments have been put together again by another self." This "look," from—so to speak—the place of the Other, fixes us, not only in its violence, hostility and aggression, but in the ambivalence of its desire.

Spaces of agency exist for Black people, wherein we can both interrogate the gaze of the Other but also look back, and at one another, naming what we see. The "gaze" has been and is a site of resistance for colonized Black people globally. Subordinates in relations of power learn experientially that there is a critical gaze, one that "looks" to document, one that is oppositional. In resistance struggle, the power of the dominated to assert agency by claiming and cultivating "awareness" politicizes looking relations—one learns to look a certain way in order to resist.

When most Black people in the United States first had the opportunity to look at film and television, they did so fully aware that mass media as a system of knowledge and power was reproducing and maintaining White supremacy. To stare at the television, or mainstream movies, to engage its images, was to engage its negation of Black representation. It was the oppositional Black gaze that responded to these looking relations by developing independent Black cinema. Black viewers of mainstream cinema and television could chart the progress of political movements for racial equality via the construction of images, and did so. Within the Southern, Black, working-class home of my growing up, in a racially segregated neighborhood, watching television was one way to develop critical spectatorship. Unless you went to work in the White world, across the tracks, you learned to look at White people by staring at them on the screen. Black looks, as they were constituted in the context of social movements for racial uplift, were interrogating gazes. We laughed at television shows like *Our Gang* and *Amos n' Andy*, at these White representations of Blackness, but we also looked at them critically. Before racial integration, Black viewers of movies and television experienced visual pleasure in a context where looking was also about contestation and confrontation. Writing about Black looking relations in "Black British Cinema: Spectatorship and Identity Formation in Territories," Manthia Diawara identifies the power of the spectator: "Every narration places the spectator in a position of agency; and race, class and sexual relations influence the way in which this subjecthood is filled by the spectator." Of particular concern for him are moments of "rupture" when the spectator resists "complete identifications with the film's discourse." These ruptures define the relation between Black spectators and dominant cinema prior to racial integration. Then, one's enjoyment of a film wherein representations of Blackness were stereotypically degrading and dehumanizing coexisted with a critical practice that restored presence where it was negated. Critical discussion of the film while it was in progress or at its conclusion maintained the distance between spectator and the image. Black films were also subject to critical interrogation. Since they came into being in part as a response to the failure of White-dominated cinema to represent Blackness in a manner that did not reinforce White supremacy, they too were critiques to see if images were seen as complicit with dominant cinematic practices.

Critical, interrogating, Black looks were mainly concerned with issues of race and racism, the way racial domination of Blacks by Whites overdetermined representation; they were rarely concerned with gender. As spectators, Black men could repudiate the reproduction of racism in cinema and television, the negation of Black presence, even as they could feel as though they were rebelling against White supremacy by daring to look, by engaging phallocentric politics of spectatorship. Given the real-life public circumstances wherein Black men were murdered/lynched for looking at White womanhood, where the Black male gaze was always subject to control and/or punishment by the powerful White other, the private realm of television screens or dark theaters could unleash the repressed gaze. There they could "look" at White womanhood without a structure of domination overseeing the gaze, interpreting, punishing. That White-supremacist structure that had murdered Emmett Till after interpreting his look as violation, as "rape" of White womanhood, could not control Black male responses to screen images. In their role as spectators, Black men could enter an imaginative space of phallocentric power that mediated racial negation. This gendered relation to looking made the experience of the Black male spectator radically different from that of the Black female spectator. Major, early, Black, male, independent filmmakers represented Black women in their films as objects of male gaze. Whether looking through the camera or as spectators watching films, mainstream cinema or "race" movies, the Black male gaze had a different scope from that of the Black female.

Black women have written little about Black female spectatorship, about our moviegoing practices. A growing body of film theory and criticism by Black women has only begun to emerge. The prolonged silence of Black women as spectators and critics was a response to absence, to cinematic negation. Writing on "The Technology of Gender," Teresa de Lauretis, drawing on the work of Monique Wittig, calls attention to "the power of discourses to 'do violence' to people, a violence which is material and physical, although produced by abstract and scientific discourses as well as the discourses of the mass media." With the possible exception of early race movies, Black female spectators have had to develop looking relations within a cinematic context that constructs our presence as absence, that must deny the "body" of the Black female so as to perpetuate White supremacy, and with it a phallocentric spectatorship where the woman to be looked at, and desired, is "white." (Recent movies do not conform to this paradigm, but I am turning to the past with the intent of charting the development of Black female spectatorship.) Talking with Black women of all ages and classes, in different areas of the United States, about their filmic looking relations, I heard, again and again, ambivalent responses to cinema. Only a few of the Black women I talked with remembered the pleasure of race movies, and even those who did, felt that pleasure interrupted and usurped by Hollywood. Most of the Black women I talked with were adamant that they never went to movies expecting to see compelling representations of Black femaleness. They were all acutely aware of cinematic racism—its violent erasure of Black womanhood. In Anne Friedberg's essay "A Denial of Difference: Theories of Cinematic Identification" she stresses that "identification can only be made through recognition, and all recognition is itself an implicit confirmation of the ideology of the status quo." Even when representations of Black women were present in film, our bodies and being were there to serve—to enhance and maintain White womanhood as object of the phallocentric gaze. Commenting on Hollywood's characterization of Black women in *Girls on Film,* Julie Burchell desribes this absent presence:

Black women have been mothers without children (Mammies—who can ever forget the sickening spectacle of Hattie MacDaniels waiting on the simpering Vivien Leigh hand and foot and enquiring like a ninny, "What's ma lamb gonna wear?" as strategic interlude? and sex-dreams without sex—Lena Horne, the first black performer signed to a long term contract with a major company (MGM), looked gutless but was actually quite spirited. She seethed when Tallulah Bankhead complimented her on the paleness of her skin and the non-Negroidness of her features.

When Black women actresses like Lena Horne appeared in mainstream cinema most White viewers were not aware that they were looking at a Black female unless the film was specifically coded as being about Blacks. Burchell is one of the few White women film critics who had dared to examine the intersection of race and gender in relation to the construction of the category "woman" in film as object of the phallocenteric gaze. With characteristic wit she asserts: "What does it say about racial purity that the best blondes have all been brunettes (Harlow, Monroe, Bardot)? I think it says that we are not as White as we think." Burchell could easily have said "we are not as White as we want to be," for clearly the obsession to have White women film stars be ultra-White was a cinematic practice that sought to maintain a distance, a separation between that image and the Black female Other; it was a way to perpetuate White supremacy. Politics of race and gender were inscribed into mainstream cinematic narrative from *The Birth of A Nation* on. As a seminal work, this film identified what the place and function of White womanhood would be in cinema. There was clearly no place for Black women.

Remembering my past in relation to screen images of Black woman-hood, I wrote a short essay, "Do you remember Sapphire" which explored both the negation of Black female representation in cinema and television, and our rejection of these images. Identifying the character of "Sapphire" from *Amos n' Andy* as that screen representation of Black femaleness I first saw in childhood, I wrote:

She was even then backdrop, foil. She was bitch—nag. She was there to soften images of black men, to make them seem vulnerable, easygoing, funny, not threatening to a white audience. She was there as man in drag, as castrating bitch, as someone to be lied to, someone to be tricked, someone the white and black audience could hate. Scapegoated on all sides. She was not us. We laughed with the black men, with the white people. We laughed at this black woman who was not us. And we did not even long to be there on the screen. How could we long to be there when our image, visually constructed, was so ugly. We did not long to be there. We did not long for her. We did not want our construction to be this hated black female thing—foil, backdrop. Her black female image was not the body of desire. There was nothing to see. She was not us.

Grown Black women had a different response to Sapphire; they identified with her frustrations and her woes. They resented the way she was mocked. They resented the way these screen images could assault Black womanhood, could name us bitches, nags. And in opposition they claimed Sapphire as their own, as the symbol of that angry part of themselves White folks and Black men could not even begin to understand.

Conventional representations of Black women have done violence to the image. Responding to this assault, many Black women spectators shut out the image, looked the other way, accorded cinema no importance in their lives. Of course there were those spectators whose gaze was one of desire and complicity. Assuming a posture of subordination, they submitted to cinema's capacity to seduce and betray. They were cinematically "gaslighted." Every Black woman I spoke with who was/is an ardent moviegoer, a lover of the Hollywood film, testified that to fully experience the pleasure of mainstream cinema they had to close down critique, analysis; they had to forget racism. And mostly they did not think about sexism. What was the nature then of this adoring Black female gaze—this look that could bring pleasure in the midst of negation? In her first novel, *The Bluest Eye,* Toni Morrison constructs a portrait of the Black female spectator; her gaze is the masochistic look of victimization. Describing her looking relations, Miss Pauline Breedlove, a poor working woman, maid in the house of a prosperous White family, asserts:

> The onliest time I be happy seem like was when I was in the picture show. Everytime I got, I went, I'd go early, before the show started. They's cut off the lights, and everything be black. Then the screen would light up, and I's move right on in them picture. White men taking such good care of they women, and they all dressed up in big clean houses with the bath tubs right in the same room with the toilet. Them pictures gave me a lot of pleasure.

To experience pleasure, Miss Pauline, sitting in the dark, must imagine herself transformed, turned into the White woman portrayed on the screen. After watching movies, feeling the pleasure, she says "but it made coming home hard."

We come home to ourselves. Not all Black women spectators submitted to that spectacle of regression through identification called for by Hollywood. Most of the women I talked with felt they consciously resisted identification with films—that this tension made moviegoing less than pleasurable, at times it caused pain. As one Black woman put it, "I could always get pleasure from movies as long as I did not look too deep." For Black female spectators who have "looked too deep" the encounter with the screen has hurt. That some of us chose to stop looking was a gesture of resistance; turning away was one way to protest, to reject negation. My pleasure in the screen ended abruptly when I and my sisters first watched *Imitation of Life*. Writing about this experience in the "Sapphire" piece, I addressed the movie directly, confessing:

> I had until now forgotten you, that screen image seen in adolescence, those images that made me stop looking. It was there in *Imitation of Life* first that comfortable mammy image. There was something familiar about this hard working black woman who loved her daughter so much, loved her in a way that hurt.

Indeed, as young, Southern, Black girls watching this film, Peola's mother reminded us of the hardworking, churchgoing, Big Mamas we knew and loved. Consequently, it was not this image that captured our gaze; we were fascinated by Peola. Addressing her, I wrote:

> You were different. There was something scary in this image of young sexual sensual black beauty betrayed—that daughter who did not want to be confined by blackness, that "tragic mulatto" who did not want to be negated. Just let me escape this image forever she could have said. I will always remember that image. I remembered how we cried for her, for our unrealized desiring selves. She was tragic because there was no place in the cinema for her, no loving pictures. She too was absent image. It was better then, that we were absent, for when we were there it was humiliating, strange, sad. We cried all night for you, for the cinema that had no place for you. And like you, we stopped thinking it would one day be different.

When I returned to films as a young woman, after a long period of silence, I felt armed with an oppositional gaze. Not only would I not be hurt by the absence of Black female presence, or the insertion of violating representation, I interrogated work and cultivated a way to look past race and gender for aspects of content, form, language. Foreign films and US independent cinema were the primary locations of my filmic looking relations, even though I also watched Hollywood films.

From "jump," Black female spectators have gone to films with awareness of the way in which race and racism determined the visual construction of gender. Whether it was *The Birth of A Nation* or Shirley Temple shows, we knew that White womanhood was the racialized sexual difference occupying the place of stardom in mainstream narrative film. We assumed

White women knew it too. Reading Laura Mulvey's provocative essay, "Visual Pleasure and Narrative Cinema" from a standpoint that acknowledges race, one sees clearly why Black women spectators not duped by mainstream cinema would develop an oppositional gaze. Placing ourselves outside that pleasure in looking Mulvey argues was determined by a "split between active/male and passive/female," Black female spectators actively chose not to identify with the film's iminaginary subject, because such identification was disenabling. Looking at films with an oppositional gaze, Black women were able to critically assess the cinema's construction of White womanhood as object of phallocentric gaze, and choose not to identify with either the victim or the perpetrator. Black female spectators who refused to identify with White womanhood, who would not take on the phallocentric gaze of desire and possession, created a critical space where the binary opposition Mulvey posits of "woman as image, man as bearer of the look" was continually deconstructed. As critical spectators Black women looked from a location that disrupted, one akin to that described by Annette Kuhn in *The Power of The Image*:

> . . . the acts of analysis, of deconstruction and of reading "against the grain" offer an additional pleasure—the pleasure of resistance, of saying "no": not to "unsophisticated" enjoyment, by ourselves and others, of culturally dominant images, but to the structures of power which ask us to consume them uncritically and in highly circumscribed ways.

Mainstream feminist film criticism in no way acknowledges Black female spectatorship. It does not even consider the possibility that women can construct an oppositional gaze via an understanding and awareness of the politics of race and racism. Feminist film theory rooted in an ahistorical psychoanalytic framework that privileges sexual difference actively suppresses recognition of race, reenacting and mirroring the erasure of Black womanhood that occurs in films, silencing any discussion of racial difference—of racialized sexual difference. Despite feminist critical interventions aimed at deconstructing the category "woman" which highlight the significance of race, many feminist film critics continue to structure their discourse as though it speaks about "women" which highlight the significance of race, many feminist film critics continue to structure their discourse as though it speaks about "women" when in actuality it speaks only about White women. It seems ironic that the cover of the recent anthology *Feminism and Film Theory* edited by Constance Penley has a graphic reproducing a photo of White women actresses Rosalind Russell and Dorothy Arzner on the 1936 set of the film *Craig's Wife,* yet there is no acknowledgement in any essay in this collection that the woman "subject" under discussion is always White. Even though there are photos of Black women from films reproduced in the text, there is no acknowledgement of racial difference. It would be too simplistic to interpret this failure of insight solely as a gesture of racism. Importantly, it speaks to the problem of structuring feminist film theory around a totalizing narrative of woman-as-object whose image functions solely to reaffirm and reinscribe patriarchy. Mary Ann Doane addresses this issue in the essay "Remembering Women: Psychical and Historical Construction in Film Theory":

> This attachment to the figure of a degeneralizable Woman as the product of the apparatus indicates why, for many, feminist film theory seems to have reached an impasse, a certain blockage in its theorization. . . . In focusing upon the task of delineating in great detail the attributes of woman as effect of the apparatus, feminist film theory participates in the abstraction of women. The concept "Woman" effaces the difference between women in specific socio-historical contexts, between women defined precisely as historical subjects rather than as a psychical subject (or non-subject).

Though Doane does not focus on race, her comments speak directly to the problem of its erasure. For it is only as one imagines "woman" in the abstract, when woman becomes fiction or fantasy, can race not be seen as significant. Are we to really imagine that feminist theorists writing only about images of White women, who subsume this specific historical subject under the totalizing category "woman," do not "see" the Whiteness of the image? It may very well be that they engage in a process of denial, that eliminates the necessity of revisioning conventional ways of thinking about psychoanalysis as a paradigm of analysis and the need to rethink a body of feminist film theory that is firmly rooted in a denial of the reality that sex/sexuality may not be the primary and/or exclusive signifier of difference. Doane's essay appears in a very recent anthology, *Psychoanalysis and Cinema,* edited by E. Ann Kaplan, where again none of the theory presented acknowledges or discusses racial difference with the exception of one essay, "Not Speaking with Language, Speaking with No Language," which problematizes notions of orientalism in its examination of Leslie Thornton's film, *Adynata.* Yet in most of the essays, the theories espoused are rendered problematic if one includes race as a category of analysis.

Constructing feminist film theory along these lines enables the production of a discursive practice that need never theorize any aspect of Black female representations or spectatorship. Yet the existence of Black women within White-supremacist culture problematizes, makes complex, the overall issue of female identity, representation, and spectatorship. If as, Friedberg suggests," . . . identification is a process which commands the subject to be displaced by an other; it is a procedure which refuses and recuperates the separation between self and other, and in this way replicates the very structure of patriarchy" and if it "demands sameness, necessitates similarity, disallows difference"—must we then surmise that many feminist film critics, who are "overidentified" with the mainstream cinematic apparatus, produce theories that replicate its totalizing agenda. Why is it that feminist film criticism, that has most claimed the terrain of woman's identity, representation, subjectivity as its field of analysis, remains aggressively silent on the subject of Blackness, and specifically on representations of Black womanhood. Just as mainstream cinema has historically forced aware Black female spectators not to look, much feminist film criticism disallows the possibility of a theoretical dialogue that might include Black women's voices. It is difficult to talk when you feel no one is listening, when you feel as though a special jargon or narrative has been created that only the chosen can understand. No wonder then that Black women have for the most part confined our critical commentary on film to conversations. And it must be reiterated that this gesture is a strategy that protects us from the violence perpetuated and advocated by discourses of mass media. Current focus on issues of race and representation in the field of film theory critically intervene on the historical repression reproduced in some arenas of contemporary critical practice, making a discursive space for discussion of Black female spectatorship possible.

When I asked a Black woman in her twenties, an obsessive moviegoer, why she thought we had not written about Black female spectatorship, she commented: "We are afraid to talk about ourselves as spectators because we have been so abused by 'the gaze'." An aspect of that abuse was the imposition of the assumption that Black female looking relations were not important enough to theorize. Film theory as a critical "turf" in the United States has been, and continues to be, influenced by and to reflect White racial domination. Since feminist film criticism was initially rooted in a Women's Liberation Movement informed by racist practices, it did not open up the discursive terrain, making it more inclusive. Recently, even those White film theorists who include an analysis of race show no interest in Black female spectatorship. In her introduction to the collection of essays, *Visual and Other Pleasures,* Laura Mulvey describes her initial romantic absorption in Hollywood cinema, stating,

> Although this great, previously unquestioned and unanalyzed love was put in crisis by the impact of feminism on my thought in the early 1970s, it also had an enormous influence on the development of my critical work and ideas and the debate within film culture with which I became preoccupied over the next fifteen years or so. Watched through eyes that were affected by the changing climate of consciousness, the movies lost their magic.

Watching movies from a feminist perspective, Mulvey arrived at that location of disaffectation that is the starting point for many Black women approaching cinema within the lived harsh reality of racism. Yet her account of being a part of a film culture whose roots rest on a founding relationship of adoration and love indicates how difficult it would have been to enter that world from "jump" as a critical spectator whose gaze had been formed in opposition.

Given the context of class exploitation, racist and sexist domination, it has only been through resistance struggle, reading, and looking "against the grain," that Black women have been able to value our process of looking enough to publicly name it. Centrally, those Black female spectators who attest to the oppositionality of their gaze deconstruct theories of female spectatorship that have relied heavily on the assumption, that, as, Doane suggests in her essay, "Woman's Stake: Filming the Female Body," "woman can only mimic man's relation to language, that is assume a position defined by the penis-phallus as the supreme arbitrer of lack." Identifying with neither the phallocentric gaze nor the construction of White womanhood as lack, critical Black female spectators construct a theory of looking relations where cinematic visual delight is the pleasure of interrogation. Every Black woman spectator I talked to, with rare exception, spoke of being "on guard" at the movies. Talking about the way being a critical spectator of Hollywood films influenced her, Black woman filmmaker Julie Dash exclaims, "I make films because I was such a spectator!" Looking at Hollywood cinema from a distance, from that critical politicized standpoint that did not want to be seduced by narratives reproducing her negation, Dash watched mainstream movies over and over again for the pleasuring of deconstructing them. And of course there is that added delight if one happens, in the process of interrogation, to come across a filmic narrative that invites the Black female spectator to engage the text with no threat of violation.

Significantly, I began to write film criticism in response to the first Spike Lee movie, *She's Gotta Have It,* contesting his replication of mainstream, patriarchal, cinematic practices that explicitly represent woman (in this instance Black woman) as the object of phallocentric gaze. Lee's investment in patriarchal filmic practices that mirror dominant patterns makes him the perfect Black candidate for entrance into the Hollywood canon. His work mimics the cinematic construction of White womanhood as object, replacing her body as text on which to write male desire with the Black female body. It is transference without transformation. Entering the discourse of film criticism from the politicized location of resistance, of not wanting, as a working-class Black woman I interviewed stated, "to see Black women in the position White women have occupied in film forever," I begin to think critically about Black female spectatorship.

For years I went to independent and/or foreign films where I was the only Black female present in the theater. I often imagined that in every theater in the United States there was another Black woman watching the same film wondering why she was the only visible Black female spectator. I remember trying to share with one of my five sisters the cinema I liked so much. She was "enraged" that I brought her to a theater where she would have to read subtitles. To her it was a violation of Hollywood notions of spectatorship, that had socialized her to believe one comes to movies solely to be entertained. When I interviewed her to ask what had changed her mind over the years, led her to embrace the cinema, she connected it to coming to critical consciousness, saying "I learned that there was more to looking than I had been exposed to in ordinary (Hollywood) movies." I shared that, though most of the films I loved were all-White, I could engage them because they did not have in their deep structure a subtext reproducing the narrative of White supremacy. Her response was to say that these films dymystified "Whiteness," since the lives they depicted seemed less rooted in fantasies of escape. They were, she suggested, more like "what we knew life to be, the deeper side of life as well." Always more seduced and enchanted with Hollywood cinema than me, she stressed that unaware Black female spectators must "break out," no longer be imprisoned by images that enact a drama of our negation. Though she still sees Hollywod films, because "they are a major influence in the culture," she no longer feels duped or victimized.

Talking with Black female spectators, looking at written discussions either in fiction or academic essays about Black women, I noted the connection made between the realm of representation in mass media and the capacity of Black women to construct ourselves as subjects in daily life. The extent to which Black women feel devalued, objectified, dehumanized in this society determines the scope and texture of their looking relations. Those Black women whose identities were constructed in resistance, by practices that oppose the dominant order, were most inclined to develop an oppositional gaze. Now that there is a growing interest in films produced by Black women and those films have become more accessible to viewers, it is possible to talk about Black female spectatorship in relation to that work. So far most discussions of Black spectatorship I have come across focus on men. In "Black Spectatorship: Problems of Identification and Resistance" Manthia Diawara suggests that "the components of 'difference' among elements of sex, gender, and sexuality give rise to different readings of the same material," adding that these conditions produce a "resisting" spectator. He focuses his critical discussion on Black masculinity. The recent publication of the anthology, *The Female Gaze: Women as Viewers of Popular Culture,* excited me, especially as it included an essay, "Black Looks," by Jacqui Roach and Petal Felix that attempts to address

Black female spectatorship. The essay posed provocative questions that were not answered: "Is there a black female gaze? How do black women relate to the gender politics of representation?" Concluding, the authors assert that Black females have "our own reality, our own history, our own gaze—one which she sees the world rather differently from 'anyone else.' " They do not name/describe this experience of seeing "rather differently". The absence of definition and explanation suggests they are assuming an essentialist stance, wherein it is presumed that Black women, as victims of race and gender oppression, have an inherently different field of vision. Many Black women do not "see differently" precisely because their perceptions of reality are so profoundly colonized, shaped by dominant ways of knowing. As Trinh T. Minh-ha points out in "Outside in Inside Out": "Subjectivity does not merely consist of talking about oneself. Be this talking indulgent or critical."

Critical Black female spectatorship emerges as a site of resistance only when individual Black women active resist the imposition of dominant ways of knowing and looking. While every Black woman I talked to was aware of racism, that awareness did not automatically correspond with politicization, the development of an oppositional gaze. When it did, individual Black women consciously named the process. Manthia Diawara's "resisting spectatorship" is a term that does not adequately describe the terrain of Black female spectatorship. We do more than resist. We create alternative texts, ones that are born not solely in reaction against. As critical spectators, Black women participate in a broad range of looking relations, contest, resist, revise, interrogate, and invent on multiple levels. Certainly when I watch the work of Black women filmmakers Camille Billops, Kathleen Collins, Julie Dash, Ayoka Chenzira, Zeinabu Davis, I do not need to "resist" the images, even as I still choose to watch their work with a critical eye.

Black female critical thinkers concerned with creating space for the construction of radical Black female subjectivity, and with the way cultural production informs this possibility, fully acknowledge the importance of mass madia, film in particular, as a powerful site for critical intervention. Certainly Julie Dash's film *Illusions* not only identifies the terrain of Hollywood cinema as a space of knowledge production that has enormous power, but also creates a filmic narrative wherein the Black female protagonist subversively claims that space. Inverting the "real-life" power structure, Dash offers the Black female spectator representations that challenge stereotypical notions placing us outside the realm of filmic discursive practices. Within the film she uses the strategy of Hollywood suspense films to undermine those cinematic practices that deny Black women a place in this structure. Problematizing the question of "racial" identity by depicting passing, suddenly it is the White male's capacity to gaze, define, and know that is called into question. When Mary Ann Doane describes, in "Woman's Stake: Filming the Female Body," the way in which feminist filmmaking practice can elaborate "a special syntax for a different articulation of the female body," she names a critical process that "undoes the structure of the classical narrative through an insistence upon its repressions." An eloquent description, this names precisely Dash's strategy in *Illusions,* even though the film is not unproblematic and works within certain conventions that are not successfully challenged. For example, there is no indication in the film that Mignon will make Hollywood films that subvert and transform the genre or will simply assimilate and perpetuate the norm. Still subversively, *Illusions* problematizes the issue of race and spectatorship. White people in the film are unable to "see" that race informs their looking relations. Though she is "passing" to gain access to the machinery of cultural production represented by film, Mignon continually asserts her ties to Black community. The bond between her and the young, Black, woman singer Esther Jeeter is affirmed by caring gestures of affirmation, often expressed by eye-to-eye contact, the direct unmediated gaze of recognition. Ironically, it is the desiring, objectifying, sexualized, White, male gaze that threatens to penetrate her "secrets" and disrupt her process. Metaphorically, Dash suggests the power of Black women to make films will be threatened and undermined by that White male gaze that seeks to reinscribe the Black female body in a narrative of voyeuristic pleasure, where the only relevant opposition is that of male/female, and the only location for the female that of victimization. These tensions are not resolved by the narrative. It is not evident that Mignon will triumph over the White-supremacist, capitalist, imperialist, dominating "gaze."

Throughout *Illusions,* Mignon's power is affirmed by her contact with the younger Black woman whom she nurtures and protects. It is this process of mirrored recognition that enables both Black women to define their reality, apart from the reality imposed upon them by structures of domination. The shared gaze of the two women reinforces their solidarity. As the younger subject, Esther represents a potential audience for films that Mignon might produce, films wherein Black females will be the narrative focus.

Another representation of Black females nurturing one another via recognition of their common struggle for subjectivity is depicted in Sankofa's collective work *A Passion of Remembrance.* Two Black women friends, possibly lovers, Louise and Maggie, are from the onset of the narrative struggling with the issue of subjectivity, of their place in progressive Black Liberation Movements that have been sexist. They challenge old norms, and want to replace them with new understandings of the complexity of Black identify, and the need for liberation struggles that address that complexity. Dressing to go to a party, Louise and Maggie claim the "gaze." Looking at one another, staring in mirrors, they appear completely focused on their encounter with Black femaleness. How they see themselves is most important, not how they will be stared at by others. Dancing to the tune "Let's Get Loose," they display their bodies not for a voyeuristic colonizing gaze but for that look of recognition that affirms their subjectivity—that constitutes them as spectators. Mutually empowered, they eagerly leave the privatized domain to confront the public. Disrupting conventional, racist and sexist, stereotypical representations of Black female bodies, these scenes invite the audience to look differently. They act to critically intervene and transform conventional filmic practices, changing notions of spectatorship.

Illusions and A Passion of Remembrance employ a deconstructive filmic practice to undermine existing grand cinematic narratives even as they retheorize subjectivity in the realm of the visual. Without providing "realistic" positive representations that emerge only as a response to the totalizing nature of existing narratives, they offer points of radical departure. Opening up a space for the assertion of a critical, Black, female spectatorship, they do not simply offer diverse representations, they imagine new transgressive possibilities for the formulation of identity. In this sense they make explicit a critical practice that provides us with different ways to think about Black female subjectivity and Black female spectatorship. Cinematically, they provide new points of recognition, embodying Stuart Hall's vision of a critical practice that acknowledges that identity is constituted "not outside but within representation," and invites us to see film "not as a second-order mirror held up to reflect what already exists, but as that form of representation which is able to constitute us as new kinds of subjects, and therby enable us to discover who we are." It is this critical practice that enables production of feminist film theory that theorizes Black female spectatorship. Looking and looking back, Black women involve ourselves in a process whereby we see our history as counter-memory, and use it as a way to know the present and invent the future.

Bibliography

compiled by Stephen M. Best

Akomfrah, John, and Pervaiz Khan, "Third Scenario: Theory and the Politics of Location," *Framework 36.*

Arbuthnot, Lucie, and Gail Senece, "Pre-Text and Text in *Gentlemen Prefer Blonds*," *Film Reader* 5 (Winter 1981), 13–23.

Armes, Roy, *Third World Film Making and the West* (Berkeley: University of California Press, 1987).

Asendio, James, "History of Negro Motion Pictures," *International Photographer* (January 1940).

Austin, J. L., *Sense and Sensibilia* (New York: Oxford University Press, 1962).

Austin, Regina, " 'The Black Community,' Its Law Breakers and a Politics of Identification," *Southern California Law Review,* May, 1992.

Barrett, Michele, *Women's Oppression Today* (London: Verso, 1980).

Brandy, Leo, Marshall Cohen, and Gerald Mast, eds., *Film Theory and Criticism,* 4th ed. (New York: Oxford University Press, 1992).

Benjamin, Jessica, "Master and Slave," *Powers of Desire: The Politics of Sexuality,* Ann Snitow, Christine Stansell, and Sharon Thompson, eds. (New York: Monthly Review Press, 1983), 280–299.

Bennett, Tony, et al., eds., *Popular Film and Television* (London: British Film Institute, 1981).

Bhabha, Homi, "The Other Question," *Screen* 24 (November-December 1983), 6, 18–36.

Birmingham, Stephen, *Certain People* (Boston and Toronto: Little, Brown, and Co., 1977).

Bobo, Jacqueline, "Sifting Through the Controversy: Reading *The Color Purple*," *Callaloo: A Journal of Afro-American and African Arts and Letters* 12 (Spring 1989), 2, 332–342.

———, "*The Color Purple*: Black Women as Cultural Readers," *Female Spectators Looking at Film and Television,* E. Deidre Pribram, ed. (London and New York: Verso, 1988), 90–109.

Bogle, Donald, *Toms, Coons, Mulattoes, Mammies and Bucks* (New York: Bantam, 1974).

Bone, Robert A., *The Negro Novel in America*, rev. ed. (New Haven: Yale University Press, 1965).

Boskin, Joseph, *Sambo: The Rise and Demise of an American Jester* (New York: Oxford University Press, 1986).

Brown, Nick, "Griffith's Family Discourse: Griffith and Freud," *Quarterly Review of Film Studies* 6 (Winter 1981), 79.

Buckley, Bruce, "Frankie and Her Man: A Study of the Interrelationships of Popular and Folk Traditions," Diss., Indiana University, 1961.

Campbell, Edward D.C., Jr., *The Celluloid South: Hollywood and the Southern Myth* (Knoxville, Tenn., 1981).

Carby, Hazel, *Reconstructing Womanhood: The Emergence of the Afro-American Woman Novelist* (New York: Oxford University Press, 1987).

———, "It Jus Be's Dat Way Sometime: The Sexual Politics of Women's Blues," *Radical America* 20 (1986), 4, 9–24.

Cham, Mbye, ed., *Ex-iles: Essays on Caribbean Cinema* (Trenton: Africa World Press, Inc., 1992).

Christian, Barbara, "From the Inside Out: Afro-American Women's Literary Tradition and the State," *Center for Humanistic Studies Occasional Papers,* Wlad Godzich, Nancy Kobrin, and Dayna Anderson, eds. (Minneapolis: University of Minnesota Press, 1987).

———, "Trajectories of Self-Definition: Placing Contemporary Afro-American Women's Fiction," *Conjuring: Black Women's Fiction and Literary Tradition,* Marjorie Pryse and Hortense J. Spillers, eds. (Bloomington, Indiana: Indiana University Press, 1985), 233–248.

———, *Black Women Novelists: The Development of a Tradition, 1892–1976* (Westport, CT: Greenwood Press, 1980).

Collins, Glenn, "Spielberg Films *The Color Purple,*" *The New York Times* (15 December 1985), sec. 2: 23+.

Cripps, Thomas, " 'Race Movies' as Voices of the Black Bourgeoisie: *The Scar of Shame,*" *American History/American Film,* John E. O'Connor and Martin A. Jackson, eds. (New York: Ungar, 1979).

———, *Black Film as Genre* (Bloomington: Indiana University Press, 1978).

———, *Slow Fade to Black* (New York: Oxford University Press, 1977).

———, "Black Films and Film Makers: Movies in the Ghetto, B.P. (Before Poitier)," *Negro Digest* (February 1969), 25.

Cruz, Robert, "Black Cinemas, Film Theory and Dependent Knowledge," *Screen* 26 (May–August 1985), 3–4.

Dandridge, Rita, "The Little Book (and Film) that Started the Big War," *Black Film Review* 2 (1986), 2.

Davis, Angela, *Women, Race and Class* (New York: Random House, 1983).

———, "The Black Woman's Role in the Community of Slaves," *The Black Scholar* (December 1971).

DeLauretis, Theresa, *Technologies of Gender: Essays on Theory, Film, and Fiction* (Bloomington: Indiana University Press, 1987).

Diawara, Manthia, *African Cinema: Politics and Culture* (Bloomington: Indiana University Press, 1992).

———, "The Nature of Mother in *Dreaming Rivers,*" *Third Text* 13 (1991), 73–84.

———, "Black British Cinema: Spectatorship and Identity Formation in *Territories,*" *Public Culture* 3 (1990), 1.

———, "Black Spectatorship: Problems of Identification and Resistance," *Screen* Vol. 29, No. 4 (Winter 1988).

Diawara, Manthia, and Phyllis Klotman, *"Ganja and Hess*: Vampires, Sex, and Addictions," *Jump Cut* (April 1990), 35.

Dill, Bonnie Thornton, "Race, Class, and Gender: Prospects for an All-Inclusive Sisterhood," *Feminist Studies* 9 (Spring 1983), 1.

Dubois, Ellen, and Linda Gordon, "Seeking Ecstasy on the Battlefield: Danger and Pleasure in Nineteenth Century Feminist Sexual Thought," *Feminist Review* 13 (Spring 1983).

DuBois, W. E. B., *The Souls of Black Folk,* in *Three Negro Classics* (New York: Avon, 1965), 206–389.

Dyer, Richard, *"Mahogany," Films for Women,* Charlotte Brunsdon, ed. (London: British Film Institute, 1986).

———, *Heavenly Bodies: Film Stars and Society* (New York: St. Martin's Press, 1986).

Ellis, Trey, "The Gay Subtext in *Beverly Hills Cop,*" *Black Film Review* 3 (Spring 1987), 15–17.

Ellison, Ralph, *Shadow and Act* (New York: Random House, 1964).

Ellsworth, Elizabeth, "Illicit Pleasures: Feminist Spectators and *Personal Best,*" *Wide Angle* 8 (1986), 2, 46–56.

Elsaesser, Thomas, "Tales of Sound and Fury: Observations on the Family Melodrama," *Movies and Methods,* Vol. II, Bill Nichols, ed. (Berkeley: University of California Press, 1985).

Erens, Patricia, ed., *Sexual Stratagems* (New York: Horizon, 1979).

Fanon, Frantz, *Black Skin, White Masks* (New York: Grove Press, 1967).

———, *The Wretched of the Earth* (New York: Grove Press, 1966).

Foucault, Michel, *The History of Sexuality* (New York: Vintage Books, 1980).

Fredrickson, George M., *The Black Image in the White Mind* (New York: Harper & Row, 1972).

Frith, Simon, *Sound Effects* (New York: Pantheon, 1981).

Frye, Marilyn, *The Poltiics of Reality* (Trumansburg, New York: The Crossing Press, 1984).

Gabler, Neal, *An Empire of Their Own: How the Jews Invented Hollywood* (New York: Crown Publishers, 1988).

Gabriel, Teshome, *Third Cinema in the Third World* (Ann Arbor: University of Michigan Research Press, 1982).

Gaines, Jane, *"The Scar of Shame*: Skin Color and Caste in Black Silent Melodrama," *Cinema Journal* 26 (Summer 1987), 4, 3–21.

Gates, Henry Louis, Jr., "Must Buppiehood Cost Homeboy His Soul?" *The New York Times* (March 1, 1922), H:11.

———, *"Race," Writing and Difference* (Chicago: University of Chicago Press, 1986).

————, *Black Literature and Literary Theory* (London: Methuen, 1984).

Geduld, Harry M., *The Birth of the Talkies: From Edison to Jolson* (Bloomington: Indiana University Press, 1975).

Gibson, Gloria, "Michelle Parkerson *is* the Eye of the Storm," *Black Film Review,* 4 (Winter 1987–88), 1, 12–16.

————, "The Cultural Significance of Music to Black Independent Filmmakers," Diss., Indiana University, 1986.

Gilroy, Paul, *There Ain't No Black In the Union Jack* (London: Hutchinson, 1987).

————, "Steppin out of Babylon—Race, Class, and Autonomy," *The Empire Strikes Back* Centre for Contemporary Cultural Studies (London: Hutchinson, 1982).

Green, J. Ronald, and Horace Neal Jr., "Oscar Micheaux and Racial Slur: A Response to 'The Rediscovery of Oscar Micheaux'," *Journal of Film and Video* 40 (Fall 1988), 4, 66–71.

Grossberg, Lawrence, Cary Nelson, and Paula Treichler, *Cultural Studies* (New York and London: Routledge, Chapman and Hall, Inc., 1992).

Grossberg, Lawrence, "History, Politics and Postmodernism: Stuart Hall and Cultural Studies," *Journal of Communication Inquiry* 10 (1986), 2, 61–75.

Hall, Jacquelyn Dowd, *The Revolt Against Chivalry* (New York: Columbia University Press, 1979).

Hall, Stuart, "Cultural Identity and Cinematic Representation," *Framework* 36 (1989), 68–81.

————, "Gramsci's Relevance for the Study of Race and Ethnicity," *Journal of Communication Inquiry* 10 (Summer 1986), 2.

————, ""On Postmodernism and Articulation: An Interview," *Journal of Communication Inquiry* 10 (Summer 1986), 2.

————, "Notes on Deconstructing 'The Popular'," *People's History and Socialist Theory,* Raphael Samuel, eds. (Boston: Routledge & Kegan Paul, 1981).

————, "The Whites of their Eyes: Racist Ideologies and the Media," *Silver Linings,* Bridges and Brunt, eds. (London: Lawrence & Wishart, 1981).

————, "Debate: Psychology, Ideology and the Human Subject," *Ideology and Consciousness* (October 1977).

Hall-Duncan, Nancy, *The History of Fashion Photography* (New York: Alpine Books, 1979).

Hofstadter, Richard, *America at 1750: A Social Portrait* (New York: Vintage Books, 1973).

hooks, bell [Gloria Watkins], *Feminist Theory: From Margin to Center* (Boston: South End Press, 1984).

————, *Black Looks: Race and Representation* (Boston: South End Press, 1992).

Hughes, James E., *Eugenic Sterilization in the United States: A Comparative Summary of Statutes and Review of Court Decisions,* Supplement No. 162 to the Public Health Reports (Washington, D.C.: U.S. Government Printing Office, 1940).

Jacobs, Harriet [Linda Brent], *Incidents in the Life of a Slave Girl, Written by Herself,* L. Maria Child, ed. (Boston: privately printed, 1861), introduction and ed. Jean Fagan Yellin (Cambridge: Harvard University Press, 1987).

Jaggar, Alison, *Feminist Politics and Human Nature* (Sussex: The Harvester Press, 1983).

Jameson, Fredric, "Pleasure: A Political Issue," *Formations of Pleasure* (Boston and London: Routledge & Kegan Paul, 1983).

Johnson, Albert, "Moods Indigo: A Long View," *Film Quarterly* 44 (Winter 1990–91), 2, 13–27.

———, "Moods Indigo: A Long View (Part II)," *Film Quarterly* 44 (Winter 1990–91), 3, 15–29.

Johnston, Claire, "Women's Cinema as Counter-Cinema," *Notes on Women's Cinema,* Claire Johnston, ed. (London: Society for Education in Film and Television, 1973).

Johnson, Randall and Robert Stam, eds., *Brazilian Cinema* (Cranbury, NJ: Farleigh Dickinson University Press, 1982).

Jones, Jacquie, "The Ghetto Aesthetic," *Wide Angle* 13 (1991) 3 & 4, 32–43.

Jones, LeRoi (Amiri Baraka), *Home: Social Essays* (New York: William Morrow & Co., 1966).

Joseph, Gloria, "The Incompatible Menage a Trois: Marxism, Feminism, and Racism," *Women and Revolution,* Lydia Sargent, ed. (Boston: South End Press, 1981).

Julien, Isaac, and Colin MacCabe, *Diary of a Young Soul Rebel* (London: British Film Institute, 1991).

Kellner, Douglas, and Michael Ryan, eds., *Camera Politica: The Politics and Ideology of Contemporary Hollywood Film* (Bloomington: Indiana University Press, 1988).

Klotman, Phyllis, *Frame by Frame: A Black Filmography* (Bloomington: Indiana University Press, 1979).

Kolodny, Annette, "Respectability is Eroding the Revolutionary Potential of Feminist Criticism," *The Chronicle of Higher Education* (4 May, 1988), A52.

Larkin, Alile Sharon, "Black Women Film-making Defining Ourselves: Feminism in Our Own Voice," *Female Spectators: Looking at Film and Television,* Deidre Pribram, ed. (New York: Verso, 1988), 157–173.

Leab, Daniel, *From Sambo to Superspade: The Black Experience in Motion Pictures* (Boston: Houghton Mifflin, 1975).

Lee, Spike and David Lee, eds., *Five for Five: The Films of Spike Lee* (New York: Stewart, Tabori & Chang, 1991).

Lessinger, Hanna, and Amy Swerdlow, eds., *Class, Race, and Sex: The Dynamics of Control* (Boston: G.K. Hall, 1983).

Lorde, Audre, *Sister Outsider* (Trumansburg, New York: The Crossing Press, 1984).

———, "The Master's Tolls Will Never Dismantle the Master's House," *This Bridge Called My Back: Writings by Radical Women of Color,* Cherrie Moraga and Gloria Anzaldua, eds. (New York: Kitchen Table/Women of Color Press, 1983), 98–101.

Lott, Tommy L., "A No-Theory Theory of Contemporary Black Cinema," *Black American Literature Forum,* 25 (1991), 2.

Lovell, Terry, *Pictures of Reality* (London: British Film Institute, 1980).

Mapp, Edward, *Blacks in American Films: Today and Yesterday* (City Metuchen: Scarecrow Press, 1972).

Marable, Manning, *How Capitalism Underdeveloped Black America* (Boston: South End Press, 1983).

Mayne, Judith, "Feminist Film Theory and Criticism," *Signs* 11 (Autumn 1985), 1.

Mcdowell, Deborah E., " 'The Changing Same': Generational Connections and Black Women Novelists," *New Literary History* 18 (1987), 2.

Memmi, Albert, *The Colonizer and the Colonized* (New York: Orion Press, 1965).

Mercer, Kobena, "Recoding Narratives of Race and Nation," *The Independent* 12 (January–February 1989), 1, 19–26.

Miller, Mark Crispin, *Boxed In: The Culture of Television* (Evanston, IL: Northwestern University Press, 1988).

Morley, David, "Texts, Readers, Subjects," *Culture, Media, Language,* Stuart Hall, et al., eds. (London: Hutchinson, 1980), 163–173.

Morrison, Toni, *The Bluest Eye* (New York: Holt, Rinehart and Winston, Inc. 1970).

Mulvey, Laura, "Visual Pleasure and Narrative Cinema," *Screen* 16 (Autumn 1985), 3.

Murray, James P., *To Find an Image: Blacks in Films from Uncle Tom to Superfly* (Indianapolis: Bobbs Merrow, 1973).

Nesteby, James, *Black Images in American Films, 1896–1954: The Interplay Between Civil Rights and Film Culture* (New York: Lanham, 1982).

Nichols, Bill, ed., *Movies and Methods* (Berkeley and Los Angeles: University of California Press, 1976).

———, *Movies and Methods II* (Berkeley and Los Angeles: University of California Press, 1985).

Nicholson, David, "A Commitment to Writing: A Conversation with Kathleen Collins Prettyman." *Black Film Review* 5 (Winter 1988–89), 1, 6–15.

Noble, Peter, *The Negro in Films* (London: Skelton Robinson, 1948).

Nell, Gary, *Black Hollywood* (Secaucus: Citadel Press, 1975).

Omolade, Barbara, "Hearts of Darkness," *Powers of Desire: The Politics of Sexuality,* Ann Snitow, Christine Stansell, and Sharon Thompson, eds. (New York: Monthly Review Press, 1983).

Perkins, Kathy A., ed., *Black Female Playwrights: An Anthology of Plays Before 1950* (Bloomington, Indiana: Indiana University Press, 1989).

Perkins, T.E., "Rethinking Stereotypes," *Ideology and Cultural Production,* Michelle Barrett, et al., eds. (London: Croom Helm, 1979).

Pines, Jim, *Blacks in Film: A Study of Racial Themes and Images in the American Film* (London: Cassell & Collier Macmillan, 1975).

Pines, Jim, and Paul Willemen, *Questions of Third Cinema* (London: British Film Institute, 1989).

Pryse, Marjorie, "Introduction," *Conjuring: Black Women Fiction and Literary Tradition,* Marjoie Pryse and Hortense J. Spillers, eds., (Bloomington, Indiana: Indiana University Press, 1985), 1–24.

Purdy, Jim, and Peter Roffman, *The Hollywood Social Problem Film: Madness, Despair, and Politics from the Depression to the Fifties* (Bloomington, Indiana: Indiana University Press, 1981).

Richolson, Janice Mosier, "He's Gotta Have It: An Interview with Spike Lee," *Cineaste* 28 (1992), 4.

Rogin, Michael, "Blankface, White Noise: The Jewish Jazz Singer Finds His Voice," *Critical Inquiry* 18 (Spring 1992), 417–453.

————, *"Ronald Reagan," the Movie and Other Episodes in Political Demonology* (Berkeley: University of California Press, 1987).

————, "The Great Mother Domesticated: Sexual Difference and Sexual Indifference in D. W. Griffith's *Intolerance*," *Critical Inquiry* 15 (Spring 1989).

Rose, Peter, *Mainstream and Margins: Jews, Blacks and Other Americans* (New Brunswick, N.J.: Rutgers University Press, 1983).

Rose, Vattel. "Afro-American Literature as a Cultural Resource for a Black Cinematic Aesthetic," *Black Cinema Aesthetics: Issues in Independent Black Filmmaking*, Gladstone L. Yearwood, ed. (Athens, Ohio: Center for Afro-American Studies, 1982), 27–40.

Ross, Andrew, *No Respect: Intellectuals & Popular Culture* (New York and London: Routledge, Chapman and Hall, Inc., 1989).

Rowbotham, Sheila, "The Trouble with Patriarchy," *People's History and Socialist Theory*, Raphael Samuel, ed. (London and Boston: Routledge & Kegan Paul, 1981).

Rubin, Gayle, "Thinking Sex: Notes for a Radical Theory of the Politics of Sexuality," *Pleasure and Danger*, Carol Vance, ed. (Boston and London: Routledge & Kegan Paul, 1984), 267–319.

Russo, Vito, *The Celluloid Closet: Homosexuality in the Movies* (New York: Harper & Row, 1981).

Sampson, Harry T., *Blacks in Black and White: A Source Book on Black Films* (Metuchen, NJ: Scarecrow Press, 1977).

Seiter, Ellen, et al., eds., *Remote Control: Television, Audiences and Cultural Power* (New York: Routledge, 1989).

Seiter, Ellen, "The Promise of Melodrama: Recent Women's Films and Soap Opera," Diss., Northwestern University, 1981.

Silver, Fred, ed., *Focus on "The Birth of a Nation"* (Englewood, NJ: Prentice-Hall, 1971).

Simpson, Rennie, "The Afro-American Female: The Historical Context of the Construction of Sexual Identity," *Powers of Desire: The Politics of Sexuality*, Ann Snitow, Christine Stansell, and Sharon Thompson, eds. (New York: Monthly Review Press, 1983).

Smith, Barbara, "Towards a Black Feminist Criticism," *The New Feminist Criticism*, Elaine Showalter, ed. (New York: Pantheon, 1985), 4–18.

————, ed., *Home Girls* (New York: Kitchen Table Press, 1983).

Smith, Valerie, *Self-Discovery and Authority in Afro-American Narrative* (Cambridge: Harvard University Press, 1987).

Spillers, Hortense J., "Interstices: A Small Drama of Words," *Pleasure and Danger*, Carol Vance, ed. (Boston and London: Routledge & Kegan Paul, 1984), 73–100.

Straayer, Chris, *"Personal Best*: Lesbian/Feminist Audience," *Jump Cut* 29 (February 1984), 40–44.

Tate, Claudia, *Black Women Writers At Work* (New York: Continuum, 1988).

Taylor, Clyde, "The Birth of Black Cinema: Overview," *Black International Cinema Berlin: 1–5 February 1989* (West Berlin: Arsenal Cinema, 1989), 115–117.

————, "The LA Rebellion: New Spirit in American Film" *Black Film Review* 2 (1986), 2.

————, "New U.S. Black Cinema," *Jump Cut* 28 (1983).

————, "One Struggle, Many Fronts," *Jump Cut* 23 (1980).

Toll, Robert C., *Blacking Up: The Minstrel Show in Nineteenth Century America* (New York, 1974).

Vertreace, Martha, "Toni Cade Bambara: The Dance of Character and Community," Mickey Pearlman, ed., *American Women Writing Fiction: Memory, Identity, Family, and Space* (Lexington, Kentucky: The University of Kentucky Press, 1989), 154–171.

Walker, Alice, "Oppressed Hair Puts a Ceiling on the Brain," *Ms. Magazine* 16 (June 1988), 12, 51–53.

Wallis, Brian, ed., *Art After Modernism: Rethinking Representation* (New York: The New Museum of Contemporary Art, 1984).

Washington, Mary Helen, *Invented Lives: Narratives of Black Women, 1860–1960* (New York: Doubleday, 1987).

West, Cornel, "Nihilism in Black America," *Dissent* (Spring 1991).

Winston, Michael R., "Racial Consciousness and the Evolution of Mass Communications in the United States," *Daedalus: Journal of the Academy of Arts and Sciences* 3 (Fall 1982), 4, 171–182.

Wittig, Monique, "The Straight Mind," *Feminist Issues* (Summer 1980), 107–111.

Yearwood, Gladstone L., *Black Cinema Aesthetics: Issues in Independent Black Filmmaking* (Athens: Ohio University Center for Afro-American Studies, 1982).

Zito, Stephen, "The Black Film Experience," *American Film Heritage: Impressions from the American Film Institute Archives* Tom Shales and Kevin Brownlow, eds. (Washington, D.C.: Acropolis Books, 1972).

Special Issues on Black Film

"Special Issue on Black Cinema," *The Black Scholar* 21 (March–April–May 1990), 2, 12–19.

Andrade-Watkins, Claire, Mbye B. Cham, eds., "Critical Perspectives on Black Independent Cinema," *Blackframes* (Cambridge: The MIT Press, 1988).

Bailey, David, ed., "Black Experiences," *Ten 8* (Summer 1986), 22.

Bassan, Raphael, et al., "Le cinéma noir américain," *CinemAction* (1977).

Billops, Camille, Ada Griffin, and Valerie Smith, eds., "Special Issue on Black Film" *Black American Literature Forum* 25 (Summer 1991), 2.

Diawara, Manthia, ed., "Black Cinema," *Wide Angle* 13 (July–October 1991), 3 & 4.

Julien, Isaac, and Kobena Mercer, eds., "The Last 'Special' Issue on Race?" *Screen* 29 (1988), 4.

Mercer, Kobena, ed., "Black Film/British Cinema," *ICA Documents 7*.

Contributors

MANTHIA DIAWARA teaches film and comparative literature at New York University. He is the author of *African Cinema: Politics and Culture.*

J. RONALD GREEN teaches film at Ohio State University. He is currently writing a book on Oscar Micheaux.

JANE GAINES teaches film and cultural studies at Duke University. She is the author of *Contested Culture: The Image, the Voice, and Law.*

THOMAS CRIPPS teaches film and history at Morgan State University. He is the author of *Black Film Genre.*

PHYLLIS KLOTMAN teaches film and literature at Indiana University. She is the author of *Frame by Frame: A Black Filmography.*

RICHARD DYER teaches film and cultural studies at the University of Warwick. He is the author of *Heavenly Bodies.*

NTONGELA MASILELA teaches English at Pitzer College. He is writing a book on Black dance theory.

TONI CADE BAMBARA is a writer and filmmaker. She is the author of *The Salt Eaters.*

AMIRI BARAKA teaches at SUNY Stony Brook. He is a poet, essayist, and playwright, author of *Dutchman.*

HOUSTON BAKER, JR. teaches English at the University of Pennsylvania. He is the author of *Modernism and the Harlem Renaissance.*

CLYDE TAYLOR teaches film and cultural studies at Tufts University. His book, *Breaking the Aesthetic Contract* is forthcoming.

HENRY LOUIS GATES, JR. teaches English at Harvard University. He is the author of *Figures in Black.*

DAN STREIBLE is a doctoral candidate in film at the University of Texas, Austin.

ED GUERRERO teaches film and literature at the University of Delaware. He is now writing a book on African-American cinema.

JACQUIE JONES is a cultural critic and editor of *The Black Film Review*.

MICHÈLE WALLACE teaches cultural studies and feminism at City College of New York. She is the author of *Invisibility Blues*.

JACQUELINE BOBO teaches film at the University of North Carolina at Chapel Hill. She is writing a book on Black women and reception theory.

bell hooks teaches feminism and cultural studies at Oberlin College. She is the author of *Black Looks*.

STEPHEN BEST is a doctoral candidate at the University of Pennsylvania.

Index

Abolitionist fiction, 57
Activism, Black women's, 285
Adynata, 296
Aesthetics, Black cinema, 8–25, 177–198
Africa, history of and cinema, 108–109,
    111, 114–115
Africanism, 19
After Winter: Sterling Brown (1985), 116
Agency, Black spectators, 289, 290
Alea, Tomas, Guitterez, 110
Alien Nation (1988), 240
All in the Family (television series), 132
Als, Hilton, 202
Altman, Rick, 58, 69n.34
America Becoming (1991), 113
American Hunger (Wright), 109
Ames, Jessie Daniel, 53
Amos n' Andy, 292–293
Anderson, Adisa, 121
Anderson, Jervis, 75
Andrews, J. Dudley, 76
Angel Heart (1987), 253
Ansah, Kwah, 128
Anti-Semitism, 151
Apocalypse Now, 14
Argentina, 111
Armstrong, Louis, 42
Ashes and Embers (1982), 116, 119, 131–
    132
Audience. *See* Spectators

Austin, J. L., 36
Austin, Texas, 221–232
The Autobiography of Malcolm H, 109
Avant-garde, 63

*Babylon is Falling: A Visual Ritual for
    Peace* (1983), 115
Baker, Houston, A., 113
Baldwin, James, 108, 200, 202, 203, 267
Bambara, Toni Cade, 9, 197
Baraka, Amiri, 113, 200, 203
Barbara O, 121, 122, 126–127, 140
Bell, Lonnie, 223, 232n.9
Beloved (Morrison), 126
Benjamin, Jessica, 252, 255
Benjamin, Walter, 179
Bentley, Eric, 58
Beverly Hills Cop I and II (1984, 1987),
    215, 241, 243, 244, 251
Billy Budd (Melville), 189, 190, 192–193
The Birth of a Nation (1915)
    Black musicality in White cinema, 98
    Black spectators and alternative read-
        ings, 212–214, 217–219
    Black womanhood in mainstream
        cimema, 292
    Cripps's critique of *The Symbol of the
        Unconquered,* 37
    as focal point for racial responses to
        Hollywood practices, 261

influence on race relations and govern-
ment policy, 258
interpretation of history in, 49
legacy of suppression of Black culture
and history in Hollywood cimena,
3, 74
protests as publicity for, 68n.9
racial and sexual stereotypes in, 260
Within Our Gates compared to, 50–51,
52, 60, 61
Birth of a Race, 261–262
Birthright, 72
Black Arts Movement, 108, 200
Black Audio Film/Video Collective, 16,
205
Black British Cinema, 200–207
The Blacker the Berry (Thurman), 88
Black Film Review, 4
Black Girl (1963), 111
Black history. *See also* History; Migra-
tion
analysis of *Within Our Gates,* 49–67
in *Daughters of the Dust,* 14–19
Spike Lee and American society, 146–
147
Blacula (1972), 138
Blaxploitation films
Black realism films and, 24–25
formula of, 118
White spectators and, 213
Bless Their Little Hearts (1984), 112
The Blood of Jesus (1941), 98
Blue, Carroll Parrot, 141
The Bluest Eye (Morrison), 285, 293
Bobo, Jacqueline, 263
Body and Soul (1924), 31, 38–39, 63, 75
Bogle, Donald
commentaries on Micheaux, 71, 72,
73–74, 75
contemporary biracial buddy films,
240
on Hurst's *Imitation of Life,* 88–89
racial and sexual stereotypes in main-
stream cinema, 260, 261
Bolivia, film and national culture, 110
Bone, Robert A., 29, 47n.16
Bourne, St. Clair, 128

Bowser, Pearl, 143
Boyz N the Hood, 19–23
Braudel, Ferdinand, 73
Brazil, Cinema Novo, 110
Breathless (1959), 5
Brenkman, John, 179
Brieux, Eugene, 83
Brown, Derek, 201
Brown, Georgia, 117n.9
Brown, Richard H., 178
Brown, William Wells, 59
The Brownsville Raid (Fuller), 193
Buddy movies, biracial formula, 238–
245, 251
Bullock, Wynn, 42
Burchell, Julie, 291–292
Burglar (1987), 238
Burnett, Charles
Black community-as-colony theorem,
120
financing of independent productions,
6
images of Black sexuality, 255–256
Los Angeles school of Black filmmak-
ers, 107, 111–114, 117n.9–11
Bush Mama (1974), 111–112, 113, 120

Cabin in the Sky (1942), 93, 98, 265–
266
Cabral, Amilcar, 108, 109
Caldwell, Ben, 115
Caldwell, Larry, 109
Camp de Thieroy, 128
Carbine, Mary, 77
Carby, Hazel, 65
Carmen Jones, 93
Carter, Benny, 43
Car Wash, 93–105
Castro, Fidel, 108
Catholic Church, 85, 92n.7
Ceddo, 124, 127, 128
Censorship, 51–52, 85
Chan is Missing (1981), 245
Chenzira, Ayoka, 141
Chesnutt, Charles, 40
Child of Resistance (1972), 116, 120
Christian, Barbara, 274

Cinematography
in *Daughters of the Dust,* 133–134, 135, 136
in *Looking for Langston,* 203–204
Micheaux's style and production values, 42–43
Civil rights, 74, 186–187. *See also* Racism
Clark, Ben, 109
Clark, Larry, 116, 138, 219
Class, 65, 77, 146–153. *See also* Middle class; Working class
Classicism, film, 34, 35
Cleaver, Eldridge, 203
Clotel: Or, the President's Daughter (Brown), 59
Coincidence, in melodrama, 58–59
College, Black tradition, 167–168
Collins, Kathleen, 139
Colonialism, 112, 114, 174
The Color Purple (film–1985)
Black women as audience, 272–273, 284–286
formal structures of film and novel, 278–284
presentation of historical setting, 130
spectatorial resistance to racial stereotypes in, 212, 214, 217–219
Colors (1988), 249
Coming to America (1987), 241
Communist Party, 65
The Conjure Woman (Chesnutt), 40
Conrack (1974), 136
Conroy, Pat, 135
Coppola, Francis Ford, 14
A Corner in Wheat (1909), 59
Crime and Punishment (Dostoevsky), 190
Cripps, Thomas, 26–39, 67n.8, 71, 261
Criticism. *See* Feminist criticism; Film criticism
Crocodile Tears, 128
Cross-cutting, 55–59, 69n.34
Crossroads, 128
Cry Freedom (1987), 239
Cuba, national cinema, 110

Culture, Black
authenticity and diaspora, 128
bourgeois cinema and, 63–67
in *Do The Right Thing,* 168–175
impact of mainstream cinema on, 248–249, 258
in *Joe's Bed-Stuy Barber Shop,* 154–161
Micheaux and cultural identity, 26–39
narrative and repetition in, 95
practice of representational politics, 177–198
in *School Daze,* 167–168
in *She's Gotta Have It,* 161–166
women writers and women's social and cultural history, 273, 278
Cycles, 128

Damaged Goods (Brieux), 83
Dandridge, Rita, 214
Dark Exodus, 134
Darnton, Robert, 73
Dash, Julie. *See also Daughters of the Dust*
and Black female spectator, 298, 300–301
documentary form mixed with fiction, 219
financing of independent productions, 6
mise-en-scene and agenda in short features, 120
Daughters of the Dust
development of Black independent cinema, 121–129
financing of, 6
portrayals of women in, 139–143
space and identity in, 13–19
spectator and empowerment, 132–139
themes of loss and recovery, 129–132
Davis, Zeinabu, 128, 141
Day, Cora Lee, 121
A Day at the Races (1937), 98
Debray, Regis, 111
Deconstruction, 259–260, 298, 302
Deep Cover, 24
The Defiant Ones (1958), 242
De Lauretis, Teresa, 291

DePriest, Oscar, 76
De Roy, Felix, 127
Desire, Black artistic/creative, 159, 163
The Devil Finds Work (Baldwin), 267
Diary of an African Nun, 124
Diaspora, African, 128
Diawara, Manthia, 206, 290, 299, 300
Dickens, Charles, 279, 281–284
Dickty, definition of, 47n.16
A Different Image (1982), 120
Diop, Cheikh Anta, 114
Directors, Black, 6, 31, 74–75, 287n.19
Directors Guild of America, 31, 74–75
Diva (1982), 137
Dixon, Melvin, 203
Dixon, Thomas, 37
Doane, Mary Ann, 296, 298, 301
Documentary, 219
Dostoevsky, Fyodor Mikhaylovich, 190
Do the Right Thing (1988)
  analysis of, 168–175
  devaluation of women in, 254
  jump-cuts, 5–6
  political thematization of music, 99
  politics of representation, 194
  portrayal of Black sexuality, 255
  race and class, 148–149
  repetition and narrative structure, 102
Driving Miss Daisy (1989), 245
A Dry White Season, 128
DuBois, W. E. B.
  Black intellectual and "double-con-
    sciousness," 66
  Ethiopian and African history, 114
  evolution of ideas, 73
  nationalism and socialism criticized by
    NAACP, 200
  race and American society, 145
  "twoness" of American racial codes,
    27–31
Duncan, Hugh Danziel, 179
Dunston, Geraldine, 121, 134
Dylan, Bob, 42

Eco, Umberto, 77
Economics. *See also* Financing
  in *Do The Right Thing,* 170, 173

in *Joe's Bed-Stuy Barber Shop,* 154–
  161
and lynching, 53–54
of motion picture and bourgeois cin-
  ema, 65
Eisenstein, Sergi, 61–62, 69n.34
Ellington, Duke, 35–36
Ellis, Trey, 251
Ellison, Ralph, 200
Elsaesser, Thomas, 279
Emma Mae (1976), 115
An Empire of Their Own (Gabler), 40
Empowerment, 132–139, 160. *See also*
  Power
English, Black and standard, 64
Enlightenment, 180–181
Espinosa, Julio Garcia, 111
Ethiopia, history of, 114
Ethnic Notions, 182
Eugenics, 82. *See also* Sterilization
Eva and Gabriella, 127
Evans, Erick Ray, 202
Evans, Walker, 43
The Exile (1931), 64

Family, Los Angeles school of filmmak-
  ing and images of Black, 111–114,
  120
Fanaka, Jamaa, 115, 117n.13
Fanon, Frantz, 108, 109, 111, 112, 219
Farm Security Administration, 43
Felix, Petal, 299–300
Feminism. *See also* Feminist criticism
  critique of *Do The Right Thing,* 175
  mainstream film criticism and Black
    female spectatorship, 295–298
  race and racism in mainstream, 265
  She's Gotta Have It as allegorical, 164
  Third World in *Bush Mama,* 113–114
Feminist criticism
  fetishization of female figure in classi-
    cal Hollywood film, 263
  gender and cultural practice in visual
    media, 258
  image of Black male in contemporary
    Hollywood films, 214–215

mainstream and Black female specta-
torship, 295–298
Feuer, Jane, 106n.2
Fiedler, Arthur Jafa, 133–134
Film criticism. *See also* Feminist criti-
cism
acclaim of *To Sleep with Anger,* 117n.9
Black female spectatorship, 291
reception of Micheaux's films, 32–39
reviews of Thurman's *High School
Girl,* 89–90
Film history, 3–13, 39. *See also The Birth
of a Nation*
Film noir, 262
Financing, independent film production,
6–7, 44, 285
Flaherty Seminar, 143
Flashbacks, 63
Flying, theme of, 22
Folktales, 131
Ford Foundation, 113
Forty-Eight Hours (1984), 215–216,
241–242, 244, 250, 252
Foucault, Michel, 288, 289
Four Women, 126
Foy, Brian, 80, 90
France, independent cinema, 5
Frank, Leo, 67n.8
Freeman, Monica J., 141
The French Connection (1971), 242
Friedberg, Anne, 291
Fuller, Charles, 185

Gabler, Neal, 40
Gabriel, Teshome, 107
Gaines, Jane, 8–9, 46–47n.12
Galbraith, John Kenneth, 77
Ganja and Hess (1973), 9–10, 11, 12–13,
138–139
Gardens of Stone (1987), 244–245
Gaze, Black female spectator and opposi-
tional, 288–302
Gender. *See also* Male, Black; Women,
Black
Black and White musicals compared,
105

and race in *Birth of a Nation* and *The
Color Purple,* 217–219
race and psychoanalysis in films of
1940s, 257–269
Gerima, Haile
cultural authenticity and African dias-
pora, 128
fundraising for independent produc-
tions, 6
healing power of folktales, 131–132
influence of *Sweet Sweetback's Baad-
assss Song,* 119
Los Angeles school of Black filmmak-
ers, 107, 108–109, 111–115, 116,
120
Getino, Octavio, 110–111
Gillespie, Dizzy, 133
Gilroy, Paul, 206
Giral, Sergio, 111
The Girl from Chicago (1932), 40–45
Givens, Dr. Everett H., 222, 223,
232n.11, 233n.25
Godard, Jean-Luc, 5, 116n.8
God's Stepchildren (1937), 65
Goldberg, Whoopi, 238
Golddiggers of 1933, 94
The Golden Child (1986), 241
Gone With the Wind (1939), 39, 264
Gramsci, Antonio, 66, 77
Gren, Ron, 8, 64–65, 71–78
The Green Pastures, 31–32
Griemas, A. J., 213
Griffith, D. W., 59, 61–62, 69n.34. *See
also The Birth of a Nation*
Grupenhoff, Richard, 71
Guerra, Ruy, 110
Gullah, language of, 127
Gunn, Bill, 9–10, 138–139
Gunning, Tom, 57
The Gunsaulus Mystery (1921), 38, 67n.8

Hall, Jacqueline Dowd, 53, 54
Hall, Stuart
Black spectatorship, 289, 302
concept of hegemony and ethnic studies, 66

hegemonic politics and cultural pro-
ductions, 279
identity and historical narrative, 201,
204
in *Looking for Langston,* 202
Hallelujah! (1929), 76, 98
Hansberry, Lorraine, 287n.19
Hansen, Miriam, 69n.34
Harlem is Heaven, 75
Harlem Nights (1989), 241
Harlem Renaissance, 42, 90–91, 113,
200–207
Harlem Theater (Austin, Texas), 224–
234
Harvest: 3,000 Years (1976), 114–115,
128, 140
Hegemony, concept of, 46–47n.12, 66,
70n.49
Hello Dolly!, 95
Heritage Africa, 128
Hicks, Tommy, 121
High School Girl (1935), 89–90
History. *See also* Black history; Film his-
tory
Black women writers and cultural
transformation, 273, 278
Ethiopian and Africa, 114
Looking for Langston as counterhis-
tory, 204
Los Angeles school of Black filmmak-
ers and, 108–109, 111–114
Hoberman, Jay, 63
Hofstadter, Richard, 253
Home of the Brave (1949), 267, 268
Homecoming (Thiongo), 109
The Homesteader (1918), 49
Homosexuality, 202–203, 251–252
Hoosier, Trula, 121, 134
Hopper, Dennis, 249
Horne, Lena, 265–266, 271n.29, 292
The Hour of the Furnaces (1968), 111,
219
House Party (1990), 97, 102, 104
Hudlin, Warrington, 240
Hughes, Langston
Black aesthetic and twoness dilemma,
28

Black urban representation, 169
Cripps's citations of, 46n.6
on Harlem Renaissance, 201
interest in film industry, 90–91
as "Representative Negro," 206
Hurston, Zora Neale, 91, 161–162, 274,
277

I and I: An African Allegory (1977), 115
Identification, Black spectators, 211–
219, 293–294
Identity, Black, 13–19, 26–39, 256
Ideology
construction of Black women in *The
Color Purple,* 273–278
domination and liberation in *Daugh-
ters of the Dust,* 125–126
ethnocentrism of liberal-modernism,
182–183
Looking for Langston and historical
narrative, 201, 204–205
Los Angeles school of filmmaking and,
109
Illusions (1982)
Black female subjectivity and Holly-
wood cinema, 300–301
deconstructive filmic practice in, 302
multicultural solidarity theme, 121,
134, 140–141
I'm Gonna Git You Sucka (1988), 245
Imitation of Life (1934), 88–89, 294
Incest, 60–61
Incidents in the Life of a Slave Girl
(Jacobs), 57, 273–274
Industrial revolution, American, 40
In the Heat of the Night (1967), 196–197,
241, 242
The Interne (Thurman), 81
Intertextuality, as facet of
interpretation, 186
Intolerance (1916), 69n.34
Invisibility, cultural phenomenon of, 259,
269n.8
Invisible Man, 9
Irony, politics of representation, 178–198

Jackson, Blyden, 102
Jacobs, Harriet A., 57, 273–274

Jailhouse Rock, 93
The Jazz Singer, 80
Jerome, V. J., 75
Joe's Bed-Stuy Barber Shop: We Cut Heads, 154–161, 173
Johnson, Robert, 113
Jones, George F., 225, 228, 233n.19
Jones, L. C., 223, 228
Jones, LeRoi, 108, 180. *See also* Baraka, Amiri
Jones, Philip Mallory, 128
Jubilee (Walker), 273–274
Juice, 24
Julien, Isaac, 202, 206
Jump-cuts, 5–6, 172
Jumpin' Jack Flash (1986), 238

Kanafani, Ghassan, 127
Kaplan, E. Ann, 296
Kellgren, Nina, 203–204
Killer of Sheep (1977), 112–114, 136, 255–256
Kincaid, Jamaica, 264
King, Martin Luther, 74, 200
King, Tony, 122
Kitt, Eartha, 200
Knowles, Jay, 227
Kuhn, Annette, 295

Lafayette Players, 83
Lane, Charles, 134
Lang, Fritz, 195–196
Language, Black and standard English, 127–128
Larkin, Alile Sharon, 120, 219
Last Supper (1977), 110
Latin America, national cinemas, 110–111
Lattimore, Lewis, 134
Leab, Daniel J., 71, 72–73, 73–74, 75
Lee, Russell, 43
Lee, Spike
   analysis of films, 154–175
   devaluation of women in films of, 254–255
   financing and commercial success, 6–7
   jump-cuts, 5–6

performers and audiences, 137
politics of representation, 194
race and American society, 145–153
replication of mainstream, patriarchal, cinematic practices, 298
Lethal Weapon (1987), 244–245, 252–253
Let There Be Light (1946), 267–268
Lewis, Jerry, 34
Lights of New York (1928), 80
Lincoln, Abbey, 142
Literature. *See also* Writers, Black
   abolitionist fiction, 57
   melodrama form and African-American fiction, 59–63
   repetition and narrative structure in African-American fiction, 102
Littin, Miguel, 110
The Lonely Villa (1909), 69n.34
Looking for Langston (1989), 200–207
Los Angeles Black filmmaking movement, 107–116, 117n.12, 118–129
Losing Ground (1982), 139
Lost Boundaries (1949), 266–267, 268
Lucchese, Frank and Sam, 228–230, 233n.35
Lucia (1968), 110
Lynching, 49–51, 52, 53–62, 122

MacCann, Richard Dyer, 76
McDaniels, Hattie, 264
McDowell, Deborah, 284–285
McQueen, Butterfly, 263, 264
Malcolm H., 74, 109, 188
Male, Black. *See also* Gender; Sexuality
   image of sexuality in mainstream cinema, 247–256
   in *She's Gotta Have It,* 163–166
   as spectator and image of Black male character, 214–219
   as spectators and phallocentrism, 290–291
Malloy, Jim, 233n.31, 234n.39
Mapplethorpe, Robert, 203
Marion, Horace, 227
Marshall, Paule, 130–131
Marxism, 62, 77, 109

Masilela, Ntongela, 109
Match cutting, 35
Media racial codes, 273
Meet Me in St. Louis, 94
Melodrama
  and African-American fiction, 59–63
  Micheaux's *Within Our Gates,* 55–59
  structure of *The Color Purple,* 279–284
Melville, Herman, 189, 190, 192–193
Memmi, Albert, 70n.49
Memories of Underdevelopment (1967), 110
Mercer, Kobena, 204, 206
Methodist Episcopal Ministers' Alliance, 49
Micheaux, Oscar
  aesthetics of black cinema, 8–9
  African-American writers in 1930s, 91
  analysis of *Within Our Gates,* 49–67
  cultural identity in films of, 26–39
  financing of films, 6
  hegemony and race, 46–47n.12
  Los Angeles school of Black filmmakers and, 108
  new theoretical tools and analysis of, 71–78
  production values and style of, 39–46
Micheaux Book and Film Company, 49
Middle class, 147, 197. *See also* Class
Migration, South-to-North
  in *Daughters of the Dust,* 13–19, 124–125
  Micheaux's portrayal of, 44–45
  in *To Sleep with Anger,* 113
Mildred Pierce, 262–263, 265
Minh-ha, Trinh T., 300
Minstrel shows, 183
Mise-en-scene, 11–13. *See also* Space
Mississippi Burning (1989), 239
Mo' Better Blues, 149–152, 254–255
Modernism, 11, 200–207
Mona Lisa, 254
Moore, Kaycee, 121
Morrison, Toni
  allusions to *Beloved* in *Daughters of the Dust,* 126

Black female spectator in *The Bluest Eye,* 285, 293
  culture and commerce in *Sula,* 158
  Ibo legend in *Tar Baby,* 130
  image of in *Looking for Langston,* 202
Mulvey, Laura
  on Black female spectatorship, 297–298
  Black male spectator and image of Black male in classical Hollywood film, 214–215
  cinematic objectification of female body, 238
  race and construction of gender in visual media, 258, 295
Murphy, Eddie
  biracial formula in buddy movies, 240, 241–244
  identification between Black male spectator and Black male character, 214–219
  images of Black male sexuality, 250, 251, 252
Muse, Clarence, 91
Music, Black. *See also* Musicals
  active use of in Black cinema, 98–99
  analogies between Black cinema and, 47n.22
  Micheaux and African-American culture, 35–36, 43, 64–65
  original-instruments movement, 48n.38
  sequences in *Do The Right Thing,* 172–173
Musicals, 93–105, 106n.2
The Music Man, 94
My Brother's Wedding (1983), 112

Narrative structure, 95–105, 123–124
Nationalism, Black, 9, 109
National Association for the Advancement of Colored People (NAACP), 50, 200, 261
Native Americans, 117n.11, 120, 134
Native Son (Wright), 22, 113, 170
Neal, Larry, 108
La Negra. See Within Our Gates

The Negro Novel in America (Bone), 29
Neoconservatism, 186–187, 196, 239
Nesteby, James, 26
New Wave, 5–6
9 1/2 Weeks, 250
Noble, Peter, 75
The Notorious Elinor Lee (1940), 36
Nugent, Bruce, 202
Nunu (in progress), 6, 128

O, Barbara, 121, 122, 126–127, 140
Oedipus myth, 213–214, 216
An Officer and a Gentleman (1982), 237–238
Oliver Twist (Dickens), 281–284
On the Town (1949), 94–95
Ottley, Roi, 32–33
Ouaga, 122
Our Nig (Wilson), 273–274

Palcy, Euzhan, 127, 128
Parkerson, Michelle, 141
Parks, Gordon, Sr., 118
Passing, subject of, 89, 266–267
Passing Through (1977), 116, 138, 219
A Passion of Remembrance (1986), 98–99, 133, 301–302
Patriarchy, 214, 298
Penitentiary (1979), 115
Penley, Constance, 295–296
Pereira dos Santos, Nelson, 110
Pinky (1949), 266
Platoon, 195
Politics
    Los Angeles school of Black filmmakers and ideology, 107–108
    music and Black culture, 99
    neoconservatism and race, 186–187, 196, 239
    practice of representational, 177–198
Popular culture, 248
Postmodernism, 11
Power. *See also* Empowerment
    domination and the oppositional gaze, 288–289, 290
    practice of representational politics, 177–198

Praise House (1991), 141–142
Praisesong For the Widow (Marshall), 130–131
Prettyman, Kathy Collins, 139
Production values, 39–46, 63–67
Pryor, Richard, 240–241
Psychoanalysis, 257–269
Puig, Manuel, 263
Purple Rain, 93

The Quiet One (1948), 267, 268
Quilt-making, 162

Race
    buddy movies and, 238–245
    feminist film criticism and Black female spectatorship, 295–298
    gender and psychoanalysis in films of 1940s, 257–269
    identification and resistance in Black spectatorship, 211–219
    Micheaux's treatment of issues, 39–46
    neoconservatism and, 186–187, 196, 239
    Spielberg's view of *The Color Purple,* 279
Racism
    Black female spectatorship and, 291, 294–295
    criticism and protest of works containing, 286
    in *Daughters of the Dust,* 17–18
    film and novel of *The Color Purple* compared, 281
    mainstream cinema in 1930s, 91
    Spike Lee's treatment of, 153
Ramey, Josephine, 230–231, 233n.34
Rape, 55–59, 59–61
Rap music, 97
Rapp, William Jourdan, 80–81
Reagan, Ronald, 186–187, 239
Realism, 23–25, 160, 219
Reconstruction, history of, 52–53, 273
Reid, Thomas, 92n.8
Religion, 16–19, 86, 132
Repetition, narrative structure and, 95–96, 101, 102, 104–105

Representation, 177–198, 200–207
Resistance, Black spectatorship, 211–219, 289, 298, 299, 300
Revolution in the Revolution, 111
Rhone, Trevor, 127
Riggs, Marlon, 256
Riots, race, 50
Rites of passage, 12, 20–23, 24–25
Ritual, lynching as, 54–55
Roach, Jacqui, 299–300
Robinson, Bill, 75
Robinson, Debbie, 141
Rocha, Glauber, 110, 111, 116n.8
Rocky II, 216
Rogers, Alva, 121–122
Roosevelt, Theodore, 73
Rudwick, Elliott, 72

St. Louis Blues, 95–96, 102
Sambo image, 257–258, 269n.4
Sampson, Harry T., 67n.8
Sanchez, Sonia, 203
Sandler, Kathe, 141
Sankofa, 133, 200, 205, 301–302
Sapphire (1959), 98
Sarris, Andrew, 76
The Scar of Shame (1928), 7
School Daze, 148, 167–168, 254
Schuyler, George S., 28, 46n.6
Scott, Hazel, 265
Segregation, 232
Seiter, Ellen, 284
Sembene, Ousmane, 111, 127, 128
Sexism, 120, 218–219
Sexuality
    Black male and homophobia, 203
    Black women's in *The Color Purple,* 274–277, 278
    image of Black in mainstream cinema, 247–256
    lynching and, 53–54
    portrayals of in *She's Gotta Have It,* 166
Shaft (1971), 118
Shange, Ntozake, 200
She's Gotta Have It (1985)
    analysis of, 161–166, 167, 175

bourgeois feminism, 147–148
jump-cuts, 6
mainstream, patriarchal, cinematic practices, 298
sexism in, 152, 254
Show Boat (1936), 89
"Show the Right Thing: A National Multicultural Conference on Film and Video Exhibition," 142–143
Shrader, Paul, 193–194
Sidewalk Stories, 134
Silverman, Kaja, 265
Silver Streak (1976), 241
Sinclair, Upton, 83
Singin' in the Rain, 141
Slavery, 182, 246n.8, 288
To Sleep With Anger (1990), 6, 112–113, 117n.9, 136
Slow Fade to Black (Cripps), 26–31, 71
Smart-Grovesnor, Verta Mae, 121, 126–127, 138, 139–140
Smile Orange, 127
Smith, Vernon L., 230–231
Snead, James, 77, 95
Solanes, Fernando, 110–111
Solas, Humberto, 110
A Soldier's Story (1981), 185–198, 216–217
Song of Ceylon (1938), 112
Song of Solomon (Morrison), 22
The Souls of Black Folk (DuBois), 29–31
South Pacific, 94
Space, theme of, 13–19, 19–23. *See also* Mise-en-scene
Spain, version of *Within Our Gates,* 51
Spectators and spectatorship
    as approach to film criticism, 258–259
    Black aesthetics and independent cinema, 7
    Black female and identification, 263–265
    Black female and oppositional gaze, 288–302
    Black women and *The Color Purple,* 272–273, 284–286
    empowerment in *Daughters of the Dust,* 132–139

identification and resistance of Black, 211–219
interpretation of text, 287n.17
Spence, Eulalie, 90
Spielberg, Steven, 214, 272, 273, 278–284. *See also The Color Purple*
Steffens, Lincoln, 83
Sterilization, government programs, 81–82, 85–88, 89, 91n.6, 92n.7
Stir Crazy (1980), 241
Stop (1975), 138, 139
Stormy Weather (1943), 98, 265–266
Stowe, Harriet Beecher, 61, 260
Street Wars (1991), 117n.13
Sugar Cane Alley, 127
Sula (Morrison), 158
Supreme Court, 87–88
Sweet Sweetback's Baadassss Song (1971)
  cinematic style, 11, 12–13
  commercial success, 108
  development of Black independent cinema, 118–119
  psychoanalytical reading of, 260–261
  spectators and Black experience, 9, 10
The Symbol of the Unconquered (1921), 36–37, 71
Syvilla: They Dance to Her Drum (1979), 141

Tar Baby (Morrison), 130
Tate, Allen, 178, 197
Taxi Driver, 194
Taylor, Clyde, 119, 219
Taylor, John Russell, 93
Television, Black viewers, 289–290
Testament, 16
Theaters, Black film, 221–232, 263
Their Eyes Were Watching God (Hurston), 161–162, 274
Thiongo, Ngugi wa, 109, 127
Third Cinema, 62, 65
Third World, 108, 110–111, 115
Thornton, Leslie, 296
Thurman, Wallace, 80–91
Time, cinematic construction of, 12, 13, 19–23

Toddy, Ted, 233n.27
Tomorrow's Children (1934), 81–82, 83–88, 92n.7
Tongues Untied, 256
Top Hat, 93
Townsend, Robert, 239
The Toy (1983), 241
Trading Places (1983), 241, 244

Uncle Tom's Cabin (Stowe), 52, 55, 61, 260
Under Fire, 138
University of California, Los Angeles, 107. *See also* Los Angeles Black filmmaking movement
Urbanization, 40. *See also* Migration
The Usurer (1910), 59
Utopianism, 104

Vanishing Rooms (Dixon), 203
Van Peebles, Melvin, 9, 77. *See also Sweet Sweetback's Baadasssss Song*
Vega, Pastor, 111
Veiled Aristocrats, 71
Vidor, King, 76
Vigilantism, 53

Walker, Alice, 200, 278, 284–285. *See also The Color Purple*
Walker, Margaret, 273–274
Wallace, Michele, 200
Waller, Gregory, 77
Wang, Wayne, 245
Warner Bros., 80
Washington, Denzel, 188
The Water is Wide (Conroy), 135
Watkins, Gloria, 203
Wayans, Keenen Ivory, 245
Way Down South (1939), 90–91
Wells, Ida B., 53, 54, 60
West, Cornel, 19, 66
White, Hayden, 178–179
White, Iverson, 134
Wilbur, Crane, 90
Wilde, Oscar, 204–205
Williams, Spencer, 72

Wilmington Ten—U.S.A., 10,000 (1978), 116, 128
Wilson, August, 287n.19
Wilson, Harriet, 273–274
Wilson, Woodrow, 73
Wind from the East (1969), 116n.8
Winston, Michael, 273
Winter, Sylvia, 246n.15
Within Our Gates, 37–38, 47n.28, 49–67, 67n.8
Women, Black. *See also* Gender; Sexuality
  as audience for *The Color Purple,* 272–273, 284–286
  and Black male sexuality in mainstream cinema, 252–255
  in *Daughters of the Dust,* 13–19, 139–143
  female-bashing in *Boyz in the Hood,* 25n.4
  in *Do The Right Thing,* 174–175
  in films of 1930s, 88
  in *Joe's Bed-Stuy Barber Shop,* 157, 160
  in *School Daze,* 167
  in *She's Gotta Have It,* 161–166
  as spectators and oppositional gaze, 288–302
Wood, Robin, 239
Woodbury, Billy, 112–114
Working class, 169. *See also* Class
World War II, 262
The Wretched of the Earth (Fanon), 109, 112
Wright, Basil, 112
Wright, Richard, 109, 113, 170
Writers, Black, 80–91, 273, 287n.19

Yearwood, Gladstone L., 72, 238
Young, Joseph A., 70n.50
You Only Live Once (1937), 195–196

Zajota and the Boogie Spirit (1989), 141
Zollar, Jawole Willa Jo, 141–142
Zooman and the Sign (1978), 187